Seven Barrel Brewery
Brewers'
Handbook

by Gregory J. Noonan

Seven Barrel Brewery
BREWERS' HANDBOOK

Published by G. W. Kent, Inc.
3667 Morgan Rd.
Ann Arbor, MI 48108 USA

ISBN # 1-887167-00-5

Printed in the United States of America

CONTENTS

INTRODUCTION 1

CHAPTER 1
BASIC HOMEBREWING TERMINOLOGY 5

CHAPTER 2
BASIC HOMEBREWING EQUIPMENT 13

CHAPTER 3
BASIC HOMEBREWING FROM KITS 17
    BASIC INGREDIENTS 20
    HOMEBREWING STEP-BY-STEP 22
    DON'T FOLLOW BOGUS DIRECTIONS 22
    SANITIZING 26
    BREW DAY 28
    FERMENTATION 32
    PRIMING AND BOTTLING 33

CHAPTER 4
INGREDIENTS 37
    MALT EXTRACTS 38
    DRY MALT EXTRACTS 40
    GRAINS 40
    BASE MALTS 41
    CARAMEL/CRYSTAL MALTS 42
    ROASTED MALTS 44
    OTHER MALTS 44
    FLAKED GRAINS 45
    SUGARS 45
    HOPS 47
    HOP VARIETIES 49
    HOP VARIETIES 50
    WATER TREATMENT 51
    MINERAL SALTS 52
    PH / ALKALINITY CORRECTION 53
    COPPER FININGS 54
    YEAST 54
    FININGS 56

CHAPTER 5
WORLD BEER STYLES 59
    REINVENTING THE WHEEL 60

    FAMILY: ALE

    AMERICAN ALE 62
    BROWN ALE 62
    SCOTTISH ALE 62
    ENGLISH PALE ALE 63
    PORTER 63
    STRONG ALE 64
    BELGIAN ALE 64
    MIXED STYLE 65
    CALIFORNIA COMMON BEER 65

WHEAT BEER 65
GERMAN-STYLE ALE 65

SPECIALTY BEER

SMOKED BEER 65
FAMILY: LAGER 66
GERMAN LIGHT LAGER 66
PILSENER 66
BAVARIAN DARK 66
VIENNA/OKTOBERFEST/MAERZEN 66
BOCK.. 67

CHAPTER 6
POWER TOOLS.. **69**

CHAPTER 7
RECIPES FROM UNHOPPED MALT EXTRACT **77**
STEP BY STEP BREWING PROCEDURE 79
AMERICAN WHEAT ALE
BREADBASKET AMERICAN WHEAT BEER 82
ENGLISH BROWN ALE
COAL SHUTTLE BROWN ALE 83
ENGLISH MILD ALE
THE VICAR'S MILD ALE 84
AMERICAN BROWN ALE
SWEET GEORGIA BROWN ALE 85
SCOTTISH LIGHT, HEAVY, EXPORT ALES
SCOTS ALE 86
CUMMINGS' LIGHT ALE (60/-) 86
MITCHELL'S HEAVY ALE (70/-) 87
BARNET'S EXPORT ALE (80/-) 87
ORDINARY BITTER
PERFECTLY ORDINARY BITTER 88
EXTRA SPECIAL BITTER
SANDS OF TIME ESB 89
CLASSIC PALE ALE
DARTBOARD PALE ALE 90
INDIA PALE ALE
MARJORIBANKS' IPA 91
ROBUST PORTER
DARKLING ROBUST PORTER 92
BROWN PORTER
EXISTENTIAL BROWN PORTER 93
CLASSIC DRY STOUT
LUNCHBUCKET DRY STOUT 94
SWEET STOUT
BIGMOUTH SWEET STOUT 95
IMPERIAL STOUT
DARTH VADER IMPERIAL STOUT 96
OLD ALE
OLDE DOG ALE 97
SCOTCH ALE
MACMAC SCOTCH ALE 98
BARLEYWINE
BIG SLEEPER BARLEYWINE... 99

FLANDERS BROWN ALE
WATT'S BRUIN 100
BELGIAN DUBBEL
YOGI'S DUBBEL 101
BELGIAN TRIPPEL
OFF THE WALL TRIPPEL 102
WIT
SPARKLING WIT 103
CALIFORNIA COMMON BEER
REPAIRMAN'S BLUES COMMON BEER 104
WEIZEN
WEIZEN A NAME? 105
DUNKELWEIZEN
COUSIN WERNER'S OLD BAVARIAN DUNKELWEIZEN 106
DÜSSELDORF ALT
'ALT 'OO GOES THERE 107
KÖLSCH
PINK ELEPHANT KÖLSCH 108
FRUIT BEER
"STRAWBERRY FIELDS" 109
RAUCHBIER
HOKISMOKES RAUCHBIER... 110
AMERICAN PREMIUM LAGER
THREE-GRAIN PREMIUM LAGER 111
CREAM ALE/LAGER
HOLD THE PEACHES CREAM ALE... 112
DORTMUND/EXPORT
DORT-THE-SHORT EXPORT 113
MUNICH HELLES
THERE AND BACK HELLES 114
GERMAN PILSENER
BÖHMERWALD PILSNER LAGER 115
MUNICH DUNKEL
TWILIGHT DUNKEL 116
SCHWARZBIER
MAY THE SCHWARZBIER WITH YOU 117
VIENNA
MR. FINGERS' VIENNA.. 118
MÄRZEN/OKTOBERFEST
MY FAVORITE MÄRZEN 119
TRADITIONAL BOCK
OFFENBOCK 120
HELLESBOCK
WE'LL BE LIGHT BOCK 121
DOPPELBOCK
TRANSLATOR DOPPELBOCK 122

CHAPTER 8
PART 1:
USING WORLD BEER STYLES TO FORMULATE RECIPES 124

PART 2:
USING FRUITS, HERBS AND VEGETABLES IN BREWING...................... 128
HERBS 128

FRUIT 129
VEGETABLES AND THE REST... 131

CHAPTER 9
MASHING 101 .... **133**
THE PSEUDO-ANTHROPOLOGICALLY-CORRECT ORIGINS
    OF BREWING 135
MALTING BARLEY 136
MALT 138
EXTRACT POTENTIAL 139
MASHING 140
SPARGING 143

CHAPTER 10
BREWING LAB 101 .... **145**
HOME MASH-O-NOMICS
HOW TO CRUSH MALT 145
HOW TO MAKE A PARTIAL MASH 146
HOW TO INFUSION MASH 149
HOW TO STEP-MASH 153
MASH RESTS 154
HOW TO DECOCTION MASH 156

CHAPTER 11
MASHING: EQUIPMENT **161**
PARTIAL MASH SYSTEMS. 162
FULL-MASH SYSTEMS 163
OTHER EQUIPMENT 166

CHAPTER 12
PARTIAL MASH RECIPES **169**
AMERICAN WHEAT ALE
    FILLMIMUG WHEAT 170
ENGLISH MILD
    PIPE-CUM-LYDE MILD 171
ENGLISH BROWN ALE
    DOUBLE CROSS XX BROWN 172
AMERICAN BROWN ALE
    MORE-BITTER-MORE-BETTER BROWN 173
SCOTTISH LIGHT
    HELLSTER KILTER 174
SCOTTISH HEAVY
    THISTLE BOG ALE 175
SCOTTISH EXPORT
    OLD 80 WEIGHT 176
ORDINARY BITTER
    BURPING ON THE TRENT ALE 177
EXTRA SPECIAL BITTER
    TOBY'S TIPPLE 178
CLASSIC PALE ALE
    BOMBAY GRAB PALE ALE 179
INDIA PALE ALE
    HUMULUS LUDICROUS IPA 180
ROBUST PORTER
    FLYCASTER PORTER 181

BROWN PORTER
HE-SHE KISS 182
CLASSIC DRY STOUT
DISCIPLE'S GATE STOUT 183
SWEET STOUT
DOUBLE DRAGON STOUT 184
IMPERIAL STOUT
R.I.P. XXX STOUT 185
OLD ALE
OLD BAGGY KNEES 186
SCOTCH ALE
REAL MEN WEAR SKIRTS SCOTCH ALE 187
BARLEY WINE
BIG BOOM BARLEY WINE 188
FLANDERS BROWN ALE
OLD BRUIN BROWN 189
BELGIUM DUBBEL
ABBOT'S HABIT 190
BELGIUM TRIPEL
TIPPLE-NIPPLE TRIPEL 191
WIT
INFINITE WIT 192
CALIFORNIA COMMON BEER
CALIFORNIA STEAM'N 193
WEIZEN
OLDER AND WEIZER 194
DUNKELWEIZEN
SLAMDUNKEL WEIZEN 195
DUSSELDORF ALT
BRUNHILDA BRAU 196
KÖLSCH
HELLESMALTZ HOFBRAU 197
FRUIT BEER
NECTARINE OF THE GODS 198
HERB BEER
CERVEZA CON CHILE 199
RAUCHBIER
SMOKEHOUSE RAUCH 200
AMERICAN PREMIUM LAGER
FIZZWASSER LAGER 201
CREAM ALE/LAGER
CREAM CORN ALE 202
DORTMUNDER/EXPORT
BREWERS' GUILD LAGER 203
MUNICH HELLES
DEUTSCHER MALZ 204
GERMAN PILSENER
GUDENHOPT 205
BOHEMIAN PILSNER
CZECHMATE PILSNER 206
MUNICH DUNKEL
ALT MALT DUNKEL 207
SCHWARZBIER
BLACK KAT LAGER 208

VIENNA
   WIENERMALZ LAGER 209
MÄRZEN/OKTOBERFEST
   OCTANE OBERFEST 210
TRADITIONAL BOCK
   REBOCK 211
HELLESBOCK
   BEELZEBUB BOCK 212
DOPPELBOCK
   SEEULATOR 213

CHAPTER 13
MASH/ALL-GRAIN RECIPES **215**
   AMERICAN WHEAT ALE
      LAWN BOY 216
   ENGLISH BROWN ALE
      NEW DUBLIN BROWN ALE 217
   ENGLISH MILD ALE
      MR. ROGER'S LOCAL 218
   AMERICAN BROWN ALE
      EUGENE BROWN 219
   SCOTTISH LIGHT
      HORNE'S 60 SHILLING ALE 220
   SCOTTISH HEAVY
      DUNCAN'S 70 SHILLING HEAVY 221
   SCOTTISH EXPORT
      JOHN BARLEYCORN 80 SHILLING EXPORT 222
   ORDINARY BITTER
      BULL & BLADDER BITTER 223
   EXTRA SPECIAL BITTER
      DOG & DEVIL ESB 224
   CLASSIC PALE ALE
      OLD NO. 7 PALE ALE 225
   INDIA PALE ALE
      CHAMPION RESERVE IPA 226
   ROBUST PORTER
      SHOREDITCH PORTER 227
   BROWN PORTER
      POOR RICHARD'S PORTER 228
   CLASSIC DRY STOUT
      OLD DUBLIN STOUT 229
   SWEET STOUT
      MILK-CHOCOLATE STOUT 230
   IMPERIAL STOUT
      CATHERINE THE GREAT TIPPLE 231
   OLD ALE
      OLD GODESGOOD STRONG ALE 232
   SCOTCH ALE
      LAIRD OF THE BORDERS WEE HEAVY 233
   BARLEYWINE
      SLEEPWALKER BARLEYWINE 234
   FLANDERS' BROWN ALE
      OUDENAARDE BROWN ALE 235

DUBBEL
FAT ABBOT ALE 236
BELGIAN TRIPEL
STANDUP TRIPLE 237
WIT
CHEVAL BLANC 238
CALIFORNIA COMMON BEER
FRITZ LAGER 239
WEIZEN
BEETLEJUICE/BETELGEUSE 240
DUNKELWEIZEN
SCHWARZ UND WEISS 241
DÜSSELDORF ALT
ZUM RUMDUM ALTBIER 242
KÖLSCH
HAUSBRAUEREI LITEN 243
FRUIT BEER
BLUEBERRY CREAM ALE 244
RAUCHBIER
RAUCHEN ROLL BRAU 245
AMERICAN PREMIUM LAGER
CORN QUEEN LAGER 246
CREAM ALE/LAGER
OTTAQUEECHIE CREAM ALE 247
DORTMUND EXPORT
MEIN KELLER SUDZWERKS XX EXPORT 248
MUNICH HELLES
SMALLBRAUHAUS HELL 249
GERMAN PILSENER
HOPFEN UND MALZ PILS 250
BOHEMIAN PILSENER
ZATEC WIRGIN PILSENER 251
MUNICH DUNKEL
BIERBAUCH LAGER 252
SCHWARZBIER
BLACKGOLD SCHWARZPILS 253
VIENNA
INNSBRUCK ALPEN SPEZIAL 254
MÄRZEN/OKTOBERFEST
ROCKTOBERFEST 255
TRADITIONAL BOCK
EMPEROR OF LEBANON BOCK 256
HELLESBOCK
BILLYBUCK MAIBOCK 257
DOPPELBOCK
SAINT LUBRICATOR 258

CHAPTER 14
KEGGING **259**
REAL ALE 261
KEGGING PROCEDURES 262
ARTIFICIAL CARBONATION 264

CHAPTER 15
"YUCCH! WHAT WENT WRONG??!!" **267**
  TROUBLE-SHOOTING 267
  PROBLEMS AND SOLUTIONS 270
  SMELLS "DIFFERENT" 270
  SMELLS BAD 273
  TASTES "DIFFERENT" 274
  TASTES BAD 275

CHAPTER 16
JUDGING YOUR BEER AND ANYONE ELSE'S **279**

CHAPTER 17
THE SEVEN BARREL BREWERY **285**
  WEIGHTS AND MEASURES 291
  VOLUME 291
  WEIGHT 292
  LINEAR MEASURE 292
  SQUARE MEASURE 292
  PRESSURE 292
  BREWLOG: BEERKITS 302
  BREWLOG: EXTRACTS 303
  BREWLOG: PARTIAL MASH 304
  BREWLOG: FULL MASH 305

INTRODUCTION

eer is nothing new; people have been brewing for almost as long as there have been people. Beer begins with malted (sprouted) barley that is "stewed" to extract sugars from it. This process is called mashing, and yields a sugar-rich liquid called wort. Yeast are allowed to ferment the wort, creating carbon dioxide and alcohol and producing beer.

It used to be, way back in the old days, lots of people knew how to brew. A thousand years ago most people brewed their own beer. Over time, individuals made discoveries about brewing that improved their beer. Over time people that made discoveries began hoarding their new knowledge and prospered because they held a secret to brewing better beer. Over time, guilds formed to protect established brewers and their secret knowledge. Over time, fewer and fewer people knew how to brew.

There was probably no time in recorded history that fewer people knew how to brew beer than in the 1960s and 70s. In America, the number of breweries had fallen from the thousands to fewer than forty. From Prohibition in the twenties until 1978, homebrewing was illegal in the United States.

The roots of the modern-day homebrewing revival lie in the back-to- basics movements of the late sixties. The increased epicurean awareness of the 80's, however, is what really got a critical mass of Americans interested in homebrewing. People realized that they could make great beer themselves. The growing market fueled an increase in the availability of ingredients, of better-quality and greater diversity, as well as specialized equipment and a vast increase in available information. Small craft breweries began appearing in America, making fresh, flavorful beers available to people who didn't already homebrew. Awareness of the

possibilities increased, and homebrewing and craft-brewing blossomed side-by-side throughout the 80's. It is a safe bet that more Americans homebrew now than at any time since Prohibition, and interest in homebrewing is mushrooming.

This book is the accumulation of three brewers' knowledge and experience. Greg Noonan began as a homebrewer in the 70's. He is the author of "Brewing Lager Beer" (Brewers Publications, 1985), "Scotch Ale" (Brewers Publications, 1993) and numerous articles in periodicals and journals. Greg opened the Vermont Pub and Brewery with his wife Nancy in 1988. He designed, installed and opened The Seven Barrel Brewery, which opened in West Lebanon, New Hampshire in April of 1994.

Mikel Redman was the original head brewer at the Seven Barrel Brewery. He began homebrewing in the mid-80s, gaining brewing knowledge through managing a homebrew supply shop in Burlington, Vermont. Mike's love for brewing led to an apprenticeship at another craft brewery before he came to The Seven Barrel Brewery in March of 1994.

Scott Russell is the author of "The Basics of Homebrewing" (Optimus, 1994) and is a contributing writer for *Brew Your Own* magazine. He has been the manager of the homebrew shop at The Seven Barrel Brewery since it opened in 1994. Homebrewing has occupied most of Scott's "spare time" for the past few years, when he is not teaching French in a high-school classroom or translating technical manuals for industrial clients.

The purpose of this book is to give simple instructions on how to make great beer at home. We begin with what are called "kits". Kits are hopped malt extract that yield a specific style of beer, and usually include a package of dried yeast. The beauty of kits is that you don't need to know a lot about brewing to brew good beer. You can buy a Brown Ale kit and brew a Brown Ale. You don't need to know which malts and hops to use and how much of each and when to add them to brew a Brown Ale. You only need to know the basics of brewing to brew from kits.

Some people want to know how to brew Brown Ale and other styles of beer from unhopped extracts. These brewers need to know a lot more about the beer styles themselves, and about malt extracts and hops and which ones to use and how much to add and when.

Other homebrewers go all the way and brew "from scratch". These enterprising few also need to know about malt and adjunct grains and mashing, and how much of which grains to use and how to mash them for each particular beer style. Brewing at this level requires a great deal of knowledge and dedication. This book is geared to all three levels of interest.

Brewing only needs to be as complicated as you want to make it. You don't need to bury yourself under a mountain of technical information to brew good beer from malt extract. If you want to mash, on the other hand, be prepared to absorb a lot of information, and be patient. First you'll need to get some experience boiling wort and fermenting it and learn what differentiates beer styles, and then you'll need to learn about malts and how to mash them.

However far you may take it in the end, everyone needs to learn the same basics to homebrew. Section One of this book will introduce you to brewing terminology and brewing from kits. Section Two addresses brewing from unhopped extract. Section Three addresses mashing and kegging. In case something goes wrong, the troubleshooting chapter will help you remedy the problem.

The information is here. You want to homebrew, we can show you how. Are you ready? Let's brew it!

Many of the recipes in this book use the trade names of beers brewed by The Seven Barrel Brewery. Greg Noonan and the Seven Barrel Brewery authorize the use of those names by this book and by amateur brewers, but expressedly retain the exclusive right to use these names in trade.

The Seven Barrel Brewery licenses the use of its name to the publisher of this book, and grants the publisher limited rights to use the name The Seven Barrel Brewery promoting and selling the book. The Seven Barrel Brewery retains all other rights associated with its trademark.

CHAPTER 1

BASIC HOMEBREWING TERMINOLOGY

I f you want to walk the walk, you've got to talk the talk. Like deadheads, trekkies and nuclear physicists, brewers have their own specialized vocabulary. You will naturally and pain-lessly learn the language of brewing as you go along. But that would be too easy, so we are sticking the imposing glossary of new words in front of you right off the bat. Don't be overwhelmed.

Don't worry about learning all these brewing terms cold. Don't even think about trying to memorize them. In fact, don't even bother reading them. They are only here so that you, the novice brewer, will know that the vocabulary exists, and because posi-tioning the glossary right at the front of the book makes it easy to find. Go on to Chapter 2 and shop for equipment. Just remem-ber to flip back to this glossary, handily positioned for ready ref-erence at the front of the book, whenever you encounter brewing terms that you don't know, and as you brew, you'll learn the lan-guage of brewing painlessly. We'll see you at Chapter 2!

AAU: Alpha Acid Unit. A measurement of the alpha acidity and potential bitterness of hops. One AAU equals one ounce of a one-percent alpha acid hop. One ounce of Cascade hops at 5% alpha acid, then, (see <u>HBU</u>) gives 5 AAUS, and so on...

ABV: Alcohol By Volume (%V/V).

Adjunct: Any ingredient used in brewing other than malted bar-ley or hops.

Aeration: The process of infusing oxygen into wort to aid yeast in reproduction.

Aerobic (Phase): The first, active phase of fermentation (respi-ration) during which yeast cells use molecular oxygen to fuel re-production. Large quantities of CO_2 are produced. (see <u>anerobic</u>).

Airlock: A device for sealing a fermenting vessel, allowing the escape of CO_2 but preventing contamination from outside, by means of a water trap.

Ale: A family of beer brewed using a top-fermenting yeast strain, and, generally, relatively warmer temperatures.

Alpha Acid: Acid from resins in hops that contributes bitterness. (see beta-acid).

Amylase: Enzymes responsible for the conversion of starch to fermentable sugar. Alpha-amylase works on soluble starch, reducing it to shorter-chain dextrins, while beta-amylase changes dextrins to glucose and maltose.

Anaerobic (Phase): The second and longer phase of fermentation, during which yeast cells metabolize simple sugars producing CO_2, ethanol and a host of minor flavor constituents.

Aroma: The smell or odor of beer.

Aromatics: Qualities pertaining to aroma.

Attenuation: The drop in density of beer, due to fermentation. A reasonable basis for the measurement of alcohol in beer.

Beta Acid: Acid contained in hops, largely insoluble, that can contribute a harsh bitterness to the flavor of beer.

Body: Texture and feel of beer, sensed with the whole mouth (mouthfeel).

Break: The coagulation of proteins during boiling (hot break) or cooling (cold break).

Carbonate: 1)(v) To charge with CO_2. 2)(adj) Water that is high in chalk ($CaCO_3$).

Carbonation: Dissolved CO_2 in beer, resulting in the head (bubbles) and effervescence. A highly carbonated beer will contain 2 1/2 to 3 times the volume of CO_2 as beer that is uncarbonated.

Carboy: A glass bottle, usually 5 or 6 gallons, used as a fermenting and/or lagering vessel.

Conditioning: 1) Bottle/cask condition: Process, in bottles, casks, etc., of promoting and/or creating carbonation in beer. 2) Aging or lagering of beer.

Decanting: Pouring technique for homebrew which prevents the yeast sediment from flowing into the glass.

Decoction: Method of mashing involving boiling part of the mash to gradually increase the temperature of the whole mash.

Dextrins: Partially-fermentable and unfermentable sugars that contribute to the sweetness and viscosity of beer.

Diacetyl: A buttery to butterscotch flavor in beer, appropriate in some styles, a defect in others.

Diastase: The enzymes involved in starch-to-sugar conversion (see amylase).

DME: See drymalt.

Doppel: The German word for double, used with bocks to indicate increased strength.

Dubbel: The Flemish word for double, used for the abbey-style beers of Belgium to indicate increased strength.

Dunkel: The German word for dark, as in color of beer.

Drymalt (or DME, also known as spraymalt): Powdered form of malt extract that has been flash-evaporated to remove 97% of liquid.

Ester: Flavor or aroma compound caused by fermentation processes, often described in terms of fruits or spices (pear, clove, apple, banana, etc.).

Extract: 1) In mashing, the fermentable sugars collected from the mashed grains. 2) In home-brewing general terms, "malt extract" is a syrup condensed/evaporated from brewer's wort by professional maltsters.

Fermentables: Sugars that can be converted into alcohol.

Fermentation: The process of converting sugars (fermentables) into alcohol and CO_2 by anerobic yeast metabolism.

Fining: Process of clarifying a fermented beer.

Finings: Substance used to clarify beer.

Flocculation: Tendency of yeast to clump into colonies. Flocculent strains tend to clear quicker than non-flocculent (or dusty) strains.

Grist: Cracked or milled grain used in mashing.

Gypsum: Calcium Sulfate, a slightly acidic salt that is commonly found dissolved in water and is beneficial in the brewing process.

Haze: Cloudiness in beer, often the result of suspended bacterial infections. May or may not affect beer flavors.

HBU: Homebrew Bitterness Unit. Also known as AAU. A standardized method for duplicating bitterness in any recipe. 1 HBU = 1 oz. of hops at 1% alpha acid.

Head: The foam on top of a poured beer, the result of proteins clinging to CO_2 bubbles.

Helles: German word for "light", as in color.

Hops: The "flower" of the hop vine (*humulus lupulus*), used for bittering beer and as an aromatic "spice".

Hydrometer: Device for measuring the dissolved sugar in a solution (density, or specific gravity) and thus indirectly the alcohol content.

IBU: International Bittering Units. Internationally accepted measurement of hop bitterness. Laboratory measurement of IBUs is outside the scope and budget of homebrewers. (see HBU).

Infusion: Mashing technique involving one-step, one temperature mashing, used with highly modified grains.

Irish Moss: Carrageenan, a seaweed which is used to aid precipitation of haze proteins in the kettle. Also known as Copper Finings.

Kilning: Process of drying, or roasting, of malted grains by heat. Creates increased color of malts.

Knock-out, Kettle: The end of the wort boil.

Kraüsening: Process of priming fermented beer with fresh unfermented wort or freshly fermenting beer.

Lager: Family of beers fermented and aged at colder temperatures with bottom-fermenting yeasts, developed in the early 19th century. From the German word "*lagern*", to store.

Lagering: The process of conditioning beer at cold temperatures for an extended period of time. Lagering produces a smoother flavor.

Lambic: (Flemish name of a town: Lambeek) Style of beer particular to a small region of Belgium, based on the use of wild yeasts and bacteria in the fermentation.

Lautering: Filtering or straining of the wort to separate it from the spent grains.

Lauter tun: Container serving as a strainer during the lautering process.

Liquor: Water, treated or otherwise, ready for brewing.

Lovibond: Color-rating system used in America to compare and categorize grains, wort and beer by the darkness of color. (see SRM).

Malt: Grain (usually barley) that has been sprouted, or "malted"; malt extract (see extract).

Malting: Process of sprouting raw grains to begin conversion of starch to sugar, and kilning them to stop growth.

Mash Tun: The vessel, which may be insulated, in which crushed malt is infused with hot liquor to convert starches to fermentable sugars.

Mashing: Process of extracting, reducing and dissolving sugars from grains, involving heat and enzymes. (see infusion and decoction)

Original Gravity (OG): The density of the wort before fermentation.

Oxidation: Oxidative spoiling of beer, due to exposure to air.

Pitching: The act of adding yeast to wort.

Primary Fermenter: 1st fermenting vessel used in a 2-stage fermentation system, in which the highly active phase of fermentation takes place. (see secondary)

Priming: Process of adding a dose of fermentable sugar to the beer at packaging to carbonate the beer in the bottle or cask.

Racking: The process of siphoning or transferring wort or beer from one vessel to another.

Rehydration: The process of reactivating a yeast culture by dissolving in water at approximately 200°F (95°C)

Reinheitsgebot: The Bavarian Purity Law of 1516 which (still!) governs the way beer is made in Germany, and in some other countries as well. Simply, it says that only malt, hops and water may be used in making beer.

Rest: A pause, or maintained temperature-controlled "stay" in the mashing process.

Secondary Fermenter: In a 2-stage fermentation system, the second vessel into which the fermenting beer is racked, after the intense activity of fermentation has fallen off.

Sediment: Particles and debris (mostly hops and yeast cells) accumulated on the bottom of the fermenting vessel or bottle. Not harmful, but not very tasty; beer is usually separated from it by racking.

Slurry: The liquid suspension in which an active yeast culture is pitched.

Sparging: The process of rinsing the mashed grains to collect as much of their extract as possible; accomplished by sprinkling hot water over grains submerged in a lauter tun.

Specific Gravity: Metric-system measurement of the density of a liquid solution, commonly used in homebrewing. Read at the beginning and end of fermentation to determine attenuation and alcohol content.

SRM (Standard Reference Method): see Lovibond.

Strike: 1) The target temperature for a given mash rest. 2) Synonym for Kettle Knock-out, or the end of the wort boil.

Sulfate: Water that has more gypsum dissolved in it than chalk.

Terminal Gravity (TG): The density of a beer after fermentation is complete.

Trub: Proteins and other debris precipitated in the boiling kettle or fermenter. Trub should be removed if possible, or the beer separated from it by racking, to produce the cleanest-possible tasting beer.

Two-stage Fermentation: Method of using a primary fermenter for the first, active stage of fermentation, and transferring the beer off the trub/sediment to complete the fermentation in a clean vessel. This generally results in a crisper, cleaner-flavored beer.

Wort: The liquid containing malt extract. In essence, the beer before it's beer. Sweet Wort becomes Bitter Wort when hops are added to it.

CHAPTER 2

BASIC HOMEBREWING EQUIPMENT

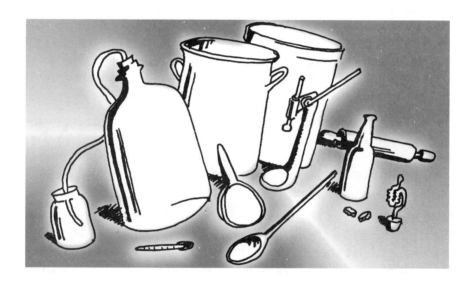

You ought to have this book in hand, open to this chapter, when you shop for your first brewery. Whether at your friendly homebrewing supplies retail shop or with catalogue in hand, look at the bewildering array of ingredients, gadgets and tools of the trade available to you. Most of what you see could be of use to you, even as a beginner, but it is advisable to get started and get a feel for brewing with a very simple set-up. Once you get a few brews under your belt, you'll have a better idea of which gadgets you'd really like to own. You will probably find that you already have some of the basic tools and equipment in your own kitchen; as for the rest, let's shop!

How-to Book: You already have the first and perhaps most important piece of equipment in your hands — this book. A reference book with plenty of no-nonsense information, expert advice and great recipes is sort of like having a brewer-in-a-bottle at your beck and call 24 hours a day.

Kettle: (Brewpot) The first step in beginning brewing is simply boiling a mixture of water and malt extract. Your kettle should be a solid, clean stainless steel, copper, or enameled-steel stockpot or canning kettle, the bigger the better (remember to remove the lobsters before you begin), with a well-fitting lid. Please note that many brewers feel that aluminum kettles should be avoided. You can get by with a 12- or 16-quart pot to start, but you will probably outgrow it. If you need to go out and buy a new pot anyway, keep in mind that if you stick with brewing, eventually you will probably want a 24-quart to 40-quart kettle. If you don't own a 12-16 quart pot already, then buy the 24 quart size.

Rubber Spatula: to scrape all the malt extract out of the can.

Spoon or paddle: Long-handled (12 - 20 inches); again, stainless steel is ideal, although plastic or clean wood may be used as well.

Measuring Spoons: Any inexpensive set will do.

Measuring Cup: 1-quart Pyrex® cup is the most useful, although any size will do.

Jugs: You will need three 1-gallon jugs or six 2-liter bottles, or the equivalent, to prepare 3 gallons of sterile water.

Spray Bottle: Any misting-type spray bottle that didn't previously contain poisonous chemicals will do, so long as it is thoroughly cleaned and rinsed, but we would advise you to buy a virgin bottle from your homebrew supplier.

Fermenter: A food-grade plastic bucket of 6.5 gallon (25 liter) capacity or greater, with a tight-fitting lid.

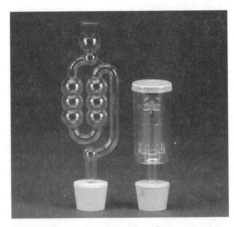

Airlock (also known as a trap, bubbler, waterlock...): These are not the sealed entryways on sophisticated interplanetary spaceships. They are a simple device, sometimes glass but usually plastic, designed to allow CO_2 to escape without allowing airborne contaminants or dust to fall into the beer. They are normally inserted into a:

Drilled, Food-grade Rubber Stopper sized to fit the opening of the hole drilled in the lid of the bucket; some bucket lids come with an airlock-sized hole fitted with a grommet, obviating the need for a stopper.

Siphon set-up: To transfer beer from one vessel to another and for bottling. Three to four feet of flexible 1/4" to 3/8" food-grade vinyl tubing, a rigid 24 - 30" "racking cane" (a curved plastic tube) and a tubing clamp.

Bottle-filler: A valve that fits on a length of tubing; reduces spilled beer, oxidation and anxiety.

Bottling bucket: (Priming bucket). A vessel into which the beer is siphoned before bottling, usually a 5 or 6 gallon food-grade plastic bucket with a spigot.

Thermometer: A solid kitchen thermometer (candy-type, not meat-type) that can measure <u>at least</u> between 60°F(15°C) and 120°F(49°C). Floating aquarium thermometers may also work — check the temperature range. The best overall thermometer to have is the floating thermometer available from your homebrew supply store.

Hydrometer: A device which measures the density of a liquid, and thus the sugar content. Readings are taken at the beginning and end of fermentation to determine the alcohol content of the beer. Made in both plastic and glass, hydrometer trial tubes are sized to hold your hydrometer and enough beer to get a density reading.

Bottle capper: Two basic varieties are sold to homebrewers, one involving a double- or triple-levered action, the other a straight-downward motion. Essential for sealing up your bottled beer.

Bottles: 50-55 twelve-ounce beer bottles, or 40 sixteen-ounce, or the equivalent in whatever size bottle you want to use. The bottles should be clean, heavy-duty glass beer bottles or screw-top PET plastic bottles.

Bottle caps: crown-type, unless you are using screw-top PET bottles or swing-top bottles with gasketed ceramic caps.

Funnel: You will need a large funnel. One fitted with a screen is especially useful.

Okay, that's your shopping list. But, you may be asking," What do I do with all this stuff?" Read on...

CHAPTER 3

BASIC HOMEBREWING FROM KITS

The longest journeys start somewhere. No matter what level of brewing you aspire to, you need to begin at the begin ning. Homebrewing begins with brewing from beer kits.

Being able to brew great tasting beer has been made easier than ever by the wide availability of beer kits. Beer kits are specifically-designed ingredients packaged to enable you to make a particular style of beer.

There are kits available for just about any style of beer. Here is a list of some beer kits available to the home brewer.

SELECTED BEER KITS

STYLE	BRAND
American Wheat:	Premier Wheat Beer
English Brown Ale:	Ironmaster Northern Brown
English Mild Ale:	Edme Mild
American Brown Ale:	Premier Brown Ale
Scots Light Ale:	Glenbrew Special 70/Ale
Scots Heavy Ale:	Brewmaker Scottish Heavy
Scots Export Ale:	Geordie Scottish Export
Bitter (Ordinary):	John Bull traditional Bitter
ESB:	Edme Dogbolter
Pale Ale:	Mahogany Coast English Ale
IPA:	Mahogany Coast India Pale Ale
Robust Porter:	Ironmaster London Porter
Brown Porter:	Telford's Porter
Dry Stout:	Mountmellick's Irish Stout
Sweet Stout:	Laaglander Stout
Imperial Stout:	Munton's Gold Imperial Stout
Old/Strong Ale:	Munton's Old Ale
Scotch Ale:	Brewferm Scotch Ale
Barleywine:	John Bull Premium Barleywine
Flanders Brown:	Brewferm Oud Bruin
Dubbel:	Brewferm Ambiorix
Tripel:	Brewferm Tripel
Wit:	Brewferm Tarwebier
California Common Beer:	William's Brewing California Lager
Weizen:	Mahogany Coast Wheat Beer
Fruit Beer:	Brewferm Kriek/Frambozen
American Premium Lager:	Mahogany Coast American Lager
Dortmunder:	Glenbrew Dortmunder Export
Munich Helles:	Otto Hoxheim Helles
German Pilsner:	Mahogany Coast Berliner Pils
Bohemian Pils:	John Bull Export Pilsner
Bock:	Munton's Bock
Doppelbock:	Otto Hoxheim Doppelbock

There are hundreds of other kits available besides these; they are ones we know and like. They fit approximately within the American Homebrewers Association Beer Style Categories (see chapter 5). We recommend these kits, but don't be afraid to use a kit in the same style that is made by a different manufacturer.

You want to know about the ingredients you will be using, so we'll get you started off right and tell you about them now. There is a lot of information packed into these next few pages, so crack a good brew, sit back, and take your time. Refer back to Chapter 1 whenever you need to sort things out.

BASIC INGREDIENTS

Malt extract, hops, yeast and water are the basic ingredients in most homebrew. Brewing kits consist of hopped malt-extract, and usually come with a package of dried, granulated yeast. Malt extract is condensed brewers wort. What's wort? Wort is the sugar-rich liquid that brewers boil with hops. Wort is cooled after boiling and brewers' yeast is added, or as a brewer would say, "pitched". The yeast ferments the wort by absorbing fermentable sugars and using them as an energy supply to fuel its own metabolism, and to reproduce. In the process, yeast produces alcohol (primarily ethyl alcohol, or ethanol) and carbon dioxide. Carbon dioxide is what carbonates beer.

Have you got that? Maybe we should have titled this section "Read This Twice". We didn't, but perhaps you should read it again. There ought to be a couple questions that this has raised, like, what in blazes is malt extract?

Malt extract is made from wort; wort is made from malt. Malt is the brewers' name for sprouted-and-dried barley. Barley, which is a grain of the same family as wheat and rye, is too steely and complex to be brewed with. Malting and kilning barley simplifies its structure so that it can be mashed.

The mash is essentially a porridge of crushed malt and hot water. Under the carefully-controlled conditions of the mash, enzymes in the grain reduce malt starch to dextrins and fermentable sugars. Dextrins are unfermentable polysaccharides, an intermediate between starch and sugar, that give beer fullness and character. Most of the sugars derived from malt are glucose, the simplest grain sugar (it is only a single molecule), and maltose, which is two molecules of glucose. Brewers' yeast will ferment all of the glucose and maltose in a wort. Most brewers' yeast also ferments maltotriose, the three-molecule malt sugar, as well, but can't ferment dextrins. Dextrins are four-to-twenty-molecule long chains of glucose. One influence over how sweet and full a beer tastes is what ratio of dextrins to fermentable sugars has been created in the mash.

So, mashing is converting malt starch to a mix of simple, fermentable sugars and non-fermentable dextrins called wort. Malt extract is condensed from wort by evaporating the water off.

Wort is about 95% water. If the water content is reduced to about 22%, you get malt-extract syrup. If all the water is evaporated, you get dry malt extract. Most kits come with a can, or pouch, of malt extract syrup, which is usually called just extract, or malt extract. Most kits need more fermentables added to them. Dry malt extract is referred to as DME, and is what homebrewers should add to kits, instead of table sugar or brewers' corn sugar.

The malt extract in kits is pre-hopped. In a usual brewery wort-boil, hops are added to the boiling kettle. They are the traditional "spice" in beer, adding bitterness and flavor to round out the sweet and roasty tastes obtained from the malt. Beer kits rarely have any hop aroma, so for styles that call for it, even novice homebrewers add a little hops at the end of their own wort boil.

Brewers' yeast comes in all shapes and sizes. Actually they all look remarkably similar under the microscope, but different strains produce rather radically different flavors. The flavor impact of certain types and strains of yeast are associated with specific beer styles. It would be nice if the yeast that comes with beer kits were strains that specifically enhanced the style of beer the kit is supposed to produce, but this is rarely the case. Most homebrewers trash the kit yeast in favor of strains that they, or their local homebrew shop, know something about.

Be aware that one package of yeast (usually 5-7 grams) is not enough yeast to produce good beer. You should always pitch 10-14 grams (usually two packages), and even 15-21 grams for very strong beers.

Now that you know something about the ingredients that you will be working with, it's time for a quiz (careful, there are some curve balls here). If you can answer 2-out-of-3, go on to the next section. Question #1: what yeast pitched a no-hitter in the 1994 World Series? Question #2: Is a dextrin fermentable? Question #3: What is DME?

HOMEBREWING STEP-BY-STEP

These are the steps to basic homebrewing. The rest of this chapter is devoted to explaining the process in detail:

The day before you brew:
Sterilize and chill 3 gallons of water.
Sterilize your fermenter and brewing equipment.

Brewday:
Boil the malt extract with 2 gallons of water for 45 minutes.
While the wort is boiling, rehydrate 2 packages of yeast.
Add finishing hops 5 minutes before the end of the boil.
Splash the sterile water and hot wort into sterile fermenter.
Chill the wort in the fermenter to 70-75°F (21-24°C).
Pitch the activated yeast.
Maintain the fermentation temperature for 2 weeks.
Transfer the clear beer to your priming bucket.
Prime the beer with corn sugar.
Bottle your beer, cap it, and let it condition for at least two weeks.
Taste a bottle. If it seems well-carbonated and tastes good, invite over some friends. Impress them with your new-found skills as a home-brewmeister.

DON'T FOLLOW BOGUS DIRECTIONS

If one fault can be found with most kits, it is the instructions printed on the can. Making beer from kits is easy, but the kit instructions often either oversimplify it or just plain give bad advice. By adding a couple more steps, and changing a few, we can guarantee that you will be much more satisfied with the finished product.

Most kits tell you that a 3.3 pound (1.5 kg) can is all that is needed to make a 5 gallon recipe. But if you look closer, they advise you to add 2 to 3 additional pounds of sugar to the 3.3 pound can of extract. Why? Because corn sugar and table sugar are cheap! When you add such large ratios of sugar to malt in a recipe, the resulting beer will be very alcoholic, but it will also be very thin and insipid. If you follow sugar-beer instructions, what you brew won't taste very much like the beer style you are emulating, or for that matter, beer at all.

There is a simple solution to this, and it's been time-tested and proven in millions of homebrews: merely substitute malt extract for the sugar called for in the kit's instructions. The results are a much fuller, richer and tastier beer. For every pound of sugar, you will need to substitute 1-1/4 pounds (562 grams) of DME or 1-1/2 pounds (680 grams) of malt-extract syrup. Since cans of malt extract generally come packaged as 3.3 lbs (1.5 kg), most homebrewers use DME, so that they don't end up with a partial can of syrup hanging around getting stale until they brew again.

So whenever you buy a brew-kit, while you are at the shop ask to borrow their calculator. Read the kit's label, and multiply the pounds of sugar that it calls for times 1.25. Buy that amount of Dry Malt Extract too.

Another problem arises with kits that call for a "No Boil" shortcut. Yes, it makes homebrewing sound easy: "Just open a can, mix it into warm water, pour it into a pail and add yeast." It's simple, alright; it's a simple way to make undrinkable homebrew.

What's wrong with it? Bacteria and wild yeast, for starters. First of all, they're everywhere. Depending on the season, the weather, the humidity, where you live, whether your windows are open, and how clean your kitchen is, there are more or less microbes in the air, but there are invariably some. None of them are good for your homebrew, and most of them will make your beer undrinkable if they get into it. Bacteria love malt extract, and they love wort. The only way to be sure that there are no bacteria in your wort is to boil it.

Some cans of extract tell you to boil with two gallons of water, and add three gallons of tap water to it to cool it and bring the volume up to 5 gallons at the same time. This is half-bad advice. Why? The idea of cooling your wort with make-up water is sound, but using tap water isn't. When you mix three gallons of tap water with two gallons of boiling-hot wort, the resulting temperature will be somewhere between 100-120°F (38-46°C). At best, brewers' yeast only barely survives at even 100°F (38°C) in wort, and only makes good beer at below about 75°F (24°C). Most bacteria, on the other hand, absolutely blossom at 100-120°F (38-46°C), and some survive temperatures right up to 140°F (60°C). If there is bacteria in your tap water, the batch of beer will be on its way to ruin before you even get the yeast into it.

If your water source is a deep well, there is a fair chance that, most of the time, there are no bacteria in your water. However, there is no guarantee that there are always no bacteria in well water.

One day a homebrewer came into the homebrew shop complaining about off-flavors in his beer. He described his problems, and it was obvious that his brews were being contaminated by bacteria. We examined possible causes. All his procedures seemed OK, except that he was adding cold well water to his cooled wort. Even though he was adamant that his well water was clean, we advised him to boil all of his brewing water. The contamination disappeared. His case is not unusual...

If you ever get a chance, look at your water through a microscope. You'll be amazed at what is floating around in that clear, "clean" glass of water. We can almost guarantee that there is some sort of bacteria in there. If you boil all the water that goes into your brew, you will kill all the bacteria that might be there.

If your water supply is a municipal system, the water department adds chlorine to it. Why? It's not to improve the flavor. It's to kill the bacteria in it. It usually doesn't get them all, and at best only retards their growth. Even if your water doesn't have an off odor to it, there are probably bacteria in it. Don't take a chance. Assume that there are. Boil all your brewing water. An added benefit is that boiling water drives off chlorine. Chlorine in beer can create unpleasant medicinal, "phenolic" flavors. If you've boiled off the chlorine, it isn't there to spoil your beer.

If for some reason you can't boil all your water, there are just two options open to you. The first is to crank your hot-water heater up to 140°F (60°C) a few hours before you pull off any brewing water. It won't get rid of the chlorine, but a couple of hours at 140°F (60°C) will kill any bacteria that are in it.

The second option is to purchase an activated-carbon water filter that is silver-impregnated. You don't even need to install it into your plumbing; just take it to the hardware store and get the fittings that will enable you to convert from your faucet threads to the nylon hose that supplies the filter. Then you can just screw it onto your faucet when you are ready to brew. Activated carbon filters, also known as charcoal or "taste-and-odor" filters, remove chlorine. If the charcoal is silver-impregnated, it kills bacteria as long as it remains "clean". Depending on your water supply, that may be 500 or 2,000 gallons throughput. Replace any cartridge when it gets the least bit discolored or has any aroma

Don't get ripped off buying a filter. A 10"(25 cm) activated-carbon filter and housing should only cost about $50, and replacement cartridges $25 or less; silver-impregnated cartridges cost substantially more. Whatever you do, don't let a fast-talking salesman sell you an ion-exchange water softener. You don't need one, and it will hurt, rather than help, your brewing water. Ditto for reverse-osmosis; it's nice, but at ten times the price. If you already have such a filter, you will need to add a teaspoon of gypsum and 1/4 teaspoon of table salt to virtually every beer you brew, above and beyond the treatment required in the recipe. Reverse-osmosis strips all minerals out of the water, and the brewing process requires minerals.

So ignore any advice you ever hear that recommends adding water straight from your tap to your brew. Always treat any water that will be added by boiling, filtering or tapping it from a hot-water heater set at over 140°F (60°C).

Speaking of water, when it's ready to brew with, stop calling it water. Call it "liquor". Once brewers have treated water, that's what we call it. Why? To avoid confusing untreated water with treated water. Once it's treated, it's liquor. Now that we have you talking like a brewer, let's get on to how much liquor you will need.

You will only need to boil the malt extract with about two gallons of liquor, but you will need 5 gallons of wort going into the fermenter. It is absolutely important that this 3 gallons of "make-up" liquor be sterile. Since you're going to have two gallons of boiling-hot wort that needs to be cooled down to below 80°F (27°C) before you pitch it with the yeast, you can kill two birds with one stone by boiling, and then refrigerating, three gallons of water the day before you brew. That way your water is really cold, and your wort in the fermenter will be cooled down to 100°F (38°C) instead of 120°F (49°C) or so.

You can't put your sterile water into a dirty milk jug, though. It would be defeating the purpose to sterilize your water and then put it into any container that you don't know is absolutely sterile.

SANITIZING

The very first thing that you are going to do to start brewing is to learn how to sterilize equipment. It's really one of the most important things you will need to know about brewing anyway!

You can't sterilize anything that isn't already essentially clean. Whether you accumulate three plastic milk jugs or six two-liter soda bottles, you need to rinse out every trace of their contents immediately after they are emptied. Put a little detergent and hot water in one, screw the rinsed lid on, and shake it well. Uncap the bottle and pour the detergent solution into the next container, and so on down the line. Go back to the first jug or bottle, and rinse it with very hot water. Repeat this step a couple of times after the last traces of soap bubbles have disappeared. Detergent will ruin a batch of beer, so play it safe. If you use spring-water jugs, you can skip the detergent and just proceed from here.

Pour 3/4 teaspoon (that's teaspoon, not tablespoon) of bleach into each 2-liter bottle, or 1 teaspoon into each gallon jug. Don't guess; measure each addition into a measuring spoon over your kitchen sink, and pour it into each bottle. Fill each bottle with tap water to the top, and let them sit and sterilize. This concentration is more-or-less standard for sterilizing homebrew equipment: up to 1 1/2 teaspoons per gallon, or one fluid ounce to four gallons. Memorize this, and you won't wear out this page, because you will use these ratios over and over again: 1 fluid ounce of bleach per 4 gallons of water.

WATER	BLEACH
1 gallon or 4 liters	1-1/2 teaspoons (7 ml)
4 gallons or 15 liters	1 fluid ounce (30 ml)
5 gallons or 19 liters	1-1/4 fluid ounces (40 ml)
6-1/2 gallons or 25 liters	1-1/2 fluid ounces (50 ml)

Allow this "homebrew sterilant solution" to remain in contact with whatever needs to be sterilized for an hour or more. At The Seven Barrel Brewery, we keep all our fermentation equipment soaking in sterilant whenever it isn't actually being used.

We recommended that you buy a misting-type spray bottle in the previous chapter. Now is a good time to put a teaspoon of bleach into it, and fill it with tap water. This solution is stronger than the soaking solution, but not so strong that it should harm any tabletops or counters that you may spray it onto. It's not a good idea to save a buck here and just use an empty Windex® bottle, because ammonia and chlorine make poisonous chlorine gas. Other sprays may contain oils or other chemicals that could ruin your beer. Spend the money, and buy a new spray bottle!

In commercial breweries, from the smallest micro to the largest mega, more time is spent cleaning and sterilizing than actually brewing. It's not much different for homebrewing. It takes about 3 hours to brew a batch of extract homebrew, and half that time is spent cleaning and sterilizing. If you don't conscientiously rinse, clean and sterilize bottles, jugs, pails and equipment as they are emptied, if you let residues harden on or become contaminated, you can expect to either spend twice as much time cleaning, or brew bad beer. The choice is obvious.

Set the jugs or bottles aside to soak and see what leftovers in the refrigerator you can eat or feed to the dog to make room for your water. Then, sanitize your fermenter so it will be ready for tomorrow's brew.

The fermenter should be either a 6 or 7 gallon food-grade plastic pail with no visible scratches and with a lid, or a 5 or 6 gallon carboy. Why? Because either of these can be easily sanitized. Overall, beginning brewers are best advised to go with the cheaper food-grade plastic bucket. How do you sanitize it? Put in an ounce to an ounce-and-a-half of bleach, and fill it with water.

If you fill it one quart at a time, you can calibrate its volume at the same time. Why? Because at various times, you will need to know how much volume you have in your fermenter. The simplest way to do this is to mark levels on the outside of the bucket with an indelible marker. While you're at it, calibrate your kettle too. But don't try to etch marks right into the stainless steel, instead immerse your long-handled brewing spoon and scratch measuring lines corresponding to the water level into the edge of the spoon.

Fill the fermenter. Put everything that won't rust that you will use brewing, all your spoons, funnels, strainers, airlocks and stoppers or grommets, right into the sterilant solution. Cover it and leave it overnight.

Go back to getting your sterile make-up liquor ready. Get out your kettle and boil up a little over three gallons of water.

Empty out your sterile-water-chilling jugs. With a very-clean, just scrubbed-and-rinsed funnel, and a Pyrex® measuring cup for a ladle, pour a cup or so of boiling water into each jug, swirl it around to rinse out the chlorine, and dump the rinse. Leave your jugs draining on a paper towel and top-up your boiling kettle to a bit over three gallons. If you let the water boil for ten minutes or so, it will drive off most of the chlorine.

Put a clean lid on the kettle, stopper up your sink and put enough cold water into it so that it comes at least half-way up the sides of your boiling kettle as you immerse the kettle into the water bath. After five minutes or so, drain and refill the sink. The brewing liquor should be cooled down to near body temperature. Using your measuring cup and funnel, fill the bottles with the sterile water, cap them, and refrigerate them.

Go to bed. You're done. Tomorrow, you will brew your first homebrew.

BREW DAY

On brew day, fill your kettle with less than two gallons of water and heat it to boiling. If you are using malt extract in the syrup form, open the can and set it in another pan or a kettle of hot water, to heat it so that the warmed syrup will run out more readily. When your brewing liquor comes to a boil, remove it from the heat to a countertop that won't be difficult to clean if you spill any extract. Using a rubber spatula, slowly scrape the extract out of the can and into the kettle. Stir the liquor and extract to mix them. Scrape the can clean, mix the wort very thoroughly, and return it to the heat. Scrape around the bottom of your brewpot with your spatula to be sure that all the extract is dissolved into the wort. Do it a couple of times, so that the extract doesn't scorch on the bottom of your brewpot.

Boil your extract wort for 45 minutes. Ignore directions that imply otherwise. Besides the fact that a 45 minute boil will ensure that any bacteria are killed, changes in wort constituents that are essential to flavor development require a boil of at least 45 minutes.

Be aware that simmering the wort just won't do. Brewing requires a steady, rolling boil. You need to see strong motion on the surface of the wort as heat "rolls" the wort around. Don't put a lid on the kettle, because it will cause it to boil over. Do adjust your burner's output to give you as intense a boil as you can get, without boiling the wort over. Boiling wort usually causes a sticky foam head to form. Wort that overflows your kettle and gets onto your range's burner is incredibly difficult to get off. Pay attention, and it won't happen.

If you are cursed with an electric range top, you should use a trivet under your brewpot to keep from scalding wort on the bottom of your pan. Trivets are essentially flat spirals of wire that dissipate heat, and are readily available at kitchen shops.

While your wort is boiling, empty the sanitizing solution out of your fermenting bucket, and invert it onto clean paper towels on a clean drainboard to drain. You are probably asking why you shouldn't be rinsing the chlorine out of it. Well, you can, and overall it's a good idea to, if you are willing to boil up a quart or so of water and rinse away the residue of the sanitizing solution. Otherwise, it is a choice between possibly picking up a slight aroma of eau-de-bandaids, or risking contamination that could entirely ruin the batch.

The reason that homebrewers use a one-ounce-per-bucket sanitizing solution is because the solution is strong enough to kill stray bacteria and wild yeast, but dilute enough so that its residue won't cause off-flavors in the beer.

Our experience is that this is 90% true; sometimes a barely-perceptible phenolic flavor occurs in brews where a film of sanitizing solution was left on equipment. All-in-all, we feel that it is worth the risk, because it averts the greater risk of losing a batch to contamination.

You should be getting near the end of the boil. If you want to personalize the batch with aroma hops, refer to the description in Chapter 5 of the style of beer you are brewing. If it mentions hop aroma, you can dramatically improve the aroma and flavor of the brew by adding "finishing" hops five minutes before the end of the brew.

Finishing hops are not meant to increase the bitterness. They provide a fresh hop aroma and flavor. If the aroma should be low to medium, add 1/4 ounce of an aroma variety of pelletized hops. If it should have a medium hop aroma, use 1/2 ounce. If it should have high hop aroma, add 1 ounce. Just gently drop the pellets into the wort. After the boil, they will settle out on the bottom of the kettle, along with proteins and other wort constituents that have come out of solution to form trub.

Trub is nasty-tasting stuff, and you will need to separate your wort from it as you transfer it into your fermenter. Cover your kettle and remove it from the burner. Get any sort of block that will hold the kettle tipped up an inch or so, and block it up to let the trub and any hop pellets settle to one side of the bottom.

In the meantime, wash your hands and spray the area where you are going to transfer into the fermenter with your sanitizing spray. Use a little common sense here; don't spray chlorine onto anything that it might bleach out. Set up your clean, sanitized fermenting bucket at a convenient height for filling, away from any drafts, and splash your 3 gallons of chilled liquor into the fermenter. Let it splash right in, because it is very important for the yeast that air becomes entrained in the liquid. Freshly-pitched yeast absolutely requires dissolved oxygen to grow, and beer always tastes better if the yeast has gone through a healthy growth cycle.

Cover the fermenter loosely with the lid until the wort in the kettle has cleared. It generally takes about ten minutes for the trub to settle out of two gallons of wort. When the wort is bright above the compactly-settled trub, start to rack the hot wort into the fermenter. Don't risk serious burns; don't try to pour the whole lot from the bucket into the fermenter. Wort burns can be serious, because the sugary solution sticks to what it strikes, and burns deeply. Use your measuring cup to ladle most of it over to the fermenting bucket, and splash it in.

Get all the clear wort out of the boiling kettle that you can, but don't go crazy about it. Leave what is mixed up with trub behind. You should collect five gallons into your fermenter.

Because it is impossible not to expose your wort to air at this point, and in fact it is essential that you cause as much air as possible to become entrained in the wort as you fill the fermenter, develop some sanitation awareness and use it at this critical point. Avoid breathing your hot, moist, bacteria-laden breath into the fermenter. Don't drip sweat into it. Shower the day you brew. Wear fresh clothing. Keep your hands clean.

After you have filled the fermenter, lock the lid down onto it,

AIRLOCK
Properly
filled with
sterilant
solution.

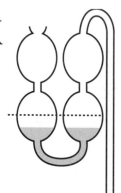

and fit the airlock through the grommet or stopper in the lid; don't forget to fill the airlock with sterilant solution. The bulges in the airlock should be filled 1/3 - 1/2 with a standard sterilant solution. If you have spilled any wort on the sides of your fermenting bucket, clean it off now, and spray around just below the lid with your sanitizing spray to keep any bacteria from growing in the crack.

You will need to cool the wort to below 80°F (27°C) before you pitch the yeast. This can be accomplished in about an hour by filling your kitchen sink with water and ice cubes and immersing the bucket into it. Don't fill it so much that the bucket floats; you don't want to risk dumping the fermenter over.

In the meantime, rehydrate your dry yeast. Dried yeast always performs better if it is rehydrated before it is pitched. Warm, sterile water works better than wort. Boil up a cup or so of water, thoroughly clean and rinse your Pyrex® measuring cup, and pour the water into it. Cover it tightly with a plastic wrap or tin foil, and put it into your refrigerator's freezer compartment for ten or fifteen minutes. You want to cool it to body temperature, or a little over. When you hold your hand against the side, it should feel warm, but not hot. You are shooting for about 95-110°F (35-43°C).

When you judge that the temperature is right, tear a corner off of each of the yeast packages, peel back a corner of your "lid", and shake the yeast into the measuring cup.

You should see the yeast begin to react after 15-30 minutes. The yeast rehydrates with a flourish, throwing up a frothy head.

When the wort in the fermenter has cooled, pop the lid off it and pitch the yeast. Give the fermenter a few good circular twists to disperse the yeast, clamp the lid back down, and set it somewhere out of harm's way, away from children, pets, and curious passersby. For ales, you generally want the room temperature to be cool, in the range of 60-70°F (16-21°C), and even cooler for lagers.

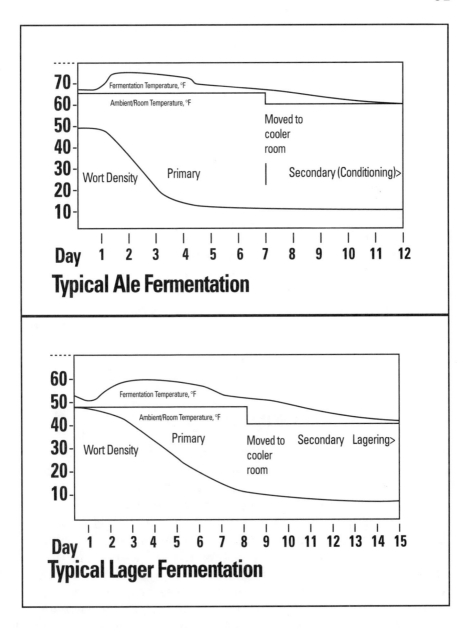

Typical Ale Fermentation

Typical Lager Fermentation

FERMENTATION

You will know when fermentation gets underway, because the carbon dioxide from fermentation creates pressure, and that pressure escapes by bubbling out through the airlock. You can learn to gauge the intensity of the fermentation by the intensity of the bubbling.

Active fermentation should be evident within 12 to 36 hours of pitching. If it isn't, check the obvious things first. If you can smell it fermenting, is there actually any liquid in the trap of the airlock? Does the lid form a seal? There is usually nothing wrong with the yeast or the wort.

The fastest fermentation is rarely the best fermentation. High temperatures and fast fermentations usually produce poorer-quality beer. Very fruity ales should generally take three to five days after pitching to ferment out; lagers should take six, seven or even ten days. A very effective trick for lowering the fermentation temperature 5-10°F (3-5°C) is to place the fermenter in a pan of cold water, and place one end of a dampened towel into that water. Drape the rest of the towel up and over as much of the fermenter as possible. The evaporation that takes place from the towel will draw heat out of the fermenter.

Plan to bottle your brew about two weeks after fermentation started. If you monitor the bubbling through the airlock, it is generally safe to bottle when bubbling has gone from active and rapid, to slow and occasional, to no bubbling at all for three or four days.

PRIMING AND BOTTLING

Bottled homebrew is primed with brewers' corn sugar (or cane sugar or DME) to carbonate it. After bottling, the few yeast cells left in suspension in your beer will use the priming sugar to produce enough carbon dioxide to carbonate your beer.

How much carbonation is right? If the kit, or recipe, doesn't recommend an amount of corn sugar to use as bottle priming, 3/4 of a cup (200 ml) is a pretty standard happy-median. If you want the carbonation to be more true to style, look at one of the recipes further along in this book, for the same style of beer.

If you substitute DME, honey or table sugar for corn sugar at bottling, use 1 cup (240 ml) of DME (or honey), or a little less than about 3/4 cup of table sugar, in place of 3/4 of a cup of corn sugar.

Bottling goes a lot easier if you have willing help to cap the bottles as you fill them. If you don't have willing help, don't worry about it, will just take a little longer.

You need to sterilize all your bottles as the first step to bottling. If your dishwasher has a "sanitizing" cycle, you can load it

up with your bottles and run the machine without detergent to sterilize them. Or you can soak them overnight in a clean 15-20 gallon (60-75 liter) bucket of water treated with the standard sanitizing solution, or just fill each one with the sterilizing solution. Finally, you can put a half-ounce (15 ml) of water into each bottle and stack them all in your oven, set at 200°F (95°C) for an hour, and shut the heat off about an hour or so before you will begin bottling. Any one of these methods works just fine. It is a good idea to sanitize your crown caps as well. This can be done by soaking them for 1/2 hour in your sterilant solution, or by boiling in a small pot with a quart of water for 5 minutes. Leave them in the pot until you start to use them.

In the meantime, gently carry your fermenter over and place it on a sturdy, solid chair, blocking it up at a slightly tilted angle with a book. You want to leave it there to settle for an hour or so to let the sediment that inevitably gets roiled up settle back down.

Boil up a pint or so of water, and stir your priming sugar into it. Leave it to cool while you set up your sanitized priming bucket and racking cane, tubing and bottle-filler on the floor next to the sturdy, solid chair in an area that is free from drafts, and that is easy to clean up, because you are likely to spill a little beer filling the bottles.

You are going to have to start a siphon to get clear beer from your fermenter into the priming bucket. You can depress the valve on the end of your bottle filler and suck to get the siphon going, but it's pretty likely that you are going to end up contaminating your beer by doing it. Just in case you think your mouth isn't oozing bacteria, let us assure you that it is. We all know homebrewers that rinse and gargle with bleach solution before starting a siphon to prevent contaminating the tubing, but there is no guarantee that it actually works, and we can't recommend it, for health reasons alone.

Homebrewers have devised dozens of more sanitary methods for starting a siphon. One of them is to boil a quart or so of water in another pan, and then pour it into one of your chilled-water bottles. Cut a 2 or 3" (50-75mm) piece off one end of your tubing, and put both pieces back into the sterilant solution. Wash your hands very thoroughly (you should do this again before you prime your beer, and again before you bottle), and drain the three pieces of your racking assembly. Assemble your racking cane to one end of the tubing and your bottle filler to the other end. Pull the plastic cap off the working- end of the racking cane, and slide the short piece of tubing over the end of the cane.

Now stand the bottle filler back in the sanitizing solution, press down on it so that the valve opens, and suck on the end of the short piece of tubing until you get sterilant in your mouth. Cap the end with your thumb, and lower it back into the sanitizer. Pull off the short piece of tubing. Put the trub cap back onto the end of the racking cane. As long as both ends of the bottling rig are submerged, it will stay full of sanitizer.

Drain a bottle, and set it on the floor. Keeping the end of the racking cane submerged, pull the bottle filler out, and set it into the bottle. Press down on it to start the siphon, just to check that everything is working.

Next, carefully lift the racking cane out of the sanitizing solution and quickly plunge it into the bottle of hot water. Press down on the bottle filler again, so that hot water replaces the sanitizing solution in the tubing. Make sure the rig isn't going to fall over, and set up for priming.

Empty the sanitizing solution out of your priming bucket and invert it on clean paper towels to drain. Wash your hands. Make sure that the windows in the room are closed.

Set up your bottles ready to fill. Drain any water or sanitizing solution out of them. Set up your crown caps and capper within easy reach.

Set the priming bucket upright on the floor next to your chair and fermenter, and gently pour the priming solution into it. Pop the lid off your fermenter, and slide it aside so that the fermenter is partially uncovered. Bring the bottle and racking cane up near the opening. Quickly pull out the cane and submerse the racking cane into the beer. Check to see that you still have a siphon going, and run beer all the way into the bottle filler. If you still have a siphon, depress the bottle filler, and rack the beer into the priming bucket. Position the racking cane so that you pull the beer from the uptilted side of the fermenter, so that you won't pull sediment into the racking cane.

As you get near the bottom, watch the end of the racking cane. Try to get all the beer you can, but leave the sediment behind and enough beer to take a hydrometer reading. The hydrometer reading gives you the Terminal Gravity (TG). Tilt the fermenting bucket a little bit more, keeping the racking cane submerged until you have collected all the wort but a cup or so. If you can keep from losing the siphon now, you won't have to get it going again. When you are through, lift the fermenter off the chair and prop it up nearby, tilted.

Lift the priming bucket up onto the chair. With your sterilized spoon, gently stir the beer to mix in the priming solution, but try not to splash the beer around doing it. Lift the racking cane out of the fermenter and submerge it in the priming bucket.

You are ready to bottle. The bottle-filler lets you control the start and finish of each fill. Fill each bottle with beer until it comes up nearly level with the rim of each bottle. Then lift out the filler and transfer it to the next bottle. If you are alone, stop and set a cap loosely on top of each bottle after it is filled. If you have a helper, have them do it. Set the first bottles that you fill an arm's-length away, so that you won't knock the caps off as you accumulate more and more full bottles.

Tilt your priming bucket as you get near the bottom, so that you get all the beer you can. When the racking cane sucks air, you will lose the siphon.

Go back now and crimp the caps onto the bottles. Take a break. Have a brew.

Rinse off the bottles, set the bottles in their cases, and put them out of the way, but at room temperature. Now you get to clean up the mess (you will get better at doing this, and you'll learn to make less of a mess). Really clean and rinse your fermenter, priming bucket and equipment well, but don't scratch the plastic in your zeal.

Leave your bottles at room temperature for 48 hours to a week, so that the yeast will go about the business of carbonating the beer in the bottles. If you chill the bottles too early, your beer probably won't carbonate.

Put the bottles in a cool place after a week or so to let the beer condition. If you can be patient, your first taste of your own beer will be that much better. If you are like most people, you won't wait, but try to anyway.

CHAPTER 4

INGREDIENTS

U p to now, you have been using pre-hopped malt extract at the simplest level of homebrewing. By basing your brews on plain, unhopped malt extracts, adjusting the water to a mineral content that suits the beer style, and adding hops yourself you will gain much more control over the flavor of the finished beer, and have more fun brewing it.

Let us guide you through the brewer's ingredients warehouse. We'll take a look at extracts, base and specialty malts, grain and sugar adjuncts, hops and hop pellets, mineral salts and acid, finings and yeast options:

MALT EXTRACTS

Not all extracts are equal. Some are just plain better than others, because some are all-malt, and others contain unmalted barley, sugar or other adjuncts. Some extracts are specifically designed to do particular things.

A good example is extra-light extract. It has only about one-third the color of light/gold extracts. Part of the reason why it is lighter is because it is condensed less than other extracts. Consequently, it gives only about 90% of the density that most other extracts do. If you are going to substitute light extract for extra-light in a recipe, you will need to reduce the amount by 10%, or cut the DME (Dry Malt Extract) in the recipe back by about 8%.

Alexander's extra-light extract is also more fermentable than most others. It seems to be about 10% more fermentable than most others, while John Bull, Geordie and Mountmellick give a 10% or so higher Terminal Gravity than others.

Which brand of extract should you use in a recipe? Ask for advice at the brewshop. Look at the recipe; divide the OG by the TG. If the result is less than 4, you should use one of the less-fermentable brands of extract, if the answer is greater than 4, use a more fermentable extract.

It is inevitable that you will have to substitute an ingredient for the one specified in a recipe. Just try to do it logically. Look at the Color and Utilization Table in the Appendix. Any substitutions in a recipe should be made conservatively, and the item should be as similar as possible to what is specified. If the recipe calls for amber extract, don't substitute light unless you have a particular reason for doing so. Moreover, expect that British extracts will give British ale recipes a more authentic character than German or American extracts will. German lager recipes, on the other hand, are always best suited by German malt extracts.

LIGHT MALT EXTRACT: Light malt extract is also known as pale or gold malt extract. It is made from pale, pilsener or lager malts. The color ranges from a light straw to pale golden. This malt extract is used when you want a light-colored beer or if you want to add your own specialty malts to control the flavor and color of your finished beer. The color range is from 4-8 SRM.

AMBER MALT EXTRACT: This extract starts with same base as light malt extract, with the addition of crystal malts and/or colorings. Amber malt extract tends to give your finished beer more body and a sweeter taste. This is a good malt extract to use when you want to make a full-bodied beer with a residual caramel sweetness. The color of this malt extract ranges from a light reddish gold to a deep amber. The color range is from 8-15 SRM.

DARK MALT EXTRACT: Dark malt extract also uses the same base malts, but with the addition of dark malts like black malt or roasted barley. Some dark malt extracts may use colorings to darken them. The color of dark malt extract ranges from a dark reddish brown to a deep ruby black. This malt extract will give your beer a deep roasted, malty taste. The color range is from 20-35 SRM.

EXTRA LIGHT MALT EXTRACT: The lightest of all the malt extracts, this extract is made from very lightly colored base malts. Use to make very pale or light colored lagers and ales. The color range is from 2-4 SRM .

WHEAT MALT EXTRACT: Because wheat malt is low in the enzymes needed to convert starches to sugars, wheat malt extracts are made with proportions of malted wheat and malted barley. The malted barley lends some of its enzymes to enable the full conversion of the malted wheat. Wheat malt extract is used to make the many different styles of wheat beers.

DRY MALT EXTRACTS

Malt extracts can also be found in a dried form. The same classifications, light, amber, dark, extra light; are available. Dry malt extract, since it contains no water, is about 10% stronger than liquid malt extract. You will need to adjust your recipes if you substitute dry malt for liquid malt extract.

All of the extracts are sold prepacked in a variety of sizes. Malt extract syrups come prepackaged in 3.3 LBS (1.5 KG), 4 LBS (1.8 KG) and 6.6 LBS (3 KG) containers. Dry malt extracts come in 1 LB (.45 KG) and 3 LB (1.4 KG) bags. Most, if not all, of the malt extracts are also available in bulk containers. These barrels and bags of malt extract can be found at most good homebrew stores, allowing you to buy as much or as little malt extract as you want and at substantial savings.

GRAINS

By definition, beer is a grain-based fermented beverage. Most grains are difficult to brew with. Malting (sprouting and kilning) grains simplifies them, making them better-suited to brewing.

Malted grains, then, are the building blocks for all beers. Malted barley is the grain that is best suited to brewing. From it, we are able to extract fermentable sugars, non-fermentable dextrins and soluble proteins which will give beer body, fullness, flavor and color.

Barley is malted by first steeping it in water, then allowing it to sprout. The sprouted grain is dried in a kiln. The degree to which it is sprouted and kilned gives each type of malt individual flavor and brewing characteristics.

As far as brewing is concerned, grains can be divided into four families: Base malts, roasted malts, crystal malts, and adjunct grains. Generally, base malts and grain adjuncts need to be mashed to be used in brewing, because they are largely starch and complex proteins. Roasted and crystal malts can either be mashed or used as-is in extract-based brews.

Roasted and crystallized malts and grain adjuncts are often grouped together as specialty grains. These contribute very unique flavors and other characteristics to beer.

BASE MALTS

Certain malts are used as the "base" for different styles of beer. These malts compose the greatest percentage of goods in mash-based brews. The base malts are:

PILSENER MALT: The lightest-colored of all malts (1.3-1.8° SRM), and the most delicate in flavor. Genuine Pilsener malt is "undermodified", which means that it is sprouted (converted) less fully than other malts, so that it is more starchy and "steely". Consequently, it generally needs to be step- or decoction-mashed.

LAGER MALT: Traditionally, lager malt was also undermodified. German and European lager malt generally needs to be step- or decoction-mashed. American, Australian and New Zealand lager malt is fairly-well modified in comparison and can be simply infusion mashed. It is also known as "brewers' malt". In all cases, lager malt has a light color (1.5-2° SRM) and flavor. When lager or brewers' malt is specified, two-row malt is called for. Six-row malt, widely used by large American breweries in combination with corn or rice for American lager, has a coarser flavor, and is normally only used where a high percentage of grain adjuncts are called for as well.

PALE MALT: A bit darker-colored (2.5-3° SRM) and fuller-flavored, but still quite light compared with specialty malts. It is probably the most widely-used base malt among all-grain homebrewers. It can be mashed by a single saccharification rest. It is used in a great many beers, from bitters to barley-wines.

MILD ALE MALT: A slightly darker (3.2° SRM) pale malt. It gives a somewhat drier, toastier flavor. Traditionally used in brown and mild ales, although substituting pale malt won't radically alter the flavor or the color of the beer.

VIENNA AND MUNICH MALT: Darker versions of lager malt. Vienna malt is the lighter of the two at 4-7° SRM. Munich malt commonly ranges between 5 and 15° SRM, depending upon the source. Both of these malts have a pleasant "toasted" flavor, and can form the base for Vienna and Oktoberfest brews.

CARAMEL/CRYSTAL MALTS

Caramel and Crystal malts are kilned from freshly-sprouted barley that is stewed at 140-167°F (60-75°C) before it is dried and roasted. Caramel malt is produced if the starches are partially saccharified during the stewing; crystal malt is kilned from completely saccharified kernels. These malts may be used interchangeably.

Caramel/Crystal malts increase residual sweetness, mouthfeel, head retention and the body of beer, because crystalline sugars are less fermentable than usual malt sugars and give a higher Terminal Gravity, and because the process simplifies protein complexes; simple proteins give beer a more substantial, silky body, and make great foam. The longer and the hotter the temperature that the malt is kilned off at, the darker the color and the more intense the flavor of the malt.

Brewers rely heavily on the range of flavors of these malts, choosing them by their color. We list them in the order of their increasing color:

CARAPILS MALT: The palest of the caramel/crystal malts. It has a color of from 1.5-2.5° SRM. Carapils increases a beer's Terminal Gravity, body and head without substantially increasing its color. It is very commonly used in recipes where residual sweetness is desired, often in combination with darker-colored caramel malts.

CARAVIENNE MALT: The caramelized equivalent of Vienna malt; it gives a little more flavor than carapils malt.

CARAMUNICH MALT: The caramelized equivalent of, that's right, Munich malt! Again, an exceptionally-nice flavored malt.

CARASTAN MALT: A malt that is commonly used interchangeably with carapils malt, although it is much darker and more caramel-like in flavor. It is commonly less caramelized than other caramel malts. All in all, it is sort of a compromise malt; its color may range from 10-20° SRM.

LIGHT CARAMEL/CRYSTAL MALT: Available as 20°, 30° and 40° SRM, or variations within the range of 20-40° SRM. These malts are very similar in flavor throughout the color range, although the crystal malts have a very much finer and crisper flavor than the caramel malts.

CRYSTAL MALT: The most commonly used of the caramel/crystal malts, it has a mild roasty character that the lighter malts don't. Either caramel or fully-crystallized malts of 50-60° SRM are both sold as crystal malt, and generally considered to be interchangeable.

DARK CRYSTAL MALT: A broad range of colors are sold as dark crystal; color may be anywhere from 70-120° SRM. The darker it is kilned, the more intensely-roasty these malts become.

ROASTED MALTS

Roasted malts are kilned at high temperatures to give them fuller flavor and color. Amber malt has enough raw starch remaining in it that it should be mashed, but the other roasted malts can be used as kettle adjuncts. All the roasted malts give very unique flavors to beer.

AMBER MALT: Malt that is roasted to a toasty color and flavor. It gives a coppery color to beer, with a dry, biscuity flavor. Biscuit malt is the Belgian version. It ranges between 20 and 40° SRM.

BROWN MALT: A darker version of amber malt (40-80° SRM), with a strong, dry, biscuity flavor.

CHOCOLATE MALT: Gives beer a nutty, chocolate-to-coffee-like flavor. Depending on the amount used, it contributes a rusty-brown to deep-mahogany hue. Although it is very dark (400-550° SRM), it can be used fairly liberally without becoming too intense or phenolic.

BLACK MALT: Also known as Black Patent malt. Malt is roasted to 500-650° SRM; it is very crisp, almost to the point of charcoal. Black malt gives a very sharp, almost burnt character to beer.

ROASTED BARLEY: Kilned from unmalted barley. Very dark in color (450-650° SRM), with an acrid and roasty flavor much like French-roast coffee. Used in small amounts it gives beer a reddish-brown hue, and in larger quantities it accounts for the black color of stouts.

OTHER MALTS

Grains other than barley can be malted. It is usually advisable to mash these in combination with malted barley to ensure that the starches in them will be converted.

MALTED WHEAT: This is the malt that you need to use to make the great German-style wheat beers. Malted wheat has no husk, so you will need to use a percentage of malted barley to add malt enzymes and to aid in lautering.

MALTED RYE: Used by some of the smaller craft breweries to make their specialty beers. Rye malt gives a dry, crisp nuttiness to a beer.

FLAKED GRAINS

Flaked grains are the easiest way to add unmalted grain to a mash. Flaked grains are made by passing the wet grains through rollers under great pressure. The heat produced by the rolling of the grains gelatinizes the starches in the unmalted grains. The starches from flaked or rolled grains can be easily mixed into your mash allowing the enzymes in malted barley to convert them to sugars.

FLAKED BARLEY: This is what Guinness uses in their world famous stout. Flaked barley adds a smoothness to beers. It also adds body and aids in head retention.

FLAKED CORN (also called flaked maize): Corn is used in most of the American-style pilsners made here in the United States. It is used to lighten the body, color and flavor in beer.

FLAKED OATS: Oats add body and a silky smoothness to a beer. Great for adding to dark beers like stouts. Use instant oats in a mash as they are more readily converted and do not tend to stick as much in a mash as regular rolled oats.

FLAKED WHEAT: Flaked wheat is used to replicate the character of many Belgian ales. Flaked wheat adds body and improves head formation and retention.

FLAKED RICE: Another adjunct used by some of the big American breweries in making their pilsners. Used like flaked maize to lighten the body and flavor in a beer, flaked rice gives a beer a dry crispness.

SUGARS

There are many different types of sugars used in brewing. Particular sugars are needed to give certain beers a particular flavor and aroma. Some of the most famous breweries in the world use some form of sugar in their beers. Do not be afraid to experiment with different types of sugars in your beer, just remember not to use large amounts. The use of sugars in large amounts will leave the finished beer thin and cidery, not very beer-like. A good general rule to follow is to use no more than 10-15% sugars in any recipe.

BROWN SUGAR: Made from adding a small amount of molasses to refined sugar. Brown sugar gives your beer a unique rummy sweetness. Try using 1/2 LB (.23 KG) to 1-1/2 LB (.68 KG) in your next brown ale.

CORN SUGAR: Also called dextrose, it is a highly fermentable sugar. When used in small amounts, 10-15 % of the total fermentables, corn sugar will lighten the body of a beer while raising its alcohol content. Corn sugar is best used in priming your beer.

TABLE SUGAR: Table sugar is sucrose. Can be used as a substitute for corn sugar in a pinch although corn sugar is preferred.

LACTOSE: Used in milk stouts, lactose is an unfermentable sugar. It will give your beer sweetness. Add lactose at the same time you add priming sugar.

MALTO-DEXTRINE: An unfermentable dextrine that will add body and smoothness to a finished beer. Can be used to adjust a finished beer to give it extra body.

MOLASSES: Molasses is the uncrystallized sugars and impurities left behind in the refining of cane sugar. Its addition to a beer will impart a definite strong, buttery, rum-like flavor and aroma.

MAPLE SYRUP: We use maple syrup here at the brewery to make our seasonal maple ale. Maple syrup, especially the darker grade, will lend its own special aroma and flavor to a beer. Use from 1 PINT (.48 L) in lighter beers to 3 PINTS (1.4 L) in darker styles.

HONEY: A great adjunct to use in brewing, honey will give your beer a delicate, floral and herbal aroma and flavor. When used in large amounts honey will give your beer a winy, hot, alcoholic taste. Honey can lend a nice subtleness to your brew.

HOPS

Hops are as much a customary ingredient of modern beers as is malt. The hop's bitterness balances the sweetness derived from the malt, and its flavor and aroma adds spice to the beer.

Hops grow on annual vines from perennial rootstock. The small flowerlike cones of the hops are what is used in brewing. Brewers call these flowers "whole hops", as opposed to processed hops, such as hop pellets and hop extracts. Many homebrewers grow at least some of their own hops right in their own backyards; the tall vines are very hardy, and rather decorative to boot.

The essence of the hop flower is its sticky yellow lupulin, which contains the resins that brewing will transmute into "alpha acids" (the bittering elements in beer), and essential oils that give off aromatic floral and spicy esters. The fresher that the hops are and the more conscientiously that they have been stored, the more bitterness and aroma that they retain. Don't buy brown hops. Always buy hops that have been stored refrigerated.

One very efficient method of preserving hop quality is to pelletize them. Hops are ground, then extruded into pellets. "Type 90 Pellets" take up only about 10% of the space of whole hops, which makes handling and storage easier. Pellets also settle out nicely on the bottom of the brew kettle at the end of the boil. Even better, they can easily be compacted out of the way into a cone at the center of the kettle's bottom, by whirlpooling the wort with a paddle for a minute or two after the boil is over. The density of the pellets also gives them good protection from oxidation, hop freshness' biggest enemy, so pellets lose less bitterness over time than whole hops do. Its not a perfect world, however, and pelletizing dramatically diminishes hop aromatics. For this reason, although the majority of homebrewers rely on hop pellets for bitterness, most homebrewers rely on a small percentage of whole hops added at, or even after the end of the wort boil for beer styles that require significant hop flavor and aroma.

Hops are organic, and therefore inconsistent. Their bitterness changes from year to year, and even from lot to lot. For that reason, an "alpha acid" (%AA; bitterness) analysis accompanies each lot of hops, so that brewers know how much bitterness that hop will give to the beer. Alpha acids are the bittering substance in beer. An ounce of 12% AA hops will make a beer twice as bitter as an ounce of 4% AA hops.

Commercial brewers also have the beer bitterness analyzed,

so that they can adjust hopping rates to keep the beer consistent. Beer bitterness is measured in a lab, and is expressed as International Bitterness Units (IBU). Homebrewers don't have the resources of a lab, but still must deal with duplicating bitterness levels given in recipes.

Why? Let's look at an example. A recipe says to add an ounce of Cascades. You brew it once from an ounce of Cascades that are 6% alpha acid, and you just love the beer. You brew it again, but this time the Cascades that the shop has in stock are 4% alpha acid. When you drink this brew, you don't like it. It's only 2/3 as bitter and hoppy. The problem is that hops' bitterness cannot be predicted by weight.

Dave Line (the English homebrewer and author whose Big Book of Brewing more or less launched the craft homebrewing revival in America) solved the problem by devising Alpha Acid Units (AAUs), adopted by the American Homebrewers Association as Homebrew Bitterness Units (HBUs). (We use HBUs in this book.) HBUs are a simple way of defining the amount of hops to add. Each HBU represents one ounce (28.35 GRAMS) of 1% AA hops. For example, 6 HBUs specifies one ounce of Cascades when they are 6% alpha acid, and one-and-a half ounces (42.5 GRAMS) of Cascades when they are 4% alpha acid. Whoever knew that math could be so useful...

Shop for hops armed with your recipe. Look at the %AA marked on the package. Look at the recipe. For each addition:

divide the HBUs in the recipe
by the % alpha acidity (%AA) of the hops on hand.

Weigh out many ounces. It is really simple. Math rules!

We recommend using hop pellets, and whole hops only where a hop flavor and aroma is characteristic of the style, and only for hops that are called for at, near or after the end of the boil. If whole hops are substituted for pellets, increase the HBUs that the recipe calls for by about 20%, because whole hops do not release as much lupulin as pellets do (because pellets are ground, and the grinding breaks the lupulin sacs, releasing more of it into the wort).

One more thing. The amount of alpha acid that makes it into solution decreases as wort density increases. If you are doing a partial boil, the density of the wort in the kettle is about 2-1/2 times greater than the same wort in a full five-gallon boil. All of the extract recipes in this book are based upon a 2-gallon (partial) boil, while the mash recipes are for a full 5-gallon boil. If you change the volume of the boil, you will also change its density, and you will need to adjust the recipe to reflect the difference in utilization. See Chapter 8 and the appendices for more on hop utilization.

HOP VARIETIES

A large proportion of all the hops grown worldwide are grown right here in America, but the major varieties grown here have not been very well respected. Elsewhere in the world, brewers often disparage a particular hop by inferring that it is "American". Most homebrewers would choose to use British and German varieties for aroma and flavor if it weren't for the fact that if and when they are available, European-grown whole hops are invariably more expensive and usually in far poorer shape than domestic hops. Happily, some American hop growers have reacted to the craft brewing revolution by planting European varieties, so that more and more domestically-grown British and German hop types are becoming available. Given the choice, homebrewers are well-advised to choose domestically-grown whole hops.

Hop varieties can be basically separated into two types: ale hops and lager hops. Although the line between them is fairly hazy, it is a fact that most of the geographic beer styles rely on particular hops for their individual characters. German hop types generally best-suit German beers and British beers are complemented by English hop types.

HOP VARIETIES

Distinctively-ale hops	Crossover hops	Distinctively-lager hops
Brewers Gold		
Bullion		
	Cascade	
	Centennial	
Challenger		
	Chinook	
		Cluster
	Columbia	
Comet		
	Crystal	
	Eroica	
Fuggles		
	Galena	
Goldings		
		Hallertau
		Hersbruck
Kent Goldings		
		Liberty
		Mount Hood
Northdown		
	Northern Brewer	
	Nugget	
		Perle
	Olympia	
		Pride of Ringwood
		Saaz
Styrian Goldings		
		Spalt
		Talisman
		Tettnang
	Willamette	
Wye Target		

WATER TREATMENT

Remember that water is what comes out of your sink's faucet. Liquor is what you use to brew beer. Liquor is water that is being used to brew beer with. Water usually requires some sort of treatment to be good brewing liquor.

Historically, one of the very major influences on why the beers from a given location were different from beers from other places was the water available for brewing with. Munich is renown for their brown beers. Munich brewers brewed sweet, dark beers because Munich's water is very alkaline, and because brewing is very pH sensitive. To make good beer, the mash needed to be more acidic than the pH of the mix of Munich's well water and light-colored malts produced. Munich brewers used dark malts, which are naturally acidic, to overcome the high pH of their water. They also used very delicate hops, and less of them, because alkalinity renders hop bitterness more coarse. Munich Dunkel became a style of beer because of the water.

Late in the last century, Munich began to meet the demands of its growing population by piping in water from the Bavarian Alps. This water had a very low mineral content and wasn't strongly alkaline. Munich brewers could brew very nice light-colored beers from it. They did, but they retained the characteristic maltiness and low bitterness of the world-famous Dunkel style. Soon enough, the new Munich Helles style became world famous too. Water scores another point.

Two other examples of water's influence on flavor are Dortmund-Pilsener lagers and English-Scottish ales. Pilsener and Dortmund recipes are nearly identical; the major difference in their flavors being the steeliness and saltiness of the Dortmunds (hard, sulfate and chloride water) as compared to the mellower Pilseners (soft, low-mineral water). The sharpness of the English ales (hard, sulfate water) is due to the water at hand, as is the sweeter style of Scots' ales (softer, more chloride water).

The beer you brew will be better if you adjust your water's mineral content and acidity to suit the style. You don't absolutely have to do it, and in truth, a lot of homebrewers don't make mineral treatments at all. Of those that do, most make mineral additions blindly. You don't have to make liquor adjustments either, and if you prefer, you can do it haphazardly, just adding a tablespoon or two of gypsum to whatever you brew. If you want to try to brew the best beer you can, however, then make liquor adjustments rationally.

Fortunately for us brewers, this is usually relatively simple. The hardest part can be getting a mineral analysis of the water that comes out of your faucet. If your tapwater is from a community system, then you can request an analysis from them. If you have well water, have the water tested for Hardness, Alkalinity, pH and Chloride content. The test kits to accomplish this can be purchased from an aquarium supply store for about $25, or you can have it done by a water analysis service (in the yellow pages), but check with your brewshop first - they may provide mineral analysis as a service to their customers.

Once you have your water analysis, use it to guide your liquor treatment. All you need to do is match the analytic parameters of your water supply with one of these categories:

As you can see, where Alkalinity as $CaCO_3$ is a significant percentage of the Hardness as $CaCO_3$, or exceeds it, the water supply is carbonate. (For brewing purposes, alkalinity and carbonate are interchangeable terms.) Compare your water to the chart. What category does it resemble the most? Use the category it fits most closely to guide your liquor adjustments as you brew the recipes in this book.

Finally, if the chloride content of your tap water is 40 mg/l or more, cut any table salt called for in any recipes in half. If the chloride is over 70 mg/l, don't make any table salt additions at all.

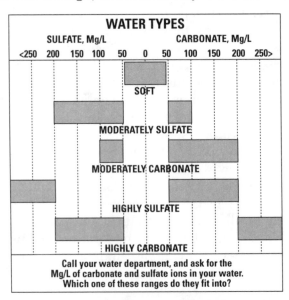

MINERAL SALTS

Homebrewers generally need only two mineral salts to prepare brewing liquor; calcium sulfate (most commonly as gypsum) and sodium chloride (table salt).

CALCIUM SULFATE OR GYPSUM: increases the calcium content of the brew, which improves mash conversion, wort clarity and yeast performance. Sulfate makes for a more pleasant hop bitterness. It is sold as gypsum (1 gram in 5 gallons = 12 mg/l Calcium, 29.5 mg/l Sulfate) or anhydrous calcium sulfate (1 gram in 5 gallons = 15.5 mg/l Calcium, 37 mg/l Sulfate).

SODIUM CHLORIDE OR COMMON TABLE SALT: brings out the overall flavor, and especially sweetness and roastiness. Sodium is pleasant to an extent, but too much sodium makes a harsh beer. Chloride accentuates roundness of flavor and improves clarity.

pH / ALKALINITY CORRECTION

The best beer comes from mashes and worts in the range of pH 5.1-5.4. Depending on your water's composition, you may end up higher than this range; for example, if you mash light colored malt with mineral-free, pure distilled water, the pH ends up around 5.5-5.8. Even using tap water, if the alkalinity is over 20 mg/l, the pH of the mash or wort for light-colored beers will always end higher than pH 5.4. Fortunately, by using small amounts of organic acids, homebrewers can easily rectify alkalinity problems.

When should you add acid to your brewing liquor? Using the recipes in this book, when and if the recipe calls for it. In general, whenever you are brewing light-colored brews, whether your water is soft, sulfate or alkaline. For amber-colored beers and darker, you probably only need to acidify your liquor if your water source is moderately to highly alkaline/carbonate.

How will you know for sure? By experience. By measuring the pH of your water, liquor and wort, before and after acid additions, and keeping records of them. It doesn't take many brews before you know what to do.

What acid should you use? We recommend dilute food-grade

lactic acid, although food-grade citric acid, phosphoric acid or sulfuric acid will do.

How much acid should you add? That depends, but usually only a few drops are required. One milliliter of standard Food-grade 85-90% Lactic Acid reduces the alkalinity of 5 gallons of water by about 25 mg/l. One milligram of Citric Acid (monohydrate, granular) reduces wort alkalinity by about 20 mg/l, while 1 ml of 85-88% Phosphoric Acid drops it about 33 mg/l, and 1 ml of 95-98% Sulfuric Acid drops it about 40 mg/l. Obviously, only tiny amounts are required for almost any water supply. A word of caution: these are very strong acids, and are dangerous to handle. Wear protective eyewear when handling any acid, or dilute the acid down with 9 parts of water to make a less-dangerous 10% solution, and use ten-times more of it making acidity adjustments. Someday, someone will package dilute lactic acid especially for homebrewers.

COPPER FININGS

Beer clarity may or may not be high on your list of priorities. In either case, it never hurts to use copper finings, or Irish Moss (carageenan). Irish moss is a gelatinous seaweed extract that aids protein coagulation, which translates into clearer beer. Copper finings are added near the end of the wort boil; generally 1/2 teaspoon (2.5 ml) of Irish Moss is a suitable amount to clear 5 gallons of wort.

YEAST

Yeast come in a variety of flavors, so to speak. There are dozens of brewers' yeast strains available to homebrewers, and they all have their own characteristic effect upon beer flavor and palate fullness. Some yeast strains ferment more sugars than others, so some yeast strains produce drier beers and others produce sweeter, fuller beers. Yeast strains that produce lots of fruity esters and butteriness, and low percentages of solvents and winey-tasting higher alcohols are ideal for hoppy British-style ales, while strains that are more "neutral" generally suit sweeter ales. Lager yeast ferment at cold temperatures and produce almost unnoticeable amounts of esters, diacetyl, solvents and higher alcohols. In all cases, brewers prefer strains that are hardy and that store well, and consistently drop out of suspension when the beer has fermented.

The amount of yeast pitched also has a marked effect upon beer flavor. Where a fruity aroma is desired, a relatively-low pitching rate is employed to increase ester formation. Carried too far, however, a low pitching rate produces off flavors from the overgrowth of cells. The culture takes longer to begin fermentation, and generally proceeds slower, inviting contamination.

A higher pitching rate is used for brews that shouldn't have a yeast character (especially lagers), but too high a pitching rate can cause off-flavors because more cells autolyze (i.e., "die") in competition for nutrients, and because over-pitched brews often do not ferment out completely. Generally, 10-14 grams of dry yeast or a pint of yeast starter are required.

"Dry", granulated yeast are the easiest and most economical to use. You just tear open the foil packaging and pour a packet or two into sterile warm water to rehydrate for a half an hour, and it's ready to pitch. Difficulties with dry yeast do arise, however, because they aren't laboratory-pure guaranteed-uncontaminated cultures, and because there is not as wide a selection of strains available as there is with "liquid" cultures.

"Liquid" yeast have been sterile-packaged, and, when fresh, have a high percentage of healthy cells. Some come packaged with nutrients, so that the culture can be reinvigorated prior to pitching. Moreover, one or two dozen different cultures are available from each of several sources. No matter what style of beer you wish to brew, the yeast used by the brewery most renown for that style is probably available in a liquid culture.

Liquid cultures do present a far greater expense, costing two-to-four times as much as a packet of dry yeast. Most require that you either pitch two packages, or that you build up the volume of yeast in a "starter". It costs more in time and money to use liquid yeasts, but they do produce consistently better lagers, and a far broader range of flavors. Many homebrewers regularly pitch dry yeast and only purchase liquid cultures when they are brewing lagers or beer styles that require idiosyncratic fermentation characteristics.

Making a starter for any yeast is no big deal. It's sort of like doing a pint-sized homebrew two to three days before the main batch. All you need is a clean beer bottle, an airlock and drilled stopper, an eighth-to-a-quarter pound (50-100 GRAMS) of DME, eight ounces (250 ML) of water and a package of yeast. Sterilize the bottle, mix the extract into eight ounces of boiling water, and pour it into the bottle. Fit the sterilized drilled stopper and airlock to the bottle, and fill the airlock with sterilant solution in the airlock.

Pack the bottle of wort in ice or put it in the refrigerator to cool. When the wort is cooled to 70-77°F (21-25°C) for ales, and to 50-60° (10-15°C) for lager strains, briefly uncap it and pitch the yeast. If it is a liquid strain, shake it up well to re-suspend the yeast that invariably settles into a paste at the bottom of the package. Let the starter ferment in the temperature range given above for two to three days before pitching. You can expect the vigorous starter to initiate fermentation faster, with less off-flavors, and for the fermentation to end sooner than if a dry yeast or an insufficient amount of yeast had been pitched.

Remember that the aromatic and flavor characteristics of every strain of yeast are temperature-dependent. Most ale yeast packed for homebrewers ferments best and give the best aroma and flavor at 68-72°F (20-22°C); sweet, less estery styles may benefit from a lower fermentation temperature, around 65-68°F (18-20°C). Lager yeasts generally perform best in the 48-55°F (9-13°C) range, although some give good results at as high as 60°F (16°C). In general, strong sulfurous aromas (burnt-match, rotten egg) during fermentation and carrying over into the finished beer indicate a temperature below the strain's preference, while winey and solvent-like aromatics result from a temperature that is too high for the particular strain. In general, liquid cultures sold for homebrewing will ferment without producing esters at up to 55°F (13°C); if you have to ferment warmer than that, then try using Wyeast 2042 or 1563, YeastLab L35 and BrewTek CL-680.

When purchasing liquid yeast, always check that the expiration date has not passed, and remember that even dry yeast lose vitality over time; purchase yeast from a supplier that keeps their stocks refrigerated.

FININGS

Many homebrewers "fine" their beer after fermentation with isinglass or gelatin, to clear the beer. More often than not, fining is unnecessary, because most times beer drops bright and clear after a short period of maturation. Sometimes, however, yeast or proteins may remain suspended, hazing an otherwise perfect beer. Finings reduce the chance of a hazy brew, and help improve head retention, so some homebrewers fine their beer as a matter of course. Fining your beer is optional; it doesn't make you a bad person if you choose not to.

Professional brewers generally prefer shredded, acidified isinglass for finings. Yes, isinglass is dried fish's swim bladder. It makes a gelatinous solution when it is mixed with water; the acidified product provides protection against contaminants by its low pH (below 3). Liquefied isinglass is more commonly used by homebrewers; shredded isinglass has to be rehydrated in 50-65°F (10-18°C) sterile water for a day or more for it to solubilize.

Isinglass combines with yeasts, proteins and fats, and settles them very firmly on the bottom of the vessel, generally within 24-72 hours in the temperature range of 39-60°F (4-16°C), at a dosing rate of about 2+ grams of isinglass dissolved in 16-20 fluid ounces (500-600 ML) of water for 5 gallons of beer.

Historically, domestic lager brewers have shown a preference for 95%-pure gelatin over isinglass. Gelatin is a slower clarifying agent, taking up to a week, and sometimes longer, to clear beer. It reacts best at temperatures below 50°F (10°C) at a rate of 4-5 grams per 5 gallons of beer. Gelatin must be rehydrated in 8-10 fluid ounces (160-180 ML) of cold water for an hour, and then heated to 150-160°F (65-71°C); it is mixed into the beer while it is still above 120°F (50°C).

Whenever finings are used, good sanitary procedure must be employed as well, and the finings should be well-distributed throughout the beer without splashing, by gently rocking or twisting the fermenter for several minutes.

CHAPTER 5

WORLD BEER STYLES

So, I'm ready to brew my own recipe! Let's head for the homebrew shop! But...wait...just what am I going to brew? I could brew a, uh, yah, a...

REINVENTING THE WHEEL

Homebrewers always have and always will brew ideosyncratic beers that aren't quite like anything that they have experienced previously...but don't be too sure that someone else hasn't brewed it before! People have been brewing for at least five thousand years, and it's a pretty safe bet that there isn't much that hasn't been tried at one time or another. How about dates and rye beer, spiced with Myrrh? The Egyptians did that already. So what about beer brewed with heather honey and spiced with, say, broom? Nobody could have brewed that, could they...? Uh, Scottish Highlanders were quaffing that since prehistory. You name it, it's probably been done before.

And of the things that have been tried before, the combinations that struck a balance of flavors that pleased the most people became beer styles. Recipes that became styles did so because they worked, and because people liked them!

And if you think about it, that's really wonderful. It saves us from brewing a lot of bad beer in search of something personal. We don't need to keep reinventing the wheel. We can refer to the accumulated knowledge of centuries of experimentation, see what worked, and proceed from that framework. It eliminates a lot of trial-and-error, and dumped batches. A serious brewer will learn to know their materials and their possibilities, and the synergy that different combinations of materials create. Five millenia of brewing has established a pretty clear definition of what works, and what doesn't!

One of the great accomplishments of the American Homebrewers Association has been the systematic categorization of beer styles. By defining the technical parameters of beer styles, the combined resources of these organizations provided the tools for homebrewers to produce a brew that is not only recognizable as say, an India Pale Ale, but that is a pleasing balance of malt, hop and yeast characteristics. The same hop bitterness, flavor and aroma that strikes a balance in an IPA would be unpleasant combined with the tart spiciness of a Weizen. The key to brewing is creating a synergy between the ingredients, and in striking a pleasing balance.

That is not to say that there is no room for creativity in homebrewing; quite to the contrary, the incredible complexity of flavor possibilities in brewing begs for experimentation. Most of the time, however, homebrewers are wise to limit the scope of their experiments to a niche within a style, a style that years, or even centuries, of brewing has proven to yield a pleasing synergy of flavor nuances.

As homebrewing has increased in popularity, homebrewers have widened their brewing horizons to encompass regional and heretofore "lost" styles on a global scale. In concert with this, the number of AHA-recognized beer styles has expanded to keep pace with increasing awareness and interest in archaic and regional beer styles. The incredible number of recipes in this book do not even approach the scope of the categories in AHA-sanctioned brewing competitions, and those categories will undoubtedly keep expanding to keep abreast of the broadening interest of the homebrewing community.

So what's the point here? Well, we may be three dumb guys, but we're not stupid. This book presents recipes that conform to the AHA guidelines. We, your ever-concerned authors, carefully reviewed each of our recipes to make sure that each and every one fits the technical parameters of its category, and can assure you that if you follow our simple instructions, you will win a gold medal, blue ribbon, white elephant or other prize beyond value in each and every brewing competition that you ever enter!
(Publisher's disclaimer: the authors have been drinking too much of their own homebrew.)

Below you will find the technical parameters for 44 AHA beer categories/subcategories that we are sharing our recipes for. By becoming familiar with the ingredients that we told you about in the last chapter and the styles in this chapter, you can even customize our recipes (although we can't imagine why you'd want to...) to suit your creative fancy, and avoid the frustration of dumping batches trying to "reinvent the wheel".

WORLD BEER STYLES Presented here with the kind permission of the American Homebrewers Association. Every style conforms to this format:

BEER STYLE	ORIGINAL GRAVITY	TERMINAL GRAVITY	ALCOHOL BY VOLUME	BITTERING UNITS	COLOR
SUBSTYLE	(OG)	(TG)	(ABV)	(IBU)	(SRM)

Color, aroma and flavor notes

Please note that we use Brewers' Gravity (eg, 1048) in our recipes, as opposed to Specific Gravity (eg, 1.048). For years brewers have dropped the decimal point, for convenience, and to conform to how density is verbally communicated, "ten-forty eight" being more readily understood than "one point oh-four-eight".

FAMILY: ALE

AMERICAN ALE

	OG	TG	ABV	IBU	SRM
AMERICAN WHEAT	1.030-1.050	1.004-1.018	4.3-5.5%	5-17	2-8

Pale to amber. Light to medium body. Low to medium bitterness. Malt and hop flavor and aroma OK. Low to medium fruitiness and esters. Low diacetyl OK. Lager yeast OK.

BROWN ALE

	OG	TG	ABV	BU	SRM
ENGLISH BROWN	1.040-1.050	1.008-1.014	4.5-5.0%	5-25	15-22

Medium to dark brown. Sweet and malty. Low bitterness.
Hop flavor and aroma low. Some fruitiness and esters. Medium body. Low diacetyl OK.

	OG	TG	ABV	IBU	SRM
ENGLISH MILD	1.032-1.036	1.004-1.008	2.5-3.6%	14-20	17-34

Low alcohol. Medium to very dark brown. Low hop
bitterness, flavor and aroma. Mild maltiness. Light body. Low esters.

	OG	TG	ABV	IBU	SRM
AMERICAN BROWN	1.040-1.055	1.010-1.018	4.5-6.0%	25-60	15-22

Medium to dark brown. High hop bitterness, flavor and
aroma. Medium maltiness and body. Low diacetyl OK.

SCOTTISH ALE

	OG	TG	ABV	IBU	SRM
LIGHT	1.030-1.035	1.006-1.012	3.0-4.0%	9-15	8-17

Gold to amber. Low carbonation. Low bitterness. May or may not have hop flavor and aroma. Medium maltiness. Medium body. Low to medium diacetyl OK. Fruitiness/esters OK. Faint smoky character OK.

	OG	TG	ABV	IBU	SRM
HEAVY	1.035-1.040	1.010-1.014	3.5-4.0%	12-17	10-19

Gold to amber to dark brown. Low carbonation. Low bitterness. May or may not have hop flavor and aroma. Medium to high maltiness. Medium body. Low to medium diacetyl OK. Fruitiness/esters OK. Faint smoky character OK.

	OG	TG	ABV	IBU	SRM
EXPORT	1.040-1.050	1.010-1.018	4.0-4.5%	15-20	10-19

Gold to amber to dark brown. Low carbonation. Low to medium bitterness. May or may not have hop flavor and aroma. High maltiness. Medium to full body. Low to medium diacetyl OK. Fruitiness/esters OK. Faint smoky character OK.

ENGLISH BITTER

Gold to copper. Low carbonation. Medium bitterness. May or may not have hop flavor or aroma. Low to medium maltiness. Light to medium body. Low to medium diacetyl OK. Fruitiness/esters OK.

	OG	TG	ABV	IBU	SRM
ORDINARY	1.035-1.038	1.006-10.12	3.0-3.5%	20-25	8-12

Mildest.

	OG	TG	ABV	IBU	SRM
EXTRA SPECIAL	1.042-1.055	1.010-1.015	4.5-6.0%	30-35	12-14

Strong Bitter. Maltiness evident. Hop bitterness balanced with malt sweetness.

ENGLISH PALE ALE

	OG	TG	ABV	IBU	SRM
CLASSIC PALE ALE	1.044-1.056	1.008-1.016	4.5-5.5%	20-40	4-11

Pale to deep amber/copper. Low to medium maltiness. High hop bitterness. Medium hop flavor and aroma. Use of English hops such as Goldings, Fuggles, etc. Fruity/estery. Low diacetyl OK. Medium body.

	OG	TG	ABV	IBU	SRM
INDIA PALE ALE	1.050-1.065	1.012-1.018	5.0-6.5%	40-65	8-14

Pale to deep amber/copper. Medium body. Medium maltiness. High hop bitterness. Hop flavor and aroma medium to high. Fruity/estery. Alcohol strength evident. Low diacetyl OK.

PORTER

	OG	TG	ABV	IBU	SRM
ROBUST PORTER	1.044-1.060	1.008-1.016	5.0-6.5%	25-40	30+

Black. No roast barley character. Sharp bitterness of black malt, without high burnt/charcoal-like flavor. Medium to full bodied. Malty sweet. Hop bitterness medium to high. Hop flavor and aroma: none to medium. Fruitiness/esters OK. Low diacetyl OK.

	OG	TG	ABV	IBU	SRM
BROWN PORTER	1.040-1.050	1.006-1.010	4.5-6.0%	20-30	20-35

Medium to dark brown. No roast barley or strong burnt malt character. Light to medium body. Low to medium malt sweetness. Medium hop bitterness. Hop flavor and aroma: none to medium. Fruitiness/esters OK. Low diacetyl OK.

STOUT

	OG	TG	ABV	IBU	SRM
DRY STOUT	1.038-1.048	1.008-1.014	3.8-5.0%	30-40	40+

Black opaque. Light to full body. Medium to high hop bitterness. Absence of, or low levels of, roasted barley (coffeelike) character OK. Sweet maltiness and caramel malt evident. No hop flavor or aroma. Slight sourness/acidity OK. Low to medium alcohol. Diacetyl low to medium.

	OG	TG	ABV	IBU	SRM
SWEET STOUT	1.045-1.056	1.012-1.020	3.0-6.0%	15-25	40+

Overall character sweet. Black opaque. Medium to full body. Hop bitterness low. Roasted barley (coffeelike) character mild. No hop flavor or aroma. Sweet malty and caramel evident. Low to medium alcohol. Low diacetyl OK.

	OG	TG	ABV	IBU	SRM
IMPERIAL STOUT	1.075-1.095	1.020-1.030	7.0-9.0%	50-80	20+

Dark copper color to black. Hop bitterness, flavor and aroma medium to high. Alcohol strength evident. Rich maltiness. Fruitiness/esters OK. Full bodied. Low diacetyl OK.

STRONG ALE

	OG	TG	ABV	IBU	SRM
OLD/STRONG ALE	1.060-1.075	1.008-1.020	6.5-8.5%	30-40	10-16

Light amber to deep amber/copper. Medium to full body. Malty. Hop bitterness apparent but not aggressive, flavor and aroma can be assertive. Fruitiness/esters high. Alcoholic strength recognizable. Low diacetyl OK.

	OG	TG	ABV	IBU	SRM
SCOTCH ALE	1.072-1.085	1.016-1.028	6.2-8.0%	25-35	10-47

Similar to English Old/Strong Ale. Stronger malty character. Deep copper to very black. Hop bitterness low. Diacetyl medium to high.

	OG	TG	ABV	IBU	SRM
BARLEY WINE	1.090-1.120	1.024-1.032	8.4-12%	50-100	14-22

Copper to medium-brown color. Malty sweetness. Fruity/estery. Low to high bitterness. Medium to full body. Low to high hop aroma and flavor. Alcoholic taste. Low to medium diacetyl OK.

BELGIAN ALE

	OG	TG	ABV	IBU	SRM
FLANDERS BROWN	1.045-1.056	1.008-1.016	4.8-5.2%	15-25	10-20

Slight sourness and spiciness. Deep copper to brown. Fruity/estery. Low to medium bitterness. Medium to full body. Low to high hop aroma and flavor. Alcoholic taste. Low to medium diacetyl OK.

	OG	TG	ABV	IBU	SRM
DUBBEL	1.050-1.070	1.012-1.016	6.0-7.5%	18-25	10-14

Dark amber to brown. Sweet, malty, nutty aroma. Faint hoppy aroma OK. Medium to full body. Low bitterness. Low diacetyl OK.

	OG	TG	ABV	IBU	SRM
TRIPEL	1.070-1.095	1.016-1.024	7.0-10.0%	20-25	3.5-5.5

Light/pale color. Light malty and hop aroma. Neutral hop/malt balance. Finish may be sweet. Medium to full body. Alcoholic, but best examples do not taste strongly of alcohol.

	OG	TG	ABV	IBU	SRM
WIT	1.044-1.054	1.006-1.010	4.5-5.2%	15-25	2-4

Unmalted wheat and malted barley. Oats OK. Often spiced with coriander seed and dried, bitter orange peel. Hop flavor and aroma "noble-type" desired. Low to medium bitterness. Low to medium body. Dry. Low diacetyl OK. Low to medium esters.

MIXED STYLE
CALIFORNIA COMMON BEER

	OG	TG	ABV	IBU	SRM
CALIFORNIA COMMON BEER	1.040-1.055	1.012-1.018	3.6-5.0%	35-45	8-12

Light amber to copper. Medium body. Toasted or caramel-like maltiness in aroma and flavor. Medium to high hop bitterness. Hop flavor medium to high. Aroma medium. Fruitiness and esters low. Low diacetyl OK. Lager yeast, fermented warm but aged cold.

WHEAT BEER

	OG	TG	ABV	IBU	SRM
WEIZEN/WEISSBIER	1.048-1.056	1.008-1.016	4.8-5.4%	10-15	3-9

Pale to golden. Light to medium body. About 50 percent wheat malt. Clove and slight banana character. Fruity/estery. Clove, vanilla, nutmeg, smoke and cinnamonlike phenolics permissable. Mild sourness OK. Highly effervescent. Cloudiness OK. Low bitterness. Low hop flavor and aroma OK. No diacetyl.

	OG	TG	ABV	IBU	SRM
DUNKELWEIZEN	1.048-1.056	1.008-1.016	4.8-5.4%	10-15	17-22

Deep copper to brown. Dark version of Weizen. Chocolate maltiness evident. Banana and cloves and other phenolics may still be evident, but to a lesser degree. Stronger than Weizen. Medium body. Low diacetyl OK. Low hop flavor and aroma OK.

GERMAN-STYLE ALE

	OG	TG	ABV	IBU	SRM
DUSSELDORF ALT	1.044-1.048	1.008-1.014	4.3-5.0%	25-35	11-19

Copper to dark brown. Medium to high bitterness. Very low hop flavor. No hop aroma. Light to medium body. Low fruitiness and esters. Traditionally fermented warm but aged at cold temperatures. Very low diacetyl OK.

	OG	TG	ABV	IBU	SRM
KÖLSCH	1.042-1.046	1.006-1.010	4.0-4.5%	20-30	3.5-5.0

Pale gold. Low hop flavor and aroma. Medium bitterness. Light to medium body. Slightly dry, winy palate. Malted wheat OK. Lager or ale yeast or combination of yeasts OK.

	OG	TG	ABV	IBU	SRM
FRUIT BEER	1.030-1.110	1.006-1.030	2.5-12%	5-70	5-50

Any ale or lager made with fruit. Character of fruit should be evident in color, aroma and flavor. Body, color, hop character and strength can vary greatly.

	OG	TG	ABV	IBU	SRM
HERB BEER	1.030-1.110	1.006-1.030	2.5-12%	5-70	5-50

Any ale or lager with herbs. Character of herb or spice should be evident in aroma and flavor. Body, color, hop character and strength can vary greatly.

SPECIALTY BEER

Any ale or lager brewed with unusual techniques and/or fermentable ingredients other than (or in addition to) malted barley as a unique contribution to the overall character of the beer.

SMOKED BEER

	OG	TG	ABV	IBU	SRM
RAUCHBIER	1.048-1.052	1.012-1.016	4.3-4.8%	20-30	10-20

Oktoberfest style with a sweet smoky aroma and flavor. Dark amber to dark brown. Intensity of smoke medium to high. Low diacetyl OK.

FAMILY: LAGER

	OG	TG	ABV	IBU	SRM
AMERICAN PREMIUM	1.046-1.050	1.010-1.014	4.3-5.0%	13-23	2-8

Very pale to golden. Light body. Low to medium bitterness. Low malt aroma and flavor OK. Low hop flavor and aroma OK. Effervescent. No fruitiness, esters or diacetyl.

	OG	TG	ABV	IBU	SRM
CREAM ALE/LAGER	1.040-1.055	1.004-1.010	4.5-5.0%	14-20	2-4

Very pale. Effervescent. Light body. Low to medium bitterness. Low hop flavor and aroma OK. Low fruitiness/esters OK. Can use ale or lager yeasts or combination of both.

GERMAN LIGHT LAGER

	OG	TG	ABV	IBU	SRM
DORTMUND/EXPORT	1.048-1.056	1.010-1.014	4.8-6.0%	23-29	4-6

Pale to golden. Medium body. Medium malty sweetness. Medium bitterness. Hop flavor and aroma, "noble-type" OK. No fruitiness, esters or diacetyl. Alcoholic warmth evident.

	OG	TG	ABV	IBU	SRM
MUNICH HELLES	1.044-1.052	1.008-1.012	4.5-5.5%	18-25	3-5

Pale to golden. Medium body. Medium malty sweetness. Low bitterness. Hop flavor and aroma, "noble-type" OK. No fruitiness, esters. Low diacetyl OK.

PILSENER

	OG	TG	ABV	IBU	SRM
GERMAN	1.044-1.050	1.006-1.012	4.0-5.0%	30-40	2.5-4

Pale to golden. Light to medium body. High hop bitterness. Medium hop flavor and aroma, "noble-type". Low maltiness in aroma and flavor. No fruitiness, esters. Very low diacetyl OK.

	OG	TG	ABV	IBU	SRM
BOHEMIAN	1.044-1.056	1.014-1.020	4.0-5.0%	35-45	3-5

Pale to golden. Light to medium body. Medium to high bitterness. Low to medium hop flavor and aroma "noble-type". Low to medium maltiness in aroma and flavor. No fruitiness, esters. Low diacetyl OK.

BAVARIAN DARK

	OG	TG	ABV	IBU	SRM
MUNICH DUNKEL	1.052-1.056	1.014-1.018	4.5-5.0%	16-25	17-23

Copper to dark brown. Medium body. Nutty, toasted, chocolate-like malty sweetness in aroma and flavor. Medium bitterness. Hop flavor and aroma, "noble-type" OK. No fruitiness or esters. Low diacetyl OK.

	OG	TG	ABV	IBU	SRM
SCHWARZBIER	1.044-1.052	1.012-1.026	4.5-5.5%	22-30	25-30

Dark brown to black. Medium body. Roasted malt evident. Low sweetness in aroma and flavor. Low to medium bitterness. Low bitterness from roast malt. Hop flavor and aroma, "noble-type" OK. No fruitiness, esters. Low diacetyl OK.

VIENNA/OKTOBERFEST/MAERZEN

	OG	TG	ABV	IBU	SRM
VIENNA	1.048-1.055	1.012-1.018	4.4-6.0%	22-28	8-12

Amber to deep copper/light brown. Toasted malt aroma and flavor. Low malt sweetness. Light to medium body. Hop bitterness "noble-type" low to medium. Low hop flavor and aroma, "noble-type" OK. No fruitiness, esters. Low diacetyl OK.

	OG	TG	ABV	IBU	SRM
MAERZEN/FEST	1.052-1.064	1.012-1.020	4.8-6.5%	22-28	7-14

Amber to deep copper/orange. Malty sweetness, toasted malt aroma and flavor dominant. Medium body. Low to medium bitterness. Low hop flavor and aroma, "noble-type" OK. No fruitiness, esters or diacetyl.

BOCK

	OG	TG	ABV	IBU	SRM
TRADITIONAL	1.066-1.074	1.018-1.024	6.0-7.5%	20-30	20-30

Copper to dark brown. Full body. Malty sweet character predominates in aroma and flavor with some toasted chocolate malt character. Low bitterness. Low hop flavor, "noble-type" OK. No hop aroma. No fruitiness or esters. Low to medium diacetyl OK.

	OG	TG	ABV	IBU	SRM
HELLESBOCK	1.066-1.068	1.012-1.020	6.0-7.5%	20-35	4.5-6

Pale to amber. Medium body. Malty sweet character predominates in aroma and flavor with some toasted chocolate malt character. Low bitterness. Low hop flavor, "noble-type" OK. No hop aroma. No fruitiness or esters. Low to medium diacetyl OK.

	OG	TG	ABV	IBU	SRM
DOPPELBOCK	1.074-1.080	1.020-1.028	6.5-8.0%	17-27	12-30

Light to very dark; amber to dark brown. Very full body. Malty sweetness evident in aroma and flavor can be intense. High alcoholic flavor. Slight fruitiness and esters OK, but not very desirable. Low bitterness. Low hop flavor, "noble -type" OK. No hop aroma. Low diacetyl OK.

Refer to this list when you are getting ready to brew, especially to the description notes. With experience, you can learn how to manipulate ingredients and process to emphasize desirable characteristics...but you need to know what those are for each style; hence, this list.

CHAPTER 6

POWER TOOLS

N ow that you're hooked, here's some more equipment you can hook up with. Because if you've gotten this far, you're ready to buy more stuff. Brewing can be done with very basic equipment, but the beer you make can be improved with more sophisticated equipment... that's right, "power tools"!

Specific pieces of equipment can make your life easier... but you don't necessarily need to own one of everything in the brewshop. Start off by deciding exactly what ought to improve your beer the most, or simplify brewing the most for you.

This chapter should help you decide what's important, and how important. We have listed equipment that we think you ought to add to your brewery, in the order that you ought to purchase it.

So cut open the mattress and head for the brewshop. You'll be happy to know that the first upgrade you ought to acquire is cheap:

HOP BAG: Whole leaf hops are much easier to manage if they are contained in a fine-mesh nylon or muslin hop bag. It looks like a giant tea bag, and works like one too. Instead of hops plugging your siphon tube, or fishing for stray hops with a strainer and struggling to balance a colander over your kettle, your hops are neatly contained in the bag, and are easy to remove from the kettle. Even kit brewers can use it to add hop aromatics to their brews. It's simple, it's elegant, and you ought to own a hop bag. (Hop bags don't work if you're brewing with pellet hops, because pellets are ground too fine.)

pH STRIPS: pH papers work by undergoing a color change corresponding to the acidity of the solution that they are dipped in. Most pH strips are incredibly inaccurate, which makes them next to useless. Look for the trademarks pHyhydrion or ColorpHast; both of these are accurate to better than pH .3. The range should cover between 3 and 9 for water, although strips with a range between 4.2 and 6.2 are fine for wort and beer.

GLASS CARBOY/SECONDARY FERMENTER: One of the greatest improvements to your beer's quality that you can make is to step-up to two-stage fermenting. Carboys are available in 5 and 6 gallon (18.9 and 23 L) sizes. Don't drop it, and it will last you a lifetime. A carboy is the perfect secondary fermenter. By transferring ("racking") your beer to secondary as fermentation falls off, you separate the beer from the trub. Trub tastes awful, and the less it contacts your beer, the better your beer will taste. The only reason that we didn't recommend that you start off with two-stage fermenting is because it requires racking the beer an extra time. When you're inexperienced, this is one more chance for your beer to become contaminated. By now, you've learned to work with a sanitation-mindset, so you ought to be able to improve your beer at little-or-no risk.

Carboys also make great primary fermenters. The larger size has enough "head space" so that the fermentation won't foam out of it, although some brewers intentionally ferment in the smaller size, letting some of the fermentation head "blow-off" (see below). Some of the advantages of fermenting in glass are:

1. Ease of cleaning - you can see when it is clean. Clean it with a carboy brush as soon as it is empty, rinse it out and fill it with sterilizing solution.

2. You can see what is happening during fermentation.

3. Easier racking - you can see when your racking cane is at the perfect height.

You will need a #6-1/2 or #7 drilled rubber stopper to hold your airlock. The next few items are all "parts" that you should consider in conjunction with carboys.

SIPHON STARTER: There are a bunch of options; go for the cheapest one that your supplier recommends. None of them are very expensive. You just might get away with sucking on the end of the tubing to get a siphon going forever, and never have a contamination, but then again, you might not. Buy one of these nifty units, most of which have been invented by frustrated (and clever) homebrewers.

SMALL KITCHEN SCALE: You need something to weigh out hops, malts, specialty grains and kettle adjuncts accurately. It should be marked in 1/2 ounce (10 gram) increments. Have your brewshop calibrate it for you when you purchase it, and then handle it with care. Recalibrate it regularly.

CARBOY AND BOTTLE BRUSHES: If you purchase a carboy, you will want a carboy brush to clean it with. If you are using bottles to package your beer, a bottle brush will also make cleaning them easier.

CARBOY HANDLE: This is a luxury, but it is cheap. It is the only smart way to carry a carboy around. Carboy handles are plastic-covered steel rings which attach around the neck of the carboy. Always use two hands hefting a carboy, even when using a carboy handle.

THE BREWCAP® or other inverted-carboy systems: Lager brewers swear by these time-tested "closed fermentation systems". Instead of racking your beer to secondary and to the bottling bucket, you just fit your 5-gallon (18.9 L) carboy with the cap, flip it upside-down in a milk crate, and you have the nearest thing to the closed conical fermenter favored by commercial brewers that homebrewers have ever seen. A draincock in the cap allows you to drain off trub, obviating the need for racking.

The same drain allows you to collect and repitch yeast from batch to batch without ever exposing it to the environment. The vent that goes up into the headspace inside the carboy allows the option of "blowing-off". You can even prime into it and bottle directly from it. These set-ups work well with all lager yeasts, and with most ale strains.

BLOWOFF SETUP: This fermentation method allows the pressures created during initial fermentation to carry some of the head and a lot of the trub with it. The trub would clog an airlock and cause, at the least, a big mess. Blowoffs are either made from 1" (25mm) tubing, or a short rigid piece of tubing over which flexible tubing is secured. The free end hangs in a pot, jar or bucket of sanitizing solution which serves as an airlock. There are proponents of this method that say it gives cleaner beer (they're right), and detractors that say that it wastes a pint to a quart each brew (they're right too). This one's up to you.

LIQUID CRYSTAL THERMOMETER STRIP: This adhesive-backed thermometer strip allows you to monitor fermentation temperatures by just sticking it onto the side of your fermenter. You won't have to guess what the temperature is at. Besides, they're pretty cheap. Go for it.

WORT CHILLER: Why should you get a wort chiller? A wort chiller enables you to do a full wort boil, and chill your 200 plus degree wort down to a temperature at which you can safely add your yeast in as little as 15 minutes. By being able to pitch your yeast as soon as possible, you cut down the window of opportunity that bacteria has to infect your beer before the yeast starts fermenting, 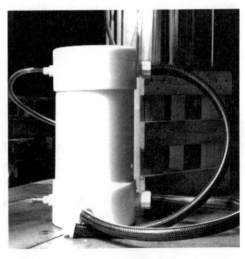 creating positive pressure and a CO_2 blanket to protect it. Start doing full wort boils instead of a two-gallon partial boil. We recommend that you also buy a wort chiller.

There are many different wort chillers out there, but they can be broken down into two basic types; immersion wort chillers and counterflow wort chillers.

The immersion type wort chiller is just what it sounds like. It's a coil of copper or stainless-steel tubing that you immerse into the hot wort in your kettle. They are usually made from 1/4 - 1/2" (6-12mm) diameter copper tubing. You hook up one end to a faucet, and let the other end hang in a sink. Drop the chiller into the brew kettle and the hot wort sterilizes it. After a couple of minutes, you turn on the faucet and run cold water through it. It cools your wort before you rack it to your fermenter. Both the hot and cold trub stay in your kettle.

A counterflow wort chiller is a bit more complicated. Hot wort is siphoned through a coil of copper or stainless-steel contained inside the chiller housing or coiled inside an equal length of garden hose. One end of the housing connects to your faucet, and cold tap-water flows in the opposite direction around the tubing. It chills your wort as it is being run into your fermenter.

Both styles have their champions. One school of homebrewing points out that the immersion chiller is basically self-sterilizing, and that it drastically reduces the amount of trub that ends up in the fermenter. They claim that counterflow chillers are difficult to clean out if you get sloppy and let one get contaminated. The other school of homebrewing scoffs at that, and makes the point that when the wort is chilled in the kettle, it is more subject to infection.

Both schools have legitimate arguments. Which method do we recommend? The immersion chiller, by split decision: 2:1.

PROPANE COOKER: Propane cookers are a godsend. You can bring your wort, or your mash water or sparge water to temperature in minutes. Most are three-legged stands constructed of wrought iron, with a cast iron burner ring that hooks-up to a gas-grille propane tank. With their high heat output, 25,000 to 50,000 BTU's, there is no waiting around for your wort to boil on the kitchen stove. The big disadvantage, as you can probably guess, is that their use is restricted to the outdoors, or a very-well ventilated space.

BOTTLE WASHER: Unless you own an electric dishwasher with a sanitize cycle, the task of cleaning out bottles is simplified by a faucet-attachment bottle-washer, a jet-spray nozzle that forces a strong stream of water into the bottle.

BOTTLE TREE: It doesn't grow bottles for you; it's a drying rack. You don't need this, but one is nice to have, instead of bottles everywhere.

LARGE STRAINER: You can use it to strain leaf hops out of your wort. You can use it to drain specialty grains after they have been steeped. If you need one, and you don't have one in your kitchen, buy one.

BENCH CAPPER: Bottles won't tip over while you're trying to balance capper and caps on top of them. They seal every bottle completely, and you don't crack the bottlenecks. There are several bench cappers to choose from. Buy the best you can afford and you will be rewarded with an easy-to-use capper that will last you for years.

BREW BELT: A heating element that wraps around your fermenter. Controlled by a thermostat, it will keep your beer fermenting at a constant temperature. It is a good option if you live in a cold climate.

SPARE REFRIGERATOR & THERMOSTAT CONTROL:
Refrigerators are not just for homebrewers who live in hot climates. With a refrigerator, you can control the temperature well enough to brew lagers year 'round, and lager (age/condition) two or even three batches at a time, at real lager temperatures.

If you shop around you may be able to find a used fridge for as little as $50. If you pick one up, it's a good idea to add an aftermarket thermostat. This allows you to bypass the imprecise and narrow-range thermostat built into the refrigerator. Most refrigerators only run at between 32 and 40°F (0-4°C), which is great for lagering, but too cold for fermenting. A thermostat will cost you another $50 or so.

The list stops here. The power tools that are available don't. There are all kinds of neat and useful gadgets made for homebrewing. Win the lottery and shop 'til you drop. Remember, whoever amasses the most toys wins.

CHAPTER 7

RECIPES FROM UNHOPPED MALT EXTRACT

B rewing from kits is easy, you say? Too easy? You say you want a new challenge? We've got one for you, but you'll be disappointed if you're looking for something difficult. Instead, we're going to show you how to use some basic "plain" ingredients and brew from scratch (well, not quite as "from scratch" as you will in chapters 11 and especially 12), and you're going to see that it really isn't any more difficult, although it is more satisfying. You will be free of the yoke of the kits, free to play and adjust, free to invent and improvise. But before you do all that, go back again and look at the AHA World Beer Styles we just talked about in chapter 5. The purpose of this chapter is double: we want you to see how the different components of the brewing process influence and change the final product. To do that, we give you recipes for many of the AHA recognized styles, but without the crutch of a pre-packaged kit. You're not quite on your own yet, but you're getting closer.

Two caveats: Remember that not all extracts are alike. Some are just plain better than others, because some are all-malt while others may have unmalted barley syrup, sugar, caramel coloring, etc. Some extracts are designed to do specific things. Refer back to chapter 4's discussion of ingredients for recommendations on extract selection for particular beer styles.

Second: Each time you brew, go over the ingredients list and procedures carefully before you start. Make sure that you have everything you need and that you have enough time planned for brewing. Rushing to finish is as sure a way to brew bad beer as using dirty equipment.

These recipes follow a standard brewing procedure, and are designed to yield 5 gallons of a true-to-style beer, in line with the AHA style guidelines already discussed. They are a step up from the kit recipes, although much of the process is the same. This time you will brew from unhopped extract, however, and tailor the wort with grains, water treatments, bittering and aroma hops, etc. The standard brewing procedure is roughly the same for each beer; follow the specifics of each recipe as given for hopping schedules, boiling times, yeast types, bottle conditioning and temperature guidelines. Refer to the step-by-step outline given below in general. Remember that an ale yeast works best and quickest at 65°F to 75°F (18°-24°C), a lager yeast prefers 45°F to 60°F (7°-16°C), and longer-term and colder storage.

Feel free to play with these recipes as suits your personal taste and the availability of ingredients. We have designed these recipes along "traditional", "accepted" standards, but the homebrewer need only satisfy himself or herself. If you plan to enter your brew in any AHA-sanctioned competition, however, be warned that judges are fairly particular about the style guidelines used. See chapter 15, "I brew better than that!" for more on judging and competitions.

STEP BY STEP BREWING PROCEDURE

0. SANITIZE ANYTHING AND EVERYTHING THAT WILL COME IN CONTACT WITH THE BOILED WORT OR BEER BEFORE YOU EVEN BEGIN. CLEAN AND RE-SANITIZE EQUIPMENT AS YOU FINISH WITH IT.

1. The day before brewing, boil 3 or 4 gallons (11.4 - 15 L) of water to sterilize it. Bottle this "liquor" in pre-sanitized gallon jugs or 2-liter soda bottles and chill it overnight. This liquor will be added to the fermenter to make up 5 gallons (19 L) of beer and will be used to cool the wort at the same time. If you have a wort chiller (cool! new toy!) and a kettle of at least 24-quart (23 L) capacity, you should do a "full wort boil" and you don't need to chill liquor ahead of time. On the other hand, you will need to add enough liquor to the kettle at the start of the boil to make up 5-1/4 gallons (20 L) of wort.

2. Measure 2 gallons (7.5 L) of cold water into your kettle, and treat it with mineral salts as per the recipe you are brewing. Coarsely crack the specialty grains specified in the recipe, and secure them in a muslin grain bag. Place the bag into the kettle and let it steep while you are heating the liquor up.

3. Gradually bring the liquor to a boil. Remove the grains when the liquor temperature reaches 170°F (77°C); place the mesh bag in a colander suspended over your kettle and pour 1 quart (.95 L) of liquor from the kettle through them to rinse free any extract that may remain (this is a primitive form of the process called "sparging").

4. If you are using malt extract syrup, warm up the container to make the syrup run easier (and use a rubber spatula to get it all out of the container!). Put the malt extract and any adjuncts that the recipe calls for into the kettle; stir to avoid scorching.

5. Add bittering hops (as per recipe). Boil according to the schedule specified in the recipe.

6. As per recipe, add any additional hops and Irish moss (copper finings) along the way.

7. Remove the kettle from the heat, cover and chill the wort as quickly as possible, either by immersing the kettle in a cold (ice) water bath or by using a wort chiller if you are making a full wort boil.

8. Splash the wort into the fermenter and bring the liquid volume up to 5 gallons (19 L) with your chilled, sterile liquor. You will generally need 3 - 3-1/2 gallons (11.5-13 L) of chilled liquor. It is helpful if you have already measured and marked the 5 gallon (19 L) level in your fermenter beforehand.

9. When the wort has cooled to between 70°F and 80°F (21°-27°C; in this range, wort does not feel perceptibly "warm"), pitch the yeast. Rehydrate dry yeasts by sprinkling into 1 cup (.23 L) of 100°F - 120°F (38°-46°C) water at least 1/2 hour before pitching.

10. Close the lid tightly on the fermenter, install the airlock, and let it sit at the fermentation temperature specified in the recipe. Initial fermentation should begin in 12 to 36 hours. Keep the fermenter's temperature within the range recommended for the beer style and type of yeast.

11. When the yeast has fermented most of the available sugars, bubbling in the airlock will slow down to one bubble every 30 or 40 seconds. Siphon (rack) the beer to the secondary fermenter, adding any "dry-hop" aroma hops (as per recipe). Close with an airlock and let continue for three to twenty-one more days. Take a hydrometer reading to see if your beer has fermented to somewhere near your expected Terminal Gravity

(TG). If your OG was high or low, your TG will be too.

12. Rack the beer back to your sanitized primary fermenter or to a bottling bucket. One more time, take a hydrometer reading. Your beer has essentially finished fermenting at this point, so the TG and alcohol content indicated now is how it will be. Dissolve priming sugar (3/4 cup (170 ML) of corn sugar or 1 cup (230 mL) of DME are standard — some styles require higher or lower carbonation levels... see the recipes) into 1 pint (.5 L) of boiling water. Use your siphon tube to stir the priming solution in well, but without splashing.

13. Siphon the beer into bottles, cap and put them away to condition. Follow the recipe regarding aging, but all beer should be stored away from light and heat. It is a good idea to let your bottled beer stand at room temperature for at least 24 hours to begin carbonation, but UV light is a definite taboo.

14. When the beer is mature, chill, open and decant.

15. Imbibe, relax, and enjoy. It's your beer.

AMERICAN WHEAT ALE

BREADBASKET AMERICAN WHEAT BEER

Less spicy and less full-bodied than the Bavarian styles, this is nevertheless a thirst-quenching and eminently enjoyable beer.

OG 1040   TG 1007   ABV 4.3%   SRM 2.5   IBU 14

WATER SUPPLY:	TREAT WATER:
Soft	ACIDIFY TO BELOW pH 7.0
Moderately sulfate	ACIDIFY TO BELOW pH 7.0
Moderately carbonate	ACIDIFY TO BELOW pH 7.0
Highly sulfate	DILUTE 1:1 AND ACIDIFY TO BELOW pH 7.0
Highly carbonate	BOIL OR DILUTE 1:1; ACIDIFY TO BELOW pH 7.0

Add:
2 LBS. (.9 KG) LIGHT DME
3.3 LBS. (1.5 KG) WHEAT MALT EXTRACT (50% barley/50% wheat) to enough liquor to make up two gallons in the kettle. Heat to boiling.

KETTLE SCHEDULE:
4 HBU HALLERTAU HOP PELLETS after 15 minutes.
1 OZ. (28 G) WILLAMETTE HOP PELLETS,
KETTLE KNOCKOUT at 45 minutes.

Cover the kettle and let the hops and trub settle for ten minutes. Rack the clear wort into the fermenter. Splash enough chilled sterile liquor into the fermenter to make up 5 gallons and cover it. Cool the wort in the fermenter to below 80°F (27°C) in an ice water bath, and then

Pitch with:
14 G. rehydrated DRY ALE YEAST or a LIQUID ALE YEAST (Yeast Lab A06, Wyeast 1007, BrewTek CL-10), close, affix airlock and

Ferment at:
60-68°F (16-20°C).

Prime with:
3/4 CUP (170 ML) CORN SUGAR. Bottle and cap. Condition for 1 month at below 65°F (18°C).

ENGLISH BROWN ALE

COAL SHUTTLE BROWN ALE

Brown ales are probably the most under-rated beers in the world, with all the attention paid to light lagers and dark stouts. Drinking a brown ale is like relaxing among good friends. Nothing is hidden, there are no high expectations, it's just a great glass of beer.

OG 1048   TG 1013   ABV 4.6 %   SRM 20   IBU 15

WATER SUPPLY:	TREAT WATER:
Soft	1/2 TSP (2.5 ML) OF GYPSUM
Moderately sulfate	OK AS IS
Moderately carbonate	ACIDIFY TO BELOW pH 7.2
Highly sulfate	DILUTE 1:1 OR BOIL
Highly carbonate	DILUTE 1:1, OR BOIL, AND ACIDIFY

Steep:
3/4 LB. (340 G) CRYSTAL 50°L
1/2 LB. (227 G) CHOCOLATE MALT
1 OZ. (28 GRAMS) BLACK PATENT MALT in 2 gallons (7.6 L) of cold water. Bring gradually to a boil. Remove grains when the water temperature reaches 170°F (77°C).

Add:
3.3 LBS. (1.5 KG) AMBER MALT EXTRACT
2-1/4 LBS. (1 KG) AMBER DME

KETTLE SCHEDULE:
5 HBU FUGGLES HOP PELLETS as boil commences,
1 OZ. (28 GRAMS) TETTNANG HOP PELLETS and
KETTLE KNOCKOUT at 45 minutes.

Cover the kettle and let the hops and trub settle for ten minutes. Rack the clear wort into the fermenter. Splash enough chilled sterile liquor into the fermenter to make up 5 gallons and cover it. Cool the wort in the fermenter to below 80°F (27°C) in an ice water bath, and then

Pitch with:
14 G. rehydrated DRY ALE YEAST or a LIQUID ALE YEAST (Yeast Lab A05, BrewTek CL-20, Wyeast1338). Close, affix airlock .

Ferment at:
60-68°F (16-20°C).

Prime with:
3/4 CUP (170 ML) AMBER DME. Bottle and cap. Age 3 weeks or more.

ENGLISH MILD ALE

THE VICAR'S MILD ALE

A mild ale is a kinder, gentler brown ale, less strong but no less flavorful. A soul-satisfying brew for those who prefer a lighter style but still want to taste what they're drinking.

OG 1036   TG 1012   ABV 3.2%   SRM 18   IBU 18

WATER SUPPLY:	TREAT WATER:
Soft	1/2 TSP (2.5 ML) OF GYPSUM
Moderately sulfate	OK AS IS
Moderately carbonate	ACIDIFY TO BELOW pH 7.2
Highly sulfate	DILUTE 1:1 OR BOIL
Highly carbonate	DILUTE 1:1, OR BOIL, AND ACIDIFY to 7.2

Steep:
1/4 LB. (.11 KG) CRYSTAL 120°L MALT
1/4 LB. (.11 KG) CRYSTAL 50°L MALT
1/4 LB. (.11 KG) CHOCOLATE MALT in 2 gallons (7.6 L) of cold water.

Bring gradually to a boil. Remove grains when the water temperature reaches 170°F (77°C).

Add:
3.3 LBS. (1.5 KG) AMBER MALT EXTRACT
1 LB. (.45 KG) AMBER DME

KETTLE SCHEDULE:
4 HBU FUGGLES HOP PELLETS as boil commences,
KETTLE KNOCKOUT after 45 minutes,
1/2 OZ. (14 GRAMS) GOLDINGS HOP PELLETS at knockout.

Cover the kettle and let the hops and trub settle for ten minutes. Rack the clear wort into the fermenter. Splash enough chilled sterile liquor into the fermenter to make up 5 gallons and cover it. Cool the wort in the fermenter to below 80°F (27°C) in an ice water bath, and then

Pitch with:
10 G. rehydrated DRY ALE YEAST or a LIQUID ALE YEAST (Yeast Lab A05, BrewTek CL-130, Wyeast 1087). Close, affix airlock.

Ferment at:
60-68°F (16-20°C).

Prime with:
3/4 CUP (170 ML) AMBER DME. Bottle and cap. Age 3 weeks or more.

AMERICAN BROWN ALE

SWEET GEORGIA BROWN ALE

Browner and hoppier than the English version, perhaps not as full-bodied, but every bit as satisfying. They say Americans do everything "BIG" - well, this is the Texas-sized treatment of the old standard: big hop flavor and aroma, roasty, nutty...

OG 1046   TG 1010 4.7%   ABV 4.7%   SRM 19   IBU 30

WATER SUPPLY:	TREAT WATER:
Soft	2 TSPS (10 ML) GYPSUM,
	1/2 TSP (2.5 ML) TABLE SALT
Moderately sulfate	1/2 TSP (2.5 ML) OF GYPSUM
Moderately carbonate	1 TSP (5 ML) GYPSUM,
	1/2 TSP (2.5 ML) TABLE SALT
Highly sulfate	OK AS IS
Highly carbonate	ACIDIFY TO BELOW 7.2

Steep:

1/4 LB. (.11 KG) CHOCOLATE MALT
1 OZ. (28 GRAMS) BLACK PATENT MALT in 2 gallons (7.6 L) of cold water. Bring to a gradual boil. Remove grains when the water temperature reaches 170°F (77°C).

Add:

3.3 LBS. (1.5 KG) AMBER MALT EXTRACT
2-2/3 LBS. (1.05 KG) AMBER DME

KETTLE SCHEDULE:

4.5 HBU WILLAMETTE HOP PELLETS, after 5 minutes,
1 OZ. (28 GRAMS) WILLAMETTE HOP PELLETS, after 40 minutes.
1 OZ. (28 GRAMS) GALENA HOP PELLETS and
KETTLE KNOCKOUT after 45 minutes,

Cover the kettle and let the hops and trub settle for ten minutes. Rack the clear wort into the fermenter. Splash enough chilled sterile liquor into the fermenter to make up 5 gallons and cover it. Cool the wort in the fermenter to below 80°F (27°C) in an ice water bath, and then

Pitch with:

14 G. rehydrated DRY ALE YEAST or a LIQUID ALE YEAST (Wyeast 1056, Yeast Lab A06, BrewTek CL-260). Close, affix airlock.

Ferment at:

60-68°F (16-20°C)

Prime with:

3/4 CUP (170 ML) AMBER DME. Bottle and cap. Age 3 weeks or more.

SCOTTISH LIGHT, HEAVY, EXPORT ALES

SCOTS ALE

Scots ales come in a variety of shapes and sizes. Well, actually that's not entirely accurate, but they do come in different strengths and shades of color. They are labeled with the tax price (in shillings, /-) according to their strength. Traditionally, Scots ales are not highly hopped but are very malty and aromatic, with a hint (but not an overpowering flavor) of roasted barley.

WATER SUPPLY:	TREAT WATER:
Soft	2 TSPS (10 ML) GYPSUM,
	1/2 TSP (2.5 ML) TABLE SALT
Moderately sulfate	1/2 TSP (2.5 ML) OF GYPSUM
Moderately carbonate	1/2 TSP (2.5 ML) GYPSUM,
	1/2 TSP (2.5 ML) TABLE SALT
Highly sulfate	OK AS IS
Highly carbonate	ACIDIFY TO BELOW 7.2

For each of the recipes below,

Steep:
grains in 2 gallons (7.6 L) of cold liquor, bringing it up to a boil gradually. Remove the grains when the liquor temperature reaches 170°F (77°C).

Add:
extracts and hops, boil for 45 minutes. Cover the kettle and let the hops and trub settle for ten minutes. Rack the clear wort into the fermenter. Splash enough chilled sterile liquor into the fermenter to make up 5 gallons and cover it. Cool the wort in the fermenter to below 80°F (27°C) in an ice water bath, and then

Pitch with:
14 g. of rehydrated DRY ALE YEAST or a LIQUID ALE strain (Wyeast 1728 or 1084, Yeast Lab A05, BrewTek CL-160). Close, affix airlock .

Ferment at:
60 - 68°F (16 - 20°C)

Prime with:
2/3 to 3/4 CUP (150-170 ML) brown sugar, bottle and cap. Age four weeks or more.

CUMMINGS' LIGHT ALE (60/-)

1 OZ. (28 GRAMS) ROASTED BARLEY
3.3 LBS. (150 G) LIGHT MALT EXTRACT
1 LB. (454 G) LIGHT DME
3-1/2 HBU KENT GOLDINGS
ALE YEAST

OG 1032   TG 1010   ABV 3%   SRM 11   IBU 14

MITCHELL'S HEAVY ALE (70/-)

1 OZ. (28 GRAMS) ROASTED BARLEY
3.3 LBS. (1.5 KG) AMBER MALT EXTRACT
2 LBS. (.9 KG) LIGHT DME
4 HBU KENT GOLDINGS
ALE YEAST

OG 1040   TG 1012   ABV 3.6%   SRM 17   IBU 16

BARNET'S EXPORT ALE (80/-)

1 OZ. (28 GRAMS) ROASTED BARLEY
1/2 LB. (.23 KG) CRYSTAL 35°L MALT
3.3 LBS. (1.5 KG) LIGHT MALT EXTRACT
2-1/4 LBS. (1 KG) LIGHT DME
5 HBU KENT GOLDINGS
ALE YEAST

OG 1046   TG 1012   ABV 4.5%   SRM 13   IBU 20

ORDINARY BITTER

PERFECTLY ORDINARY BITTER

There's actually nothing ordinary about this Bitter, except the fact that it is one of the most popular beverages in Britain. Usually found on draught in every local pub, we homebrewers can enjoy it without the expense of travelling to England.

OG 1038   TG 1010   ABV 3.7 %   SRM 12   IBU 25

WATER SUPPLY:	TREAT WATER:
Soft	3 TSPS (15 ML) GYPSUM,
	1/2 TSP (2.5 ML) TABLE SALT
Moderately sulfate	1 TSP (5 ML) OF GYPSUM
Moderately carbonate	1 TSP (5 ML) GYPSUM,
	1/2 TSP (2.5 ML) TABLE SALT
Highly sulfate	ACIDIFY TO BELOW 7.0
Highly carbonate	ACIDIFY TO BELOW 7.0

Steep:
1/2 LB. (.23 KG) 120°L CRYSTAL MALT in 2 gallons (7.6 L) of cold water. Bring gradually to a boil. Remove grains when the water temperature reaches 170°F (77°C).

Add:
1-1/2 LBS. (.68 KG) LIGHT DME
3.3 LBS. (1.5 KG) AMBER PLAIN MALT EXTRACT

KETTLE SCHEDULE:
8 HBU FUGGLES HOP PELLETS, after 15 minutes.
5 HBU CHINOOK HOP PELLETS, after 30 minutes.
KETTLE KNOCKOUT after 45 minutes.

Cover the kettle and let the hops and trub settle for ten minutes. Rack the clear wort into the fermenter. Splash enough chilled sterile liquor into the fermenter to make up 5 gallons and cover it. Cool the wort in the fermenter to below 80°F (27°C) in an ice water bath, and then

Pitch with:
14 G. rehydrated DRY ALE YEAST or a LIQUID STRAIN (Wyeast 1028, Yeast Lab A04, BrewTek CL-160), close, affix airlock and

Ferment at:
60-68°F (16-20°C).

Prime with:
2/3 CUP (150 ML) LIGHT DME, cap and bottle. Age ten days.

EXTRA SPECIAL BITTER

SANDS OF TIME ESB

Extra Strong Bitter. Extra Special Bitter. Either way, you will want to savor this one. Be sure and put some aside for yourself before you start giving this brew away. Like the sand in an hourglass, it will be gone all too quickly.

OG 1050 TG 1012 ABV 5% SRM 14 IBU 30

WATER SUPPLY:	TREAT WATER:
Soft	1/2 TSP (2.5 ML) OF GYPSUM
Moderately sulfate	OK AS IS
Moderately carbonate	ACIDIFY TO BELOW 7.2
Highly sulfate	DILUTE 1:1
Highly carbonate	BOIL OR DILUTE 1:1; ACIDIFY TO BELOW 7.2

Steep:
1/2 OZ. (14 GRAMS) ROASTED BARLEY
1/2 LB. (.23 KG) 35° L CRYSTAL in 2 gallons (7.6 L) of cold water. Bring gradually to a boil, remove grains when the water temperature reaches 170°F (77°C).

Add:
3.3 LBS. (1.5 KG) AMBER MALT EXTRACT
3 LBS. (1.4 KG) AMBER DME

KETTLE SCHEDULE:
4 HBU BULLION HOP PELLETS as boil commences,
6 HBU BULLION HOP PELLETS after 30 minutes.
1 OZ. (28 GRAMS) KENT GOLDINGS HOP PELLETS AFTER 40 minutes.
KETTLE KNOCKOUT after 45 minutes.
1 OZ. (28 GRAMS) KENT GOLDINGS HOP PELLETS at knockout.

Cover the kettle and let the hops and trub settle for ten minutes. Rack the clear wort into the fermenter. Splash enough chilled sterile liquor into the fermenter to make up 5 gallons and cover it. Cool the wort in the fermenter to below 80°F (27°C) in an ice water bath, and then

Pitch with:
14 G. rehydrated DRY ALE YEAST or a LIQUID ALE YEAST (Yeast Lab A08, BrewTek CL-120, Wyeast 1098), close, affix airlock .

Ferment at:
60-68°F (16-20°C)

Prime with:
1 CUP (.23 L) AMBER DME, bottle and cap. Age 6 weeks.

CLASSIC PALE ALE

DARTBOARD PALE ALE

A classic English pub beer, light amber in color, hoppy with a brisk hop aroma that's a real bullseye. It's only pale in comparison with brown ales — this is a tasty and satisfying beer to brew and to enjoy.

OG 1045   TG 1010   ABV 4.5   SRM 8   IBU 37

WATER SUPPLY:	TREAT WATER:
Soft	2 TSPS (10 ML) GYPSUM,
	1/2 TSP (2.5 ML) TABLE SALT
Moderately sulfate	1/2 TSP (2.5 ML) OF GYPSUM
Moderately carbonate	1 TSP (5 ML) GYPSUM,
	1/2 TSP (2.5 ML) TABLE SALT
Highly sulfate	OK AS IS
Highly carbonate	ACIDIFY TO BELOW 7.0

Steep:
1/2 LB. (.23 KG) 50°L CRYSTAL MALT in 2 gallons (7.6 L) of cold water. Bring gradually to a boil. Remove grains when the water temperature reaches 170°F (77°C).

Add:
3.3 LBS. (1.5 KG) LIGHT PLAIN MALT EXTRACT
2-1/2 LBS. (1.1 KG) LIGHT DME

KETTLE SCHEDULE:
8 HBU CHINOOK HOP PELLETS after 5 minutes.
1 OZ. (28 GRAMS) PERLE HOP PELLETS after 40 minutes.
KETTLE KNOCKOUT after 45 minutes.

Cover the kettle and let the hops and trub settle for ten minutes. Rack the clear wort into the fermenter. Splash enough chilled sterile liquor into the fermenter to make up 5 gallons and cover it. Cool the wort in the fermenter to below 80°F (27°C) in an ice water bath, and then

Pitch with:
14 G. rehydrated DRY ALE YEAST or a LIQUID STRAIN (Wyeast 1028, Yeast Lab A03, BrewTek CL-170). Close, affix airlock and

Ferment at:
60-68°F (16-20°C)

Prime with:
1 CUP (.23 L) LIGHT DME, cap and bottle. Age ten days.

INDIA PALE ALE

MARJORIBANKS' IPA

This strong, highly hopped style of ale was made in the British Isles for shipment to colonial troops in India at the height of the British empire. It was shipped in oak casks; many homebrewers try to give their IPA some of that oak flavor through the use of oak chips in the fermenter. Don't be afraid to experiment with this yourself. Mr. Marjoribanks, by the way, was Director of the British East India Company in 1821, one of the men indirectly responsible for the creation of this style.

OG 1063   TG 1017   ABV 6%   SRM 11 - 12   IBU 51

WATER SUPPLY:	TREAT WATER:
Soft	6 TSPS (30 ML) GYPSUM,
	1/4 TSP (1.2 ML) TABLE SALT
Moderately sulfate	4 TSPS (20 ML) GYPSUM,
	1/4 TSP (1.2 ML) TABLE SALT
Moderately carbonate	5 TSPS (25 ML) GYPSUM,
	1/4 TSP (1.2 ML) TABLE SALT
Highly sulfate	UP TO 3 TSPS (15 ML) OF GYPSUM
Highly carbonate	UP TO 3 TSPS (15 ML) OF GYPSUM, ACIDIFY TO 7.0

Steep:
1 LB. (.45 KG) 50°L CRYSTAL MALT in 2 gallons (7.6 L) of cold water.
Bring gradually to a boil. Remove grains when the water temperature reaches 170°F (77°C).

Add:
1-1/2 LBS. (.68 KG) LIGHT DME
6.6 LBS. (3 KG) LIGHT PLAIN MALT EXTRACT, boil 10 minutes.

KETTLE SCHEDULE:
10 HBU CHINOOK HOP PELLETS, after 10 minutes.
6 HBU CASCADE HOP PELLETS after 50 minutes,
KETTLE KNOCKOUT at 60 minutes.

Cover the kettle and let the hops and trub settle for ten minutes. Rack the clear wort into the fermenter. Splash enough chilled sterile liquor into the fermenter to make up 5 gallons and cover it. Cool the wort in the fermenter to below 80°F (27°C) in an ice water bath, and then

Pitch with:
15 - 20 G. DRY ALE YEAST OR A LIQUID YEAST (Wyeast 1087, Yeast Lab A07, BrewTek CL-130). Close, affix airlock. (Optional: steam, in a vegetable steamer, and toast , on a cookie sheet at 350°F, 177°C, for 10 minutes, 2 OZ. (57 GRAMS) OAK CHIPS, place in primary fermenter before you add wort and water)

Ferment at:
60 -68°F (16 - 20°C)

When racking to secondary, add in:
1 OZ. (28 GRAMS) CHINOOK HOP PELLETS, continue fermentation as normal.

Prime with:
3/4 CUP (170 ML) CORN SUGAR, cap and bottle. Age 6 weeks or more.

ROBUST PORTER

DARKLING ROBUST PORTER

This beer carries the title robust because it is. Dark, with a hint of red, porters in general are a rich, hearty class of brews. This is one to enjoy with your "darkling", perhaps.

OG 1054   TG 1010   ABV 5.8%   SRM 35   IBU 36

WATER SUPPLY:	TREAT WATER:
Soft	1/2 TSP (2.5 ML) OF GYPSUM
Moderately sulfate	OK AS IS
Moderately carbonate	ACIDIFY TO BELOW 7.2
Highly sulfate	DILUTE 1:1
Highly carbonate	BOIL OR DILUTE 1:1; ACIDIFY TO BELOW 7.2

Steep:
1/2 LB. (.23 KG) 120°L CRYSTAL MALT
2 OZ. (57 GRAMS) BLACK PATENT MALT
1/2 LB. (.23 KG) CHOCOLATE MALT in 2 gallons (7.6 L) of cold water.
Bring gradually to a boil, remove grains when the water temperature reaches 170°F (77°C). With these dark grains it is important to "sparge" as described in step 2 of our general instructions (see above).

Add to boil:
6.6 LBS. (3 KG) AMBER MALT EXTRACT
7 HBU NORTHERN BREWER HOP PELLETS

KETTLE SCHEDULE:
1 OZ. (28 GRAMS) TETTNANG HOP PELLETS after 45 minutes.
KETTLE KNOCKOUT after 50 minutes.

Cover the kettle and let the hops and trub settle for ten minutes. Rack the clear wort into the fermenter. Splash enough chilled sterile liquor into the fermenter to make up 5 gallons and cover it. Cool the wort in the fermenter to below 80°F (27°C) in an ice water bath, and then

Pitch with:
10 G. DRY ALE YEAST OR A LIQUID ALE YEAST STRAIN (Wyeast 1028, Yeast Lab A03, BrewTek CL-130). Close, affix airlock.

Ferment at:
60 - 68°F (16 - 20°C)

When racking to your secondary fermenter,

Add:
1 OZ. (28 GRAMS) NORTHERN BREWER HOP PELLETS, close and continue fermentation as normal.

Prime with:
3/4 CUP (170 ML) CORN SUGAR, bottle and cap. Age three weeks.

BROWN PORTER

EXISTENTIAL BROWN PORTER

A "mild" version of the above recipe, brown porter is less dark, less bitter, smoother and less alcoholic than its robust cousin. This does not make it inferior, by any means; indeed brown porter has been known to inspire writers, poets and philosophers. In the world of brewing, this is a beer that just is.

OG 1046   TG 1010   ABV 4.7%   SRM 24   IBU 26

WATER SUPPLY:	TREAT WATER:
Soft	1/2 TSP (2.5 ML) OF GYPSUM
Moderately sulfate	OK AS IS
Moderately carbonate	ACIDIFY TO BELOW 7.2
Highly sulfate	DILUTE 1:1
Highly carbonate	BOIL OR DILUTE 1:1; ACIDIFY TO BELOW 7.2

Steep:
1 LB. (.45 KG) 50°L CRYSTAL MALT
2 OZ. (57 GRAMS) BLACK PATENT MALT
1/3 LB. (.15 KG) CHOCOLATE MALT in 2 gallons (7.6 L) of cold water.

Bring gradually to a boil, remove grains when the water temperature reaches 170°F (77°C). "Sparge" the grains as described in step 2 of our general instructions (see above).

Add to boil:
3.3 LBS. (1.5 KG) AMBER MALT EXTRACT
1-1/2 LBS. (.68 KG) AMBER DME
10 HBU NORTHERN BREWER HOP PELLETS

KETTLE SCHEDULE:
2 HBU TETTNANG HOP PELLETS after 30 minutes.
KETTLE KNOCKOUT after 45 minutes.

Cover the kettle and let the hops and trub settle for ten minutes. Rack the clear wort into the fermenter. Splash enough chilled sterile liquor into the fermenter to make up 5 gallons and cover it. Cool the wort in the fermenter to below 80°F (27°C) in an ice water bath, and then

Pitch with:
10 G. DRY ALE YEAST OR A LIQUID ALE YEAST STRAIN (Wyeast 1028, Yeast Lab A03, BrewTek CL-130). Close, affix airlock .

Ferment at:
60-68°F (16 - 20°C)

Prime with:
3/4 CUP (170 ML) CORN SUGAR, bottle and cap. Age three weeks.

CLASSIC DRY STOUT

LUNCHBUCKET DRY STOUT

For many years, stouts were considered food as much as they were drink. In Ireland, but also in Wales, Australia, New Zealand and parts of Africa, stout was considered a part of a miner's daily nutritional requirement. This dry stout recipe is almost rich enough to make a meal on even if you don't have to go underground to dig for coal or diamonds.

OG 1044   TG 1012   ABV 4.2%   SRM 45   IBU 33

WATER SUPPLY:	TREAT WATER:
Soft	1/2 TSP (2.5 ML) OF GYPSUM
Moderately sulfate	OK AS IS
Moderately carbonate	OK AS IS
Highly sulfate	OK AS IS
Highly carbonate	ACIDIFY TO BELOW 7.2

Steep:
1/2 LB. (.23 KG) 120°L CRYSTAL MALT
1/4 LB. (.11 KG) BLACK PATENT MALT
1/2 LB. (.23 KG) ROASTED BARLEY in 2 gallons (7.6 L) cold water.

Bring to a gradual boil and remove grains when the water temperature reaches 170°F (77°C). "Sparge" the grains, as described in Step 2 above.

Add:
3.3 LBS. (1.5 KG) DARK MALT EXTRACT
1-1/2 LBS. (.68 KG) AMBER DME

KETTLE SCHEDULE:
6 HBU NORTHERN BREWER HOP PELLETS as boil commences
7.5 HBU FUGGLES HOP PELLETS after 30 minutes.
KETTLE KNOCKOUT at 45 minutes.

Cover the kettle and let the hops and trub settle for ten minutes. Rack the clear wort into the fermenter. Splash enough chilled sterile liquor into the fermenter to make up 5 gallons and cover it. Cool the wort in the fermenter to below 80°F (27°C) in an ice water bath, and then

Pitch with:
10 G. DRY ALE YEAST OR A LIQUID ALE YEAST (Wyeast 1084, Yeast lab A05, BrewTek CL-240). Close, affix airlock.

Ferment at:
60 - 68°F (16 - 20 °C)

Prime with:
3/4 CUP (170 ML) AMBER DME, bottle and cap. Age three weeks.

SWEET STOUT

BIGMOUTH SWEET STOUT

A little richer yet, sweet stout has a sweeter, often wine-like finish while still maintaining the roasted and hoppy balance of a dry stout. This brew has a fuller mouth-feel due to the presence of unfermented dextrin. Even quiet people will enjoy the company of a Bigmouth from time to time.

OG 1050   TG 1018   ABV 4.2%   SRM 40   IBU 18

WATER SUPPLY:	TREAT WATER:
Soft	1/2 TSP (2.5 ML) OF GYPSUM
Moderately sulfate	OK AS IS
Moderately carbonate	OK AS IS
Highly sulfate	DILUTE UP TO 1:1
Highly carbonate	ACIDIFY TO BELOW 7.2

Steep:
3/4 LB. (.34 KG) CRYSTAL 35°L MALT
1/4 LB. (.11 KG) BLACK PATENT MALT
1/4 LB. (.11 KG) ROASTED BARLEY
1/4 LB. (.11 KG) CHOCOLATE MALT in 2 gallons (7.6 L) of cold water.

Bring gradually to a boil, remove grains when the water temperature reaches 170°F (77°C).

Add:
3.3 LBS. (1.5 KG) DARK MALT EXTRACT
1-1/2 LBS. (.68 KG) AMBER DME
1/2 LB. (.23 KG) MALTO-DEXTRIN POWDER

KETTLE SCHEDULE:
6 HBU CASCADE HOP PELLETS after 5 minutes.
1/2 OZ. (14 GRAMS) NORTHERN BREWER HOP PELLETS and
KETTLE KNOCKOUT at 45 minutes.

Cover the kettle and let the hops and trub settle for ten minutes. Rack the clear wort into the fermenter. Splash enough chilled sterile liquor into the fermenter to make up 5 gallons and cover it. Cool the wort in the fermenter to below 80°F (27°C) in an ice water bath, and then

Pitch with:
10 G. OF DRY ALE YEAST OR A LIQUID ALE YEAST CULTURE
(Wyeast 1084, Yeast Lab A05, BrewTek CL-240). Close, affix airlock .

Ferment at:
60 - 68°F (16 -20°C)

Prime with:
3/4 CUP (170 ML) AMBER DME, bottle and cap. Age three weeks.

IMPERIAL STOUT

DARTH VADER IMPERIAL STOUT

Whatever your favorite empire, you are sure to appreciate this thick, rich and strong brew. The addition of chopped sultanas adds an interesting fruitiness like that found in some of the Russian and Baltic commercial versions. A beer this strong and roasty absolutely requires months of bottle-conditioning, and will be none the worse after a light year or so.

OG 1092   TG 1022   ABV 9%   SRM 50   IBU 60

WATER SUPPLY:	TREAT WATER:
Soft	6 TSPS(30 ML) GYPSUM,
	1/4 TSP (1.2 ML) TABLE SALT
Moderately sulfate	4 TSPS (20 ML) GYPSUM,
	1/4 TSP (1.2 ML) TABLE SALT
Moderately carbonate	5 TSPS (25 ML) GYPSUM,
	1/4 TSP (1.2 ML) TABLE SALT
Highly sulfate	UP TO 3 TSPS (15 ML) OF GYPSUM
Highly carbonate	UP TO 3 TSPS (15 ML) OF GYPSUM, ACIDIFY TO 7.0

Steep:
1/2 LB. (.23 KG) CHOCOLATE MALT
1/2 LB. (.23 KG) ROASTED BARLEY
1/2 LB. (.23 KG) CARAPILS MALT in 2 gallons (7.6 L) of cold water.

Bring gradually to a boil, remove grains when the water temperature reaches 170°F (77°C). "Sparge" the grains (see the General Instructions, step 3).

Add:
6.6 LBS. (3 KG) AMBER MALT EXTRACT
2-3/4 LBS. (1.2 KG) AMBER DME
1 LB. (.45 KG) BREWER'S CORN SUGAR
1/2 LB. (.23 KG) CHOPPED SULTANAS OR GOLDEN RAISINS (optional)

KETTLE SCHEDULE:
15 HBU NORTHERN BREWER HOP PELLETS as boil commences,
7.5 HBU NORTHERN BREWER HOP PELLETS after 30 minutes,
1 OZ. (28 GRAMS) GALENA HOP PELLETS, after 45 minutes,
1 OZ. (28 GRAMS) SPALT HOP PELLETS after 50 minutes.
KETTLE KNOCKOUT at 52 minutes.

Cover the kettle and let the hops and trub settle for ten minutes. Rack the clear wort into the fermenter. Splash enough chilled sterile liquor into the fermenter to make up 5 gallons and cover it. Cool the wort in the fermenter to below 80°F (27°C) in an ice water bath, and then

Pitch with:
15 - 20 G. DRY ALE YEAST OR CHAMPAGNE YEAST , OR A LIQUID ALE YEAST (Wyeast 1084, Yeast Lab A05, BrewTek CL-240). Close, affix airlock.

Ferment at:
60 - 68°F (16 - 20°C)

Prime with:
3/4 CUP (170 ML) CORN SUGAR, bottle and cap. Age 3 months, but will last considerably longer.

OLD ALE

OLDE DOG ALE

English old ales and strong ales have acquired over the years a kind of cult following. Many connoisseurs go out of their way to purchase vintage dated bottles of such brews as Thomas Hardy's Old Ale, and hide them away for several years in their cellars. Olde Dog is one of those, keeping for years and mellowing like a fine wine. Who needs to learn new tricks when there's an Olde Dog around?

OG 1062   TG 1012   ABV 6.5%   SRM 16   IBU 36

WATER SUPPLY:	TREAT WATER:
Soft	2 TSPS (10 ML) GYPSUM,
	1/2 TSP (2.5 ML) TABLE SALT
Moderately sulfate	1/2 TSP (2.5 ML) OF GYPSUM
Moderately carbonate	1/2 TSP (2.5 ML) GYPSUM,
	1/2 TSP (2.5 ML) TABLE SALT
Highly sulfate	OK AS IS
Highly carbonate	ACIDIFY TO BELOW 7.2

Steep:
1/3 LB. (.15 KG) CRYSTAL 120°L MALT
2 OZ. (57 GRAMS) CHOCOLATE MALT in 2 gallons (7.6 L) of cold water, bring gradually to a boil. Remove grains when the water temperature reaches 170°F (77°C).

Add:
6.6 LBS. (3 KG) LIGHT MALT EXTRACT
1-3/4 LBS. (.79 KG) AMBER DME

KETTLE SCHEDULE:
5 HBU GOLDINGS HOP PELLETS as boil commences,
4 HBU BULLION HOP PELLETS as boil commences,
4 HBU BULLION HOP PELLETS after 45 minutes.
KETTLE KNOCKOUT at 60 minutes.

Cover the kettle and let the hops and trub settle for ten minutes. Rack the clear wort into the fermenter. Splash enough chilled sterile liquor into the fermenter to make up 5 gallons and cover it. Cool the wort in the fermenter to below 80°F (27°C) in an ice water bath, and then

Pitch with:
15 - 20 G. DRY ALE YEAST OR A LIQUID ALE YEAST (Wyeast 1728, Yeast Lab A05, BrewTek CL-160). Close, affix airlock .

Ferment at:
60 - 68°F (16 - 20°C)

When racking to your secondary,

Add:
1 OZ. (28 GRAMS) FUGGLES HOP PELLETS, reseal and continue fermentation as normal.

Prime with:
3/4 CUP (170 ML) DME, bottle and cap.

Age for at least 2 months, the longer the better. And do put some away for the long-term.

SCOTCH ALE

MACMAC SCOTCH ALE

A strong, sweet, malty brew that will have you adding Mac to your name, whatever it may be. (MacDoe? MacSmith? MacSchwartz? MacDeLucia? Why not?) The absence of aromatic hops leaves the clean maltiness and roasted flavor of the barley to stand alone.

OG 1075   TG 1025   ABV 6.6%   SRM 18   IBU 26

WATER SUPPLY:	TREAT WATER:
Soft	2 TSPS (10 ML) GYPSUM,
	1/2 TSP (2.5 ML) TABLE SALT
Moderately sulfate	1/2 TSP (2.5 ML) OF GYPSUM
Moderately carbonate	1/2 TSP (2.5 ML) GYPSUM,
	1/2 TSP (2.5 ML) TABLE SALT
Highly sulfate	OK AS IS
Highly carbonate	ACIDIFY TO BELOW 7.2

Steep:
1 LB. (.45 KG) CRYSTAL 50°L MALT
2 OZ. (57 GRAMS) ROASTED BARLEY in 2 gallons (7.6 L) of cold water, bring gradually to a boil. Remove grains when the water temperature reaches 170°F (77°C).

Add:
6.6 LBS. (3 KG) PALE MALT EXTRACT
2-3/4 LBS. (1.2 KG) GOLD DME

KETTLE SCHEDULE:
8 HBU FUGGLES HOP PELLETS as boil commences,
KETTLE KNOCKOUT at 45 minutes.

Cover the kettle and let the hops and trub settle for ten minutes. Rack the clear wort into the fermenter. Splash enough chilled sterile liquor into the fermenter to make up 5 gallons and cover it. Cool the wort in the fermenter to below 80°F (27°C) in an ice water bath, and then

Pitch with:
15 - 20 G. OF A DRY ALE YEAST OR A LIQUID ALE YEAST CULTURE
(Wyeast 1728, Yeast Lab A05, BrewTek CL-160). Close, affix airlock.

Ferment at:
60 - 68°F (16 - 20°C)

Prime with:
3/4 CUP (170 ML) GOLD DME, bottle and cap. Age 2 months.

BARLEYWINE

BIG SLEEPER BARLEYWINE

A strong, amber to light brown ale with a highly hopped flavor and aroma. One of those beers that you can take all night enjoying. Also a good brew to age for a long time. Put it to sleep in champagne bottles and save it for a special occasion.

OG 1095   TG 1025   ABV 9.0 %   SRM 14   IBU 85

WATER SUPPLY:	TREAT WATER:
Soft	1/2 TSP (2.5 ML) OF GYPSUM
Moderately sulfate	OK AS IS
Moderately carbonate	ACIDIFY TO BELOW pH 7.2
Highly sulfate	DILUTE 1:1 OR BOIL
Highly carbonate	DILUTE 1:1, OR BOIL, AND ACIDIFY

Boil 2 gallons (7.6 L) of water

Add:
6.6 LBS. (3 KG) AMBER MALT EXTRACT
6 LBS. (2.7 KG) LIGHT DME

KETTLE SCHEDULE:
20 HBU GALENA HOP PELLETS as boil commences,
1 OZ. (28 GRAMS) WILLAMETTE HOP PELLETS after 45 minutes,
KETTLE KNOCKOUT at 47 minutes.

Cover the kettle and let the hops and trub settle for ten minutes. Rack the clear wort into the fermenter. Splash enough chilled sterile liquor into the fermenter to make up 5 gallons and cover it. Cool the wort in the fermenter to below 80°F (27°C) in an ice water bath, and then

Pitch with:
15 - 20 G. DRY CHAMPAGNE YEAST, OR A LIQUID ALE YEAST
(Wyeast 1028, Yeast Lab A02). Close, affix airlock.

Ferment at:
60 - 68°F (16 - 20°C)

Prime with:
2/3 - 3/4 CUP (150-170 ML) CORN SUGAR, bottle and age as long as you can wait. Six months is not a long time for this beer; it will mellow and keep for two years or more.

FLANDERS BROWN ALE

WATT'S BRUIN

Brown ales and tart Belgian funkiness collide in this recipe, although it will not be as sour as the traditional Flanders Browns (which require lactobacillus and other weird stuff). But hey, it's a nice beer. For more authenticity, use a Belgian Abbey liquid yeast (Wyeast 1214, for example).

OG 1055   TG 1015   ABV 5.1%   SRM 12.5   IBU 20

WATER SUPPLY:	TREAT WATER:
Soft or Moderately sulfate	OK AS IS
Moderately carbonate	OK AS IS
Highly sulfate	DILUTE 1:1; ACIDIFY TO BELOW 7.2
Highly carbonate	DILUTE 1:1, OR BOIL, AND ACIDIFY

Steep:
1/2 LB. (.23 KG) MALTED WHEAT
1/2 LB. (.23 KG) CRYSTAL 50°L
1/2 LB. (.23 KG) BELGIAN BISCUIT MALT in 2 gallons (7.6 L) of cold water. Bring gradually to a boil. Remove grains when the water temperature reaches 170°F (77°C).

Add:
6.6 LBS. (3 KG) AMBER MALT EXTRACT

KETTLE SCHEDULE:
4 HBU CASCADE HOP PELLETS as boil commences,
2 HBU TETTNANG HOP PELLETS after 45 minutes.
1/2 OZ. (14 GRAMS) TETTNANG HOP PELLETS and
KETTLE KNOCKOUT after 55 minutes.

Cover the kettle and let the hops and trub settle for ten minutes. Rack the clear wort into the fermenter. Splash enough chilled sterile liquor into the fermenter to make up 5 gallons and cover it. Cool the wort in the fermenter to below 80°F (27°C) in an ice water bath, and then

Pitch with:
10 G. DRY ALE YEAST OR A LIQUID ALE YEAST (BrewTek CL-320, Wyeast 2565, Yeast Lab A08). Close, affix airlock .

Ferment at:
 60 - 68°F (16 - 20°C)

At bottling, add:
4 OR 5 DROPS .88N LACTIC ACID diluted 9:1 with sterile water

Prime with:
2/3 CUP (150 ML) BROWN SUGAR. Bottle and cap. Age 3 months or more.

BELGIAN DUBBEL

YOGI'S DUBBEL

Richer and stronger than your average bear, er... beer. Hey-ey, Boo-Boo! Maybe this is what Ranger Smith had in his pic-a-nic basket!

OG 1064   TG 1014   ABV 6.5%   SRM 14   IBU 22

WATER SUPPLY: TREAT WATER:
Soft/Moderately sulfate   OK AS IS
Moderately carbonate   ACIDIFY TO BELOW 7.2
Highly sulfate   DILUTE 1:1 AND ACIDIFY TO BELOW 7.2
Highly carbonate   DILUTE 1:1, OR BOIL, AND ACIDIFY

Steep:
1/2 LB. (.23 KG) CRYSTAL 50°L in 2 gallons (7.6 L) of cold water. Bring gradually to a boil. Remove grains when the water temperature reaches 170°F (77°C).

Add:
6.6 LBS. (3 KG) PALE MALT EXTRACT
1 LB. (.45 KG) AMBER DME
1 LB. (.45 KG) BROWN SUGAR (or dark candi sugar, if you can find it)

KETTLE SCHEDULE:
5 HBU NORTHERN BREWER HOP PELLETS as boil commences,
1/2 OZ. (14 GRAMS) GOLDINGS PELLETS after 45 minutes,
KETTLE KNOCKOUT at 46 minutes.

Cover the kettle and let the hops and trub settle for ten minutes. Rack the clear wort into the fermenter. Splash enough chilled sterile liquor into the fermenter to make up 5 gallons and cover it. Cool the wort in the fermenter to below 80°F (27°C) in an ice water bath, and then

Pitch with:
15 - 20 G. DRY ALE YEAST OR A LIQUID BELGIAN STRAIN (Wyeast 1214, Yeast Lab A08, BrewTek CL-340). Close, affix airlock .

Ferment at:
60 - 68°F (16 - 20°C)

Prime with:
1 CUP (.23 L) AMBER DME. Bottle and cap. Age 6 weeks or more.

BELGIAN TRIPPEL

OFF THE WALL TRIPPEL

Actually, there's nothing terribly off the wall about this recipe. It's a lighter-colored strong ale, a little hoppier and a little stronger than a dubbel. If you have more than one of these, though, do watch out for the wall...

OG 1091   TG 1024   ABV 8.8%   SRM 5.5   IBU 24

WATER SUPPLY:	TREAT WATER:
Soft/Moderately sulfate	OK AS IS
Moderately carbonate	ACIDIFY TO BELOW 7.0
Highly sulfate	DILUTE 1:1; ACIDIFY TO BELOW 7.0
Highly carbonate	DILUTE 1:1, OR BOIL, AND ACIDIFY

Steep:
1/2 LB. (.23 KG) CARAPILS MALT in 2 gallons (7.6 L) of cold water. Bring gradually to a boil. Remove grains when the water temperature reaches 170°F (77°C).

Add:
9.9 LBS. (4.5 KG) EXTRA-LIGHT MALT EXTRACT
2 LBS. (.9 KG) GOLD DME
1/2 LB. (.23 KG) CANDI SUGAR OR CORN SUGAR

KETTLE SCHEDULE:
4 HBU NORTHERN BREWER HOP PELLETS as boil commences,
6.5 HBU PERLE HOP PELLETS after 45 minutes,
1/2 oz. GOLDINGS HOP PELLETS after 60 minutes,
KETTLE KNOCKOUT at 61 minutes.

Cover the kettle and let the hops and trub settle for ten minutes. Rack the clear wort into the fermenter. Splash enough chilled sterile liquor into the fermenter to make up 5 gallons and cover it. Cool the wort in the fermenter to below 80°F (27°C) in an ice water bath, and then

Pitch with:
15 - 20 G. DRY ALE YEAST OR A LIQUID BELGIAN STRAIN (Wyeast 1214, Yeast lab A08, BrewTek CL-300). Close, affix airlock.

Ferment at:
60 - 68°F (16 - 20°C)

Prime with:
1 CUP (.23 L) LIGHT DME. Bottle and cap. Age 3 months or more.

WIT

SPARKLING WIT

A Belgian specialty, a light and spicy wheat beer, made with herbs and orange peel and only lightly hopped. Hazy and opalescent, this beer hides a mystery. It's different, and once you have tasted a real Wit, nothing else will ever taste the same. Witbiers are one of the rare instances where the homebrewer can appropriately use malted wheat and/or oats as kettle adjuncts.

OG 1050   TG 1010   ABV 5.2%   SRM 4   IBU 25

WATER SUPPLY:	TREAT WATER:
Soft or Moderately sulfate	OK AS IS
Moderately carbonate	ACIDIFY TO BELOW 7.0
Highly sulfate	DILUTE 1:1; ACIDIFY TO BELOW 7.0
Highly carbonate	DILUTE 1:1, OR BOIL, AND ACIDIFY

Steep:
1/2 LB. (.23 KG) MALTED WHEAT
6 OZ. (170 GRAMS) FLAKED OATS in 2 gallons (7.6 L) of cold water. Bring gradually to a boil. Remove grains when the water temperature reaches 170°F (77°C).

Add:
3.3 LBS. (1.5 KG) WHEAT MALT EXTRACT (50% barley/50% wheat)
2-1/4 LBS. (1.1 KG) WEIZEN DME
1/2 LB. (.23 KG) LIGHT HONEY

KETTLE SCHEDULE:
5 HBU SAAZ HOP PELLETS as boil commences,
1 OZ. (28 GRAMS) CRUSHED CORIANDER SEED after 45 minutes,
KETTLE KNOCKOUT and
3/4 OZ. (21 GRAMS) GRATED DRIED CURAÇAO ORANGE PEEL after 47 minutes.

Cover the kettle and let the hops and trub settle for ten minutes. Rack the clear wort into the fermenter. Splash enough chilled sterile liquor into the fermenter to make up 5 gallons and cover it. Cool the wort in the fermenter to below 80°F (27°C) in an ice water bath, and then

Pitch with:
10 G. DRY ALE YEAST OR A LIQUID BELGIAN YEAST (Wyeast 1214 or 3944, Yeast Lab W52, BrewTek CL-390). Close, affix airlock.

Ferment at:
60 - 68°F (16 - 20 °C)

Prime with:
3/4 CUP (170 ML) CORN SUGAR,

Add:
1 WHOLE CORIANDER SEED per bottle.
Bottle and cap. Bottle condition two weeks or more.

CALIFORNIA COMMON BEER

REPAIRMAN'S BLUES COMMON BEER

When Fritz Maytag rescued the Anchor brewery in San Francisco in the mid-1960's, he did the beer-drinking world a real favor by preventing this style from becoming extinct. Raise a glass to Fritz, then, and brew a batch of Repairman's Blues. You won't be lonely long.

OG 1048   TG 1012   ABV 4.8%   SRM 12   IBU 38

WATER SUPPLY:	TREAT WATER:
Soft	OK AS IS
Moderately sulfate	OK AS IS
Moderately carbonate	ACIDIFY TO BELOW pH 7.2
Highly sulfate	DILUTE 1:1
Highly carbonate	BOIL, AND ACIDIFY TO BELOW pH 7.2

Steep:
1/2 LB. TOASTED PALE MALT
1/2 LB. CRYSTAL 35°L MALT in 2 gallons (7.6 L) of cold water. Bring gradually to a boil. Remove grains when the water temperature reaches 170°F (77°C).

Add:
3.3 LBS. LIGHT MALT EXTRACT
2-1/4 LBS. LIGHT DME

KETTLE SCHEDULE:
8-1/2 HBU CASCADE HOP PELLETS as boil commences,
1 OZ. CASCADE HOP PELLETS after 45 minutes,
KETTLE KNOCKOUT at 47 minutes.

Cover the kettle and let the hops and trub settle for ten minutes. Rack the clear wort into the fermenter. Splash enough chilled sterile liquor into the fermenter to make up 5 gallons and cover it. Cool the wort in the fermenter to below 80°F (27°C) in an ice water bath, and then

Pitch with:
10 G. DRY LAGER YEAST or a warm-temperature tolerant liquid lager yeast culture (Wyeast 2112, Yeast Lab L35, or BrewTek CL-690). Close, affix airlock.

Ferment at:
60 - 68°F (16 - 20°C).

Into the secondary fermenter

Add:
1 OZ. CASCADE HOP PELLETS, reseal and condition in secondary at around 45°F or 50°F (7°-10°C)

Prime with:
3/4 CUP (170 ML) CORN SUGAR, bottle and cap. Store at room temperature for 48 hours, then condition cool (below 50°F / 10°C) for 6 weeks.

WEIZEN A NAME?

The wheat beer family goes by a number of different appellations, depending on where they are made: weizenbiers in Bavaria, weissbiers in Berlin, witbiers in Belgium, bières blanches in France and Québec, and simply wheat beers in the US. They are all generally refreshing, smooth drinking brews, of varying strengths and characters, however. This recipe is intended to emulate the moderately strong, spicy, estery version common to southern Germany. Using one of the special liquid yeast strains will make a huge difference in this brew. Can you taste the cloves and bananas? Then you used the right yeast!

Adjust the wort to below pH 5.4 with lemon juice before boiling.

OG 1049   TG 1010   ABV 5.3%   SRM 5   IBU 15

WATER SUPPLY:	TREAT WATER:
Soft	1 TSP (5 ML) GYPSUM,
	1 TSP (5 ML) TABLE SALT
Moderately sulfate	1/2 TSP (2.5 ML) GYPSUM,
	1 TSP (5 ML) TABLE SALT
Moderately carbonate	1 TSP (5 ML) GYPSUM,
	1/2 TSP (2.5 ML) TABLE SALT
Highly sulfate	DILUTE 1:1, 1/2 TSP (2.5 ML) TABLE SALT
Highly carbonate	BOIL; 1/2 TSP (2.5 ML) TABLE SALT

Steep:
3/4 LB. (.34 KG) CRACKED WHEAT MALT in 2 gallons (7.6 L) of cold water. Bring gradually to a boil, remove grains when the water temperature reaches 170°F (77°C).

Add:
1 LB. (.45 KG) WEIZEN DME
3.3 LBS. (1.5 KG) WEIZEN MALT EXTRACT
1 LB. (.45 KG) LIGHT DME

KETTLE SCHEDULE:
2.5 HBU HALLERTAU HOP PELLETS as boil commences,
1 OZ. (28 GRAMS) PERLE HOP PELLETS after 45 minutes.
KETTLE KNOCKOUT at 47 minutes.

Cover the kettle and let the hops and trub settle for ten minutes. Rack the clear wort into the fermenter. Splash enough chilled sterile liquor into the fermenter to make up 5 gallons and cover it. Cool the wort in the fermenter to below 80°F (27°C) in an ice water bath, and then

Pitch with:
10 G. DRY ALE YEAST or a liquid wheat beer yeast culture (Wyeast 3068 or 3056, Yeast Lab W51, BrewTek CL-920 or CL-930). Close, affix airlock

Ferment at:
60 - 68 °F (16 - 20°C)

Prime with:
1 CUP (.23 L) LIGHT DME, bottle and cap. Store at room temperature for 48 hours, then bottle condition cool (below 60°F / 16°C) for 4 weeks.

DUNKELWEIZEN

COUSIN WERNER'S OLD BAVARIAN DUNKELWEIZEN

Add the roasty, chocolate flavor of darker malts to the spiciness of wheat and what do you get? This stuff is rich and enchanting, balanced and full-flavored, everything you could want from a homebrew. And German enough to please your cousin Werner! or Heinz, or Ludwig...

OG 1054   TG 1013   ABV 5.4 %   SRM 19   IBU 12

WATER SUPPLY:	TREAT WATER:
Soft	1 TSP (5 ML) GYPSUM,
	1/2 TSP (2.5 ML) TABLE SALT
Moderately sulfate	1/2 TSP (2.5 ML) OF TABLE SALT
Moderately carbonate	1/2 TSP (2.5 ML) GYPSUM,
	1/2 TSP (2.5 ML) TABLE SALT
Highly sulfate	DILUTE 1:1, ADJUST ACIDITY TO pH 7.2
Highly carbonate	BOIL, ADJUST ACIDITY TO pH 7.2 OR BELOW

Steep:
1 LB. (.45 KG) CRACKED MALTED WHEAT
1/4 LB. (.11 KG) CHOCOLATE MALT
2 OZ. (57 GRAMS) BLACK PATENT MALT, bring gradually to a boil.
Remove grains when the water temperature reaches 170°F (77°C) and "sparge" them.

Add:
6.6 LBS. (3 KG) WEIZEN MALT EXTRACT

KETTLE SCHEDULE:
2.5 HBU TETTNANG HOP PELLETS as boil commences,
1/2 OZ. (14 GRAMS) TETTNANG HOP PELLETS, after 45 minutes,
KETTLE KNOCKOUT at 47 minutes.

Cover the kettle and let the hops and trub settle for ten minutes. Rack the clear wort into the fermenter. Splash enough chilled sterile liquor into the fermenter to make up 5 gallons and cover it. Cool the wort in the fermenter to below 80°F (27°C) in an ice water bath, and then

Pitch with:
10 G. DRY ALE YEAST or a liquid wheat beer yeast culture (Wyeast 3068 or 3056, Yeast Lab W51, BrewTek CL-920 or CL-930). Close and affix airlock.

Ferment at:
60 - 68°F (16 - 20°C)

Prime with:
1 CUP (.23 L) DARK DME, bottle and cap. Store at room temperature for 48 hours, then age cool (below 60°F / 16°C) for 4 weeks.

DÜSSELDORF ALT

'ALT 'OO GOES THERE

This brew, a traditional copper-colored, cold-conditioned ale from the Düsseldorf area of Germany, will amaze your non-homebrewing friends. It tastes complex, rich and smooth, but is very easy to brew. Commercial Altbiers are now made the world over, and homebrewers make their share too.

OG 1047   TG 1012   ABV 4.6%   SRM 14   IBU 27

WATER SUPPLY:	TREAT WATER:
Soft	1-1/2 TSPS (7.4 ML) GYPSUM,
	1/2 TSP (2.5 ML) SALT
Moderately sulfate	1/2 TSP (2.5 ML) GYPSUM,
	1/2 TSP (2.5 ML) TABLE SALT
Moderately carbonate	1/2 TSP (2.5 ML) GYPSUM,
	1/2 TSP (2.5 ML) TABLE SALT
Highly sulfate	ACIDIFY TO BELOW pH 7.2
Highly carbonate	BOIL, ACIDIFY TO BELOW pH 7.2

Steep:

1/2 LB. (.23 KG) CRYSTAL 50°L MALT
2 OZ. (57 GRAMS) CHOCOLATE MALT in 2 gallons (7.6 L) of cold water. Bring gradually to a boil, remove grains when the water temperature reaches 170°F (77°C).

Add:

3.3 LBS. (1.5 KG) GOLD MALT EXTRACT
2-1/2 LBS. (1.1 KG) GOLD DME

KETTLE SCHEDULE:

4.5 HBU HALLERTAU HOP PELLETS as boil commences,
1 OZ. (28 GRAMS) NORTHERN BREWER HOP PELLETS after 45 minutes,
KETTLE KNOCKOUT at 60 minutes.

Cover the kettle and let the hops and trub settle for ten minutes. Rack the clear wort into the fermenter. Splash enough chilled sterile liquor into the fermenter to make up 5 gallons and cover it. Cool the wort in the fermenter to below 80°F (27°C) in an ice water bath, and then

Pitch with:

10 G. OF A DRY ALE YEAST OR A LIQUID ALE YEAST CULTURE
(Wyeast 1338, 1007, Yeast Lab A06, BrewTek CL-400). Close and affix airlock.

Ferment at:

50° to 55°F (10° - 13° C).

Transfer to secondary after the first phase of fermentation, condition at 35° to 40°F (2° - 4° C) for 3 to 4 weeks.

Prime with:

3/4 CUP (170 ML) CORN SUGAR, bottle and cap. Store at room temperature for 48 hours, then store cool (below 50°F / 10°C) for 6 weeks.

KÖLSCH

PINK ELEPHANT KÖLSCH

If you went through Köln (Cologne) on a train a few years ago, you may have seen, framed by the windows of the Hauptbanhof, the Dom or cathedral. There was also a sign in the station, framed against the Dom, promoting the year of the German railroad... Its emblem, almost large as life, was a pink elephant... A Kölsch-drinker's delirium? A symbol of things to come? Who knows?

OG 1044   TG 1010   ABV 4.4%   SRM 4   IBU 24

WATER SUPPLY:	TREAT WATER:
Soft	ACIDIFY TO BELOW pH 7.0
Moderately sulfate	ACIDIFY TO BELOW pH 7.0
Moderately carbonate	BOIL, ACIDIFY TO BELOW pH 7.0
Highly sulfate	DILUTE AT LEAST 1:1, ACIDIFY BELOW 7.0
Highly carbonate	BOIL, DILUTE 1:1, ACIDIFY BELOW 7.0

Steep:
1 LB. (.45 KG) FLAKED WHEAT in 2 gallons (7.6 L) of cold water. Bring gradually to a boil, remove grains when the water temperature reaches 170°F (77°C).

Add:
3.3 LBS. (1.5 KG) LIGHT PLAIN EXTRACT
1.5 LBS. (.79 KG) LIGHT DME

KETTLE SCHEDULE:
6 HBU TETTNANG HOP PELLETS as boil commences
KETTLE KNOCKOUT at 45 minutes.

Cover the kettle and let the hops and trub settle for ten minutes. Rack the clear wort into the fermenter. Splash enough chilled sterile liquor into the fermenter to make up 5 gallons and cover it. Cool the wort in the fermenter to below 80°F (27°C) in an ice water bath, and then

Pitch with:
10 G. DRY ALE YEAST OR A LIQUID ALE YEAST CULTURE (Wyeast 1007, 2565, Yeast Lab L32, L33, BrewTek CL-450). Close, affix airlock .

Ferment at:
50° to 55°F (10° - 13° C). Transfer : to secondary after the first phase of fermentation, condition at 35° to 40°F (2° - 4° C) for 3 to 4 weeks.

Prime with:
2/3 CUP (150 ML) CORN SUGAR, bottle and cap. Store at room temperature for 48 hours, then age cool (below 50°F / 10°C) for six weeks.

FRUIT BEER

"STRAWBERRY FIELDS"

Let us take you down... Nothing to get hung about... It all works out... A really basic fruit-flavored ale, easy to make, easy to drink, with just a hint of 1960's psychedelia... See the section in Chapter 8 on fruit and herb beers for suggestions on how to make this even better.

OG 1050   TG 1010   ABV 5.2%   SRM 3   IBU 17

WATER SUPPLY:	TREAT WATER:
Soft	1-1/2 TSPS (7.4 ML) OF GYPSUM, ACIDIFY TO pH 7.0
Moderately sulfate	ACIDIFY TO BELOW pH 7.0
Moderately carbonate	1/2 TSP (2.5 ML) OF GYPSUM, ACIDIFY TO pH 7.0
Highly sulfate	ACIDIFY TO BELOW pH 7.0
Highly carbonate	BOIL, ACIDIFY TO BELOW pH 7.0

Boil: 2 gallons (7.6 L) of water.

Add:
6.6 LBS. (3 KG) EXTRA-LIGHT MALT EXTRACT
2/3 LB. (.3 KG) LIGHT DME

KETTLE SCHEDULE:
4 HBU CASCADE HOP PELLETS as boil commences,
1/2 OZ. (14 GRAMS) CASCADE HOP PELLETS after 45 minutes,
KETTLE KNOCKOUT at 47 minutes.

Cover the kettle and let the hops and trub settle for ten minutes. Rack the clear wort into the fermenter. Splash enough chilled sterile liquor into the fermenter to make up 5 gallons and cover it. Cool the wort in the fermenter to below 80°F (27°C) in an ice water bath, and then

Pitch with:
10 G. OF DRY ALE YEAST OR A LIQUID ALE YEAST CULTURE
(almost any one will work, each will give a unique twist — try Wyeast 1084, 1224, 1338, Yeast Lab A08, BrewTek CL-300, CL-320). Close and affix airlock.

Ferment at:
60 - 68°F (16 - 20°C)

At bottling time,

Add:
4 OZ. STRAWBERRY WINE FLAVORING

Prime with:
3/4 CUP (170 ML) CORN SUGAR. Bottle and cap. Store at room temperature for 48 hours, then age cool (below 60°F / 16°C) for 4 weeks.

RAUCHBIER

HOKISMOKES RAUCHBIER

Bamberg, Germany is the origin of this style, although there are now a few commercial examples in the US as well. Homebrewers and some microbrewers have experimented with smoked malts and smoke flavor in a variety of other styles (porters, weizens, scots ales...), but beech-smoked rauchbiers remain characteristically unique. We don't know if they brew smoked beers in Frostbite Falls, Minnesota, but if they did, surely Rocky and Bullwinkle would be involved...

OG 1048   TG 1015   ABV 4.7%   SRM 15   IBU 21

WATER SUPPLY:	TREAT WATER:
Soft	1-1/2 TSPS (7.4 ML) OF GYPSUM
Moderately sulfate	1/2 TSP (2.5 ML) OF GYPSUM
Moderately carbonate	1 TSP (5 ML) OF GYPSUM
Highly sulfate	OK AS IS
Highly carbonate	ACIDIFY TO 7.2

Steep:
1 LB. (.45 KG) GERMAN RAUCHMALT (or home-smoked pale malt)
(or use 1 lb. carapils, add 2 tsp. liquid smoke, see below)
1/2 LB. (.23 KG) CRYSTAL 35°L
2 OZ. (57 GRAMS) CHOCOLATE MALT in 2 gallons (7.6 L) of cold water. Bring gradually to a boil, remove grains when the water temperature reaches 170°F (77°C). Sparge grains with 1 quart (.95 L) of boiling water.

Add:
3.3 LBS. (1.5 KG) AMBER MALT EXTRACT
1-3/4 LBS. (.79 KG) AMBER DME

KETTLE SCHEDULE:
4.5 HBU HALLERTAU HOP PELLETS as boil commences,
1 OZ. (28 GRAMS) TETTNANG HOP PELLETS after 45 minutes,
KETTLE KNOCKOUT after 48 minutes.

Cover the kettle and let the hops and trub settle for ten minutes. Rack the clear wort into the fermenter. Splash enough chilled sterile liquor into the fermenter to make up 5 gallons and cover it. Cool the wort in the fermenter to below 80°F (27°C) in an ice water bath, and then

Pitch with:
10 G. DRY ALE OR LAGER YEAST, OR A LIQUID YEAST CULTURE
(Wyeast 1007, 1084, 2308, 2035, Yeast Lab A01, A05, L32, L33, BrewTek CL-240, CL-320, CL-680). Close and affix airlock .

Ferment at:
60 - 68°F (16 - 20°C)

Prime with:
3/4 CUP (170 ML) CORN SUGAR, add liquid smoke if using it, bottle and cap. Store at room temperature for 48 hours, then age cool (below 60°F / 16°C) for 6 weeks.

*If you can't find rauchmalts, smoke your own using a barbecue and a hardware screen - dampen the grain, smoke slowly over a smoldering fruit- or nut-wood fire, covered for 1/2 hour then uncovered for 15 minutes. If liquid smoke is to be used at bottling, avoid those with preservatives, vinegar, spices... 'Nuff said.

AMERICAN PREMIUM LAGER

THREE-GRAIN PREMIUM LAGER

On a small scale, homebrewers can produce a good, clean, refreshing American style lager; using high quality ingredients and care in the process, you will be surprised how good this style can taste.

OG 1048 TG 1011   ABV 4.9%   SRM 4   IBU 15

WATER SUPPLY:	TREAT WATER:
Soft	1-1/2 TSPS (7.4 ML) GYPSUM, ACIDIFY TO BELOW 7.0
Moderately sulfate	ACIDIFY TO BELOW pH 7.0
Moderately carbonate	ACIDIFY TO BELOW pH 7.0
Highly sulfate	ACIDIFY TO BELOW pH 7.0
Highly carbonate	BOIL, ACIDIFY TO BELOW pH 7.0

Boil : 2 gallons (7.6 L) of water.

Add:
4-3/4 IBS. (2.2 KG) LIGHT DME
1/2 LB. (.23 KG) RICE SYRUP SOLIDS
1/2 LB. (.23 KG) CORN SUGAR

KETTLE SCHEDULE:
4.5 HBU WILLAMETTE HOP PELLETS as boil commences,
1/2 OZ. (14 GRAMS) CASCADE HOP PELLETS after 45 minutes,
KETTLE KNOCKOUT at 50 minutes.

Cover the kettle and let the hops and trub settle for ten minutes. Rack the clear wort into the fermenter. Splash enough chilled sterile liquor into the fermenter to make up 5 gallons and cover it. Cool the wort in the fermenter to below 80°F (27°C) in an ice water bath, and then

Pitch with:
10 G. DRY LAGER YEAST OR A LIQUID LAGER YEAST CULTURE
(Wyeast 2112, Yeast Lab L34, BrewTek CL-690). Close, affix airlock.

Ferment at:
50° to 55°F (10° - 13° C).

Transfer to secondary after the first phase of fermentation, seal and condition at 35° to 40°F (2° - 4° C) for 3 to 4 weeks.

Prime with:
3/4 CUP (170 ML) CORN SUGAR, bottle and cap. Store at room temperature for 48 hours, then store cold (below 50°F) for three to four weeks.

CREAM ALE/LAGER

HOLD THE PEACHES CREAM ALE

No, this is not a fruit ale! The mixture of ale and lager yeasts do make for an interesting and somewhat fruity flavor, though. A good old-fashioned chilling-out beer, light and effervescent, hoppy but not very bitter...

OG 1045   TG 1008   ABV 4.9 %   SRM 4   IBU 15

WATER SUPPLY:	TREAT WATER:
Soft	1-1/2 TSPS (7.4 ML) OF GYPSUM, ACIDIFY TO pH 7.0
Moderately sulfate	ACIDIFY TO BELOW pH 7.0
Moderately carbonate	1/2 TSP (2.5 ML) OF GYPSUM, , ACIDIFY TO pH 7.0
Highly sulfate	ACIDIFY TO BELOW pH 7.0
Highly carbonate	BOIL, ACIDIFY TO BELOW pH 7.0

Steep:
1/2 LB. (.23 KG) CARAPILS MALT in 2 gallons (7.6 L) of cold water. Bring gradually to a boil, remove grains when the water temperature reaches 170°F (77°C).

Add:
3.3 LBS. (1.5 KG) EXTRA-LIGHT MALT EXTRACT
1 LB. (.45 KG) LIGHT DME
1-1/2 LBS. (.68 KG) RICE SYRUP SOLIDS

KETTLE SCHEDULE:
5.5 HBU SPALT HOP PELLETS as boil commences, 45 minutes.
1/2 OZ. (14 GRAMS) SPALT HOP PELLETS after 45 minutes,
KETTLE KNOCKOUT at 50 minutes.

Cover the kettle and let the hops and trub settle for ten minutes. Rack the clear wort into the fermenter. Splash enough chilled sterile liquor into the fermenter to make up 5 gallons and cover it. Cool the wort in the fermenter to below 80°F (27°C) in an ice water bath, and then

Pitch with:
7 G. NEUTRAL DRY ALE YEAST or a liquid lager or ale yeast culture (Wyeast 1007, 1056, Yeast Lab A07, BrewTek CL-260). Close and affix airlock.

Ferment at:
60-68°F (16-20°C).

When racking to the secondary fermenter,

Add:
1/2 OZ. (14 GRAMS) CASCADE HOP PELLETS, reseal and continue fermentation at cooler temperatures (below 60°F / 16°C) for three weeks or so.

Prime with:
3/4 CUP (170 ML) CORN SUGAR, bottle and cap. Store at room temperature for 48 hours, then store cool (below 60°F / 16°C) for 4 weeks.

DORTMUND/EXPORT

DORT-THE-SHORT EXPORT

The Dortmund area brews this light lager, and, believe it or not, until recently they didn't even get to drink it there! It was all brewed for the export market! For shame. Luckily, now they do have access to their own local specialty. And so do we homebrewers. Prosit!

OG 1054   TG 1013   ABV 5.4%   SRM 5   IBU 28

WATER SUPPLY:	TREAT WATER:
Soft	1-1/2 TSPS (7.4 ML) GYPSUM, 1/2 TSP (2.5 ML) SALT
Moderately sulfate	1/2 TSP (2.5 ML) TABLE SALT
Moderately carbonate	1/2 TSP (2.5 ML) OF TABLE SALT
Highly sulfate	OK AS IS
Highly carbonate	1/2 TSP (2.5 ML) SALT, ACIDIFY BELOW 7.0

Steep:
1/2 LB. (.23 KG) CARAPILS MALT in 2 gallons (7.6 L) of cold water. Bring to a gradual boil. Remove grains when the water temperature reaches 170°F (77°C).

Add:
6.6 LBS. (3 KG) LIGHT MALT EXTRACT
3/4 LB. (.34 KG) LIGHT DME

KETTLE SCHEDULE:
6-1/2 HBU TETTNANG HOP PELLETS as boil commences,
KETTLE KNOCKOUT at 45 minutes.

Cover the kettle and let the hops and trub settle for ten minutes. Rack the clear wort into the fermenter. Splash enough chilled sterile liquor into the fermenter to make up 5 gallons and cover it. Cool the wort in the fermenter to below 80°F (27°C) in an ice water bath, and then

Pitch with:
10 G. DRY LAGER YEAST OR A LIQUID LAGER YEAST CULTURE (Wyeast 2278 or 2042, Yeast Lab L31, BrewTek CL-660). Close and affix airlock.

Ferment at:
50° to 55°F (10° - 13° C).

Transfer to secondary after the first phase of fermentation,

Add:
1/2 OZ. (14 GRAMS) TETTNANG PELLETS, seal and condition at 35° to 40°F (2° - 4° C) for 3 to 4 weeks.

Prime with:
3/4 CUP CORN SUGAR, bottle and cap. Store at room temperature for 48 hours, then store cold (below 50°F / 10°C) for 6 weeks.

MUNICH HELLES

THERE AND BACK HELLES

If you go to Munich, you will find a beer-drinker's paradise. And if you don't go prepared with a bottle or two of Translator Doppelbock (see recipe below), here's a brief German lesson, one of two things you need to know in Munich: Helles means light. Light, as in color, but not body or flavor.

OG 1050   TG 1012   ABV 4.9%   SRM 3   IBU 20

WATER SUPPLY:	TREAT WATER:
Soft	1/2 TSP (2.5 ML) GYPSUM ACIDIFY TO pH 7.0
Moderately sulfate	ACIDIFY TO BELOW pH 7.0
Moderately carbonate	ACIDIFY TO BELOW pH 7.0
Highly sulfate	DILUTE 1:1, ACIDIFY TO BELOW pH 7.0
Highly carbonate	DILUTE 1:1, ACIDIFY TO BELOW pH 7.0

Steep:
2/3 LB. (.3 KG) CARAPILS MALT in 2 gallons (7.6 L) of cold water. Bring gradually to a boil. Remove grains when the water temperature reaches 170°F (77°C).

Add:
3.3 LBS. (1.5 KG) LIGHT MALT EXTRACT
2-3/4 LBS. (1.2 KG) LIGHT DME

KETTLE SCHEDULE:
4.5 HBU HALLERTAU HOP PELLETS as boil commences,
1/2 OZ. (14 GRAMS) HALLERTAU HOP PELLETS after 45 minutes,
KETTLE KNOCKOUT after 47 minutes.

Cover the kettle and let the hops and trub settle for ten minutes. Rack the clear wort into the fermenter. Splash enough chilled sterile liquor into the fermenter to make up 5 gallons and cover it. Cool the wort in the fermenter to below 80°F (27°C) in an ice water bath, and then

Pitch with:
10 G. DRY LAGER YEAST OR A LIQUID LAGER YEAST CULTURE (Wyeast 2308 or 2124, Yeast Lab L33, BrewTek CL-620). Close, affix airlock.

Ferment at:
50° to 55°F (10° - 13° C). Transfer to secondary after the first phase of fermentation, condition at 35° to 40°F (2° - 4° C) for 3 to 4 weeks.

Prime with:
3/4 CUP (170 ML) CORN SUGAR, bottle and cap. Store at room temperature for 48 hours, then store cold (below 50°F / 10°C) for six weeks.

GERMAN PILSENER

BÖHMERWALD PILSNER LAGER

The Böhmerwald (or Bohemian forest) hides secrets, mysteries, wonders. One such wonder, which has found its way out, is the beer of the region. The style which originated there has been more or less universally adopted. Every brewing nation in the world makes some sort of a Pilsner (whose name derives from the Bohemian city of Plzn). This recipe makes a Pilsner in the German style. For a Bohemian style, closer to the original (like Urquell or Budvar), try adding 1/2 lb. (.23 KG) 35°L crystal malt and substitute Saaz hops for the Tettnang, using 1 oz. (28 grams) at the end of the boil. If you have it, 1/2 lb. (.23 KG) of flaked rye will add a crispness and a little bit of a wry twist.

OG 1046   TG 1012   ABV 4.6%   SRM 4   IBU 35

WATER SUPPLY:	TREAT WATER:
Soft	1 TSP (5 ML) GYPSUM, ACIDIFY BELOW 7.0
Moderately sulfate	ACIDIFY TO BELOW pH 7.0
Moderately carbonate	ACIDIFY TO BELOW pH 7.0
Highly sulfate	DILUTE 1:1, AND ACIDIFY BELOW pH 7.0
Highly carbonate	DILUTE 1:1, AND ACIDIFY BELOW pH 7.0

Steep:
1/2 LB. (.23 KG) CARAPILS MALT in 2 gallons (7.6 L) of cold water. Bring gradually to a boil. Remove grains when the water temperature reaches 170°F (77°C).

Add:
3.3 LBS. (1.5 KG) EXTRA-LIGHT MALT EXTRACT
2-3/4 LBS. (1.2 KG) LIGHT DME

KETTLE SCHEDULE:
8 HBU TETTNANG HOP PELLETS as boil commences,
5 HBU TETTNANG HOP PELLETS after 45 minutes,
1/2 OZ. (14 GRAMS) TETTNANG HOP PELLETS after 60 minutes,
KETTLE KNOCKOUT at 48 minutes.

Cover the kettle and let the hops and trub settle for ten minutes. Rack the clear wort into the fermenter. Splash enough chilled sterile liquor into the fermenter to make up 5 gallons and cover it. Cool the wort in the fermenter to below 80°F (27°C) in an ice water bath, and then

Pitch with:
10 G. DRY LAGER YEAST OR A LIQUID LAGER YEAST CULTURE (Wyeast 2007 or 2278, Yeast Lab L35, BrewTek CL-660). Close, affix airlock.

Ferment at:
50° to 55°F (10° - 13° C).

Transfer to secondary after the first phase of fermentation,

Add:
1/2 OZ. (14 GRAMS) TETTNANG HOP PELLETS, seal and condition at 35° to 40°F (2° - 4° C) for 3 to 4 weeks.

Prime with:
3/4 CUP (170 ML) CORN SUGAR, bottle and cap. Let stand at room temperature for 48 hours, then store cold (below 50°F / 10°C) for four weeks.

MUNICH DUNKEL

TWILIGHT DUNKEL

Remember German lesson #1 (see There and Back Helles, above)? Well, here's part 2: Dunkel means dark. Munich Dunkels are dark brown, full-bodied and moderately hopped, roasty and... well, just try one!

OG 1054   TG 1016   ABV 5%   SRM 21   IBU 20

WATER SUPPLY:	TREAT WATER:
Soft	1/2 TSP (2.5 ML) OF GYPSUM
Moderately sulfate	OK AS IS
Moderately carbonate	OK AS IS
Highly sulfate	OK AS IS
Highly carbonate	ACIDIFY SPARGE WATER TO BELOW 7.2

Steep:
1/2 LB. (.23 KG) CRYSTAL 35°L MALT
2 OZ. (57 GRAMS) CHOCOLATE MALT
2 OZ. (57 GRAMS) BLACK PATENT MALT in 2 gallons (7.6 L) of cold water. Bring to a gradual boil. Remove grains when the water temperature reaches 170°F (77°C).

Add:
3.3 LBS. (1.5 KG) AMBER MALT EXTRACT
2-1/2 LBS. (1.1 KG) AMBER DME

KETTLE SCHEDULE:
4-1/2 HBU HALLERTAU HOP PELLETS as boil commences,
1/2 OZ. (14 GRAMS) HALLERTAU after 45 minutes,
KETTLE KNOCKOUT at 47 minutes.

Cover the kettle and let the hops and trub settle for ten minutes. Rack the clear wort into the fermenter. Splash enough chilled sterile liquor into the fermenter to make up 5 gallons and cover it. Cool the wort in the fermenter to below 80°F (27°C) in an ice water bath, and then

Pitch with:
10 G. DRY LAGER YEAST OR A LIQUID LAGER YEAST CULTURE (Wyeast 2124 or 2308, Yeast Lab L33, BrewTek CL-620). Close and affix airlock.

Ferment at:
50° to 55°F (10° - 13° C). Transfer to secondary after the first phase of fermentation, condition at 35° to 40°F (2° - 4° C) for 3 to 4 weeks.

Prime with:
3/4 CUP (170 ML) CORN SUGAR, bottle and cap. Store at room temperature for 48 hours then store cold (below 50°F / 10°C) for six weeks.

SCHWARZBIER

MAY THE SCHWARZBIER WITH YOU

The German answer to Darth Vader Imperial Stout, maybe? Actually, Schwarzbiers are not as strong as they look, despite their deep dark color. Black malt gives this beer a roasty, smoky flavor, the hops are moderate and the finish is smooth.

OG 1048   TG 1012   ABV 4.7%   SRM 28   IBU 27

WATER SUPPLY:	TREAT WATER:
Soft	UP TO 1-1/2 TSPS (7.4 ML) OF GYPSUM
Moderately sulfate	OK AS IS
Moderately carbonate	OK AS IS
Highly sulfate	OK AS IS
Highly carbonate	ACIDIFY TO BELOW 7.2

Steep:
2 OZ. (57 GRAMS) BLACK PATENT MALT
1/4 LB. (.11 KG) CRYSTAL 120°L
1/4 LB. (.11 KG) CHOCOLATE MALT in 2 gallons (7.6 L) of cold water. Bring to a gradual boil. Remove grains when the water temperature reaches 170°F (77°C).

Add:
3.3 LBS. (1.5 KG) DARK MALT EXTRACT
2-1/4 LBS. (1 KG) AMBER DME

KETTLE SCHEDULE:
9-1/2 HBU HALLERTAU HOP PELLETS as boil commences,
1 OZ. (28 GRAMS) TETTNANG HOP PELLETS after 45 minutes,
KETTLE KNOCKOUT at 45 minutes.

Cover the kettle and let the hops and trub settle for ten minutes. Rack the clear wort into the fermenter. Splash enough chilled sterile liquor into the fermenter to make up 5 gallons and cover it. Cool the wort in the fermenter to below 80°F (27°C) in an ice water bath, and then

Pitch with:
10 G. DRY LAGER YEAST OR A LIQUID LAGER YEAST CULTURE (Wyeast 2007 or 2042, Yeast Lab L31, BrewTek CL-660). Close and affix airlock.

Ferment at:
50° to 55°F (10° - 13° C). Transfer to secondary after the first phase of fermentation, condition at 35° to 40°F (2° - 4° C) for 3 to 4 weeks.

Prime with:
3/4 CUP (170 ML) CORN SUGAR, bottle and cap. Store at room temperature for 48 hours, then store cold (below 50°F / 10°C) for 6 weeks.

VIENNA

MR. FINGERS' VIENNA

Arguably one of the most elegant cities in old Europe, Vienna's brewing reputation rests on this style of amber lager, moderately hopped and full-bodied. Mr. Fingers was a harmonica player who used to entertain crowds of tourists on the sidewalks of Der Ring, Wien's equivalent of the Champs-Elysées.

OG 1050   TG 1012   ABV 5%   SRM 13   IBU 26

WATER SUPPLY:	TREAT WATER:
Soft	1-1/2 TSPS (7.4 ML) OF GYPSUM, ACIDIFY TO pH 7.2
Moderately sulfate	1/2 TSP (2.5 ML) OF GYPSUM, ACIDIFY TO pH 7.2
Moderately carbonate	1/2 TSP (2.5 ML) OF GYPSUM, ACIDIFY TO pH 7.2
Highly sulfate	ACIDIFY TO BELOW pH 7.2
Highly carbonate	ACIDIFY TO BELOW pH 7.2

Steep:

1/4 IB. (.11 KG) CRYSTAL 120°L MALT
1/2 LB. (.23 KG) CARAPILS MALT in 2 gallons (7.6 L) of cold water. Bring gradually to a boil Remove grains when the water temperature reaches 170°F (77°C).

Add:

3.3 LBS. (1.5 KG) AMBER MALT EXTRACT
2-3/4 LBS. (1.2 KG) LIGHT DME

KETTLE SCHEDULE:

10 HBU HALLERTAU HOP PELLETS as boil commences,
1/2 OZ. (14 GRAMS) TETTNANG HOP PELLETS after 30 minutes,
KETTLE KNOCKOUT after 45 minutes.

Cover the kettle and let the hops and trub settle for ten minutes. Rack the clear wort into the fermenter. Splash enough chilled sterile liquor into the fermenter to make up 5 gallons and cover it. Cool the wort in the fermenter to below 80°F (27°C) in an ice water bath, and then

Pitch with:

10 G. OF A DRY LAGER YEAST OR A LIQUID LAGER YEAST CULTURE (Wyeast 2042, 2178, 2206, Yeast Lab L32, BrewTek CL-640, CL-680). Close, affix airlock.

Ferment at:

50° to 55°F (10° - 13° C). Transfer to secondary after the first phase of fermentation,

Add:

1/2 OZ. (14 GRAMS) TETTNANG HOP PELLETS, seal and condition at 35° to 40°F (2° - 4° C) for 3 to 4 weeks.

Prime with:

3/4 CUP (170 ML) CORN SUGAR, bottle and cap. Store at room temperature for 48 hours, then store cool (below 50°F / 10°C) for 6 weeks.

MÄRZEN/OKTOBERFEST

MY FAVORITE MÄRZEN

Märzenbiers were traditionally made in March (the end of the brewing season) and were made strong and hoppy to be put away for the warmer weather of summer and fall. The last of the beer was brought out to celebrate the harvest, in late September or October, hence their other name, Oktoberfest. Lucky homebrewers that we are, we can pretend it's March right now and brew up My Favorite Märzen to enjoy in a couple of months, whether it's harvest time or not.

OG 1056   TG 1012   ABV 5.8%   SRM 12   IBU 27

WATER SUPPLY:	TREAT WATER:
Soft	1 TSP (5 ML) OF GYPSUM, ACIDIFY TO pH 7.2
Moderately sulfate	ACIDIFY TO BELOW pH 7.2
Moderately carbonate	ACIDIFY TO BELOW pH 7.2
Highly sulfate	DILUTE 1:1, ACIDIFY TO BELOW pH 7.2
Highly carbonate	BOIL, ACIDIFY TO BELOW pH 7.2

Steep:
1/2 LB. (.23 KG) CRYSTAL 35°L MALT
1/4 LB. (.11 KG) CARAPILS MALT in 2 gallons (7.6 L) of cold water. Bring gradually to a boil, remove grains when the water temperature reaches 170°F (77°C).

Add:
3.3 LBS. (1.5 KG) AMBER MALT EXTRACT
3-1/2 LBS. (1.6 KG) LIGHT DME

KETTLE SCHEDULE:
5 HBU HALLERTAU HOP PELLETS as boil commences,
5 HBU HALLERTAU HOP PELLETS after 15 minutes,
5 HBU TETTNANG HOP PELLETS after 30 minutes,
1 OZ. (28 GRAMS) TETTNANG HOP PELLETS after 45 minutes,
KETTLE KNOCKOUT at 47

Cover the kettle and let the hops and trub settle for ten minutes. Rack the clear wort into the fermenter. Splash enough chilled sterile liquor into the fermenter to make up 5 gallons and cover it. Cool the wort in the fermenter to below 80°F (27°C) in an ice water bath, and then

Pitch with:
10 G. OF A DRY LAGER YEAST OR A LIQUID LAGER YEAST CULTURE (Wyeast 2042, Yeast Lab L32, BrewTek CL-640). Close, affix airlock.

Ferment at:
50° to 55°F (10° - 13°C).

Transfer to secondary after the first phase of fermentation.

Add:
1/2 OZ. (14 GRAMS) HALLERTAU HOP PELLETS, seal and condition at 35° to 40°F (2° - 4° C) for 3 to 4 weeks.

Prime with:
3/4 CUP (170 ML) CORN SUGAR, bottle and cap. Store at room temperature for 48 hours, then store cool (below 50°F / 10°C) for 8 weeks.

TRADITIONAL BOCK

OFFENBOCK

You will want to sample this brew "offen", in fact (watch out, here comes a pun), as "offen" as you "can-can"... (The authors apologize.) It is a brown, semi-sweet lager with moderate hoppiness and a lingering, musical finish. Musical? Yes, musical!

OG 1067   TG 1018   ABV 6.3%   SRM 28   IBU 20

WATER SUPPLY:	TREAT WATER:
Soft	1-1/2 TSPS (7.4 ML) OF GYPSUM
Moderately sulfate	1/2 TSP (2.5 ML) OF GYPSUM
Moderately carbonate	1/2 TSP (2.5 ML) OF GYPSUM
Highly sulfate	OK AS IS
Highly carbonate	ACIDIFY TO BELOW 7.0

Steep:
1/2 LB. (.23 KG) CRYSTAL MALT
1/2 LB. (.23 KG) MUNICH MALT
1/2 LB. (.23 KG) TOASTED PALE MALT in 2 gallons (7.6 L) of cold water. Bring to a gradual boil. Remove grains when the water temperature reaches 170°F (77°C).

Add:
6.6 LBS. (3 KG) DARK MALT EXTRACT
1 LB. (.45 KG) AMBER DME

KETTLE SCHEDULE:
4.5 HBU HALLERTAU HOP PELLETS as boil commences,
4.5 HBU HALLERTAU HOP PELLETS after 30 minutes,
1 OZ. (28 GRAMS) SAAZ after 45 minutes,
KETTLE KNOCKOUT at 47 minutes.

Cover the kettle and let the hops and trub settle for ten minutes. Rack the clear wort into the fermenter. Splash enough chilled sterile liquor into the fermenter to make up 5 gallons and cover it. Cool the wort in the fermenter to below 80°F (27°C) in an ice water bath, and then

Pitch with:
15 - 20 G. DRY LAGER YEAST OR A LIQUID LAGER YEAST CULTURE (Wyeast 2206 or 2308, Yeast Lab L32 or L33, BrewTek CL-640). Close, affix airlock.

Ferment at:
50° to 55°F (10° - 13° C). Transfer to secondary after the first phase of fermentation. Condition at 35° to 40°F (2° - 4° C) for 3 to 4 weeks.

Prime with:
3/4 CUP (170 ML) CORN SUGAR, let stand at room temperature for 48 hours then store cold (below 50°F / 10°C) for six weeks.

HELLESBOCK

WE'LL BE LIGHT BOCK

A "helles"style bock, lighter in color but every bit as rich and full-bodied as the traditional darker style. Looks can deceive.

Toast 1/2 lb. (.23 KG) of Carapils malt on a cookie sheet at 350°F (177°C) for 20 minutes. The fresh-roasted aroma is "hellish" in this brew!

OG 1066   TG 1018   ABV 6.3%   SRM 6   IBU 30

WATER SUPPLY:	TREAT WATER:
Soft	1/2 TSP (2.5 ML) GYPSUM; ACIDIFY TO pH 7.0
Moderately sulfate	ACIDIFY TO BELOW pH 7.0
Moderately carbonate	ACIDIFY TO BELOW pH 7.0
Highly sulfate	DILUTE 1:1 AND ACIDIFY TO BELOW 7.0
Highly carbonate	BOIL OR DILUTE 1:1; ACIDIFY TO BELOW 7.0

Steep:
1/4 LB. (.11 KG) TOASTED CARAPILS MALT in 2 gallons (7.6 L) of cold water. Bring to a gradual boil. Remove grains when the water temperature reaches 170°F (77°C).

Add:
6.6 LBS. (3 KG) EXTRA-LIGHT MALT EXTRACT
2-3/4 LBS. (1.2 KG) LIGHT DME

KETTLE SCHEDULE:
10 HBU TETTNANG HOP PELLETS as boil commences,
5.5 HBU SAAZ HOP PELLETS after 30 minutes,
1/2 OZ (14 g.) TETTNANG HOP PELLETS and
KETTLE KNOCKOUT at 45 minutes.

Cover the kettle and let the hops and trub settle for ten minutes. Rack the clear wort into the fermenter. Splash enough chilled sterile liquor into the fermenter to make up 5 gallons and cover it. Cool the wort in the fermenter to below 80°F (27°C) in an ice water bath, and then

Pitch with:
15 - 20 G. DRY LAGER YEAST OR A LIQUID YEAST CULTURE (Wyeast 2124, Yeast Lab L33, BrewTek CL-680). Close, affix airlock .

Ferment at:
50° to 55°F (10° - 13° C). Transfer to secondary after the first phase of fermentation. Condition at 35° to 40°F (2° - 4° C) for 3 to 4 weeks.

Prime with:
3/4 CUP (170 ML) CORN SUGAR, bottle and cap. Store at room temperature for 48 hours then store cold (below 50 °F / 10°C) for six weeks.

DOPPELBOCK

TRANSLATOR DOPPELBOCK

This is a brew that will make you fluent in almost any language, even if you have never studied it. Well, maybe not, but it will make you feel more fluent. And if you feel fluent, other people will think you are fluent! And they'll give you presents, send you money, ask for your autograph... Oops, sorry, we got a little carried away there... But if you need a nice, rich darker lager, maybe you need a Translator.

OG 1080   TG 1022   ABV 7.6%   SRM 22   IBU 25

WATER SUPPLY:	TREAT WATER:
Soft	1/2 TSP (2.5 ML) GYPSUM; ACIDIFY TO pH 7.2
Moderately sulfate	ACIDIFY TO BELOW pH 7.2
Moderately carbonate	ACIDIFY TO BELOW pH 7.2
Highly sulfate	ACIDIFY TO BELOW 7.2
Highly carbonate	ACIDIFY TO BELOW 7.2

Steep:
1/2 LB. (.23 KG) CRYSTAL 50°L MALT
2 OZ. (57 GRAMS) CHOCOLATE MALT
2 OZ. (57 GRAMS) BLACK PATENT MALT in 2 gallons (7.6 L) of water. Bring gradually to a boil. Remove grains when the water temperature reaches 170°F (77°C).

Add:
9.9 LBS. (4.5 KG) AMBER MALT EXTRACT
1 LB. (.45 KG) DARK DME

KETTLE SCHEDULE:
5 HBU TETTNANG HOP PELLETS as boil commences,
5 HBU SAAZ HOP PELLETS after 45 minutes,
KETTLE KNOCKOUT at 55 minutes.

Cover the kettle and let the hops and trub settle for ten minutes. Rack the clear wort into the fermenter. Splash enough chilled sterile liquor into the fermenter to make up 5 gallons and cover it. Cool the wort in the fermenter to below 80°F (27°C) in an ice water bath, and then

Pitch with:
15 - 20 G. DRY LAGER YEAST OR A LIQUID LAGER YEAST CULTURE (Wyeast 2124, Yeast Lab L33, BrewTek CL-680). Close, affix airlock .

Ferment at:
50° to 55°F (10° - 13° C). Transfer to secondary after the first phase of fermentation. Condition at 35° to 40°F (2° - 4° C) for 3 to 4 weeks.

Prime with:
3/4 CUP (170 ML) CORN SUGAR, bottle and cap. Store at room temperature for 48 hours then store cold (below 50°F / 10°C) for six weeks.

CHAPTER 8

WHAT IF I ADDED A LITTLE?...

ADVENTURES IN BREWING

PART 1:
USING WORLD BEER STYLES TO
FORMULATE RECIPES

So you've got a few brews under your belt now. Perhaps you have brewed a couple dozen recipes, and you're feeling like you ought to stretch a little bit and try something new. What to do? You can go on to experimenting with fruits and herbs (see part two of this chapter), or you can start fiddling with your own recipe formulations.

This is a big step. You can just wing it, and brew a kitchen-sink brew, adding whatever you feel like to your brew kettle. Or you can continue learning, learning about styles and recipe formulation.

When we decide to brew a new beer at The Seven Barrel Brewery, we don't just grab what we have in malt and hop stores and throw it in the pot. We are already pretty familiar with the various beer styles, and we've brewed a lot of them before. We decide what style of beer we want to brew, and we talk about it. Do we want it to be reserved for the style, or very big? Do we want it on the bitter end of the scale, or not? What characteristics of the style do we want to highlight?

Even though we are pretty familiar with most of the beer styles, we always refer to the style parameters when we are creating a new recipe. We look back at the brewlogs of beers that we have brewed before in the style. We have a section on our brewlogs for comments, and we review them. Did we find that recipe weak on maltiness? Was it too alcoholic? Did we remark that it had too much of a solventy character? We will look to correct even the most miniscule misjudgments that we made with a previous recipe, as we devise a new one.

You may lack the breadth of experience to do the same, but you can use our experience to help you along the way. If you have brewed both the kit and the extract version of the India Pale Ale, you can jump ahead and look at the recipes for the partial-mash and full-mash versions. To some extent, there are different means to reaching the same end in recipe formulations. Compare the recipes; how do they use different malts, hops, yeast strains and fermentation parameters to arrive at similar results? The easiest way to customize a recipe is to grab "parts" from the other recipes for the style of beer.

Another approach is to target a particular flavor or other attribute of a beer that you would like to duplicate. Perhaps you have tasted a particular beer and said to yourself, "Self, I would like to brew a beer like this".

How can you brew it? Well, you've learned something about how different ingredients affect flavor. Trust your senses now, and pour another one of those beers that you'd like to emulate. Look at it. Look at its color and its carbonation. Smell it. Pinpoint its aromatic characters. Jot notes down as you do. Equate its aromatics with specific ingredients or processes that you have experience with. Write down what those are.

Do the same with flavor. Is it sweet or dry? Is it bitter or malty? Is it roasty or nutty? Is it spicy or floral? What have you done that has produced similar flavors? Review your brewlogs, and make notes as you see similarities.

Find out what you can about the beer you want to reproduce. Is it an ale or a lager? In what country was it brewed? What style of beer is it? If it is an English Extra Special Bitter, chances are it uses English malt, hops and yeast, and it has a relatively high bitterness and alcohol content and is well attenuated. It probably relies on British crystal malt for flavor, and the SRM color range for the style gives you an indication of how much.

Look at the ranges specified in the style guidelines, then look at the corresponding specifications for our recipes. Where do they niche in? Would you like to increase the color and fullness of the beer?

For malt and adjunct additions, use the SRM and OG ranges of the beer style to guide your calculations. The INGREDIENTS: COLOR AND UTILIZATION chart in the appendices gives the approximate SRM color and gravity increase that each pound of ingredients should increase your wort by. Figure out what you can add or change and still remain within the color and OG parameters of the style.

Would you like to brew a version that is closer to the top-end of bitterness for the style than our recipe? Then add more hops. You can use these guidelines for adjusting hop pellet additions for 5 gallon batches:

1 HBU in boiling wort for: Will increase IBUs:

	2 gallon boil	5 gallon boil
0 minutes:	.5 IBU	.7 IBU
5 minutes:	.5 IBU	.7 IBU
15 minutes:	1.0 IBU	1.25 IBUs
20 minutes:	1.1 IBUs	1.5 IBUs
30 minutes:	1.75 IBUs	2.4 IBUs
45 minutes:	2.8 IBUs	4.0 IBUs
60 minutes:	3.25 IBUs	4.25 IBUs
90 minutes:	3.25 IBUs	4.5 IBUs

2 GALLONS = 7.6 LITERS,   5 GALLONS = 18.9 LITERS

So, if you want to increase the bitterness of an ESB recipe by 6 IBUs, using Fuggles at 5% Alpha Acid, added 30 minutes before kettle knock-out in a two-gallon wort boil, this is what you need to do:

Look up the utilization in the chart above, intersecting the 2 gallon column and the 30 minute row; it gives you utilization of 1.75 IBUs per HBU of hops added.

IBUs divided by utilization equals HBUs, divided by Alpha Acid equals ounces of that hop that you should add.

This is the equation you would use, then:

6 divided by 1.75 equals 3.4. Divided by 5 equals .69 ounces of Fuggles.

So to increase the bitterness of your ESB by 6 IBUs, you need to add about 2/3 of an ounce (20 grams) of Fuggles to your two-gallon boil 30 minutes before knock-out.

You can use this simple formula (well, simple as far as brewing equations go, anyway) for increasing or decreasing bitterness in any recipe.

Fermentation characteristics are generally controlled by four parameters: the yeast strain, the amount of it that is pitched, the fermentation temperature and the duration of conditioning. Lower temperatures give mellower, more sulphury aroma and flavor, higher temperatures give fruitier flavors, and even higher temperatures give more phenolic, alcoholic and solvent flavors.

If the beer is transferred off its trub, longer conditioning will give mellower, rounder flavors.

This may seem bassackwards, but jump to the troubleshooting in Chapter 14. Why would I want to brew a BAD beer, you might ask? Well, you don't, and that's the whole point. You are going into uncharted territory, and it helps to know where the pitfalls are ahead of time. As you develop your recipe, review your intentions against the list of problems and what causes them. Take a look at the BJCP Judging Form in Chapter 15 as well, and reflect upon your recipe.

Once you are satisfied with your recipe, brew it. Keep good records! When your beer is fully matured, sit down and seriously evaluate it. Use the Judging Form to rate it, but don't limit yourself by it - write down every perception about the beer that you have. How have you done?

We really want you to play with our recipes. We think that they are great recipes, but each time that we brew them, we are likely to tweak ingredients or process one way or another, and there is no reason why you shouldn't either. If you want to create your own recipes, start with ours, and take it whichever way you want to go. And if you want to brew with stuff that's not in our recipes, read on...

PART 2:
USING FRUITS, HERBS
AND VEGETABLES IN BREWING

OK, hang on, folks, this is where it can get weird. Excited? Ready to go? OK! You've already seen a couple of fruit beer recipes, maybe you've even made one already... What you've seen so far, though, involved fruit as a beer flavor. Chances are, if you are at all a beer enthusiast or gourmet, you've tasted or at least heard of some kind of strange brew made with pumpkin, or spiced with jalapeños or nutmeg. Well, then picture a perfect brewing world, a world in which convention and limits disappear, a world in which anything goes, as long as it appeals to you, the brewer... You've just entered the "Fruit/Herb/Vegetable Zone".

Virtually any non-oily food or spice you can eat can be added to beer. No, really! The amounts will differ, the way in which those ingredients are processed and handled will differ, but the effect is the same: changing the flavor of beer, creating sometimes dramatic new taste sensations.

HERBS

Most herbs are best used in dried form, and are added either at the end of the boil, or to the cooling (but still-warm) wort. Whole seeds, like caraway, cardamon, anise, fennel, etc., need to be crushed (but not ground); cinnamon, licorice, ginger and other roots and bark should be shaved or chopped, and used in conservative doses. Other possibilities here include (but please do not consider this a complete or exhaustive list): coffee (whole beans or freshly crushed), chocolate (ground sweetened cocoa is OK, but not hot chocolate mix!), vanilla bean (chopped), spruce or juniper needles, juniper berries (crushed), gentian root (very bitter - use sparingly!), woodruff, maple sap or syrup... It is also possible to make a tincture by soaking chopped or shredded herbs in plain vodka — add this at bottling, to taste. Err on the side of caution: if you're not sure of how something is going to taste, or if you're not sure if you're going to like it, be very careful not to overdo it. Some herbs, even in small quantities, can overpower a beer's flavor. Try to achieve a balance, as you would with hops. To test the way an herb will influence the flavor of a beer, try a pinch of it in about 2 ounces of a beer of a similar style to what you are going to be brewing. Let it sit for an hour and taste it — if it's OK with you, go ahead and try it.

The following is a (partial) list of other herbs and spices that have been, or are currently used in some brewing styles, somewhere in the world. Amounts mentioned are only suggestions, for 5 gallons:

Bayberries (1 oz.), sweet gale leaves (1 gram), hedge nettle or betony (1/2 oz.), yarrow (1 - 2 g.), burnet leaves (1 g.), milk thistle stalk (1 g.), elderberry flowers (or berries) (1 g.), lavender (1/2 oz), marjoram (1 - 2 g.), rosemary (1 - 2 g.), sliced horseradish stalks or roots (1 - 2 oz.), thyme (1 g.), cinnamon (2 - 3 oz.), anise seed (1 oz.), fennel seed (1 oz.), agrimony leaves (1 - 2 oz.), fresh lemon balm leaves (2 - 4 oz), cardamon seed (5 - 8 in boil), chamomile flowers (1 oz. or more), dandelion leaves or fresh flowers (up to a gallon in a simmering wort!), sage (1/2 - 1 oz.), gentian root (1/8 - 1/4 oz.), hyssop (1 for 1 in place of hops), licorice root (1/2 - 1 oz.), fresh or dried mint, any variety (1 -3 oz.), wintergreen leaves (tincture or strong tea, 2 - 3 oz.),etc... For more information on these and other herbs, see the articles "A Brewer's Herbal" by Gary Carlin in the Summer 1987 issue of Zymurgy, "Early British Ale" by Gary Spedding in Zymurgy's 1993 Special Issue, and Scott Russells's "Spice up Your Brew" in Brew Your Own, September 1995.

FRUIT

Fruit can be trickier to work with than herbs. There are essentially three forms in which fruit flavoring can be added to beer: fresh fruit, fruit juice or flavoring essences/extracts. Dried fruits such as elderberries, orange peel, rose hips, dates and figs occasionally end up in brews as well.

The easiest thing to use are the flavoring extracts, usually sold in homebrew and winemaking shops and catalogs. They come in a wide variety of flavors and are generally unsweetened. These are not to be confused with cooking extracts, which are alcohol-based, or soft drink extracts such as root beer, cola, etc. (although both of these find their way into an occasional batch of beer as well...). Use an ounce for five gallons to get a light hint of fruit flavor, 2 or 3 ounces to fill it out and as much as 4 ounces to brew a strongly fruit-flavored beer. It is best to add these at bottling time along with priming sugar, so that they can be adjusted to taste.   Fruit juices are sometimes added to the boil, instead of, or in addition to, some of the water. Add apple juice, grape juice, cherry juice or whatever you happen to have. Be careful to use only pure juice. Any additives, preservatives, or sweeteners will adversely affect your beer. You might try priming with about 2 cups of blueberry or cherry juice, but unless you want to brew "wild", you should first pasteurize fresh squeezed-or-pressed fruit juice by heating it up to 180°F(82°C) or so.

There are a couple of different ways to use fresh fruit. The least complicated and least risky method is to put a couple of pounds of bruised cherries or strawberries, sliced peaches, etc., in a mesh bag and steep them in your wort for the last 10 or 15 minutes of the boil. Alternatively, you can heat the fruit separately with a little water to above 200°F (95°C) for 10 minutes to pasteurize it, and then place it into the secondary fermenter before racking the fermented beer onto it. This will induce some re-fermentation. Many styles, particularly Belgian, use fresh fruit, unpasteurized and unprocessed, in a significant second fermentation. This gives a sharper fruit flavor to the brew and avoids a lot of the possible haze problems and stuck fermentation that pectin from overcooked, gelatinized fruit can cause, but it also makes bacterial infection likely.

Homebrewers also use fruit liqueurs in place of priming sugar. It takes a whole 750 ml. bottle to get enough sugar from most of them to induce adequate bottle conditioning, and they up the alcohol content by 1% or more.

Traditional use of fruit in beers is essentially a Belgian province, with Kriek (cherry), Frambozen (raspberry), Pêche (peach) and Druiven (grape) being the most common. Other styles include Aardbien (strawberry) and Cassis (currant). Some US microbrewers use blueberries and cranberries, and let us not overlook the German practice of adding lemon or raspberry (or woodruff) syrups to Weizens and Berliner Weissbiers, although this usually occurs in the bar or café, at the consumer's discretion.

VEGETABLES AND THE REST...

Say what? Tomato Stout, Dandelion Helles Lager, Cucumber Bitter? Why not? Here again, the possibilities are as limitless as your garden or local market. Obviously, the fresher and more chemical-free the veggies you use, the more appropriate they will be in your brew... Use much like fresh fruit — if you can juice it, try that. If not, chop it up, or puree it and steep it in the hot wort. Strong flavors like chili peppers and garlic (yes, it's been done) will be "enhanced" (or at least increased) by putting a bit in each bottle. Try to achieve a balance of flavors, bitter/sweet, sharp/soft. Most vegetables will not do much for color, but some flowers certainly will (nasturtiums, geraniums, borage are all edible — imagine a Borage Blue Pale Ale!)

A point of philosophy: while there are a few traditional examples of brewing with fruit, a few more with herbs, modern beer drinkers have tended to shy away from them as "too exotic" or "too weird". Homebrewers here again have an advantage: if the big brewers won't make them, and the few foreign specialties are just too expensive to make a habit of frequenting, well, so what? Make your own! If you know you like it, make a big batch. If you're not sure, make a small batch! We can play with things, make a couple gallons at a time, make it again if it comes out great, whatever! Homebrewers can be adventurous: a peat-smoked scots ale with cumin seed, a ginger and spruce schwarzbier, a pilsner with caraway and honey, a raspberry and coriander wheat beer... Most fruited or herbed beers are just that — beers of a standard, recognizable style to which fruit or herbs have been added. If you're inclined to experiment, do so. If you're cautious, do so in a small way. Try repeating the recipe, varying the amount of the herb or fruit each time. You will probably hit on a combination or two that you really enjoy. Maybe you'll even discover that perfect elixir, the one that transcends the term "beer" and becomes not just your favorite brew of all time, but your connection to another reality!

CHAPTER 9

MASHING 101

It's just remotely possible that you have read this far, brewed a few batches, and still have no clue what "mashing" is. OK, so you're a little slow. Here is the definitive, abridged-and-condensed definition of mashing:

Mashing (m-a-s-h-i-n-g). The process of stewing grain to make wort.

Some homebrewers remain perfectly content to brew from extracts forever. This is not surprising, since great homebrew can be made from extracts. Just the fact that a homebrewer mashes does not mean that their beer is going to be better, either. Some extract homebrewers seriously wonder about whether mash-brewers have a very good grip on reality. Mashing adds two or three hours brewing time to each batch, and more than doubles the investment a homebrewer has to make in equipment.

Other brewers just have to move on to mashing. Some make the move because mashing is more organic. Others wish to gain the control over fermentability, color, fullness and flavor-nuances that mashing affords. A few do it just because they're geeks, and mashing is techno-geek stuff. The rest can't help it, they're just type-A personalities.

The choice of whether to mash or not is entirely yours. The only bad reason for taking up grain brewing is you think you have to. It just ain't so. Such a wide variety of malt extracts are so readily available that nearly any beer style can be brewed from extracts alone. Brews can be personalized by using grain adjuncts, or a very simple partial mash.

However, even if you never mash, it will never hurt you to know what goes on and how it's done. It may bore you to tears (remember, this is techno-geek stuff!) or put you to sleep, but it shouldn't cause permanent brain damage. If the reason that you dropped out of sixth grade is because you hated science class, then you might want to point at the words as you read them, and speak them aloud. It's too bad, but not everything in life can be as much fun as homebrewing. Finally, if you really don't care what is happening or why and you still want to mash, just skip the next sixteen pages, and go on to the "How To" section of this chapter. But if you want to become a full-fledged beer nerd, clean the Twinkie smudges off your glasses and sit up straight. Putting first things first, we'll need take a look back at how brewing began, and how barley is prepared for brewing.

THE PSEUDO-ANTHROPOLOGICALLY-CORRECT ORIGINS OF BREWING

Imagine primitive man eking out a sustenance-living, hunting and gathering, hunting and gathering. Life is good, but man has tasted the fruit of the forbidden tree. Man has experienced demon alcohol, and damned if he didn't like it! Only trouble is, the fruits don't ripen year 'round. That means there is only over-ripe, fermenting fruit for a couple of months. Man looks forward to the seasons when fruits ripen.

Early man has already figured out that if barley is dried out it stores well, and can be eaten at other times of the year. Wild barley (really just species of grass) is pretty easy to harvest when it ripens, so it's not difficult to stash away a few piles of it. And besides, the barley is as hard as steel and the husks stick between his teeth and drive him nuts for hours. So man piles barley in the corners of his cave and when the weather really sucks, he just hangs around the cave and chews barley, which beats Toledo out of having to go out hunting and gathering, hunting and gathering in the rain.

Man being man, however, man inevitably gets careless one day and leaves a heap of barley outside. It rains, the barley gets wet, and the barley begins to sprout. The sun comes back out, and the barley dries. It rains again, and the sprouted barley gets wet again. The sun comes out for awhile and heats up the wet barley. Enzymes in the barley start reducing grain-starch to sugar. The germ of the barley has withered, and so the barley doesn't start sprouting again. The barley just keeps getting sweeter and sweeter.

Man doesn't know it, but he has just stumbled on malting and mashing. Man doesn't know it because it's still wet outside, the rest of his grain isn't gone yet, and he ain't going nowhere until the weather clears up or the grain runs out. It's still damp out, and the wet sugars inside the barley are swelling up and splitting their husks. Coincidentally, or by grand design, or by opportunistic evolution (choose one), yeast love this damp air, and they're just riding droplets of condensation wherever it's going. Some of them hit payday, and settle on the barley. The yeast go right to work fermenting the grain sugars.

In the meantime man has finally eaten up the last grain of the stored barley. He's hungry. Having no other choice, he heads out hunting and gathering. Grumbling, he stumbles out of the cave and smack dab into the forgotten pile of barley, except now it smells just about like overripe fruit. Overripe fruit? The day is looking better already. Man digs right into the barley soup, and a couple pounds later the weather is just fine as far as he's concerned. Man blows off hunting and gathering, to enjoy a little quality time getting in touch with his inner self.

Over time, woman figures out what happened, and mimics the chance occurrences that led to man's first brew. Homebrewing has been discovered. The wheel is still a few millennia down the evolutionary highway, but man takes to brewing like a cat takes to kitty litter, and goes to brewing year-round, or at least until he runs out of barley.

Cultural anthropologists really do propose that mankind first settled in agrarian communities because early man wanted a reliable supply of barley to make beer from. Barley, because it is one of the hardiest and most widely-growing of the grass plants, and because it is the easiest to mash, became one of the first cultivated grains. Man became civilized not for opera, but for beer. And here's an absolute fact (and this one is correlatable) with which to bore any captive audience that you might happen to corner: the earliest known recipe of any kind is for making beer!

MALTING BARLEY

Malting and mashing, then, are nothing new. Mankind has been malting and mashing for millennia, and even improved on the methods of doing it! Moreover, we even know what's happening, and why, or at least most of what's happening, and some of the reasons why. So let's see what happens to get barley ready for brewing with.

The barley plant produces its seeds as kernels, growing in rows along the end of its stem. 6-row barley grows six rows of seeds, and 2-row barley grows only two rows of seeds. 6-row is used when brewing with a high percentage of adjuncts, because it has more enzymes in it than 2- row, and adjuncts usually have none or next to none. 2-row is preferred by most brewers in all other circumstances, because it is usually plumper and has a lower protein-and-husk to starch ratio.

The barley kernel contains an embryonic barley plant, called the germ, and a stored food supply, called the endosperm. The endosperm is made up of complex starches encased in protein matrixes. The germ and endosperm are encased by a cellulose husk. All in all, the kernel is pretty impregnable, except for the fact that close to the husk is an aleurone layer that is rich in enzymes. Enzymes are catalysts, things that cause other things to become new things. There are lots of enzymes in malt, but the ones that we mostly care about are the proteolytic enzymes that dissolve proteins, and the diastatic enzymes that reduce starches to sugars.

These enzymes aren't there in the barley just to make it convenient for us to brew with. They are the latch-keys to the kernel's food larder. In the wild, each kernel, or "corn", falls to the earth as the barley plant dries up at the end of the growing season. Spring rains hydrate the kernel, triggering the germ to grow and leaching the enzymes into the endosperm. Proteolytic enzymes break down the protein that encases starch. Diastatic enzymes mix with the mass of starch and convert it to sugars. The germ, in turn, absorbs the sugars to fuel its growth.

Malting is necessary to the brewing process, because raw barley cannot be mashed. There are not enough active enzymes in barley to saccharify the starch, and the complexity of the proteins would turn the whole works into a gummy mess. The barley has to be sprouted.

At the maltings, barley is steeped in fresh water until it is hydrated. It is then drained, let warm up, and voila! sprouting begins. Rootlets emerge from the germ, at the base of each kernel. An embryonic stem, called the acrospire, begins to grow from the germ, upward along the length of the kernel, under the husk. In the endosperm, proteolytic enzymes dissolve large protein matrixes, exposing granules of starch. Diastatic enzymes disassemble the starches, first into simpler polysaccharide chains called amylose and amylopectin, eventually into simpler fractions called dextrins, and finally down to simple fermentable sugars.

The maltster isn't just sitting on his duff while this is happening. He keeps checking the malt, seeing how far it is modified. If it's lager malt that he is malting, he terminates sprouting when the malt is still considered "under-modified". The acrospires of most of the barley will have grown to only 1/2 - 2/3 the length of the kernels. If it's pale malt he's malting, the malt will be left sprouting until it's well-modified, and the acrospires will usually have grown to about the length of the kernels. Pale malt is generally used for infusion mashes and ale brewing. Under-modified malts require more extensive conversion in the mash, and require step-mashing or decoction-mashing. American lager malt, also known as brewer's malt, is not as well-converted as pale malt, but on the other hand it is less steely than European lager malts. It may be infusion mashed or step-mashed.

The maltster terminates the sprouting by drying out the kernels in a malt kiln. Lager malt is dried to a somewhat lighter color than pale malt, and Pilsener malt is dried to the lightest color of all (it is also among the most under-modified of malts).

Some amount of kilning is necessary, to form beta-amylase, and because it improves the flavor of malt. Unkilned malt doesn't taste as good in beer.

Malted barley, then, is basic to the brewing process; even "wheat" beers use as much as two-thirds barley malt with the wheat in the mash.

MALT

The basic malts in modern brewing are pale malt, European pilsener/lager malt and American lager/brewer's malt. The beer brewed from each one differs a little from the other two, but mostly the difference among them is a matter of the manner of the mash which each one responds best to. It's other malts, called specialty malts, that make a big difference in the aroma and flavor and color and mouthfeel of different beers.

Most specialty malts contribute darker colors and fuller flavors. Roasted malts are dried at higher temperatures and for a longer time than the basic brewing malts. Crystal and caramel malts are heated while they are still wet, to temperatures that crystallize the sugars of the endosperm, sort of like hard candy with a husk.

As you know already, not all malts have to be mashed. The starch in highly-roasted or crystallized grains is completely reduced. These specialty malts can be used as flavoring in malt-extract-based brews without mashing. Just suspend them, uncrushed, in a muslin bag in the kettle while you're heating the brewing liquor to boiling. Remove them when the liquor comes up to 170° F (77° C). The heat and movement within the kettle usually splits the husk, and dissolves the malt sugars into the wort, but to be sure of good extraction, most homebrewers roughly crack specialty grains to be used as kettle adjuncts. Extract brewers commonly use this method to enhance their beer with fresh flavors.

Lighter malts, such as pale, lager, Pilsener, Vienna, Munich and amber must be mashed, because they contain high proportions of starch that need to be reduced by mashing; otherwise, the starch would ruin the beer.

EXTRACT POTENTIAL

Not all malts are equal. Depending upon the size and quality of the barley, the caliber of the malting and kilning, and the type of malt produced, the amount of soluble extract that can be obtained differs depending upon the type of malt (2-row, 6-row, lager, pale, crystal, etc), and to a lesser extent varies from supplier to supplier, and even batch to batch. Maltsters generally supply a batch analysis, or at least an average analysis, that gives coarse and fine-grind extract yields. The coarse-grind value, as is (at the moisture content of the malt when tested), is the best extraction that any brewery could achieve, but it is rarely matched in the real-world of the brewhouse. Laboratory hot-water-extract for 2-row lager malt, coarse grind, as-is at 3% moisture content will be about 78% of what the same weight of sucrose would yield. An average brewery might get 90% of that, or 70% extract by weight ($.78 \times .90 = .70$).

Homebrewers can only expect to achieve 60-70% extract efficiency from the mash. The mash recipes in this book are based upon an extract efficiency of 68% for lager and pale malt, 67% for light crystal malt, 65% for crystal and chocolate malt, etc. (see Appendix, Ingredients). Added to the kettle, the same grains yield as much as the laboratory extract, or 75%, 74% and 72%, respectively.

Every homebrewer may not get 68% yield from pale malt, because there are a large number of variables that are specific to each homebrewer's supplies and equipment. Depending upon the malt you use, how well it is crushed, how well it is hydrated, how wet the mash is, how long a time the mash "rests", whether it is infusion, decoction or step-mashed, and how efficiently it is "sparged", you may get better or worse efficiency. After you have the experience of a few brews, if you keep good records, it is a simple thing to customize recipes to your actual mash efficiency.

If the repeated use of the word 'extract' is confusing you, then it is time to clarify for you what the word extract means. Brewers call what is extracted out of the malt "extract". The condensed wort syrup that comes in a can, or "malt extract", is also abbreviated and called "extract". So when brewers are talking about the mash, or the gravity of the wort, extract means what comes out of the malt and into the liquor to make wort. (Liquor, remember, is water treated for brewing with gypsum, non-iodized table salt and/or tiny amounts of mild acids. Liquor is another confusing brewing word.) When brewers are talking about the source of the wort, extract means condensed wort syrup, aka malt extract. Whether this bit of confusion was devised by brewers to confuse and impress non-brewers, or is just a vestige of Babelian linguistic chaos is anybody's guess. In any case, you shouldn't be confused anymore, so we can stop babeling and get back to malting and mashing.

MASHING

Malt is crushed before it is mashed, so that the brewing liquor will hydrate the starches rapidly and completely. The ideal crush would be to squeeze the kernels of malt, crushing the starch into BB-sized grits and splitting the husk so that all the starch grits pop out of the kernel. With this perfect crush, the husks create a nice, porous filter bed, and mash enzymes have ready access to the starch. Extract efficiency can be 95%, and the mash never sticks during sparging... but don't expect it to happen quite this neatly.

Usually when malt is crushed there is considerable tearing of the husks, and not all of the starch gets crushed to grits. Some larger chunks of endosperm remain intact, and a small percentage is reduced to flour. All in all, a less-than-perfect crush like this doesn't cause any problems except a small drop in extract efficiency. Problems arise only if the malt is crushed too coarsely or too fine. If the crush is inadequate large chunks of the endosperm remain encased in the husk. Extract efficiency is poor, because enzymes cannot work their way through the large starch chunks before they expire. The finished beer ends up clouded with unconverted starch. Even worse, if bacteria or wild yeast that can decompose starch end up in your brew, they are served up a banquet. Since starch is too complex for brewers' yeast to use as an energy source, the yeast cannot out-compete the contaminating invaders and overwhelm them. The batch goes bad.

On the other hand, if the malt is crushed too finely, the flour produced turns the mash into a slick bucket of wallpaper paste.

Malt enzymes can't reduce that sticky mess to sugars either, and since the husks are shredded to pieces in an overly-fine grind, the whole muddle sets like concrete and cannot be sparged.

The problems that poor crushing cause are mostly related to the fact that starch itself does not dissolve in water; it is too complex. At about 149°F (65°C), starch "gelatinizes", which allows enzymes to freely contact it and reduce it over a short period of time. The mash will eventually convert at temperatures from 120°F (49°C) up, but "eventually" is the operative word here. You don't want to wait that long. 149°F(65°C) is usually the lowest practical temperature for a saccharification rest.

And what is a saccharification rest, you ask? A "rest" is a temperature that is held for a specified time. "Saccharification" is the conversion of starches to sugars. So the saccharification rest is a mash temperature of from 149-160°F (65-71°C) that is held for a period of time, usually from 45 to 90 minutes.

The actual temperature of the rest, and the amount of liquor that the malt is mixed with, are determined by the beer being brewed. The ratio between the OG and the target TG (attenuation) are what determines mash temperature and thickness. If it is a beer of a relatively usual OG (1040-1050) that is meant to ferment-out to a light finish, then the "goods" will be mashed in with a higher ratio of water and at a low temperature, for example, with a quart-and-a-half of liquor per pound of malt, at 149-150°F (65°C). If the beer is to be sweeter, with a very full mouthfeel, it might be mashed with as little as a quart of water per pound, at 155-156°F (69°C).

What do these relatively small changes in mash thickness and temperature accomplish? They accommodate the optimum ranges of the two diastatic enzymes, alpha amylase and beta amylase.

Beta amylase does not reduce complex starch to any appreciable degree, but it does chop up simpler starch chains into glucose, the single-molecule grain sugar, and maltose, which is two molecules of glucose. These mono- and disaccharides are entirely fermentable. Beta amylase is the dominant enzyme at 149-150°F (65°C), and it quickly becomes less viable as the mash temperature increases.

Alpha amylase does attack complex starch chains. Alpha amylase produces glucose and maltose, but also chops starch up into intermediate polysaccharides that are soluble, called dextrins. Where alpha amylase is dominant, the wort will be less fermentable. Since alpha amylase remains viable for a short time right up to about 160°F (71°C), mashes at temperatures progressively higher than 149-150°F (65°C) give correspondingly sweeter/fuller beer.

The acidity, or pH of the mash, and the amount of calcium present also affect enzyme viability, which is one of the reasons why brewers treat their water supplies. The pH of the mash should be between 5.2 and 5.4 for maximum effectiveness, although readings between 5.0 and 5.7 are acceptable.

The duration of the rest also affects the quality and fermentability of the wort. A saccharification rest needs to be long enough to at least reduce all the starch, or the beer will be hazy, off-flavored and more susceptible to contamination. On the other hand, the mash enzymes have a limited "lifetime", and the higher the temperature, the more quickly they expire. At 150°F (65°C), less than 50% are viable within an hour; at above 200°F (95°C) less than half survive after 45 minutes. If the mash is very thin, the enzymes are destroyed even more rapidly. Moreover, alpha amylase is more efficient in a thick mash, and beta amylase more effective in a thin mash.

Recipe design, then, needs to take into consideration mash temperature, duration, pH and thickness, relative to the fermentability of the wort desired. For "dextrinous" worts, the mash is hotter, thicker, at a higher pH and held for a short time. For example, for a full, sweet beer that will ferment out to only 30% of the Original Gravity, the program would be 149-150°F (65°C) for 45 minutes at pH 5.4 using 1-1/4 quarts of water per pound of malt . For a very fermentable wort to end up at a TG of less than 25% of the OG, the program might be 149-150°F (65°C) for 1-1/2 hours at pH 5.2 using 1-1/2 quarts of water. Since crystal and dark-roasted malts are far less fermentable than ale and lager malts, their contribution to the fullness of the finished beer needs to be taken into account as well.

This is all very complex, isn't it? It is, but it is also the reason why many homebrewers choose to mash. By manipulating mash temperature, thickness and time, and the percentages of colored malts in the mash, very different results can be produced. Moreover, it doesn't need to be approached from a strictly scientific basis; with a little experience, homebrewers will get a "feel" for mashing and the character of the beer it will produce.

How far the conversion of the starch to fermentable sugars has proceeded can be assessed by simple testing. When iodine is placed in the presence of starch, it turns blue-black. You prob-

Temperature Corrections

Page 142   line 15
at above 155°F (69°C) less than ......

Page 142   line 25
the program would be 155 - 156°F (69°C) for 45 minutes at ......

Page 147   line 5
malt to 165°F (74°C) in your 8 to 12 quart pot.

Page 147   line 35
and pour the 165°F (74°C) liquor onto the crushed grain,

Page 148   line 5
for the liquor is 165°F (74°C), under most circumstances.......

Page 148   line14
the temperature back up to about 156°F (65°C) every fiften minutes..

Page 151   line 35
temperature drops to 145°F (63°C) or so after the strike.

Page 151   line 36
its duration nearer to 145°F (63°C) ......

Page 151   line38
if the strike temperature is 155°F (65°C), and the TG...

Page 151   line 40
between 153°F (67°C) and 158°F (70°C) is very important.

Page 153   line 13
be raised up to above 165°F (74°C), but not over 168°F (76°C).

Page 154   line 11 & 12
Beta amylase awakens at above 126°F (52°C) and is very active at 149°F (60°C).

Page 154   line 14
Protein rest is 126°F (52°C) or warmer, saccharification ....

Page 154   line 18
by a rest temperature above 155°F (68°C), or above the .....

Page 155   line 22 & 23
heat the liquor to about 145°F (63°C) to hit a strike temperature of 131°F (55°C),

Page 155   line 25
only 140°F (60°C). Don't dirty your shorts worrying ....

Page 158   line 1
then heated gradually to 160°F (72°C) and quickly to ....

Page 158   line 5
heated slowly to 160°F (72°C), then to boiling ....

ably saw this phenomenon way back when you were in fourth-grade science class and the teacher had you dropper iodine onto a split potato. The iodine turned blue-black, because a potato is just a mass of starch.

In the absence of starch, iodine remains iodine-colored. So if a drop of ordinary pharmacy iodine is placed on a white porcelain plate, and a drop of wort is placed next to it so that the two drops run together, the color of the iodine indicates what the fermentability of the wort will be.

Actually doing it is easy, but seeing what the change actually is, isn't. It's easier to read about it. On the other hand it's not as hard as sixth grade science, so don't panic.

Near the end of the prescribed mash program brewers run iodine tests on wort samples drawn from the mash. Each sample needs to be free of mash grits and pieces of husks, since these always turn blue-black. Even so, very fine husk particles usually end up in the wort droplet, so one has to ignore the black "dots" in the test. A purple-to-blue reaction indicates that the mash still has a way to go. A violet color indicates a fermentability of only about 60%. A mahogany color indicates a wort that will ferment to around 1/3 gravity, and a faint- red or pink reaction fermentability of circa 71-75%. A negative reaction, or no color change in the iodine, indicates that the wort will ferment out to 1/4 gravity, or less.

The iodine test can be difficult to read, and even impossible with very dark worts. Moreover, recipes with high percentages of unfermentable adjuncts make the Terminal Gravity prediction less accurate. Once again, the brewer needs to rely upon experience to predict what TG a given mash will yield.

SPARGING

Once mashing is completed, the sweet wort needs to be separated from the spent grains. The usual manner in which this is done is called "sparging".

The objectives of sparging are to run the wort off from the spent grain and rinse the trapped extract out of it, as well as to raise the temperature as quickly as possible, so as to stop further enzyme activity. This is accomplished by running-off the wort from the mash until the spent grains are just barely submerged, and then sprinkling hotter liquor onto the submerged mash. The hotter liquor both dissolves more extract and makes it run more freely, as well as raising the temperature so that enzyme activity is terminated.

In spite of the fact that getting all the extract possible out of the mash is one of the goals of mashing, it can be carried too far. There are some very harsh-tasting elements of the malt, generically referred to as tannins, that you definitely want to leave behind. Ditto for silicates and lipids (malt fat), which will ruin a beer's ability to hold a head. Fortunately, centuries of experience have established certain criteria for when sparging should be terminated, and the rest of the runoff from the mash should be dumped. Not only that, the criteria are simple: Stop the runoff when the specific gravity drops below 1010, or the pH rises above 5.8.

One of the ways that brewers treat their water supply is to acidify it. One of the most important reasons for acidifying the liquor is because acidic liquor lowers the pH of the mash runoff. If the runoff doesn't have to be stopped because it has risen to pH 5.8, then it can keep being collected until the gravity drops to 1010. Voila, better extract-efficiency.

Good extract efficiency also relies on the submerged grains being somewhat level, with no channels running down through them, so it's usually necessary to accomplish the two tasks at hand by taking a spoon in hand and spreading the grain a bit, with the same sort of motion that you would use buttering bread.

And you thought that this mashing stuff was going to be intellectually challenging. What could be any simpler?

CHAPTER 10

BREWING LAB 101

HOME MASH-O-NOMICS
HOW TO CRUSH MALT

Small amounts of malt can be crushed with a rolling pin. Spread the malt out, cover it (plastic wrap, tin foil, waxed paper) and crack it with the rolling pin. This method is practical only when crushing a pound of malt or less, because it is very time-inefficient.

Larger quantities need to be milled. The easiest way to crush malt is to have your homebrew shop do it for you. Just pay the dime-(or so)- a-pound surcharge. If you insist on buying your own mill, you'll hit the break-even point at about grain-brew #50.

Regardless of whether you use a roller mill or a grain/grist mill, you need to experiment with the setting of the width between the rollers or the mill plates, and the speed at which they turn. The setting must be wide enough so that the malt husks are not torn to shreds, and the starch is not reduced to flour. On the other hand, the setting should not be so wide that kernels go uncracked. Keep adjusting your mill until you get the best crush possible. Grain/grist mills, such as the Corona mill, usually do a better job if an electric drill is used to turn the arbor; these mills give a more uniform crush if they are turning at higher speeds.

As you get a feel for grain-brewing, you will learn how fine you can crush your malt without getting a stuck mash or losing extract.

HOW TO MAKE A PARTIAL MASH

The partial mash is an excellent way to ease into mashing. You can botch the job and feel good about it, because it cost you at least $5 less to screw up a partial mash than a full one.

You probably have most of the equipment you need to make partial mashes right in your kitchen. Since you will only be mashing two or three pounds of grain, all you need to dig out of your cabinets is an 8- to-12 quart pot to heat water in, a 4-to-8 quart pot or insulated cooler for the partial mash, a strainer (or a mesh bag and a colander), a long- handled spoon and a measuring cup. If you cannot purchase your grains pre-crushed, then you will need a rolling pin or a wine bottle, or you will have to buy or borrow a mill to crush the grain. You will also need a thermometer, pH papers, and tincture of iodine in a dropper bottle.

The only ingredients you need are malt, gypsum, or in rare incidents calcium carbonate, and acid (see below).

Heat 2-1/2 to 3 quarts of water per pound of malt to 200°F (95°C) in your 8-to-12 quart pot. Add gypsum to the brewing liquor if the recipe calls for it. In fact, except for Pilsener beers, it doesn't hurt to add 1/4 -1/2 teaspoon of gypsum to the brewing water anyway, since the calcium helps the mash convert, and has at least a moderate effect on reducing the alkalinity of the water. You may have a good idea already about whether you need to acidify your water at all. If all your extract brews end up at below pH 5.3 after the wort boil, then you probably don't need to acidify your liquor. On the other hand, if you have carbonate water, you probably do need to acidify the liquor or the mash.

Check the pH of the mash the first time you do a partial mash; if it is above pH 5.5, pull off a cup or so of liquid from the mash, add a few drops of .1 N lactic, phosphoric, sulfuric, or hydrochloric acid. (Citric acid can be used as well, but it will be partially metabolized by the yeast in the fermentation, so the other acids are preferred if a large drop in alkalinity and pH is required.) Usually only a few drops of .1N acid are required to accomplish the drop in pH that is required. Check the mash pH again after thoroughly dispersing the acidified liquid throughout the mash; repeat the adjustment if the pH is still above 5.4.

Once the mash pH is adjusted, add about the same amount of acid that you mixed into your mash to the sparge liquor, and in the future adjust the whole volume of liquor before you begin mashing. It may take you several brews to zero in on the gypsum and acid addition to achieve a mash pH of 5.2-5.4 and runoff that doesn't rise above pH 5.8.

Place the crushed malt into the smaller pot. If you are mashing into a picnic cooler, preheat the cooler with a quart or so of hot water and then dump it out before adding the grains. Using your measuring cup, measure and pour the 200°F (95°C) liquor onto the crushed grain, mixing it in as you go along. Add a total of 1-1/4 to 1-1/2 quarts of water for each pound of malt. As you add the liquor to the mash, break up large "balls" of starch as they form; by the time that you are ready for the last liquor infusion, the malt should be evenly hydrated, with no dry pockets remaining.

Check the mash temperature with your thermometer before

you make the last liquor addition. If the mash temperature is already within the range of 149-152°F (65-67°C), cool the last liquor addition to within that range. The next time you brew, reduce the temperature that you heat your liquor to. Although the temperature specified for the liquor is 150°F (65°C), under most circumstances it needs to be only 10-12°F (5-7 °C) higher than the strike temperature, or about 160-162°F (71-72°C).

Mix the mash very well to evenly distribute the temperature, and then cover it. If you are mashing into an insulated cooler, it should hold the strike temperature reasonably well for the next hour. In any case, as long as the temperature doesn't drop more than 5°F, it is of no major consequence. If you are mashing in a stainless-steel pot, you have three options. The first is to raise the temperature back up to about 200°F (95°C) every fifteen minutes by heating it on the stovetop. The second is to put a couple inches of water into a larger skillet or pot, and heat this on the stovetop to 150-155°F (65-69°C). The mashing pot can be placed into this water-bath, and the burner turned on low for about five minutes out of every fifteen to maintain something reasonably close to the strike temperature. The third option is the easiest; place the covered pot into your oven, preheated to 140-150°F (60-65°C), and do nothing but check the temperature once or twice over the next hour.

As the end of the one hour mash period draws near, heat the remaining liquor up to 170-175°F (77-80°C) for sparging the mash. Suspend or block your strainer, or mesh-bag-in-a-colander, in any large pot, pail or bucket. Carefully (because you don't want to burn yourself!) pour the mash into the strainer/mesh bag-and-colander, letting the wort flow out of the spent grains.

Take the strainer/mesh bag-and-colander now and suspend it over your wort kettle. Gently flatten the grains, making a concave surface so that your sparge liquor will be forced to run down through the grains, and not over the top and down the sides. With your measuring cup, gently ladle the cloudy wort onto the top of the spent grains, letting it filter through them and run into your kettle. Once all the wort has been recycled through the mash filterbed, start ladling the 170-175°F (77-80°C) sparge liquor onto the spent grains. Use the back of your spoon to flatten and redistribute the spent grains as necessary, so that the sparge water does not follow only a few channels down through the mash.

Pull a sample of the runoff from the spent grains and set it aside to check the pH as you get near to the end of your sparge water. If the sample is at, near or above pH 5.8, make a note of it, because you will need to increase your liquor acidification in future brews.

Once all the liquor has run through the mash filter, remove your strainer from the kettle, do something ecologically-correct with the spent grains (they are great roughage and about 25% protein dry weight - bake a loaf of bread!) and add the malt extract and brewing water (or treated liquor, if that is what the recipe specifies) to top up to 5-1/2 gallons in your kettle. You have just made your first partial- mash, and are ready to boil your wort, which you already know how to do!

HOW TO INFUSION MASH

If you have experimented with grains in a partial mash, you already know that mashing doesn't have to be rocket science. All you need is the equipment for mashing, a couple of extra hours, and a little bit more information.

Don't let the information overwhelm you. After a few mash brews, you will be able to use it intelligently. For your first few brews, just do what you can, and don't get frantic if you miss a strike temperature by a country mile or some other seeming disaster occurs. There is no substitute for experience, so start mashing and get some!

Well, don't start just yet. First, take a cruise through this overflowing cornucopia of overwhelming choices.

Do your equipment shopping in Chapter 11, "Mashing: Equipment". You will need a mash tun, a lauter tun (or a combination of the two), a pot for heating the brewing liquor and boiling the wort in (the bigger the better; go for the 40 quart!), a long-handled spoon, a one-quart measuring cup, a thermometer, pH papers, and tincture of iodine in a dropper bottle.

Let's start with your brewing liquor, since there are fewer choices for you to face in this department. Each recipe in this book specifies the amount of water you will need, and suggests treatment for that water. The treatments are specific for each recipe, primarily to enhance the particular flavors of the style, but also to facilitate the mechanics of the mash. In general, you will have to treat 7-1/2 to 8 gallons of water for mashing and sparging. If you need to brush up on water treatment, refer back to Chapter 4 before your first mash.

If you have been treating your brewing water, and you have done at least a couple of partial mashes, you should have a good idea of how extensively you need to acidify your water supply. If you don't have a clue, acidify all of your brewing liquor to below pH 7.0, but not below pH 5.5, with dilute acid. After a few mashes, you will have a good idea of what treatment you do or don't require to achieve a mash pH of 5.2-5.35 and sparging run-off at not over pH 5.8. Usually only a drop or two of .1N acid are required when brewing with soft or sulfate water, a little more for moderately carbonate water, and rarely over a dozen or so drops even when dealing with highly carbonate water.

Once you mash in, take a pH reading, and record it. If the mash pH is below 5.0 reduce the amount of acid you add to your brewing liquor in future brews. In rare cases the mash pH may settle at below pH 5.0 with no water treatment. This condition is corrected by stirring in a little chalk (calcium carbonate) to buffer overly-acidic water. If the mash pH is above 5.4, pull a pint or so of liquid out of the mash, and stir a few drops of acid into it. Record the amount of acid, and then mix the acidified liquid back into the mash. Once it is well dispersed, read the pH again, and repeat the adjustment if necessary. As you gain experience mashing, tighten up the mash pH parameters to between 5.2 and 5.35.

You can add the crushed malt to the pre-measured liquor in the mash pot (or insulated cooler), but in general you will have a lot greater control if you put the crushed malt into the pot first, and add measured amounts of liquor to it. This allows the grain to rise in temperature evenly, and the crushed malt has time to absorb the liquor gradually. The malt will tend to ball less readily. Moreover, there is the risk that you will overshoot the strike temperature if the malt is stirred into the liquor.

The first time that you mash, you will most likely not hit or hold the strike temperature. Don't have a stroke over it. It takes a little experience to learn how to hit and hold strike temperatures, and we've never brewed with your equipment in your kitchen before, so we can't help. If you know a mash brewer, enlist their guidance for your first brew. If you don't, just do it. Whatever rules you may violate, it won't make you a bad person.

In spite of what we've just said, be aware that except for the dispensation covering your first couple of brews, the strike temperature is critical. Diastatic enzymes don't wait for you to get the temperature right. If you're brewing to a style, you can't leave the mash temperature radically different from the strike temperature for very long. Always try to get within 1°F (1/2°C) of the strike temperature within five minutes of mashing in.

The liquor temperatures in the recipes are slightly higher than they need to be; under most circumstances the liquor only needs to be 10-12°F (5-7°C) higher than the strike temperature. Again, however, this is one of those things that is specific to your equipment, as well as to the thickness of the mash, and even the temperature of the crushed malt, so you will need to brew a couple of batches to fine-tune it. In the meantime, heat your liquor to the temperature specified in the recipe.

Once the mash is doughed-in, mix the mash very thoroughly to evenly distribute the temperature, and then cover it and leave it alone as much as possible. The more you stir an infusion mash, the greater the possibility that it will "set" during sparging. If you are mashing in a picnic cooler or other insulated vessel, you probably will not need to adjust or remix the temperature again. If you are mashing in a Bruheat boiler, or Thorne Electrim, or other heated pail, you only need to stir the mash occasionally. If you are mashing in a 16-to-24 quart (15-25 liter) pot, put the covered pot into your oven, preheated to 200°F (95°C). Stir the mash and check its temperature every 15 minutes, and make adjustments to the oven temperature as necessary. If you insist on infusion mashing on the rangetop, then you will need to readjust the mash temperature more often. Plan to stir the mash at least every ten minutes, take a temperature reading with your thermometer, and then apply heat to the pot for one or two minutes, while stirring. Remove the pot from the heat and check the temperature again; it should be within a few degrees of the strike temperature.

How many degrees? It depends on what you're brewing. Look at the strike temperature, the OG and the TG of the recipe. If the strike temperature is 149-150°F (65°C), and the TG is less than one-quarter of the OG, then it is not critically important if the temperature drops to 200°F (95°C) or so after the strike. Even if the mash spends most of its duration nearer to 200°F (95°C) than 150°F (65°C), the beer will not be radically different. However, if the strike temperature is 150°F (65°C), and the TG is nearer to 33% of the OG, then keeping the temperature in a range between 200°F (95°C) and 200°F (95°C) is very important. In general, the higher the strike temperature, the more important it is to hit the strike temperature exactly, and to maintain it there.

All in all, using an insulated cooler of at least 20-quart capacity as a mash tun is probably the simplest (and therefore the most elegant) method for maintaining the temperature of the mash. If you want to have the option of step-mashing (aka upward-infusion mashing) you will need to own a twenty-quart pot, and if you can't convince the spouse that you need a picnic cooler too, placing the mash pot in your oven to maintain the strike temperature becomes the best option.

There are other solutions to the problem, and homebrewers have risen to the challenge and developed many methods of maintaining mash temperature. One is to place the mash pot into an insulated box, another is to employ a water bath by heating water in a larger pan on the rangetop and placing the mash pot into that. If you've got a streak of mad inventor in you and a good idea of your own, use it!

When you get within fifteen minutes of the end of the mash, do an iodine test. Drip a couple of separate drops of clear wort from the mash onto a clean, white porcelain plate. The easiest way to get clear wort for a sample is to put a teaspoon of mash into a coffee filter, and squeeze out a few drops onto the plate. Then place a drop of tincture of iodine right next to one of them, so the wort and iodine run together. Watch for a color change as the two liquids merge.

The iodine reaction is not absolutely definitive, because specialty malts and the fermenting strength of the particular yeast strain you will be using have an influence on the TG that the iodine test will not account for. The iodine test is still an important tool, however.

Look at the recipe you are brewing; if the TG is about 1/3 of the OG, you want a red-to-mahogany color reaction from the iodine test at the end of the mash. If the TG is a little over 1/4 of the OG, a faint pink-to-red reaction is what you want to see. If the TG is about 1/4 of the OG, the iodine should not change color by the end of the mash. If the TG is less than 1/4 of the OG, the negative reaction should be reached 10-15 minutes before the end of the mash.

Record the iodine test. Repeat the iodine test at the end of the mash.

At least for your first few mashes, stop the mash at the time specified in the recipe, regardless of the iodine reading. After a few all-grain brews, review your brewlogs and observe the correlation between the mash-iodine reaction and the attenuation of the beer. Use the iodine test in the future to increase your control over the wort's fermentability.

A mash-out is prescribed in some recipes. The mash-out generally does two things: it stops all enzyme activity at a definite point in time, and it thins the sugar-laden wort so that it runs easier. An infusion of hot water is also sometimes called for to thin the syrupy wort even more, but this practice increases the possibility of a set mash.

You have to be mashing in a pot to do a mash-out; if you are mashing in a cooler, you would have to do a partial decoction to pull it off.

If you are going to mash-out, the mash temperature needs to be raised up to above 150°F (65°C), but not over 200°F (95°C). Use discretion in heating up the mash. There are a lot of malt sugars in the mash now, and you will need to stir the mash well while heating it to prevent them from burning on the bottom of the pot. And that's how you infusion mash. Simple, huh? Well, it really isn't all that difficult, once you've had some experience at it.

HOW TO STEP-MASH

Let's just start out here by looking for a moment at what the step-mash, or upward-infusion mash is. Step mashing increases the temperature of the goods from the protein rest up to the saccharification range, and then up to the mash-out temperature. An infusion mash only rests in the diastatic-enzyme range. A step-mash also has a proteolytic-enzyme rest, and then a mash-out that shuts down all enzyme activity at a precise time. It gives the brewer much greater control.

Step-mashing is specific to particular malts, and to some extent, to particular beer styles. If you are using American malts, an infusion mash can be substituted for a step-mash, or vice-versa, without causing any glaring defects. A step-mash is sometimes called for with British malts, but it is the exception rather than the rule. If *undermodified* European lager malts constitute over half of a recipe's grain bill, then either a step or decoction mash is absolutely necessary.

In the step-mash, the grain and brewing liquor are combined at a temperature between 113°F and 140°F (45-60°C) for the protein rest. The lower end of this temperature range favors an enzyme that reduces proteins to amino acids. Recipes rarely call for a low-end rest, because any all-malt brew generally has enough amino acids to keep the yeast going during fermentation, so there is no need for more amino acids.

At the higher end of the range, large proteins that cause haze and stuck mashes are degraded into smaller proteins that improve a beer's head. It would seem that the higher end of the temperature range is where the protein rest should be made, then. Right? Well, not always.

Why? Because another enzyme becomes active within protease's range. Beta amylase awakens at above 150°F (65°C), and is very active at 200°F (95°C) . Beta amylase chops dextrins up into fermentable sugars. If the temperature of the protein rest is 200°F (95°C) or warmer, saccharification as well as proteolysis occurs. Step-mash recipes that call for a rest at between 128 and 140°F (53-60°C) are combining proteolysis and saccharification. Protein rests in this range are generally followed by a rest temperature above 150°F (65°C), or above the high-temperature limit of beta amylase. This type of step mash combines proteolysis and saccharification, and separates dextrinization from saccharification.

MASH RESTS

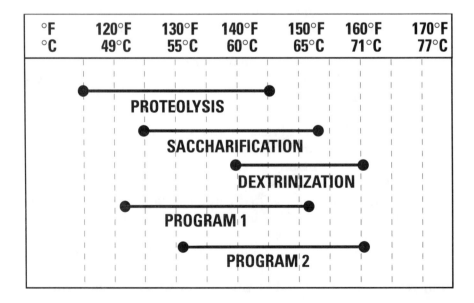

Program #1 separates proteolysis from amylosis; program #2 combines proteolysis and saccharification, and dextrinization occurs separately.

Step-mash programs most commonly call for a proteolysis rest at 122°F to 128°F (50-53°C), and combine dextrinization and saccharification at temperatures between 149°F and 155°F (65-68°C), as is usual in an infusion mash.

The two procedures are somewhat interchangeable, but a 131-158°F (55-70°C) program is better suited to "steely" malt, and a 122-152°F (50- 67°C) schedule more effective with chewier malt. A 3-step 131-149-158°F (55-65-70°C) mash or similar program is called for when a wort is meant to be highly attenuated.

Step-mashing is no more difficult than infusion mashing on a stove top. Temperature changes are accomplished in a pot, on the stove-top. You will need a pot of at least 16 quarts/liters capacity. If you are using a picnic cooler for a mash tun and don't have a 16 quart/liter pot around, you can decoction mash instead of step-mashing.

For the step-mash, heat the brewing liquor to 10-15°F (5-8°C) above the strike temperature; if you are using a thick mash (less than 1/3 gallon or 1-1/4 liters per pound of malt) you will need to heat the liquor to about 200°F (95°C) to hit a strike temperature of 150°F (65°C), but if the recipe calls for a thin mash (1-1/2 quarts or 1-1/3 liters of water per pound) the liquor might need to be only 200°F (95°C). Don't dirty your shorts worrying about it, because you'll never know exactly what temperature is "perfect" until you've step-mashed a few times, and it's easy enough to correct any temperature errors.

Like all the mash enzymes, the proteolytic group is strongest during the first few minutes of the rest. The protein rest doesn't usually need to be held for more than 10-15 minutes. Proteolysis doesn't stop after 15 minutes, however, and proteolysis can be overdone. A brew is generally better for having no protein rest than one that is too long. Except when brewing a very thin style, with wheat, 6-row malt or very steely malt, don't let the mash rest in the proteolysis range for more than 15 minutes. If you feel that a beer brewed from a step-mash is thinner than it ought to be, reduce the length of the protein rest the next time you brew it.

The temperature of the step-mash is raised to the next rest temperature by applying heat to the mash pot. Some recipes call for infusing more hot liquor to assist the temperature rise. Usually these recipes are for well-attenuated styles. Beta-amylase works better in a reasonably-thin mash than a thick one. If the recipe calls for a saccharification rest at below 150°F (65°C), it may also call for thinning the mash after the protein rest.

Thicker mashes protect enzyme viability, and alpha amylase is more effective dextrinizing starches in a thick mash. If a recipe is not meant to be well attenuated (that is, the TG is greater than 1/4 of the OG), it probably calls for a thick mash held for an hour or less at 153-160°F (67-71°C), to enhance dextrinization and depress saccharification.

When raising or maintaining temperatures on the range top, don't leave the pan on the heat for too long a period. Pull it off, stir the mash and check its temperature. Put it back onto the heat if it's not warm enough. Apply heat gradually, so that you don't wildly overshoot the strike temperature, but don't get neurotic over it. Unless the strike temperature of the recipe is already high (over 156°F/69°C), it's nothing to get excited about if you are off by 5°F(3°C) or so, as long as you correct the temperature quickly.

Some step-mash recipes call for a mash-out. As before, use discretion in heating up the mash. The mash-out is always made at 165- 168°F (74-76°C).

HOW TO DECOCTION MASH

If you have a 20-quart cooler, a pot of at least 10-quart capacity and a lauter tun, it is no big thing to decoction mash. If you don't have a pot that holds at least 16 quarts and a range top that really pumps out the BTUs, you'll find it difficult to step-mash anyway. A two-decoction mash is a very reasonable alternative to step-mashing.

A decoction mash is similar to a step-mash, except that the temperature of the goods is raised from rest-to-rest by boiling part of the mash and then remixing it into the rest. It yields the clearest- possible beer from steely malt. Moreover, extract yields from all but well-modified malt are always slightly higher when such malt is decoction mashed, and more importantly, otherwise-elusive "malty" flavors emerge in decoction-mashed beers. With styles such as Munich helles and soft pilseners, maltiness should be the dominant character of the beer. Infusion mashing at a high temperature can give these styles the residual sweetness that they require, but not the malt flavor. Decoction mashes do release "malt" flavor, and even weakly-enzymatic Vienna and Munich malts convert well enough in a decoction program so that no lager malt even needs to be used in a recipe. If you choose to use the decoction method, brew a helles for your third or fourth brew with 50% Vienna malt, and really experience the subtle allure of maltiness in a beer.

Most decoction homebrewers use a picnic cooler for their mash tun, because it holds rest temperatures so well, but any pot of at least 16 quarts/liters capacity will do. You will also need a 8-to-16 quart/liter pot to boil decoctions in. A one-quart/liter Pyrex® measuring cup makes an excellent "shovel" for moving mash from the tun to the decoction pot and back again.

The portion of the goods to be boiled ranges from about 35% up to 45% or so of the mash; the greater the temperature rise required, the more mash that needs to be boiled. In general, it is far easier to err on the high side and cool the mash temperature back down than it is to undershoot the strike temperature and try to raise it up.

It is very important not to boil any more of the free liquid in the mash than necessary when decoction mashing. Using a measuring cup for the transfer, it is simple to pull the mash against the side of the tun and squeeze most of the free liquid out of the grains before dumping it into the decoction pot. Only enough liquid to fill the spaces between the grains in the decoction pot is necessary, and any extra should be returned to the mash tun.

You can do a single, double, or triple decoction mash. Each decoction adds about an hour's time to mashing.

The triple decoction program is seldom used by homebrewers. It begins by mashing the malt in thickly with 105-120°F (41-49°C) water for an acidifying rest at 95-100°F (35-38°C) while the decoction mash boils. Brewers use a longer acid rest only if they want to combine a bacterial sourmash with the enzymatic acidulation that takes place during a short rest.

The decoction is made by removing about 1/3 of the mash, heating that to 149-150°F (65°C) and resting for 15-20 minutes, then heating it slowly until it boils. After ten minutes or so of boiling, it is remixed with the main mash for a protein rest at 122-140°F (50-60°C).

The double-decoction mash is more common, and begins with the protein rest. The crushed malt is mashed-in with liquor that is 10-15°F(6-8°C) hotter than the strike temperature. A 1/3 portion is withdrawn, heated to 149-150°F (65°C) and held for 20 minutes, then heated gradually to 200°F (95°C) and quickly to boiling. It may be boiled for 5-45 minutes before being remixed into the main mash. Depending on the recipe, the strike temperature will be from 149-160°F (65-72°C). After a rest of 5- 30 minutes, 40% is withdrawn, heated slowly to 150°F (65°C), then to boiling for 5-30 minutes, and is remixed for a mash-out temperature of 165-168°F (74-76°C).

Homebrewers also use a single-decoction mash that skips the mash-out. When brewing for malt character, how many decoctions are made is less important than that a decoction is boiled for at least 20 minutes, and for up to 45 minutes, to develop flavor.

HOW TO SPARGE

Before sparging was developed to separate the wort from the spent grain, brewers would drain the wort from the mash, mash-in again, and then repeat the process. If the worts were not re-combined in a kettle to make one beer, they would be boiled in separate kettles to yield three batches of beer: XXX, XX, and X, signifying strength.

Some British and Belgian breweries still mash in this fashion, and there is nothing to prevent homebrewers from doing the same, although there is no advantage to it unless you want to yield strong and weak beers from the same batch of mash. For the rest of us, it's sparging time.

In some way, form or manner a "false bottom" is required to sparge the mash, so that the spent grains are withheld and the wort runs out from below it. The configuration naturally creates a bed of husks and grain particles through which the wort is filtered. The holes in the false bottom need to be small enough that grain particles don't wash through them, or become lodged in them. There should be enough of these tiny holes, well-spaced, so that the wort will find its way down through, but few enough so that the false bottom creates more resistance to the passage of liquid than the mash does. Theoretically, the downward flow of liquid cannot pull the mash down and cause it to set if the false bottom gives the highest point of resistance, but as any experienced brewer knows, a mash sets whenever the brewing gods are unhappy, regardless of what you do to prevent it.

A set mash, by the way, occurs when the spent grains are pulled down so tight that liquid can't pass through them freely.

A mash is more likely to set if the spent grains aren't really spent, because unconverted starch acts like glue. Unreduced protein is even worse, which is why the more wheat malt that there is in a mash, the more likely it is that the mash will set, because wheat malt has very glutinous protein.

Unless you enjoy adversity, avoid stirring infusion mashes. Enough air usually becomes entrained in mixing in an infusion mash so that the mash "floats". Stirring it knocks the air out of the mash, and it settles more densely each time that it is stirred. For this reason, infusion mashes are disturbed as little as possible, and are kept floating during sparging, so that they don't compact.

Step and decoction mashes present less of a problem, because proteolysis should have changed the malt protein from gummy grey slime to powdery grey crumbs which conveniently float to the top of the mash.

However the malt has been mashed, it is never drained so much so that the liquid level falls below the top of the grain level. This helps prevent the mash from being pulled down and the liquor from just channeling down through the lowest surface depression. Ideally, an infusion mash drops only 10% or so from the level the mash itself was at. Step and decoction mashes drop up to 25%, and wheat-malt mashes may drop to 50% of the mash's depth.

Mashing and sparging can be combined in a cylindrical cooler fitted with a false bottom, but otherwise you will need a separate lauter tun. Your false bottom may be as simple as a mesh bag supported by a colander inside a 5-gallon plastic pail fitted with a spigot. Whatever you're using for a lauter tun, transfer the mash to it. Avoid splashing. If the goods were step or decoction mashed, give them a good stirring and allow them to settle for five or ten minutes. If you infusion mashed, wait 5 minutes before starting the runoff.

The runoff needs to be begun very slowly, at a rate of only about a cup per minute. If it is real chunky, pour it back into the lauter tun. Otherwise, it's up to you whether to recycle the first runnings. Some homebrewers recycle the wort until it starts to run clear, others don't. There are good arguments made for both options. If you do recycle, it may take up to 10 minutes for the runoff to clear, depending on how well your false-bottom/strainer works.

In either case, the best extraction of the mash will be had by taking 45 minutes or so to run off the wort, so that the mash isn't pulled down and the liquor will leach out all the extract from the spent grains. This means that the runoff rate will need to be increased to 1/2 to 2/3 of a quart per minute after the initial 5 or 10 minutes of slow runoff.

Only three things can go wrong during sparging. The mash can set; hope it doesn't. If it does, squeeze as much liquid as you can out of it, heat the liquid up to 175-180°F (80-85°C) as quickly as possible, remix it into the grain and repeat, as above, except don't do what you did that made the mash set the first time.

The second disaster occurs if you don't level-out the top of the mash before sparging, and periodically during sparging. The liquor will follow the path of least resistance; if you let the mash channel, the liquor will just run straight down and out the spigot. Channeling is no problem if you level the mash surface 3 or 4 times during sparging.

The third problem arises if either the pH or the temperature within the mash rises too high. Both things cause harsh flavors in the finished beer. Don't heat your sparge liquor above 150°F (65°C), and stop collecting the runoff when the pH rises above 5.8. Make pH readings every few minutes during the last 10 minutes of the sparge period. If the pH does rise above 5.8, make a note of it, and in the future decrease the pH of the sparge water further.

pH papers are easy to use, but don't expect too much from them. They are not 100% accurate. That's OK, since being off pH .2 or so is not going to ruin the brew, and besides, affordable pH meters are no more accurate. Dip the strip in a drop of cooled wort, shake it, and read the color against the color/pH key. Record the pH on your brewlog.

CHAPTER 11

MASHING: EQUIPMENT

Y ou know now that mashing amounts to combining crushed malt and water at a specific temperature, and letting the enzymes in the malted barley convert the starches to sugars. With that in mind, we need to satisfy two requirements:

1. We need a container large enough to hold all the grain and water and that can maintain mash "rest" temperatures, either by insulation or by being heated.

2. We need a means to effectively rinse the solution of converted sugars (wort) from the mashed grains.

Depending on your brewing set-up, this may all be done in one vessel, or you may need to use two separate containers. What configuration you end up with depends on how much you are willing to spend, unless you have the time, ability, patience and interest to make some of your own components. Fortunately, many of the "parts" needed to make your own sparging system are available from your homebrew shop.

Let's look at the options available to us:

PARTIAL MASH SYSTEMS.

You probably have a pot in your kitchen large enough to hold up to 5 or 6 pounds (2-3 kg) of grain for the mash. Either a 4 to 8 quart/liter pot or insulated cooler will suffice as a mash tun. Even in a partial mash, the problem of how to separate the wort from the spent grain comes up. You can do this by suspending a colander or strainer over your kettle, lining it with a mesh bag, and ladle the mash into it. The spent grain can then be sparged.

There are a number of disadvantages to this method, chief among them that the hot wort will be heavily oxidized, a lot of draff will end up in the wort, and extract efficiency usually isn't so good, because it's hard to get all of it rinsed out of the grains.

One option is to fit a spigot into the side of a 1-1/2 gallon (5-1/2 L) polyethylene bucket near the bottom, place a vegetable steamer inside, and line it with a mesh bag. This works immensely better, because you can control the runoff of wort out of this "lauter tun", so that the grain is kept flooded, which reduces oxidation and draff and increases extract efficiency. There is a space under the false bottom, so that the flow throughout the grain bed will be more uniform.

The other option is to buy a Phil's Mini-Lauter Tun. This product is designed for partial mashes, and improves upon the above method by virtue of a well-fitted perforated false-bottom, designed for the job at hand.

FULL-MASH SYSTEMS

We need to address both sparging and mashing as we look at various systems. In general, there are three options for mashing. The first two separate mashing from sparging, one by mashing on the stove-top in a 16-24 quart (15-25 L) pot, the other by mashing in a heavy-duty bucket equipped with its own internal heating coil. With both of these methods, sparging is carried out in a separate vessel. The third option combines mashing and sparging using an insulated picnic cooler. There are advantages and limitations to all three.

The most basic full-mash lautering system is stove-top mashing with a lauter tun made from a 5-gallon bucket, a spigot, a colander or vegetable steamer and a large mesh "sparging" bag. It is the cheapest system, it works, and a lot of good beers have been brewed using it. It's the system that most full-mash grain brewers start with.

You'll need to fit a five-gallon (20 L) food-grade polyethylene bucket with a spigot, or purchase one from your homebrew shop. Place an open stainless-steel vegetable steamer or colander in the bottom. Line the bucket with a mesh sparging bag. Secure the top of the bag securely onto the rim of the bucket with clips or rubber bands. The vegetable steamer helps raise up and support the bottom of the bag without impeding the wort flow.

A more efficient system can be made with a cylindrical insulated camping cooler, because it maintains temperatures extremely well, and the wort sugars will separate from the spent grains more freely. This system allows you to infusion-mash and sparge in the same container. If you want to do a step mash, you'll have to go back to the pot and range-top, and use this rig just for lautering/sparging.

You can upgrade this system by purchasing a Phil's Phalse Bottom® from your homebrew store. In fact, an insulated cylindrical cooler fitted with a Phil's Phalse Bottom® is probably the best mash/sparge tun possible.

Double Bucket system: For years, grain brewers have made their own false bottoms and lauter tuns using two five-gallon buckets. They are simple to make, if you own a drill. Drill a 1" (25 mm) hole into the bottom of the side of one pail and screw in a spigot. This will be your bottom bucket, from which you will draw off sweet wort. The other bucket will serve as the false bottom. Perforate it by drilling several hundred 1/16-3/32" (2 mm) holes. The holes should be close together, but not touching. 15-25% of the bottom of the bucket should be holes. The false bottom bucket sets into the bottom bucket with the spigot, creating an effective lauter tun. You can mash in this tun as well, but it won't hold temperatures very well.

Picnic Cooler System: This system requires some do-it-yourself work too, but it makes an excellent mash/lauter tun, and is especially suited for decoction mashing. You can not do step-mashes with this system. Rectangular picnic coolers are unrivalled for maintaining rest temperatures, and they come in sizes from 16 up to 120 quarts (15 - 110 L), making even 30-gallon batches of all-grain barleywine possible. If you don't own one already, picnic coolers can be purchased almost everywhere.

The major drawback is that you'll need to build a mash-filter. Depending on the spigot that comes with the cooler, you may need to modify it or replace it.

A mash filter can be constructed from common plumbing parts: 3/8" to 1/2" (10 - 12 mm) copper or PVC pipe, elbows and T's. Take a look at the illustration to see how it is constructed. Generally, you will require 4 elbows, 5 to 9 tees and 5-10' (1-1/2 - 3 meters) of pipe, depending on the size of the cooler.

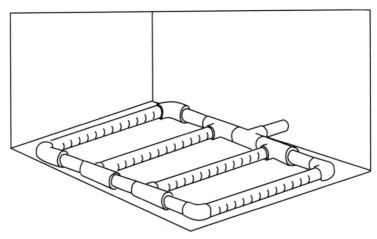

HOMEMADE PVC-PIPE MASH STRAINER

Lay the fittings into the bottom of the cooler. Measure how long the transverse pieces of pipe will need to be, and then the pieces to join the fittings along the filter's length. Mark these lengths along the piece of pipe. With a hacksaw, cut slots halfway through the pipe about a half-inch (12 mm) apart. Now go back and cut off the pieces, deburr the ends, and fit the whole thing together. Fix your mistakes, and try it again. The slots should face the bottom, at least more or less. Don't glue or solder the joints, because you will want to be able to take the whole thing apart for cleaning.

The wort flow can be routed out of the cooler by several means. A piece of 3/8" (9 mm) tubing connected to the mash filter should fit snugly through the existing drain, and can be controlled with an inexpensive nylon valve or a tubing clamp. Otherwise, drill a hole through the side, as close to the bottom as you can, and seal a threaded nipple through the wall with silicone. A FPT-by-socket fitting on the inside and a ball valve on the outside completes the arrangement.

How you control the sparge-liquor flow for any of the lautering systems is not critically important. You can devise a sparge arm or ring similar to those used by commercial brewers, but given the small diameter of homebrewing lauter tuns, it's not really necessary. Ladling sparge liquor gets old real quick, so plan at least to buy another bucket with a spigot to dispense your sparge liquor from.

Off-the-shelf Systems: If you do not have the time or the patience to make your own, commercially manufactured mashing systems, as well as lauter tuns, false bottoms, sparging devices, etc., are available from homebrew suppliers and by mail-order; check out the ads in brewing magazines.

Listermann Manufacturing makes a five-gallon (20 L) system composed of a polyethylene bucket fitted with a length of tubing and hose-clamp as a valve, a perforated false bottom, and a sparging arm to sprinkle the sparge water onto the mash.

The Bru-heat boiler and similar configurations employ an internal electric heating element to control the mash temperature. The thermostat automatically maintains mash temperatures during rests. You can do step-mashing in the Bru-heat, resetting the temperature to the strike temperature for the next rest. This isn't the cheapest option, and you'll still need a lauter tun, but a lot of homebrewers swear by them. The heavy duty buckets can be used as wort kettles as well.

OTHER EQUIPMENT

There are a couple of other pieces of equipment that you might want to consider in conjunction with mash brewing. They are:

Grain Mill: In the mashing chapter we recommend that you save the bucks and let your homebrew shop crush your grain for you, but if you do a lot of all grain brewing, you might want to purchase your own mill. Having your own grain mill allows you to brew whenever you want to brew, with freshly-crushed malt, that is crushed the way that you want it crushed.

There are many different grain mills available to the home brewer. You get more or less what you pay for with a malt mill, although even the cheapest one isn't real cheap. The basic Corona mill gives only a passable crush. It's better if you use a hand drill to turn the arbor, and quicker too, but any of the roller mills currently marketed give a better crush. If you become a dedicated mash brewer, spend the bucks and buy yourself a roller mill.

Electronic ph Meter: If you mash, pH is really important. A pH meter can enable you to make accurate pH corrections to your mash liquor, sparging liquor and wort. *Good* pH meters are much more accurate and reliable than pH test strips. There are many pH meters out there, but only ones that have resolution and accuracy better than pH 0.1 are really an improvement over pHydrion test strips. The saying that "you get what you pay for" truly applies here. Unless you are willing to drop a big chunk of cash, stick with pH strips, but use *accurate* ones!

Stop the runoff when the specific gravity drops below 1010, or the pH rises above 5.8. If you never use pH papers for anything else, use them now!

OK, so now you know everything there is to know about brewing, or at least everything you need to know for now, so let's pick a recipe, head for the homebrew shop with our shopping list, and then let's get brewing!

CHAPTER 12

PARTIAL MASH RECIPES

AMERICAN WHEAT ALE

FILLMIMUG WHEAT

A great summertime style of beer, and Fillmimug Wheat is just made for drinking when it's 93° in the shade. American Wheats should be light-bodied, refreshing, easy-drinking beers. This recipe is designed to allow you to have more than one, without worrying about falling asleep in the potted plants. So fill mi' mug, I'm havin' another wheat beer!

OG 1041   TG 1010   ABV 4.1%   SRM 2.5   IBU 15

Heat 6 gallons (23 L) of water to 165°F (74°C).

WATER SUPPLY:	TREAT WATER:
Soft	ACIDIFY TO BELOW pH 7.0
Moderately sulfate	ACIDIFY TO BELOW pH 7.0
Moderately carbonate	ACIDIFY TO BELOW pH 7.0
Highly sulfate	DILUTE 1:1 AND ACIDIFY TO BELOW pH 7.0
Highly carbonate	BOIL OR DILUTE 1:1 AND ACIDIFY TO BELOW pH 7.0

2-1/4 LBS (1 KG) LAGER MALT
1-1/2 LBS (.68 KG) WHEAT MALT

Crush the malt. Mash-in to 150°F (65°C) with 1 gallon (3.8 L) of liquor at 165°F (74°C). Cover and hold. After 1 hour, begin to runoff sweet wort to the kettle. Heat sparge liquor to 172°F (78°C). Sparge the mash with 1-1/4 gallons (4.7 L) of liquor. Add the remaining liquor to the kettle to bring the total volume to 5-1/2 gallons (21 L)

Add:
3.3 LBS (1.5 KG) EXTRA LIGHT MALT EXTRACT.

KETTLE SCHEDULE:
1.5 HBU CASCADE as soon as the wort comes to a boil,
2 HBU CASCADE after 15 minutes, and
1/2 TSP (2.5 ML) IRISH MOSS after 1 hour and fifteen minutes,
KETTLE KNOCKOUT at 1-1/2 hours.

Transfer through wort chiller into carboy, aerating the wort.
5-1/4 gallons (20 L) of wort should be collected at sg 1041.

Pitch with:
2 PKGS of neutral ale yeast (10-14 grams dry yeast) or liquid yeast (Wyeast 1007 or 1056, Yeast Lab A07, BrewTek CL-10 or CL-400).

Ferment at:
60-70°F (16-21°C). Transfer to secondary after 4-7 days, condition at 40-60°F (4-16°C) for 3-6 weeks.

Prime with:
3/4-1 cup (170-230 ML) of CORN SUGAR and bottle condition for 1 month at below 65°F (18°C)

ENGLISH MILD

PIPE-CUM-LYDE MILD

A dark, easy-drinking mild, with just a touch of characteristic sweetness, and a very light finish. Fruity esters will perfectly suit this beer, but avoid high fermentation temperatures that might produce fusels and solventy flavors. This may be the perfect beer to brew to introduce friends to homebrewing. Then invite them over for a "session" when it's ready to quaff. It's a pretty safe bet you won't have to brew all the Pipe-cum-lyde Mild for long!

OG 1040   TG 1008   ABV 4.2%   SRM 18   IBU 15

Heat 6 gallons (23 L) of water to 165°F (74°C)

WATER SUPPLY:	TREAT WATER
Soft	1/2 TEASPOON OF GYPSUM
Moderately sulfate	OK AS IS
Moderately carbonate	ACIDIFY TO BELOW pH 7.2
Highly sulfate	DILUTE 1:1 OR BOIL
Highly carbonate	DILUTE 1:1 OR BOIL AND ACIDIFY TO 7.2

2-1/4 LBS (1 KG) PALE MALT
1/4 LBS (.11 KG) WHEAT MALT
1/4 LBS (.11 KG) ROASTED BARLEY
1/4 LBS (.11 KG) 80°L CRYSTAL

Crush the malt. Mash-in to 150°F (65°C) with 1 gallon (3.8 L) of liquor at 165°F (74°C). Cover and hold. After 1 hour begin to runoff sweet wort to the kettle. Heat sparge liquor to 172°F (78°C). Sparge the mash with 1 gallon (3.8 L) liquor. Add the remaining liquor to the kettle to bring the total volume to 5-1/2 gallons (21 L)

Add:
1/4 LBS (.11 KG) DARK BROWN SUGAR
2-1/2 LBS (1.1 KG) LIGHT DME

KETTLE SCHEDULE:
1.25 HBU FUGGLES as soon as the wort comes to a boil,
2.5 HBU FUGGLES after 45 minutes, and
1/2 TSP (2.5 ML) IRISH MOSS after 1 hour and fifteen minutes
KETTLE KNOCKOUT at 1-1/2 hours.

Transfer through wort chiller into carboy, aerating the wort.
5-1/4 gallons (20 L) of wort should be collected at sg 1040.

Pitch with:
2 PKGS of malty-fruity ale yeast (10-14 grams dry yeast) or liquid yeast (Wyeast 1028 or 1084, Yeast Lab A05, BrewTek CL-20 or CL-130)

Ferment at:
68-72°F (20-22°C). Transfer to secondary after 4-7 days, condition at 50-60°F (10-16°C) for 2-3 weeks.

Prime with:
1/2-2/3 cup (115-150 ML) of CORN SUGAR and bottle condition for 1 month at below 65°F (18°C)

ENGLISH BROWN ALE

DOUBLE CROSS XX BROWN

A southern-style English brown ale, Double Cross Brown is a rich blend of soft flavors. Dark malts contribute a sweet, roasty-chocolaty flavor to this sweet and full-bodied brew, making it a great beer to go with dessert, or as dessert!

OG 1046   TG 1012   ABV 4.5%   SRM 20   IBU 20

Heat 6-3/4 gallons (25.5 L) of water to 169°F (76°C)

WATER SUPPLY:	TREAT WATER
Soft	1/2 TEASPOON OF GYPSUM
Moderately sulfate	OK AS IS
Moderately carbonate	ACIDIFY TO BELOW pH 7.2
Highly sulfate	DILUTE 1:1 OR BOIL
Highly carbonate	DILUTE 1:1 OR BOIL AND ACIDIFY TO 7.2

2-1/2 LBS (1.1 KG) PALE MALT
1/4 LB (.11 KG) WHEAT MALT
1-1/4 LBS (.57 KG) 80°L CRYSTAL
1/4 LB (.11 KG) CHOCOLATE MALT

Crush the malt. Mash-in to 154-156°F (68-69°C) with 1-1/2 gallons (5.7 L) of liquor at 165°F (74°C). Cover and hold. After 1 hour begin to runoff sweet wort to the kettle. Heat sparge liquor to 172°F (78°C). Sparge the mash with 1-1/2 gallons (5.7 L) liquor. Add the remaining liquor to the kettle to bring the total volume to 5-2/3 gallons (21.5 L)

Add:
3.3 LBS (1.5 KG) LIGHT MALT EXTRACT

KETTLE SCHEDULE:
1.5 HBU WILLAMETTE as soon as the wort comes to a boil,
3.5 HBU WILLAMETTE after 45 minutes, and
1/2 TSP (2.5 ML) IRISH MOSS after 1 hour and fifteen minutes
KETTLE KNOCKOUT at 1-1/2 hours.

Transfer through wort chiller into carboy, aerating the wort.
5-1/4 gallons (20 L) of wort should be collected at sg 1046.

Pitch with:
2 PKGS of malty-fruity ale yeast (10-14 grams dry yeast) or liquid yeast (Wyeast 1028 or 1084, Yeast Lab A05, BrewTek CL-20 or CL-130)

Ferment at:
68-72°F (20-22°C). Transfer to secondary after 4-7 days, condition at 50-60°F (10-16°C) for 2-3 weeks.

Prime with:
1/2-2/3 cup (115-150 ML) of CORN SUGAR and bottle condition for 1 month at below 65°F (18°C)

AMERICAN BROWN ALE

MORE-BITTER-MORE-BETTER BROWN

American Brown ales are kind of British-style brown ales with a pronounced hop bite to them. More-Bitter gets its definitive American-hop character from Cascade hops, and you gotta like Cascade hops. You can increase the hoppiness for More-Better Brown Ale by dry hopping in the secondary with an additional 1/2 ounce of Cascade. Don't worry about the dryhops contaminating the brew, just do it! Join the true hop-heads out there!

OG 1054 TG 1013 ABV 5.4% SRM 20 IBU 50

Heat 6-3/4 gallons (25.5 L) of water to 167°F (75°C)

WATER SUPPLY:	TREAT WATER
Soft	2 TEASPOONS GYPSUM,
	1/2 TEASPOON TABLE SALT
Moderately sulfate	1/2 TEASPOON OF GYPSUM
Moderately carbonate	1 TEASPOON GYPSUM,
	1/2 TEASPOON TABLE SALT
Highly sulfate	OK AS IS
Highly carbonate	ACIDIFY TO BELOW 7.2

3-3/4 LBS (1.7 KG) PALE MALT
1-1/2 LBS (.68 KG) 80°L CRYSTAL
1/4 LBS (.11 KG) CHOCOLATE MALT
1/4 LBS (.11 KG) WHEAT MALT

Crush the malt. Mash-in to 152°F (67°C) with 1-3/4 gallons (6.6 L) of liquor at 167°F (75°C). Cover and hold. After 1 hour begin to runoff sweet wort to the kettle. Heat sparge liquor to 172°F (78°C). Sparge the mash with 2 gallons (7.6 L) of liquor. Add the remaining liquor to the kettle to bring the total volume to 5-3/4 gallons (22 L)

Add:
3.3 LBS (1.5 KG) LIGHT MALT EXTRACT

KETTLE SCHEDULE:
1.5 HBU CASCADE as soon as the wort comes to a boil,
7.5 HBU CASCADE after 45 minutes,
5 HBU CASCADE after 1 hour,
1/2 TSP (2.5 ML) IRISH MOSS after 1 hour and fifteen minutes, and 1/2 OZ (14 GRAMS) CASCADE added at knockout,
KETTLE KNOCKOUT at 1-1/2 hours.

Transfer through wort chiller into carboy, aerating the wort.
5-1/4 gallons (20 L) of wort should be collected at sg 1054.

Pitch with:
2 PKGS of neutral ale yeast (10-14 grams dry yeast) or liquid yeast (Wyeast 1056, Yeast Lab A06, BrewTek CL-1260).

Ferment at:
68-72°F (20-22°C). Transfer to secondary after 4-7 days, condition at 50-60°F (10-16°C) for 2 weeks.

Prime with:
3/4 cup (170 ML) of CORN SUGAR and bottle condition for 1 month at below 65°F (18°C)

SCOTTISH LIGHT

HELLSTER KILTER

A light, malty brew to drink when you yearn for the highlands. Just put on something plaid and dream.........

OG 1035 TG 1010 ABV 3.3% SRM 12 IBU 15

Heat 6 gallons (23 L) of water to 170°F (77°C)

WATER SUPPLY:	TREAT WATER
Soft	2 TEASPOONS GYPSUM,
	1/2 TEASPOON TABLE SALT
Moderately sulfate	1/2 TEASPOON OF GYPSUM
Moderately carbonate	1/2 TEASPOONS GYPSUM,
	1/2 TEASPOON TABLE SALT
Highly sulfate	OK AS IS
Highly carbonate	ACIDIFY TO BELOW 7.2

2 LBS (.9 KG) PALE MALT
1/4 LBS (.11 KG) CARAPILS
1/2 OZ (14 GRAMS) ROASTED BARLEY

Crush the malt. Mash-in to 156°F (69°C) with 3 quarts (2.8 L) of liquor at 165°F (74°C). Cover and hold. After 1 hour, begin to runoff sweet wort to the kettle. Cover the bottom of the kettle and apply heat till the wort "carmelizes". Continue to run the wort into the kettle. Heat sparge liquor to 172°F (78°C). Sparge the mash with 3 quarts (2.8 L) liquor. Add the remaining liquor to the kettle to bring the total volume to 5-1/2 gallons (21 L).

Add:
3.3 LBS (1.5 KG) LIGHT MALT EXTRACT

KETTLE SCHEDULE:
1.25 HBU FUGGLES as soon as the wort comes to a boil
2.5 HBU GOLDINGS after 45 minutes
1/2 TSP (2.5 ML) IRISH MOSS after 1 hour and fifteen minutes
KETTLE KNOCKOUT at 1-1/2 hours.

Transfer through wort chiller into carboy, aerating the wort.
5-1/4 gallons (20 L) of wort should be collected at sg 1035.

Pitch with:
2 PKGS of neutral ale yeast (10-14 grams dry yeast) or liquid yeast (Wyeast 1084 or 1728, Yeast Lab A05, BrewTek CL-160).

Ferment at:
60-68°F (15-20°C). Transfer to secondary after 4-7 days, condition at 50-60°F (10-16°C) for 2-3 weeks.

Prime with:
1/2 cup (115 ML) of CORN SUGAR and bottle condition for 1 month at below 65°F (18°C).

SCOTTISH HEAVY

THISTLE BOG ALE

A smooth Scotch ale that goes down like butter. In fact, a yeast strain that leaves a good bit of buttery diacetyl is just the thing here. If you have some heather honey, substitute a pound of that for the same of pale malt for a real highland touch. After a few of these, you will be able to play the bagpipes. Well, maybe...

OG 1040 TG 1012 ABV 3.7% SRM 16 IBU 15

Heat 6 gallons (23 L) of water to 168°F (76°C)

WATER SUPPLY:	TREAT WATER
Soft	2 TEASPOONS GYPSUM,
	1/2 TEASPOON TABLE SALT
Moderately sulfate	1/2 TEASPOON OF GYPSUM
Moderately carbonate	1/2 TEASPOON GYPSUM,
	1/2 TEASPOON TABLE SALT
Highly sulfate	OK AS IS
Highly carbonate	ACIDIFY TO BELOW 7.2

2-1/2 LBS (1.1 KG) PALE MALT
1/4 LB (.11 KG) 80°L CRYSTAL
1/4 LB (.11 KG) CARAPILS
2 OZ (57 GRAMS) ROASTED BARLEY

Crush the malt. Mash-in to 155°F (68°C) with 1 gallon (3.8 L) of liquor at 168°F (76°C). Cover and hold. After 1 hour begin to runoff sweet wort to the kettle. Heat sparge liquor to 172°F (78°C). Sparge the mash with 1-1/4 gallons (4.7 L) of liquor. Add the remaining liquor to the kettle to bring the total volume to 5-2/3 gallons (21.5 L)

Add:
3.3 LBS (1.5 KG) LIGHT MALT EXTRACT.

KETTLE SCHEDULE:
1.25 HBU GOLDINGS as soon as the wort comes to a boil
2.5 HBU GOLDINGS (1.25 HBU) after 45 minutes
1/2 TSP (2.5 ML) IRISH MOSS after 1 hour and fifteen minutes
KETTLE KNOCKOUT at 1-1/2 hours

Transfer through wort chiller into carboy, aerating the wort.
5-1/4 gallons (20 L) of wort should be collected at sg 1040.

Pitch with:
2 PKGS of neutral ale yeast (10-14 grams dry yeast) or liquid yeast (Wyeast 1084 or 1728, Yeast Lab A05, BrewTek CL-160).

Ferment at:
60-68°F (15-20°C). Transfer to secondary after 4-7 days, condition at 50-60°F (10-16°C) for 2-3 weeks.

Prime with:
1/2 cup (115 ML) of CORN SUGAR and bottle condition for 1 month at below 65°F (18°C).

SCOTTISH EXPORT

OLD 80 WEIGHT

Soft, full-bodied and satisfying, OLD 80 WEIGHT is a beer to lubricate those creaky bones when the chill wind whistles through the crags of Ben Nevis, churns up sea monsters on Loch Ness, and blows icy up from the Firth and howls down old Rose Street. You won't need to stoke the fire, just break out the Old 80-Weight!

OG 1048 TG 1012 ABV 4.7% SRM 16 IBU 20

Heat 6-1/2 gallons (25 L) of water to 167°F (75°C)

WATER SUPPLY:	TREAT WATER
Soft	2 TEASPOONS GYPSUM,
	1/2 TEASPOON TABLE SALT
Moderately sulfate	1/2 TEASPOON OF GYPSUM
Moderately carbonate	1/2 TEASPOON GYPSUM,
	1/2 TEASPOON TABLE SALT
Highly sulfate	OK AS IS
Highly carbonate	ACIDIFY TO BELOW 7.2

3-1/2 LBS (1.6 KG) PALE MALT
1/2 LB (.23 KG) 55°L CRYSTAL
1/2 LB (.23 KG) CARAPILS
2 OZ (57 GRAMS) ROASTED BARLEY

Crush the malt. Mash-in to 152°F (67°C) with 1-1/2 gallons (5.7 L) of liquor at 167°F (75°C). Cover and hold. After 1 hour begin to runoff sweet wort to the kettle. Heat sparge liquor to 172°F (78°C). Sparge the mash with 1-1/2 gallons (5.7 L) liquor. Add the remaining liquor to the kettle to bring the total volume to 5-2/3 gallons (21.5 L).

Add:
3.3 LBS (1.5 KG) LIGHT MALT EXTRACT

KETTLE SCHEDULE:
4.5 HBU FUGGLES as soon as the wort comes to a boil
1/2 TSP (2.5 ML) IRISH MOSS after 1 hour and fifteen minutes
KETTLE KNOCKOUT at 1-1/2 hours.

Transfer through wort chiller into carboy, aerating the wort.
5-1/4 gallons (20 L) of wort should be collected at sg 1048.

Pitch with:
2 PKGS of neutral ale yeast (10-14 grams dry yeast) or liquid yeast (Wyeast 1084 or 1728, Yeast Lab A05, BrewTek CL-160).

Ferment at:
60-68°F (16-20°C). Transfer to secondary after 4-7 days, condition at 50-60°F (10-16°C) for 2-3 weeks.

Prime with:
1/2 cup (115 ML) of CORN SUGAR and bottle condition for 1 month at below 65°F (18°C).

ORDINARY BITTER

BURPING ON THE TRENT ALE

A British style ale that holds its own in the best of company. The addition of just the right amount of crystal malt and the "Burtonizing" water treatment round off the hop bitterness. And if you want to avoid burping, follow the recipe and don't overcarbonate this brew! English Ordinary should never be gassy, so take it easy on the priming sugar.

OG 1037 TG 1009 ABV 3.7% SRM 10 IBU 25

Heat 6 gallons (23 L) of water to 165°F (74°C)

WATER SUPPLY:	TREAT WATER
Soft	6 TEASPOONS GYPSUM, 1/4 TEASPOON TABLE SALT
Moderately sulfate	4 TEASPOONS GYPSUM, 1/4 TEASPOON TABLE SALT
Moderately carbonate	5 TEASPOONS GYPSUM, 1/4 TEASPOON TABLE SALT
Highly sulfate	Up TO 3 TEASPOONS OF GYPSUM
Highly carbonate	Up TO 3 TEASPOONS OF GYPSUM, ACIDIFY TO 7.0

2 LBS (.9 KG) PALE MALT
1/2 LB (.23 KG) 55°L CRYSTAL

Crush the malt. Mash-in to 150°F (65°C) with 3 quarts (2.8 L) of liquor at 165°F (74°C). Cover and hold. After 1 hour begin to runoff sweet wort to the kettle. Heat sparge liquor to 172°C (78°C). Sparge the mash with 1 gallon (3.8 L) liquor. Add the remaining liquor to the kettle to bring the total volume to 5-1/2 gallons (21 L)

Add:
3.3 LBS (1.5 KG) LIGHT MALT EXTRACT

KETTLE SCHEDULE:
1 HBU FUGGLES as soon as the wort comes to a boil
2.5 HBU FUGGLES after 30 minutes
2.5 HBU FUGGLES after 45 minutes
1/2 TSP (2.5 ML) IRISH MOSS after 1 hour and fifteen minutes
KETTLE KNOCKOUT at 1-1/2 hours.

Transfer through wort chiller into carboy, aerating the wort.
5-1/4 gallons (20 L) of wort should be collected at sg 1037.

Pitch with:
2 PKGS of fruity ale yeast (10-14 grams dry yeast) or liquid yeast (Wyeast 1098, 1028, Yeast Lab A04, A08, BrewTek CL-120, CL-130, CL-160, CL-170).

Ferment at:
68-72°F (20-22°C) Transfer to secondary after 3-4 days, condition at 50-60°F (10-16°C) for 1-2 weeks.

Prime with:
1/2 cup (115 ML) of CORN SUGAR and bottle condition for 1 month at below 65°F (18°C).

EXTRA SPECIAL BITTER

TOBY'S TIPPLE

ESB is just what it says it is; a stronger, more bitter version of English Bitter. Our Extra Special Bitter is a very flavorful ale, with a rummy, fruity character from the combination of Crystal malt and the raw sugar. If you can't find raw sugar, just substitute brown sugar. If you like this recipe, use it to experiment with brewing liquor. The next time you brew it, substitute the water treatment given in the last recipe, for a Burton version of an ESB.

OG 1052 TG 1012 ABV 5.3% SRM 11 IBU 32

Heat 6-3/4 gallons (25.5 L) of water to 165°F (74°C)

WATER SUPPLY:	TREAT WATER
Soft	1/2 TEASPOON OF GYPSUM
Moderately sulfate	OK AS IS
Moderately carbonate	ACIDIFY TO BELOW 7.2
Highly sulfate	DILUTE 1:1
Highly carbonate	BOIL OR DILUTE 1:1, ACIDIFY TO BELOW 7.2

3-3/4 LBS (1.7 KG) PALE MALT
1/4 LB (.11 KG) FLAKED BARLEY
1/2 LB (.23 KG) 55°L CRYSTAL

Crush the malt. Mash-in to 150°F (65°C) with 1-1/2 gallons (5.7 L) of liquor at 165°F (74°C). Cover and hold. After 1 hour begin to runoff sweet wort to the kettle. Heat sparge liquor to 172°F (78°C). Sparge the mash with 1-1/2 gallons (5.7 L) liquor. Add the remaining liquor to the kettle to bring the total volume to 6 gallons (23 L)

Add:
3.3 LBS (1.5 KG) LIGHT MALT EXTRACT
1/2 LB (.23 KG) RAW SUGAR

KETTLE SCHEDULE:
1.5 HBU GOLDINGS as soon as the wort comes to a boil
2.5 HBU GOLDINGS after 30 minutes
3.5 HBU GOLDINGS after 15 minutes
1/2 TSP (2.5 ML) IRISH MOSS after 1 hour and fifteen minutes
KETTLE KNOCKOUT at 1-1/2 hours.

Transfer through wort chiller into carboy, aerating the wort.
5-1/4 gallons (20 L) of wort should be collected at sg 1052.

Pitch with:
2 PKGS of fruity ale yeast (10-14 grams dry yeast) or liquid yeast (Wyeast 1098, 1028, or 1068, Yeast Lab A04, A08, BrewTek CL-120).

Ferment at:
68-72°F (20-22°C). Transfer to secondary after 3-4 days, condition at 50-60°F (10-16°C) for 1-2 weeks.

Prime with 1/2 cup (115 ML) of CORN SUGAR and bottle condition for 1 month at below 65°F (18°C).

CLASSIC PALE ALE

BOMBAY GRAB PALE ALE

A classic pale ale that is named after the father of pale ales. Hodgson's brewery and tap-room, the Bombay Grab, were in London, not Burton, which has come to be so famous for its pale ales. Hodgson's Pale is a London ale, drier and sharper than the fruity Burton ales. Serve it at about 50°F(10°C) for the full flavor to come through, while you lean back, relax and hoist a pint at your local pub (fake it).

OG 1050 TG 1012 ABV 5% SRM 9 IBU 36

Heat 6-1/4 gallons (24 L) of water to 165°F (74°C)

WATER SUPPLY:	TREAT WATER
Soft	3 TEASPOONS GYPSUM,
	1/2 TEASPOON TABLE SALT
Moderately sulfate	1 TEASPOON OF GYPSUM
Moderately carbonate	1 TEASPOONS GYPSUM,
	1/2 TEASPOON TABLE SALT
Highly sulfate	ACIDIFY TO BELOW 7.0
Highly carbonate	ACIDIFY TO BELOW 7.0

4 LBS (1.8 KG) PALE MALT
1/4 LB (.11 KG) 55°L CRYSTAL

Crush the malt. Mash-in to 150°F (65°C) with 1-1/4 gallons (4.7 L) of liquor at 165°F (74°C). Cover and hold. After 1 hour begin to runoff sweet wort to the kettle. Heat sparge liquor to 172°F (78°C). Sparge the mash with 1-1/2 gallons (5.7 L) liquor. Add the remaining liquor to the kettle to bring the total volume to 5-2/3 gallons (21.5 L)

Add:
1/2 LB (.23 KG) BROWN SUGAR
3.3 LBS (1.5 KG) LIGHT MALT EXTRACT

KETTLE SCHEDULE:
3 HBU CHINOOK as soon as the wort comes to a boil
2.5 HBU GOLDINGS after 45 minutes
3 HBU FUGGLES after 60 minutes
4 HBU GOLDINGS and1/2 TSP (2.5 ML) IRISH MOSS after 1 hour and fifteen minutes
KETTLE KNOCKOUT at 1-1/2 hours.

Transfer through wort chiller into carboy, aerating the wort.
5-1/4 gallons (20 L) of wort should be collected at sg 1050.

Pitch with:
2 PKGS of fruity ale yeast (10-14 grams dry yeast) or liquid yeast (Wyeast 1098, 1028, or 1068 Yeast Lab A04, A08, BrewTek CL-120).

Ferment at:
68-72°F (20-22°C) Transfer to secondary after 3-4 days,
Add:
1 OZ (28 GRAMS) GOLDINGS dry hops,
condition at 50-60°F (10-16°C) for 1-2 weeks.

Prime with:
1/2 cup (115 ML) of CORN SUGAR and bottle condition for 1 month at below 65°F (18°C).

INDIA PALE ALE

HUMULUS LUDICROUS IPA

Hops with a capital "H". Enough hops that this brew would be ludicrous if it didn't taste so good. Hops are what India Pale Ales are all about, right? Right. This IPA has LOTS of hops...bitter hopping, flavor hopping, aroma hopping, and dry hopping. Count the IBUs with every taste...

WARNING: This IPA is for hopheads only!!!!!!

OG 1063 TG 1015 ABV 6.3% SRM 13 IBU 65

Heat 6-3/4 gallons (25.5 L) of water to 165°F (74°C)

WATER SUPPLY:	TREAT WATER
Soft	6 TEASPOONS GYPSUM,
	1/4 TEASPOON TABLE SALT
Moderately sulfate	4 TEASPOONS GYPSUM,
	1/4 TEASPOON TABLE SALT
Moderately carbonate	5 TEASPOONS GYPSUM,
	1/4 TEASPOON TABLE SALT
Highly sulfate	UP TO 3 TEASPOONS OF GYPSUM
Highly carbonate	UP TO 3 TEASPOONS OF GYPSUM, ACIDIFY TO 7.0

4-1/2 LBS (2 KG) PALE MALT / 3/4 LB (.34 KG) 55°L CRYSTAL
Crush the malt. Mash-in to 150°F (65°C) with 1-3/4 gallons (6.6 L) of liquor at 165°F (74°C). Cover and hold. After 1 hour begin to runoff sweet wort to the kettle. Heat sparge liquor to 172°F (78°C). Sparge the mash with 1-3/4 gallons (6.6 L) liquor. Add the remaining liquor to the kettle to bring the total volume to 5-3/4 gallons (22 L).

Add:
3.3 LBS (1.5 KG) LIGHT MALT EXTRACT
1-1/2LBS (.68 KG) LIGHT DME.

KETTLE SCHEDULE:
4 HBU PERLE as soon as the wort comes to a boil,
5 HBU PERLE after 45 minutes,
7.5 HBU GOLDINGS after 60 minutes,
7.5 HBU FUGGLES and,
1/2 TSP (2.5 ML) IRISH MOSS after 1 hour and fifteen minutes,
KETTLE KNOCKOUT at 1-1/2 hours.

Transfer through wort chiller into carboy, aerating the wort.
5-1/4 gallons (20 L) of wort should be collected at sg 1063.

Pitch with:
2 PKGS of fruity ale yeast (10-14 grams dry yeast) or liquid yeast (Wyeast 1098, 1028, or 1068, Yeast Lab A04, A08, BrewTek CL-120).

Ferment at:
68-72°F (20-22°C). Transfer to secondary after 3-4 days, adding
2 OZ (57 GRAMS) GOLDINGS dry hops,
condition at 50-60°F (10-16°C) for 1-2 weeks.

Prime with:
1/2 cup (115 ML) of CORN SUGAR and bottle condition for 1 month at below 65°F (18°C).

ROBUST PORTER

FLYCASTER PORTER

Rich and dark, the addition of black patent malt adds an underlying dryness to this porter, balancing the sweetness of the crystal malts. Porter is a rich and satisfying style of beer to be enjoyed all by itself, but goes well with a wide variety of foods as well. Flycaster porter is especially nice with spicy foods, because the richness tames the heat of the spices.

OG 1056 TG 1014 ABV 5.5% SRM 35 IBU 35

Heat 6-1/2 gallons (25 L) of water to 167°F (75°C)

WATER SUPPLY:	TREAT WATER
Soft	1/2 TEASPOON OF GYPSUM
Moderately sulfate	OK AS IS
Moderately carbonate	ACIDIFY TO BELOW 7.2
Highly sulfate	DILUTE 1:1
Highly carbonate	BOIL OR DILUTE 1:1, ACIDIFY TO BELOW 7.2

2 LBS (.9 KG) PALE MALT
1-1/2 LBS (.68 KG) 80°L CRYSTAL
1/2 LB (.23 KG) CARAPILS
1/4 LB (.11 KG) BLACK PATENT MALT
1/2 LB (.23 KG) CHOCOLATE MALT

Crush the malt. Mash-in to 152°F (67°C) with 1-1/2 gallons (5.7 L) of liquor at 167°F (75°C). Cover and hold. After 1 hour begin to runoff sweet wort to the kettle. Heat sparge liquor to 172°F (78°C). Sparge the mash with 1-3/4 gallons (6.6 L) liquor. Add the remaining liquor to the kettle to bring the total volume to 5-3/4 gallons (22 L)

Add:
3.3 LBS (1.5 KG) LIGHT MALT EXTRACT / 1 LB (.45 KG) LIGHT DME

KETTLE SCHEDULE:
3.5 HBU EROICA as soon as the wort comes to a boil
2.5 HBU WILLAMETTE after 45 minutes
2 HBU FUGGLES after 60 minutes
4 HBU CASCADE and
1/2 TSP (2.5 ML) IRISH MOSS after 1 hour and fifteen minutes
KETTLE KNOCKOUT at 1-1/2 hours.

Transfer through wort chiller into carboy, aerating the wort.
5-1/4 gallons (20 L) of wort should be collected at sg 1056.

Pitch with:
2 PKGS of fruity ale yeast (10-14 grams dry yeast) or liquid yeast (Wyeast 1098, 1028, or 1068, Yeast Lab A04, A08, BrewTek CL-120).

Ferment at:
68-72°F (20-22°C). Transfer to secondary after 3-4 days, condition at 50-60°F (10-16°C) for 1-2 weeks.

Prime with:
1/2-2/3 cup (115-150 ML) of CORN SUGAR and bottle condition for 1 month at below 65°F (18°C).

BROWN PORTER

HE-SHE KISS

A sweeter porter than the recipe (above) for robust porter. Don't decide that this is not the brew for you just yet, though. What kind of chocolate do you prefer, milk chocolate, or baker's chocolate? Do you like Columbian-roast coffee, or the more bitter French roast? Well, porter is kind of like chocolate and coffee. If you answered milk chocolate and Columbian roast, then this is probably the recipe for you...a true dessert lover's beer. And if it's not rich enough for your tastes, just add a half-pound of fresh-ground coffee to the mash and a half-pound of baker's chocolate to the kettle!

OG 1045 TG 1012 ABV 4.5% SRM 20 IBU 25

Heat 6-1/4 gallons (24 L) of water to 165°F (74°C)

WATER SUPPLY:	TREAT WATER
Soft	1/2 TEASPOON OF GYPSUM
Moderately sulfate	OK AS IS
Moderately carbonate	ACIDIFY TO BELOW 7.2
Highly sulfate	DILUTE 1:1
Highly carbonate	BOIL OR DILUTE 1:1, ACIDIFY TO BELOW 7.2

3-1/2 LBS (1.6 KG) PALE MALT
1/2 LB (.23 KG) 80°L CRYSTAL
1/4 LB (.11 KG) CHOCOLATE MALT
1/8 LB (57 GRAMS) BLACK PATENT

Crush the malt. Mash-in to 154°F (68°C) with 1-1/4 gallons (4.7 L) of liquor at 165°F (74°C). Cover and hold. After 1 hour begin to runoff sweet wort to the kettle. Heat sparge liquor to 172°F (78°C). Sparge the mash with 1-1/2 gallons (5.7 L) of liquor. Add the remaining liquor to the kettle to bring the total volume to 5-2/3 gallons (21.5 L)

Add:
3.3 LBS (1.5 KG) LIGHT MALT EXTRACT.

KETTLE SCHEDULE:
2.5 HBU CHINOOK as soon as the wort comes to a boil
2.5 HBU PERLE after 45 minutes
2 HBU WILLAMETTE after 60 minutes
1/2 TSP (2.5 ML) IRISH MOSS after 1 hour and fifteen minutes
KETTLE KNOCKOUT at 1-1/2 hours.

Transfer through wort chiller into carboy, aerating the wort.
5-1/4 gallons (20 L) of wort should be collected at sg 1045.

Pitch with:
2 PKGS of fruity ale yeast (10-14 grams dry yeast) or liquid yeast (Wyeast 1098, 1028, or 1068, Yeast Lab A04, A08, BrewTek CL-120).

Ferment at:
68-72°F (20-22°C). Transfer to secondary after 3-4 days, condition at 50-60°F (10-16°C) for 1-2 weeks.

Prime with:
1/2 cup (115 ML) of CORN SUGAR and bottle condition for 1 month at below 65°F (18°C).

CLASSIC DRY STOUT

DISCIPLE'S GATE STOUT

This style is, of course, made famous by Guinness, the legendary brewery in Dublin, Ireland. This recipe is designed to emulate the original, with a smooth flavor, but dry and full of character from the liberal addition of roasted barley. It's stout like stout is meant to be.

OG 1045 TG 1012 ABV 4.3% SRM 45 IBU 35

Heat 6-1/4 gallons (24 L) of water to 165°F (74°C)

WATER SUPPLY:	TREAT WATER
Soft	1/2 TEASPOON OF GYPSUM
Moderately sulfate	OK AS IS
Moderately carbonate	OK AS IS
Highly sulfate	OK AS IS
Highly carbonate	ACIDIFY TO BELOW 7.2

2-3/4 LBS (1.2 KG) PALE MALT
1/2 LB (.23 KG) FLAKED BARLEY
3/4 LB (.34 KG) ROASTED BARLEY
1/2 LB (23 KG) CHOCOLATE MALT

Crush the malt. Mash-in to 150°F (65°C) with 1-1/4 gallons (4.7 L) of liquor at 165°F (74°C). Cover and hold. After 1 hour begin to runoff sweet wort to the kettle. Heat sparge liquor to 172°F (78°C). Sparge the mash with 1-1/2 gallons (5.7 L) liquor. Add the remaining liquor to the kettle to bring the total volume to 5-2/3 gallons (21.5 L)

Add:
3.3 LBS (1.5 KG) LIGHT MALT EXTRACT

KETTLE SCHEDULE:
4.5 HBU PERLE as soon as the wort comes to a boil
2.5 HBU GOLDINGS after 45 minutes
4 HBU GOLDINGS and
1/2 TSP (2.5 ML) IRISH MOSS after 1 hour and fifteen minutes
KETTLE KNOCKOUT at 1-1/2 hours.

Transfer through wort chiller into carboy, aerating the wort.
5-1/4 gallons (20 L) of wort should be collected at sg 1045.

Pitch with:
2 PKGS of fruity ale yeast (10-14 grams dry yeast) or liquid yeast (Wyeast 1084, Yeast Lab A05, BrewTek CL-240).

Ferment at:
65-72°F (18-22°C). Transfer to secondary after 3-6 days, condition at 50-60°F (10-16°C) for 1-2 weeks.

Prime with:
2/3 cup (150 ML) of CORN SUGAR and bottle condition for 1 month at below 65°F (18°C).

SWEET STOUT

DOUBLE DRAGON STOUT

Dark, rich and sweet like a chocolate dessert, this stout is rich enough by itself to give a fufilling finish to any meal. So enjoy one after dinner, and call it dessert. Have another, and call it a digestif. Go for three, and call it a nightcap. Enjoy one in the afternoon, and just call it a real nice beer!

OG 1047 TG 1012 ABV 4.6% SRM 40 IBU 25

Heat 6-1/2 gallons (25 L) of water to 169°F (76°C)

WATER SUPPLY:	TREAT WATER
Soft	1/2 TEASPOON OF GYPSUM
Moderately sulfate	OK AS IS
Moderately carbonate	OK AS IS
Highly sulfate	DILUTE UP TO 1:1
Highly carbonate	ACIDIFY TO BELOW 7.2

2-1/4 LBS (1 KG) PALE MALT
1-1/2 LBS (.68 KG) 80°L CRYSTAL
1/2 LB (.23 KG) ROASTED BARLEY
1/2 LB (.23 KG) BLACK PATENT

Crush the malt. Mash-in to 154°F (68°C) with 1-1/2 gallons (5.7 L) of liquor at 169°F (76°C). Cover and hold. After 1 hour begin to runoff sweet wort to the kettle. Heat sparge liquor to 172°C (78°C). Sparge the mash with 1-1/2 gallons (5.7 L) liquor. Add the remaining liquor to the kettle to bring the total volume to 5-3/4 gallons (22 L)

Add:
3.3 LBS (1.5 KG) LIGHT MALT EXTRACT

KETTLE SCHEDULE:
1.5 HBU PERLE as soon as the wort comes to a boil
4.5 HBU FUGGLES after 45 minutes
1/2 TSP (2.5 ML) IRISH MOSS after 1 hour and fifteen minutes
KETTLE KNOCKOUT at 1-1/2 hours.

Transfer through wort chiller into carboy, aerating the wort.
5-1/4 gallons (20 L) of wort should be collected at sg 1047.

Pitch with:
2 PKGS of fruity ale yeast (10-14 grams dry yeast) or liquid yeast (Wyeast 1084, Yeast Lab A05, BrewTek CL-240).

Ferment at:
65-72°F (18-22°C). Transfer to secondary after 3-6 days, condition at 50-60°F (10-16°C) for 1-2 weeks.

Prime with 2/3 cup (150 ML) of CORN SUGAR and bottle condition for 1 month at below 65°F (18°C).

IMPERIAL STOUT

R.I.P. XXX STOUT

Russian Imperial Stout truly is the supreme ruler of all stouts. Even dry stout pales beside its bigness and the intensity of its flavor. The sheer concentration of sensation is not for everyone! How does one know if one is ready to R.I.P.? Well, if you love fruit cakes, black licorice and barley wines, then rest in peace, and brew up a batch of Russian Imperial Stout!

OG 1086 TG 1021 ABV 8.5% SRM 70 IBU 65

Heat 6-3/4 gallons (25.5 L) of water to 167°F (75°C)

WATER SUPPLY:	TREAT WATER
Soft	6 TEASPOONS GYPSUM,
	1/4 TEASPOON TABLE SALT
Moderately sulfate	4 TEASPOONS GYPSUM,
	1/4 TEASPOON TABLE SALT
Moderately carbonate	5 TEASPOONS GYPSUM,
	1/4 TEASPOON TABLE SALT
Highly sulfate	UP TO 3 TEASPOONS OF GYPSUM
Highly carbonate	UP TO 3 TEASPOONS OF GYPSUM, ACIDIFY TO 7.0

3 LBS (1.4 KG) PALE MALT
1-3/4 LBS (.7 KG) 80°L CRYSTAL
1 LB (.45 KG) ROASTED BARLEY
1/2 LB (.23 KG) BLACK PATENT MALT
1 LB (.45 KG) CHOCOLATE MALT

Crush the malt. Mash-in to 152°F (67°C) with 2 gallons (7.6 L) of liquor at 167°F (75°C). Cover and hold. After 1 hour begin to runoff sweet wort to the kettle. Heat sparge liquor to 172°C (78°C). Sparge the mash with 2 gallons (7.6 L) liquor. Add the remaining liquor to the kettle to bring the total volume to 5-3/4 gallons (22 L)

Add:
6.6 LBS (3 KG) LIGHT MALT EXTRACT
1 LB (.45 KG) DARK DME

KETTLE SCHEDULE:
4.5 HBU GALENA as soon as the wort comes to a boil
9 HBU CHINOOK after 45 minutes
5 HBU WILLAMETTE after 60 minutes
4 HBU GOLDINGS and
1/2 TSP (2.5 ML) IRISH MOSS after 1 hour and fifteen minutes
KETTLE KNOCKOUT at 1-1/2 hours.

Transfer through wort chiller into carboy, aerating the wort.
5-1/4 gallons (20 L) of wort should be collected at sg 1086.

Pitch with:
2-3 PKGS of fruity ale yeast (10-21 grams dry yeast) or liquid yeast (Wyeast 1084, Yeast Lab A05, BrewTek CL-240).

Ferment at:
65-72°F (18-22°C). Transfer to secondary after 3-6 days, adding
1 OZ (28 GRAMS) CHINOOK dry hops, condition at 50-60°F (10-16°C) for 1-2 weeks.
Prime with:
2/3 cup (150 ML) of CORN SUGAR and bottle condition for 1 month at below 65°F (18°C).

OLD ALE

OLD BAGGY KNEES

Old ales are a favorite style of people who enjoy big, full flavors. An Old Ale is almost defined by bigness. It should be rich and warming, with fruity, caramel and rum overtones. It's really too bad that more Old Ales aren't readily available in the states, but all the more reason you should brew your own!

OG 1072 TG 1020 ABV 6.8% SRM 21 IBU 35

Heat 6-1/2 gallons (25 L) of water to 168°F (76°C)

WATER SUPPLY:	TREAT WATER
Soft	2 TEASPOONS GYPSUM,
	1/2 TEASPOON TABLE SALT
Moderately sulfate	1/2 TEASPOON OF GYPSUM
Moderately carbonate	1/2 TEASPOON GYPSUM,
	1/2 TEASPOON TABLE SALT
Highly sulfate	OK AS IS
Highly carbonate	ACIDIFY TO BELOW 7.0

3-3/4 LBS (1.7 KG) PALE MALT
1/4 LB (.11 KG) ROASTED BARLEY
1 LB (.45 KG) 55°L CRYSTAL

Crush the malt. Mash-in to 153°F (67°C) with 1-3/4 gallons (6.6 L) of liquor at 168°F (76°C). Cover and hold. After 1 hour begin to runoff sweet wort to the kettle. Heat sparge liquor to 172°C (78°C). Sparge the mash with 1-3/4 gallons (6.6 L) liquor. Add the remaining liquor to the kettle to bring the total volume to 5-3/4 gallons (22 L)

Add:
1-1/2 LBS (.68 KG) DARK BROWN SUGAR
3.3 LBS (1.5 KG) LIGHT MALT EXTRACT
1 LB (.45 KG) DARK DME

KETTLE SCHEDULE:
3.5 HBU NORTHERN BREWER as soon as the wort comes to a boil
4 HBU FUGGLES after 30 minutes
4 HBU FUGGLES after 60 minutes
1/2 TSP (2.5 ML) IRISH MOSS after 1 hour and fifteen minutes
KETTLE KNOCKOUT at 1-1/2 hours.

Transfer through wort chiller into carboy, aerating the wort.
5-1/4 gallons (20 L) of wort should be collected at sg 1072.

Pitch with:
2 PKGS of neutral ale yeast (10-14 grams dry yeast) or liquid yeast (Wyeast 1028,1084 or 1056, Yeast Lab A07 , BrewTek CL-10 or CL-400).

Ferment at:
68-72°F (20-22°C). Transfer to secondary after 4-7 days, condition at 50-60°F (10-15°C) for 3-6 weeks.

Prime with:
1/2 cup (115 ML) MOLASSES and bottle condition for 1 month at below 65°F (18°C).

REAL MEN WEAR SKIRTS SCOTCH ALE

A strong Scotch ale that deserves to have an extended aging period. Give it at least a season in the cellar. The aging will marry the flavors together to make a beautifully smooth and rich, warming beer. You know a Scotch Ale is really ready for drinking when sherry and "peaty" flavors develop, but that might take a year. A Wee Heavy is a beer to sip and savor, and revel in the complexity of its flavors. Brew one today, but don't even think about drinking it for four months...or a year.

OG 1075 TG 1019 ABV 7.4% SRM 20 IBU 30

Heat 6-3/4 gallons (25.5 L) of water to 169°F (76°C)

WATER SUPPLY:	TREAT WATER
Soft	2 TEASPOONS GYPSUM,
	1/2 TEASPOON TABLE SALT
Moderately sulfate	1/2 TEASPOON OF GYPSUM
Moderately carbonate	1/2 TEASPOON GYPSUM,
	1/2 TEASPOON TABLE SALT
Highly sulfate	OK AS IS
Highly carbonate	ACIDIFY TO BELOW 7.0

2 LBS (.9 KG) PALE MALT
2 LBS (9 KG) 55°L CRYSTAL
1/2 LB (23 KG) CARAPILS
1/8 LB (57 GRAMS) ROASTED BARLEY

Crush the malt. Mash-in to 154°F (68°C) with 1-3/4 gallons (6.6 L) of liquor at 169°F (76°C). Cover and hold. After 1 hour begin to runoff sweet wort to the kettle. Heat sparge liquor to 172°C (78°C). Sparge the mash with 2 gallons (7.6 L) liquor. Add the remaining liquor to the kettle to bring the total volume to 5-3/4 gallons (22 L)

Add:
6.6 LBS (3 KG) LIGHT MALT EXTRACT

KETTLE SCHEDULE:
2.5 HBU FUGGLES as soon as the wort comes to a boil
6 HBU FUGGLES after 45 minutes
1/2 TSP (2.5 ML) IRISH MOSS after 1 hour and fifteen minutes
KETTLE KNOCKOUT at 1-1/2 hours.

Transfer through wort chiller into carboy, aerating the wort.
5-1/4 gallons (20 L) of wort should be collected at sg 1075.

Pitch with:
2 PKGS of neutral ale yeast (10-14 grams dry yeast) or liquid yeast (Wyeast 1728, 1087 or 1084, Yeast Lab A05, BrewTek CL-160).

Ferment at:
60-68°F (15-20°C). Transfer to secondary after 5-8 days, condition at 50-60°F (10-15°C) for 3-6 weeks.

Prime with:
1/2-2/3 cup (115-150 ML) of CORN SUGAR and bottle condition for 4-10 months at below 65°F (18°C).

BARLEY WINE

BIG BOOM BARLEY WINE

The beer that started it all, Big Boom is a beer of universe-shaking strength. If you can collect some small, dark-glass bottles, they make an attractive and practical package for this "drink with caution" beer. In any case, leave as little head space as possible. Scotch Ales actually require a little oxidation during bottle-aging to mature, but oxidation will ruin a highly-hopped barley wine.

When is this Barley Wine best to drink? Go ahead and try it out after a season, but this beer won't enter its prime for at least six months. Save at least a bottle (or two), and enjoy an anniversary Big Boom a year from now! If you are very careful about avoiding oxidation when you brew and when you bottle, this beer will keep getting better for two or three years.

OG 1099 TG 1025 ABV 9.7% SRM 18 IBU 70

Heat 7-1/4 gallons (27.5 L) of water to 168°F (75°C)

WATER SUPPLY:	TREAT WATER
Soft	1/2 TEASPOON OF GYPSUM
Moderately sulfate	OK AS IS
Moderately carbonate	ACIDIFY TO BELOW 7.2
Highly sulfate	DILUTE 1:1
Highly carbonate	BOIL OR DILUTE 1:1, ACIDIFY TO BELOW 7.2

4-3/4 LBS (2.34 KG) PALE MALT
2-1/2 LBS (1.1 KG) 55°L CRYSTAL

Crush the malt. Mash-in to 153°F (67°C) with 2-1/4 gallons (8.5 L) of liquor at 168°F (75°C). Cover and hold. After 1 hour begin to runoff sweet wort to the kettle. Heat sparge liquor to 172°C (78°C). Sparge the mash with 2-1/2 gallons (9.5 L) liquor. Add the remaining liquor to the kettle to bring the total volume to 6 gallons (23 L)

Add:
2 LBS (.9 KG) CORN SUGAR, 6.6 LBS (3 KG) LIGHT MALT EXTRACT

KETTLE SCHEDULE:
3 HBU EROICA as soon as the wort comes to a boil
15 IBU EROICA after 45 minutes
10 IBU FUGGLES after 60 minutes
7.5 IBU GOLDNGS and
1/2 TSP (2.5 ML) IRISH MOSS after 1 hour and fifteen minutes
KETTLE KNOCKOUT at 1-1/2 hours.

Transfer through wort chiller into carboy, aerating the wort.
5-1/4 gallons (20 L) of wort should be collected at sg 1099.

Pitch with:
3 PKGS of fruity ale yeast (15-25 grams dry yeast) or liquid yeast (Wyeast 1728 or 1056, Yeast Lab A02, BrewTek CL-10 or CL-170).

Ferment at:
66-72°F (19-22°C) Transfer to secondary after 4-7 days, and add
2 OZ (57 GRAMS) WILLAMETTE dry hops, condition at 60-65°F (16-18°C) for 3-6 weeks.

Prime with:
1/2 cup (115 ML) of CORN SUGAR and bottle condition for 4-8 months at below 65°F (18°C).

FLANDERS BROWN ALE

OLD BRUIN BROWN

Flanders Browns have a unique sweet/sour complexity. The secret to making a true-to-style Flanders Brown is in the yeast. A good Belgian ale strain is needed to impart the characteristic sourness and spiciness. Flanders Brown Ales are great food beers. Their maltiness, acidity and aging-compounds complement even very rich foods.

OG 1056 TG 1014 ABV 5.5% SRM 16 IBU 20

Heat 6-1/2 gallons (25 L) of water to 165°F (74°C)

WATER SUPPLY:	TREAT WATER
Soft	OK AS IS
Moderately sulfate	OK AS IS
Moderately carbonate	OK AS IS
Highly sulfate	DILUTE 1:1 AND ACIDIFY TO BELOW 7.2
Highly carbonate	DILUTE 1:1, OR BOIL AND ACIDIFY TO BELOW 7.2

2-3/4 LBS (1.21 KG) PALE MALT
1 LB (.45 KG) MUNICH MALT
1 LB (.45 KG) WHEAT MALT
1/2 LB (.23 KG) 80°L CRYSTAL
1/8 LB (57 GRAMS) CHOCOLATE MALT

Crush the malt. Mash-in to 150°F (65°C) with 1-3/4 gallons (6.6 L) of liquor at 165°F (74°C). Cover and hold. After 1 hour begin to runoff sweet wort to the kettle. Heat sparge liquor to 172°F (78°C). Sparge the mash with 1-3/4 gallons (6.6 L) liquor. Add the remaining liquor to the kettle to bring the total volume to 5-3/4 gallons (22 L)

Add:
1/2 LB (.23 KG) DARK BROWN SUGAR
3.3 LBS (1.5 KG) LIGHT MALT EXTRACT

KETTLE SCHEDULE:
1.5 HBU HALLERTAU as soon as the wort comes to a boil
1 HBU SPALT after 45 minutes
4.5 HBU STYRIAN GOLDINGS after 60 minutes, and
1/2 TSP (2.5 ML) IRISH MOSS after 1 hour and fifteen minutes
KETTLE KNOCKOUT at 1-1/2 hours.

Transfer through wort chiller into carboy, aerating the wort.
5-1/4 gallons (20 L) of wort should be collected at sg 1056.

Pitch with:
2 PKGS of fruity ale yeast (10-14 grams dry yeast) or liquid yeast (Wyeast 1007 or 1056, Yeast Lab A07 or A08, BrewTek CL-320).

Ferment at:
65-72°F (18-22°C). Transfer to secondary after 5-7 days, condition at 50-60°F (10-15°C) for 4-8 weeks.

Prime with:
3/4-1 cup (170-230 ML) of CORN SUGAR and bottle condition for 1 month at below 65°F (18°C).

BELGIUM DUBBEL

ABBOT'S HABIT

This is a Belgian Trappist-style ale, one of the more complex types of beer in the world. Much of this complexity is from the interplay of the estery strains of yeasts that are used in fermentation with their big maltiness and the flavors imparted by the addition of candi sugar. You can homebrew Belgian Trappist-style ales, but again, you need to use an appropriate yeast strain and sugar or honey to even come close to the flavors of the originals.

OG 1060 TG 1015 ABV 5.9% SRM 14 IBU 20

Heat 6-3/4 gallons (25.5 L) of water to 165°F (74°C)

WATER SUPPLY:	TREAT WATER
Soft	OK AS IS
Moderately sulfate	OK AS IS
Moderately carbonate	ACIDIFY TO BELOW 7.2
Highly sulfate	DILUTE 1:1 AND ACIDIFY TO BELOW 7.2
Highly carbonate	DILUTE 1:1 OR BOIL AND ACIDIFY TO BELOW 7.2

4 LBS (1.8 KG) PALE MALT
1 LB (.45 KG) MUNICH MALT
1/2 LB (.23 KG) 80° CRYSTAL MALT

Crush the malt. Mash-in to 150°F (65°C) with 1-3/4 gallons (6.6 L) of liquor at 165°F (74°C). Cover and hold. After 1 hour begin to runoff sweet wort to the kettle. Heat sparge liquor to 172°C (78°C). Sparge the mash with 2 gallons (7.6 L) liquor. Add the remaining liquor to the kettle to bring the total volume to 5-3/4 gallons (22 L)

Add:
1 LB (.45 KG) HONEY
3.3 LBS (1.5 KG) LIGHT MALT EXTRACT

KETTLE SCHEDULE:
1.5 HBU GOLDINGS as soon as the wort comes to a boil
3.5 HBU GOLDINGS after 30 minutes
1/2 TSP (2.5 ML) IRISH MOSS after 1 hour and fifteen minutes
KETTLE KNOCKOUT at 1-1/2 hours.

Transfer through wort chiller into carboy, aerating the wort.
5-1/4 gallons (20 L) of wort should be collected at sg 1060.

Pitch with:
2 PKGS of fruity ale yeast (10-14 grams dry yeast) or liquid yeast (Wyeast 1214, Yeast Lab A08, BrewTek CL-300 or CL-340).

Ferment at:
65-68°F (18-20°C). Transfer to secondary after 5-8 days, condition at 55-60°F (13-16°C) for 3-6 weeks.

Prime with:
3/4-1 cup (170-230 ML) of CORN SUGAR and bottle condition for 1 month at below 65°F (18°C).

BELGIUM TRIPEL

TIPPLE-NIPPLE TRIPEL

A Tripel is brewed very much like a Belgium Double, but can be very different in appearance and flavor. Tripels have a higher starting gravity, and are usually of a far lighter color. Sheer alcohol strength contributes much of the flavor, along with esters produced by the yeasts. This is also a style of beer that is enhanced by aging, which allows oxidation to form raisin and sherry-like flavors that really round out the flavor of the beer.

OG 1090 TG 1020 ABV 9.2% SRM 5.5 IBU 22

Heat 6-3/4 gallons (25.5 L) of water to 165°F (74°C)

WATER SUPPLY:	TREAT WATER
Soft	OK AS IS
Moderately sulfate	OK AS IS
Moderately carbonate	ACIDIFY TO BELOW 7.0
Highly sulfate	DILUTE 1:1 AND ACIDIFY TO BELOW 7.0
Highly carbonate	DILUTE 1:1 OR BOIL AND ACIDIFY

5 LBS (2.3 KG) PILSNER MALT
1/2 LB (.23 KG) CARAPILS

Crush the malt. Mash-in to 150°F (65°C) with 1-3/4 gallons (6.6 L) of liquor at 165°F (74°C). Cover and hold. After 1 hour begin to runoff sweet wort to the kettle. Heat sparge liquor to 172°C (78°C). Sparge the mash with 1-3/4 gallons (6.6 L) liquor. Add the remaining liquor to the kettle to bring the total volume to 5-3/4 gallons (22 L)

Add:
1 LB (.45 KG) CORN SUGAR
1 LB (.45 KG) LIGHT HONEY
6.6 LBS (3 KG) EXTRA LIGHT MALT EXTRACT or 6 LBS (2.7 KG) EXTRA LIGHT DME

KETTLE SCHEDULE:
1.5 HBU PERLE as soon as the wort comes to a boil
4 HBU HALLERTAU after 30 minutes
1/2 TSP (2.5 ML) IRISH MOSS after 1 hour and fifteen minutes
KETTLE KNOCKOUT at 1-1/2 hours.

Transfer through wort chiller into carboy, aerating the wort.
5-1/4 gallons (20 L) of wort should be collected at sg 1090.

Pitch with:
2 PKGS of fruity ale yeast (10-14 grams dry yeast) or liquid yeast (Wyeast 1214, Yeast Lab A08, BrewTek CL-300 or CL-340).

Ferment at:
65-68°F (18-20°C). Transfer to secondary after 5-8 days, condition at 55-60°F (13-16°C) for 3-6 weeks.

Prime with:
3/4-1 cup (170-230 ML) of CORN SUGAR and bottle condition for 1 month at below 65°F (18°C).

WIT

INFINITE WIT

Wit beers are orangy, spicy, refreshing beers that are very drinkable. The spices that are used largely determine the aromatics and finish, but the use of an appropriate yeast strain is equally important. The unmalted wheat and the oats give this style not only its characteristic cloudiness, but contribute to the lofty head that is typical of well-brewed white beer. Just calling a pale beer a Wit doesn't make it one; you need to use the ingredients that produce the characteristics of the style.

OG 1053 TG 1013 ABV 5.3% SRM 2.8 IBU 18

Heat 6-3/4 gallons (25.5 L) of water to 165°F (74 C)

WATER SUPPLY:	TREAT WATER
Soft	OK AS IS
Moderately sulfate	OK AS IS
Moderately carbonate	ACIDIFY TO BELOW 7.0
Highly sulfate	DILUTE 1:1 AND ACIDIFY TO BELOW 7.0
Highly carbonate	DILUTE 1:1 OR BOIL AND ACIDIFY

3-3/4 LBS (1.7 KG) PILSNER MALT
1 LB (.45 KG) FLAKED WHEAT
1/2 LB (.23 KG) FLAKED OATS (INSTANT TYPE)

Crush the malt. Mash-in to 150°F (65°C) with 1-3/4 gallons (6.6 L) of liquor at 165°F (74°C). Cover and hold. After 1 hour begin to runoff sweet wort to the kettle. Heat sparge liquor to 172°F (78°C). Sparge the mash with 2 gallons (7.6 L) liquor. Add the remaining liquor to the kettle to bring the total volume to 5-3/4 gallons (22 L)

Add:
3.3 LBS (1.5 KG) WHEAT MALT EXTRACT

KETTLE SCHEDULE:
1.5 HBU SAAZ as soon as the wort comes to a boil
2.5 HBU HALLERTAU after 45 minutes
1.5 HBU SAAZ after 15 minutes
1/2 TSP (2.5 ML) IRISH MOSS after 1 hour and fifteen minutes
1-1/2 OZ (42 GRAMS) DRIED ORANGE PEEL add at the end of the boil
1/2 OZ (14 GRAMS) CORIANDER SEED add at the end of the boil
1/4 OZ (7 GRAMS) GROUND CARDAMOM add at the end of the boil
KETTLE KNOCKOUT at 1-1/2 hours.

Transfer through wort chiller into carboy, aerating the wort.
5-1/4 gallons (20 L) of wort should be collected at sg 1053.

Pitch with:
2 PKGS of neutral ale yeast (10-14 grams dry yeast) or liquid yeast (YeastLab W52, Wyeast 3944, BrewTek CL-900).

Ferment at:
60-68°F (15-20°C). Transfer to secondary after 4-7 days, condition at 50-60°F (10-15°C) for 2-3 weeks.

Prime with:
1 cup (.23 L) of CORN SUGAR and bottle condition for 1 month at below 65°F (18°C).

CALIFORNIA COMMON BEER

CALIFORNIA STEAM'N

A hybrid ale-lager, California Common beers were first brewed when West-coast breweries pitched lager yeasts, but were unable to control fermentation temperatures. The beers were fruity with the esters formed at the warmer temperatures. The style is also generously hopped, with the resulting beer sharing a lot of similarity with British ESBs.

For homebrewers without recourse to refrigeration for their fermenting lagers, California common beer offers a very reasonable alternative. Northern Brewer hops have become almost *de rigeur* for brewing this style, although substitution of Galena or Chinook hops will give good results.

OG 1046 TG 1011 ABV 4.6% SRM 12 IBU 40

Heat 6-1/2 gallons (25 L) of water to 165°F (74°C)

WATER SUPPLY:	TREAT WATER
Soft	OK AS IS
Moderately sulfate	OK AS IS
Moderately carbonate	ACIDIFY TO BELOW pH 7.2
Highly sulfate	DILUTE 1:1
Highly carbonate	BOIL AND ACIDIFY TO BELOW pH 7.2

3-1/2 LBS (1.6 KG) PALE MALT
3/4 LB (.34 KG) 55°L CRYSTAL

Crush the malt. Mash-in to 150°F (65°C) with 1-1/2 gallons (5.7 L) of liquor at 165°F (74°C). Cover and hold. After 1 hour begin to runoff sweet wort to the kettle. Heat sparge liquor to 172°F (78°C). Sparge the mash with 1-1/2 gallons (5.7 L) liquor. Add the remaining liquor to the kettle to bring the total volume to 5-3/4 gallons (22 L)

Add:
3.3 LBS (1.5 KG) LIGHT MALT EXTRACT

KETTLE SCHEDULE :
2.5 HBU NORTHERN BREWER as soon as the wort comes to a boil
6.5 HBU NORTHERN BREWER after 60 minutes, and
1/2 TSP (2.5 ML) IRISH MOSS after 1 hour and fifteen minutes
KETTLE KNOCKOUT at 1-1/2 hours.

Transfer through wort chiller into carboy, aerating the wort.
5-1/4 gallons (20 L) of wort should be collected at sg 1046.

Pitch with:
2 PKGS of neutral ale yeast (10-14 grams dry yeast) or liquid yeast (Wyeast 2112, Yeast Lab A02 or L35, BrewTek CL-10).

Ferment at:
60-70°F (16-21°C) Transfer to secondary after 4-7 days, adding
1/2 OZ (14 GRAMS) NORTHERN BREWER dry hops,
condition at 40-60°F (4-16°C) for 2-3 weeks.

Prime with:
3/4-1 cup (170-230 ML) of CORN SUGAR and bottle condition for 1 month at below 65°F (18°C).

WEIZEN

OLDER AND WEIZER

German-style wheat beers have a thirst-quenching quality about them that is just about unmatched. The subtle sweetness from the wheat malt combined with underlying acidity, the clean phenolic flavor of clove and banana esters and high levels of carbonation produce a cleansing and remarkably refreshing flavor.

Our Older and Weizer is best drunk when young and turbulent. Don't plan on cellaring this beer; give it enough time in the bottle to completely carbonate, and then get it out of the cellar and into the hot summer sunshine.

OG 1050 TG 1012 ABV 5% SRM 3.5 IBU 12

Heat 6-1/2 gallons (25 L) of water to 167°F (75°C)

(adjust to below pH 7.0 before brewing)

WATER SUPPLY:	TREAT WATER
Soft	1 TEASPOON GYPSUM,
	1 TEASPOON TABLE SALT
Moderately sulfate	1/2 TEASPOON GYPSUM,
	1TEASPOON TABLE SALT
Moderately carbonate	1 TEASPOON GYPSUM,
	1/2 TEASPOON TABLE SALT
Highly sulfate	DILUTE 1:1, 1/2 TEASPOON TABLE SALT
Highly carbonate	BOIL, ADD 1/2 TEASPOON TABLE SALT

2-3/4 LBS (1.2 KG) PALE MALT
2 LBS (.9 KG) WHEAT MALT

Crush the malt. Mash-in to 152°F (67°C) with 1-1/2 gallons (5.7 L) of liquor at 167°F (75°C). Cover and hold. After 1 hour begin to runoff sweet wort to the kettle. Heat sparge liquor to 172°C (78°C). Sparge the mash with 1-3/4 gallons (6.6 L) liquor. Add the remaining liquor to the kettle to bring the total volume to 5-3/4 gallons (22 L)

Add:
3.3 LBS (1.5 KG) WHEAT MALT EXTRACT

KETTLE SCHEDULE:
1.25 HBU HALLERTAU as soon as the wort comes to a boil,
1.5 HBU HALLERTAU after 45 minutes, and
1/2 TSP (2.5 ML) IRISH MOSS after 1 hour and fifteen minutes
KETTLE KNOCKOUT at 1-1/2 hours.

Transfer through wort chiller into carboy, aerating the wort.
5-1/4 gallons (20 L) of wort should be collected at sg 1050.

Pitch with:
2 PKGS of neutral ale yeast (10-14 grams dry yeast) or liquid yeast (Wyeast 3056 or 3068, Yeast Lab W51, BrewTek CL-920, or CL-930).

Ferment at:
65-72°F (18-22°C). Transfer to secondary after 4-7 days, condition at 35-55°F (2-13°C) for 2-3 weeks.

Prime with:
3/4-1 cup (170-230 ML) of CORN SUGAR and bottle condition for 1 month at below 65°F (18°C).

DUNKELWEIZEN

SLAMDUNKEL WEIZEN

This is a more flavorful, fuller-bodied wheat beer that has a depth of flavor gained from the addition of crystal and chocolate malts. Dunkel Weizens are everything that a Wheat beer should be, and more! They are enjoying increasing popularity as brewpub winter beers, although they make a nice summer refreshment as well. If you don't care for the phenolics of Bavarian Weizens, brew this recipe with a "neutral" ale strain, or even as a "steam-weiss" with a high-temp lager yeast. The flavor contributions of the wheat and dark malts will make an interesting brew even without the true-to-style clove flavor.

OG 1051 TG 1013 ABV 5% SRM 17 IBU 15

Heat 6-1/2 gallons (25 L) of water to 167°F (75°C)

WATER SUPPLY:	TREAT WATER
Soft	1 TEASPOON GYPSUM,
	1/2 TEASPOON TABLE SALT
Moderately sulfate	1/2 TEASPOON TABLE SALT
Moderately carbonate	1/2 TEASPOON GYPSUM,
	1/2 TEASPOONS TABLE SALT
Highly sulfate	DILUTE 1:1, ADJUST ACIDITY TO pH 7.2
Highly carbonate	BOIL, ADJUST ACIDITY TO pH 7.2 OR BELOW

2-1/2 LBS (1.1 KG) PALE MALT
2 LBS (.9 KG) WHEAT MALT
1/4 LB (.11 KG) 80°L CRYSTAL
1 OZ (28 GRAMS) BLACK MALT
1/8 LB (57 GRAMS) CHOCOLATE MALT

Crush the malt. Mash-in to 152°F (67°C) with 1-3/4 gallons (6.6 L) of liquor at 167°F (75°C). Cover and hold. After 1 hour begin to runoff sweet wort to the kettle. Heat sparge liquor to 172°C (78°C). Sparge the mash with 1-3/4 gallons (6.6 L) liquor. Add the remaining liquor to the kettle to bring the total volume to 5-3/4 gallons (22 L).

Add:
3.3 LBS (1.5 KG) WHEAT MALT EXTRACT

KETTLE SCHEDULE:
1.25 HBU HALLERTAU as soon as the wort comes to a boil,
2.25 HBU HALLERTAU after 45 minutes, and
1/2 TSP (2.5 ML) IRISH MOSS after 1 hour and fifteen minutes
KETTLE KNOCKOUT at 1-1/2 hours.

Transfer through wort chiller into carboy, aerating the wort.
5-1/4 gallons (20 L) of wort should be collected at sg 1051.

Pitch with:
2 PKGS of neutral ale yeast (10-14 grams dry yeast) or liquid yeast (Wyeast 3056 or 3068, Yeast Lab W51, BrewTek CL-920).

Ferment at:
65-72°F (18-22°C). Transfer to secondary after 4-7 days, condition at 35-55°F (2-13°C) for 2-3 weeks.

Prime with:
3/4-1 cup (170-230 ML) of CORN SUGAR and bottle condition for 1 month at below 65°F (18°C).

DUSSELDORF ALT

BRUNHILDA BRAU

An ale that is still popular in the land of lagers. No, not Australia, Germany! "Alt" means old, and refers to the beers that were popular before lager brewing changed the face of brewing in the fatherland.

Alts have a unique character of their own that sets them apart from the ales of Great Britain. The style is defined by a malty palate with a strong, even intense, bitter hop finish, and a restrained fruitiness, from cold aging, that differentiates alts from the more estery ales of England and the maltier ales of Scotland.

OG 1047 TG 1012 ABV 4.6% SRM 16 IBU 30

Heat 6-1/2 gallons (25 L) of water to 165°F (74°C)

WATER SUPPLY:	TREAT WATER
Soft	1-1/2 TEASPOONS GYPSUM, 1/2 TEASPOON TABLE SALT
Moderately sulfate	1/2 TEASPOON GYPSUM, 1/2 TEASPOON TABLE SALT
Moderately carbonate	1/2 TEASPOON GYPSUM, 1/2 TEASPOON TABLE SALT
Highly sulfate	ACIDIFY TO BELOW pH 7.2
Highly carbonate	BOIL AND ACIDIFY TO BELOW pH 7.2

2-3/4 LBS (1.2 KG) PALE MALT
1 LB (.45 KG) MUNICH MALT
1/4 LB (.11 KG) WHEAT MALT
1/4 LB (.11 KG) 80°L CRYSTAL
1/8 LB (57 GRAMS) ROASTED BARLEY

Crush the malt. Mash-in to 150°F (65°C) with 1-1/2 gallons (5.7 L) of liquor at 165°F (74°C). Cover and hold. After 1 hour begin to runoff sweet wort to the kettle. Heat sparge liquor to 172°F (78°C). Sparge the mash with 1-1/2 gallons (5.7 L) liquor. Add the remaining liquor to the kettle to bring the total volume to 5-2/3 gallons (21.5 L)

Add:
3.3 LBS (1.5 KG) LIGHT MALT EXTRACT

KETTLE SCHEDULE:
1.25 HBU SPALT as soon as the wort comes to a boil,
5 HBU SPALT after 45 minutes,
3.5 HBU SPALT and
1/2 TSP (2.5 ML) IRISH MOSS after 1 hour and fifteen minutes,
KETTLE KNOCKOUT at 1-1/2 hours.

Transfer through wort chiller into carboy, aerating the wort.
5-1/4 gallons (20 L) of wort should be collected at sg 1047.

Pitch with:
2 PKGS of neutral ale yeast (10-14 grams dry yeast) or liquid yeast (Wyeast 1338,1565 or 1007, Yeast Lab A06, BrewTek CL-450 or CL-400).

Ferment at:
60-68°F (16-20°C). Transfer to secondary after 4-8 days, condition at 35-55°F (2-13°C) for 3-6 weeks.

Prime with:
3/4-7/8 cup (170-200 ML) of CORN SUGAR and bottle condition for 2 month at below 60°F (16°C).

KÖLSCH

HELLESMALTZ HOFBRAU

Kölsch beers are very light-colored and softly-flavored, with a slightly citrusy, somewhat vinous, fruity palate. A Kölsch is a nice alternative to fizzwater when you want a beer with character that will quench your thirst without being full-bodied and filling.

OG 1045   TG 1011   ABV 4.5%   SRM 4   IBU 22

Heat 6-1/4 gallons (24 L) of water to 165°F (74°C)

WATER SUPPLY:	TREAT WATER:
Soft	ACIDIFY TO BELOW pH 7.0
Moderately sulfate	ACIDIFY TO BELOW pH 7.0
Moderately carbonate	BOIL, ACIDIFY TO BELOW pH 7.0
Highly sulfate	DILUTE AT LEAST 1:1, AND ACIDIFY TO BELOW pH 7.0
Highly carbonate	BOIL, DILUTE 1:1, ACIDIFY TO BELOW pH 7.0

3-3/4 LBS (1.7 KG) PALE MALT
1/4 LB (.11 KG) CARAPILS

Crush the malt. Mash-in to 150°F (65°C) with 1-1/4 gallons (4.7 L) of liquor at 165°F (74°C). Cover and hold. After 1 hour begin to runoff sweet wort to the kettle. Heat sparge liquor to 172°F (78°C). Sparge the mash with 1-1/2 gallons (5.7 L) liquor. Add the remaining liquor to the kettle to bring the total volume to 5-2/3 gallons (21.5 L)

Add:
3.3 LBS (1.5 KG) WHEAT MALT EXTRACT

KETTLE SCHEDULE:
1.5 HBU SAAZ as soon as the wort comes to a boil,
4 HBU SAAZ after 45 minutes, and
1/2 TSP (2.5 ML) IRISH MOSS after 1 hour and fifteen minutes,
KETTLE KNOCKOUT at 1-1/2 hours.

Transfer through wort chiller into carboy, aerating the wort.
5-1/4 gallons (20 L) of wort should be collected at sg 1045.

Pitch with:
2 PKGS of neutral ale yeast (10-14 grams dry yeast) or liquid yeast (Wyeast 1338,1565 or 1007, Yeast Lab A06, BrewTek CL-450 or CL-400).

Ferment at:
60-68°F (16-20°C). Transfer to secondary after 4-8 days, condition at 35-55°F (2-13°C) for 3-6 weeks.

Prime with:
3/4-7/8 cup (170-200 ML) of CORN SUGAR and bottle condition for 2 month at below 60°F (16°C).

FRUIT BEER

NECTARINE OF THE GODS

You really ought to brew this beer with a mind to giving it as a gift to friends, maybe for some special occasion. The use of wheat malt extract in this recipe allows the wonderful flavor of the nectarines to come through gracefully, sweetened by the residual sugars from the crystal and caramel malts.

OG 1046 TG 1012 ABV 4.5% SRM 7 IBU 15

Heat 5-1/2 gallons (21 L) of water to 165°F (74°C)

WATER SUPPLY:	TREAT WATER
Soft	1-1/2 TEASPOONS OF GYPSUM, ACIDIFY TO pH 7.0
Moderately sulfate	ACIDIFY TO BELOW pH 7.0
Moderately carbonate	1/2 TEASPOON OF GYPSUM, ACIDIFY TO pH 7.0
Highly sulfate	ACIDIFY TO BELOW pH 7.0
Highly carbonate	BOIL, ACIDIFY TO BELOW pH 7.0

2 LBS (.9 KG) PALE MALT
1/4 LB (.11 KG) 35°L CRYSTAL
1/4 LB (.11 KG) CARAPILS

Crush the malt. Mash-in to 155°F (68°C) with 3 quarts (2.8 L) of liquor at 165°F (74°C). Cover and hold. After 1 hour begin to runoff sweet wort to the kettle. Heat sparge liquor to 172°F (78°C). Sparge the mash with 1 gallon (3.8 L) liquor. Add the remaining liquor to the kettle to bring the total volume to 4-3/4 gallons (18 L)

Add:
3.3 LBS (1.5 KG) WHEAT MALT EXTRACT

KETTLE SCHEDULE:
1.5 HBU CASCADE as soon as the wort comes to a boil,
2 HBU CASCADE after 45 minutes
1/2 TSP (2.5 ML) IRISH MOSS after 1 hour and fifteen minutes
KETTLE KNOCKOUT at 1-1/2 hours.

Transfer through wort chiller into carboy, aerating the wort.
4-3/4 gallons (18 L) should be collected.

Pitch with:
2 PKGS of neutral ale yeast (10-14 grams dry yeast) or liquid yeast (Wyeast 1007 or 2565, Yeast Lab A07, BrewTek CL-10 or CL-400).

Ferment at:
60-70°F (16-21°C). Transfer to secondary after 4-7 days, then

add:
5 LBS (2.3 KG) NECTARINES (pitted and crushed)
allow the additional sugars in the nectarines to ferment out (slow to no activity in the fermenter) than transfer to an another fermenter to condition at 40-50°F (4-10°C) for 3-5 weeks.

Prime with:
3/4-1 cup (170-230 ML) of CORN SUGAR and 1 tblsp ACID BLEND. Bottle condition for 1 month at below 65°F (18°C).

HERB BEER

CERVEZA CON CHILE

Chiles in a beer?. Yes, this is a great combination of smoky heat, with the dark-but-not-overpowering sweetness of dark crystal and black malts. A beer to have with friends who enjoy both rich dark beers and hot food.

If you've never drunk a chile beer, prepare yourself to have more than one. After the hot sensation of the first taste you'll probably find yourself instinctively taking another gulp, in a vain attempt to cool things down. By the end of the bottle, you've learned to like it. By the end of the batch, you'll be brewing another!

OG 1044 TG 1011 ABV 4.3% SRM 18 IBU 15

Heat 6-1/4 gallons (24 L) of water to 165°F (74°C)

WATER SUPPLY:	TREAT WATER
Soft	1-1/2 TEASPOONS OF GYPSUM, ACIDIFY TO pH 7.0
Moderately sulfate	ACIDIFY TO BELOW pH 7.0
Moderately carbonate	1/2 TEASPOON OF GYPSUM, ACIDIFY TO pH 7.0
Highly sulfate	ACIDIFY TO BELOW pH 7.0
Highly carbonate	BOIL, ACIDIFY TO BELOW pH 7.0

2-1/2 LBS (1.1 KG) PALE MALT
1 LB (.45 KG) 80°L CRYSTAL
1/4 LB (.11 KG) WHEAT MALT
2 OZ (57 GRAMS) BLACK MALT

Crush the malt. Mash-in to 150°F (65°C) with 1-1/4 gallons (4.7 L) of liquor at 165°F (74°C). Cover and hold. After 1 hour begin to runoff sweet wort to the kettle. Heat sparge liquor to 172°F (78°C). Sparge the mash with 1-1/2 gallons (5.7 L) liquor. Add the remaining liquor to the kettle to bring the total volume to 5-2/3 gallons (21.5 L)

Add:
3.3 LBS (1.5 KG) LIGHT MALT EXTRACT

KETTLE SCHEDULE:
3.75 HBU FUGGLES after 45 minutes
1 OZ (28 GRAMS) CHIPOTLE CHILES after 45 minutes
1/2 TSP (2.5 ML) IRISH MOSS after 1 hour and fifteen minutes
KETTLE KNOCKOUT at 1-1/2 hours.

Transfer through wort chiller into carboy, aerating the wort.
5-1/4 gallons (20 L) of wort should be collected at sg 1044.

Pitch with:
2 PKGS of neutral ale yeast (10-14 grams dry yeast) or liquid yeast (Wyeast 1728 or 1056, Yeast Lab A01, BrewTek CL-10 or CL-120).

Ferment at:
60-70°F (16-21°C). Transfer to secondary after 4-7 days and

add :
1/2 OZ (14 GRAMS) CHIPOTLE CHILES
1/4 OZ (7 GRAMS) BLACK PEPPERCORNS
condition at 40-60°F (4-16°C) for 3-6 weeks.

Prime with:
3/4 cup (170 ML) of CORN SUGAR and bottle condition for 1 month at below 65°F (18°C).

RAUCHBIER

SMOKEHOUSE RAUCH

Brewing smoked beers requires finding the balance between too much and not enough. You may need to try different amounts of beechwood-smoked grains 'til you hit on the taste that is right for you.

If you can't find German Rauch malt, you will need to smoke your own. The length of time and the kind of wood that you smoke the malt over will greatly vary the flavor of the beer. Alder or a combination of fruitwood and hickory chips will closely approximate the flavor of beech. See the recipe for Hokismokes Rauchbier (in Chapter 7) for some tips on smoking malt.

OG 1052 TG 1013 ABV 5.1% SRM 14 IBU 25

Heat 6-3/4 gallons (25.5 L) of water to 167°F (75°C)

WATER SUPPLY:	TREAT WATER
Soft	1-1/2 TEASPOONS OF GYPSUM
Moderately sulfate	1/2 TEASPOON OF GYPSUM
Moderately carbonate	1 TEASPOON OF GYPSUM
Highly sulfate	OK AS IS
Highly carbonate	ACIDIFY TO 7.2

2-3/4 LBS (1.2 KG) PALE MALT
2 LBS (.9 KG) RAUCHMALZ or HOME-SMOKED MUNICH MALT
1/2 LB (.23 KG) 55°L CRYSTAL

Crush the malt. Mash-in to 152°F (67°C) with 1-3/4 gallons (6.6 L) of liquor at 167°F (75°C). Cover and hold. After 1 hour begin to runoff sweet wort to the kettle. Heat sparge liquor to 172°C (78°C). Sparge the mash with 1-3/4 gallons (6.6 L) liquor. Add the remaining liquor to the kettle to bring the total volume to 5-3/4 gallons (22 L)

Add:
3.3 LBS (1.5 KG) AMBER MALT EXTRACT

KETTLE SCHEDULE:
1.5 HBU TETTNANG as soon as the wort comes to a boil,
3.5 HBU TETTNANG after 45 minutes,
3.5 HBU SPALT and
1/2 TSP (2.5 ML) IRISH MOSS after 1 hour and fifteen minutes,
KETTLE KNOCKOUT at 1-1/2 hours.

Transfer through wort chiller into carboy, aerating the wort.
5-1/4 gallons (20 L) of wort should be collected at sg 1052.

Pitch with:
2 PKGS of lager yeast (10-14 grams dry yeast) or liquid yeast (Wyeast 2035 or 2206, Yeast Lab L32 or L34, BrewTek CL-640 or CL-680).

Ferment at:
40-55°F (4-13°C). Transfer to secondary after 7-10 days, condition at 35-50°F (2-10°C) for 4-8 weeks.

Prime with:
3/4 cup (170 ML) of CORN SUGAR and bottle condition for 2 month at below 60°F (16°C).

AMERICAN PREMIUM LAGER

FIZZWASSER LAGER

Make this beer to pique the interest of your American-Lager friends in homebrewing, or just to prove that you can brew a beer just like the big boys, or maybe because you want to brew a beer to be just the beer for when you're having more than one...(hey, wasn't that the jingle for a beer commercial?)

OG 1047 TG 1010 ABV 4.9% SRM 2.5 IBU 20

Heat 6-1/2 gallons (25 L) of water to 137°F (58°C)

WATER SUPPLY:	TREAT WATER
Soft	1-1/2 TEASPOONS OF GYPSUM, ACIDIFY TO pH 7.0
Moderately sulfate	ACIDIFY TO BELOW pH 7.0
Moderately carbonate	ACIDIFY TO BELOW pH 7.0
Highly sulfate	ACIDIFY TO BELOW pH 7.0
Highly carbonate	BOIL, ACIDIFY TO BELOW pH 7.0

3-1/4 LBS (1.5 KG) PALE 6 ROW MALT
1 LB (.45 KG) FLAKED MAIZE

Crush the malt. Mash-in to 122°F (50°C) with 1-1/2 gallons (5.7 L) of liquor at 137°F (58°C). Cover and hold. After 15 minutes raise the temperature to 150°F (65°C). After 1 hour begin to runoff sweet wort to the kettle. Heat sparge liquor to 172°F (78°C). Sparge the mash with 1-1/2 gallons (5.7 L) liquor. Add the remaining liquor to the kettle to bring the total volume to 5-3/4 gallons (22 L)

Add:
3.3 LBS (1.5 KG) EXTRA LIGHT MALT EXTRACT
OR 3 LBS (1.4 KG) EXTRA LIGHT DME

KETTLE SCHEDULE:
1.5 HBU CASCADE as soon as the wort comes to a boil,
3 HBU CASCADE after 45 minutes,
1.5 HBU CASCADE and
1/2 TSP (2.5 ML) IRISH MOSS after 1 hour and fifteen minutes,
KETTLE KNOCKOUT at 1-1/2 hours.

Transfer through wort chiller into carboy, aerating the wort.
5-1/4 gallons (20 L) of wort should be collected at sg 1047.

Pitch with:
2 PKGS of lager yeast(10-14 grams dry yeast) or liquid yeast (Wyeast 2007 or 2042, Yeast Lab L31 or L34, BrewTek CL-620 or CL-660).

Ferment at:
50-60°F (10-16°C). Transfer to secondary after 6-10 days, condition at 35-50°F (2-10°C) for 2-4 weeks.

Prime with:
3/4-1 cup (170-230 ML) of CORN SUGAR and bottle condition for 2 months at below 45°F (7°C).

CREAM ALE/LAGER

CREAM CORN ALE

American Cream ales are a hybrid-style that mix ale and lager brewing techniques and ingredients. Cream Corn Ale has the light, crisp body of an American Pilsner, with a touch of fruitiness from the restrained use of ale yeast. This is a beer to savor while relaxing in the shade when you are supposed to be mowing the yard. Thirst-quenching and just a bit sweet, mild, but with subtle character, a beer to contemplate without putting too much strain on the brain.

OG 1047 TG 1010 ABV 4.9% SRM 2.5 IBU 18

Heat 6-1/4 gallons (24 L) of water to 137°F (58°C)

WATER SUPPLY:	TREAT WATER
Soft	1-1/2 TEASPOONS OF GYPSUM, ACIDIFY TO pH 7.0
Moderately sulfate	ACIDIFY TO BELOW pH 7.0
Moderately carbonate	1/2 TEASPOON OF GYPSUM, ACIDIFY TO pH 7.0
Highly sulfate	ACIDIFY TO BELOW pH 7.0
Highly carbonate	BOIL, ACIDIFY TO BELOW pH 7.0

3-1/4 LBS (1.5 KG) PALE 6 ROW MALT
1/2 LB (.23 KG) FLAKED MAIZE

Crush the malt. Mash-in to 122°F (50°C) with 1-1/4 gallons (4.7 L) of liquor at 137°F (58°C). Cover and hold. After 15 minutes raise the temperature to 150°F (65°C). After 1 hour begin to runoff sweet wort to the kettle. Heat sparge liquor to 172°C (78°C). Sparge the mash with 1-1/4 gallons (4.7 L) liquor. Add the remaining liquor to the kettle to bring the total volume to 5-2/3 gallons (21.5 L)

Add:
1/2 LB (.23 KG) CORN SUGAR
3.3 LBS (1.5 KG) EXTRA LIGHT MALT EXTRACT OR 3 LBS (1.4 KG) EXTRA LIGHT DME

KETTLE SCHEDULE:
1.5 HBU CASCADE as soon as the wort comes to a boil,
2.5 HBU CASCADE after 45 minutes,
1.5 HBU CASCADE and
1/2 TSP (2.5 ML) IRISH MOSS after 1 hour and fifteen minutes,
KETTLE KNOCKOUT at 1-1/2 hours.

Transfer through wort chiller into carboy, aerating the wort.
5-1/4 gallons (20 L) of wort should be collected at sg 1047.

Pitch with:
2 PKGS of neutral ale yeast (10-14 grams dry yeast) or liquid yeast (Wyeast 1007, 1565 or 1056, Yeast Lab A07, BrewTek CL-10 or CL-260).

Ferment at:
60-68°F (16-20°C). Transfer to secondary after 4-7 days, condition at 40-60°F (4-16°C) for 3-6 weeks.

Prime with:
3/4-1 cup (170-230 ML) of CORN SUGAR and bottle condition for 1 month at below 65°F (18°C).

DORTMUNDER/EXPORT

BREWERS' GUILD LAGER

A Dortmunder is the perfect light lager to brew if your water source is "hard". Compared to pilseners, recipes for Dortmund Exports are almost identical, the only real differences being the hardness of the water used to brew them. It's a textbook example of how water mineral-content affects beer flavor.

In general, high levels of gypsum hardness give a cleaner, sharper bitterness to well-hopped beers, while even small amounts of table salt give a salty, minerally character. The water treatment for Dortmund brewing liquor gives a brew that is faintly salty and robust.

OG 1050   TG 1012   ABV 5%   SRM 6   IBU 29

Heat 6-1/2 gallons (25 L) of water to 137°F (58°C)

WATER SUPPLY:	TREAT WATER
Soft	1-1/2 TEASPOONS GYPSUM,
	1/2 TEASPOON TABLE SALT
Moderately sulfate	1/2 TEASPOON TABLE SALT
Moderately carbonate	1/2 TEASPOON TABLE SALT
Highly sulfate	OK AS IS
Highly carbonate	1/2 TEASPOON TABLE SALT, ACIDIFY TO BELOW 7.0

4-1/4 LBS (1.9 KG) PILSNER MALT
1/2 LB (.23 KG) CARAPILS

Crush the malt. Mash-in to 122°F (50°C) with 1-1/2 gallons (5.7 L) of liquor at 137°F (58°C). Cover and hold. After 15 minutes raise the temperature to 154°F (67°C). After 1 hour begin to runoff sweet wort to the kettle. Heat sparge liquor to 172°F (78°C). Sparge the mash with 1-3/4 gallons (6.6 L) liquor. Add the remaining liquor to the kettle to bring the total volume to 5-3/4 gallons (22 L)

Add:
3.3 LBS (1.5 KG) LIGHT MALT EXTRACT

KETTLE SCHEDULE:
1.25 HBU TETTNANG as soon as the wort comes to a boil,
4 HBU TETTNANG after 45 minutes,
2.5 HBU HALLERTAU after 60 minutes,
1.25 HBU TETTNANG and
1/2 TSP (2.5 ML) IRISH MOSS after 1 hour and fifteen minutes
KETTLE KNOCKOUT at 1-1/2 hours.

Transfer through wort chiller into carboy, aerating the wort.
5-1/4 gallons (20 L) of wort should be collected at sg 1050.

Pitch with:
2 PKGS of lager yeast (10-14 grams dry yeast) or liquid yeast (Wyeast 2308 or 2206, Yeast Lab L32 or L33, BrewTek CL-680).

Ferment at:
40-55°F (4-13°C). Transfer to secondary after 7-12 days, condition at 35-50°F (2-10°C) for 4-8 weeks.

Prime with:
2/3-3/4 cup (150-170 ML) of CORN SUGAR and bottle condition for 2 months at below 60°F (16°C).

MUNICH HELLES

DEUTSCHER MALZ

Helles literally translated means "light", but to a beer lover Helles means malty. Be sure to keep the mash saccharification temperature high, because this style is defined by fullness and sweetness. Munich lagers are malty with a capital "M', with just enough hops to balance the sweetness. A beguiling brew that invites you to have another sip, then another...

OG 1047   TG 1012   ABV 4.6%   SRM 5   IBU 20

Heat 6-1/2 gallons (25 L) of water to 137°F (58°C)

WATER SUPPLY:	TREAT WATER
Soft	1/2 TEASPOON GYPSUM, ACIDIFY TO pH 7.0
Moderately sulfate	ACIDIFY TO BELOW pH 7.0
Moderately carbonate	ACIDIFY TO BELOW pH 7.0
Highly sulfate	DILUTE 1:1, ACIDIFY TO BELOW pH 7.0
Highly carbonate	DILUTE 1:1, ACIDIFY TO BELOW pH 7.0

3-1/2 LBS (1.6 KG) PILSNER MALT
1/4 LB (.11 KG) 35°L CRYSTAL
1/2 LB (.23 KG) CARAPILS

Crush the malt. Mash-in to 122°F (50°C) with 1-1/4 gallons (4.7 L) of liquor at 137°F (58°C). Cover and hold. After 15 minutes raise the temperature to 155°F (67°C). After 1 hour begin to runoff sweet wort to the kettle. Heat sparge liquor to 172°F (78°C). Sparge the mash with 1-3/4 gallons (6.6 L) liquor. Add the remaining liquor to the kettle to bring the total volume to 5-2/3 gallons (21.5 L)

Add:
3.3 LBS (1.5 KG) EXTRA LIGHT MALT EXTRACT

KETTLE SCHEDULE:
1.25 HBU MT HOOD as soon as the wort comes to a boil,
3.75 MT HOOD after 45 minutes, and
1/2 TSP (2.5 ML) IRISH MOSS after 1 hour and fifteen minutes,
KETTLE KNOCKOUT at 1-1/2 hours.

Transfer through wort chiller into carboy, aerating the wort.
5-1/4 gallons (20 L) of wort should be collected at sg 1047.

Pitch with:
2 PKGS of lager yeast (10-14 grams dry yeast) or liquid yeast (Wyeast 2308 or 2206, Yeast Lab L32 or L33, BrewTek CL-680).

Ferment at:
40-55°F (4-13°C) Transfer to secondary after 7-12 days, condition at 35-50°F (2-10°C) for 4-8 weeks.

Prime with:
2/3-3/4 cup (150-170 ML) of CORN SUGAR and bottle condition for 2 months at below 60°F (16°C).

GERMAN PILSENER

GUDENHOPT

Helles are known for their malt character, and German Pilseners are known for their dry, hoppy bitterness. Unrestrained Pilseners are the hop lover's lager; some Pilseners approach the bitterness and hoppiness of India Pale Ales. A great beer to have when you need that hop fix, or if you just prefer a drier, less malty beer.

OG 1045   TG 1011   ABV 4.5%   SRM 2.5   IBU 35

Heat 6-1/4 gallons (24 L) of water to 137°F (58°C)

WATER SUPPLY:	TREAT WATER
Soft	1 TEASPOON OF GYPSUM, ACIDIFY TO BELOW 7.0
Moderately sulfate	ACIDIFY TO BELOW pH 7.0
Moderately carbonate	ACIDIFY TO BELOW pH 7.0
Highly sulfate	DILUTE 1:1 AND ACIDIFY TO BELOW pH 7.0
Highly carbonate	DILUTE 1:1 AND ACIDIFY TO BELOW pH 7.0

4 LBS (1.8 KG) PILSNER MALT

Crush the malt. Mash-in to 122°F (50°C) with 1-1/4 gallons (4.7 L) of liquor at 137°F (58°C). Cover and hold. After 15 minutes raise the temperature to 150°F (65°C). After 1 hour begin to runoff sweet wort to the kettle. Heat sparge liquor to 172°F (78°C). Sparge the mash with 1-1/2 gallons (5.7 L) liquor. Add the remaining liquor to the kettle to bring the total volume to 5-2/3 gallons (21.5 L)

Add:
3.3 LBS (1.5 KG) EXTRA LIGHT MALT EXTRACT OR 3 LBS (1.4 KG) EXTRA LIGHT DME

KETTLE SCHEDULE:
1.25 HBU TETTNANG as soon as the wort comes to a boil,
6.5 HBU PERLE after 45 minutes,
2.5 HBU TETTNANG and
1/2 TSP (2.5 ML) IRISH MOSS after 1 hour and fifteen minutes,
KETTLE KNOCKOUT at 1-1/2 hours.

Transfer through wort chiller into carboy, aerating the wort.
5-1/4 gallons (20 L) of wort should be collected at sg 1045.

Pitch with:
2 PKGS of lager yeast (10-14 grams dry yeast) or liquid yeast (Wyeast 2007 or 2042, Yeast Lab L31 or L34, BrewTek CL-620 or CL-660).

Ferment at:
40-55°F (4-13°C). Transfer to secondary after 7-10 days, condition at 35-50°F (2-10°C) for 4-6 weeks.

Prime with:
3/4 cup (170 ML) of CORN SUGAR and bottle condition for 2 months at below 60°F (16°C).

BOHEMIAN PILSNER

CZECHMATE PILSNER

Czechmate is modeled on the original pilsner, from Plzen, near Bavaria in the Czech Republic. Bohemian Pilseners are generally maltier and more complex than their German counterpart. This recipe is malty with a definite spiciness from the generous use of Saaz hops, the definitive pilsener hop.

OG 1045 TG 1011 ABV 4.5% SRM 3.5 IBU 40

Heat 6-1/4 gallons (24 L) of water to 137°F (58°C)

WATER SUPPLY:	TREAT WATER
Soft	ACIDIFY TO BELOW pH 7.0
Moderately sulfate	ACIDIFY TO BELOW pH 7.0
Moderately carbonate	BOIL AND ACIDIFY TO BELOW pH 7.0
Highly sulfate	DILUTE 1:1
Highly carbonate	ACIDIFY TO BELOW pH 7.0

3-1/4 LBS (1.5 KG) PILSNER MALT
1/4 LB (.11 KG) VIENNA MALT
1/2 LB (.23 KG) CARAPILS

Crush the malt. Mash-in to 122°F (50°C) with 1-1/4 gallons (4.7 L) of liquor at 137°F (58°C). Cover and hold. After 15 minutes raise the temperature to 154°F (67°C). After 1 hour begin to runoff sweet wort to the kettle. Heat sparge liquor to 172°F (78°C). Sparge the mash with 1-1/2 gallons (5.7 L) liquor. Add the remaining liquor to the kettle to bring the total volume to 5-2/3 gallons (21.5 L).

Add:
3.3 LBS (1.5 KG) EXTRA LIGHT MALT EXTRACT

KETTLE SCHEDULE:
2.5 HBU SAAZ as soon as the wort comes to a boil,
5 HBU SAAZ after 45 minutes,
2.5 HBU SAAZ after 60 minutes,
2.5 HBU SAAZ and
1/2 TSP (2.5 ML) IRISH MOSS after 1 hour and fifteen minutes,
KETTLE KNOCKOUT at 1-1/2 hours.

Transfer through wort chiller into carboy, aerating the wort.
5-1/4 gallons (20 L) of wort should be collected at sg 1045.

Pitch with:
2 PKGS of lager yeast (10-14 grams dry yeast) or liquid yeast (Wyeast 2278, Yeast Lab L31, BrewTek CL-600).

Ferment at:
40-55°F (4-13°C). Transfer to secondary after 7-10 days, condition at 35-50°F (2-10°C) for 4-6 weeks.

Prime with:
3/4 cup (170 ML) of CORN SUGAR and bottle condition for 2 months at below 60°F (16°C).

MUNICH DUNKEL

ALT MALT DUNKEL

When you think of lagers, do you usually think of light-colored beers? The dark-brown beers that Munich is famous for are lagers too. In fact, Munich was one of the first brewing centers to embrace lager techniques. The carbonate hardness of the water required the liberal use of acidic dark malts to adjust the pH of the brewing cycle.

Munich Dunkels should be brown, not black, malty and full. Belying their color, the flavor is not really "roasty" in the sense that a stout is roasty; they share more in common with the brown porters of ale breweries, or the brown alts of Bavaria. Keep your hop rates and fermentation temperatures low so that the malts come to the fore in both the aroma and flavor.

OG 1054 TG 1014 ABV 5.3% SRM 17 IBU 20

Heat 6-1/4 gallons (24 L) of water to 137°F (58°C)

WATER SUPPLY:	TREAT WATER
Soft	1/2 TEASPOON OF GYPSUM
Moderately sulfate	OK AS IS
Moderately carbonate	OK AS IS
Highly sulfate	OK AS IS
Highly carbonate	ACIDIFY SPARGE WATER TO 7.2

2-3/4 LBS (1.2 KG) MUNICH MALT
1/2 LB (.23 KG) 55°L CRYSTAL
1/8 LB (57 GRAMS) CHOCOLATE MALT

Crush the malt. Mash-in to 122°F (50°C) with 1-1/4 gallons (4.7 L) of liquor at 137°F (58°C). Cover and hold. After 15 minutes raise the temperature to 150°F (65°C). After 1 hour begin to runoff sweet wort to the kettle. Heat sparge liquor to 172°F (78°C). Sparge the mash with 1-1/4 gallons (4.7 L) liquor. Add the remaining liquor to the kettle to bring the total volume to 5-2/3 gallons (21.5 L)

Add:
3.3 LBS (1.5 KG) AMBER MALT EXTRACT
1-1/2 LBS (.68 KG) AMBER DME

KETTLE SCHEDULE:
1.25 HBU HALLERTAU as soon as the wort comes to a boil,
2.5 HBU HALLERTAU after 45 minutes,
2 HBU HALLERTAU after 60 minutes, and
1/2 TSP (2.5 ML) IRISH MOSS after 1 hour and fifteen minutes,
KETTLE KNOCKOUT at 1-1/2 hours.

Transfer through wort chiller into carboy, aerating the wort.
5-1/4 gallons (20 L) of wort should be collected at sg 1054.

Pitch with:
2 PKGS of lager yeast (10-14 grams dry yeast) or liquid yeast (Wyeast 2308 or 2206, Yeast Lab L32 or L33, or BrewTek CL-680).

Ferment at:
40-55°F (4-13°C). Transfer to secondary after 7-12 days, condition at 35-50°F (2-10°C) for 4-8 weeks.

Prime with:
2/3-3/4 cup (150-170 ML) of CORN SUGAR and bottle condition for 2 months at below 60°F (16°C).

SCHWARZBIER

BLACK KAT LAGER

A dark, crisp lager, in general schwarzbiers are more akin to light-bodied, refined and sophisticated stouts than Munich-style dunkels or porters. For those of you who love Dry Stouts, this is the lager to brew.

Schwarzpils are just one style of schwarzbiers, and Black Kat is a relatively full interpretation. If you want to experiment, try substituting honey or wheat malt for the Munich malt for a drier and crisper variation.

OG 1046   TG 1012   ABV 4.5%   SRM 25   IBU 30

Heat 6-1/4 gallons (24 L) of water to 137°F (58°C)

WATER SUPPLY:	TREAT WATER
Soft	UP TO 1-1/2 TEASPOON OF GYPSUM
Moderately sulfate	OK AS IS
Moderately carbonate	OK AS IS
Highly sulfate	OK AS IS
Highly carbonate	ACIDIFY TO BELOW pH 7.2

3-3/4 LBS (1.7 KG) MUNICH MALT
1/2 LB (.23 KG) BLACK MALT

Crush the malt. Mash-in to 122°F (50°C) with 1-1/4 gallons (4.7 L) of liquor at 137°F (58°C). Cover and hold. After 15 minutes raise the temperature to 150°F (65°C). After 1 hour begin to runoff sweet wort to the kettle. Heat sparge liquor to 172°F (78°C). Sparge the mash with 1-3/4 gallons (6.6 L) liquor. Add the remaining liquor to the kettle to bring the total volume to 5-3/4 gallons (22 L)

Add:
3.3 LBS (1.5 KG) LIGHT MALT EXTRACT

KETTLE SCHEDULE:
1.25 HBU HALLERTAU as soon as the wort comes to a boil,
3.75 HBU HALLERTAU after 45 minutes,
2.5 HBU HALLERTAU after 30 minutes,
2.5 HBU HALLERTAU and
1/2 TSP (2.5 ML) IRISH MOSS after 1 hour and fifteen minutes,
KETTLE KNOCKOUT at 1-1/2 hours.

Transfer through wort chiller into carboy, aerating the wort.
5-1/4 gallons (20 L) of wort should be collected at sg 1046.

Pitch with:
2 PKGS of lager yeast (10-14 grams dry yeast) or liquid yeast (Wyeast 2007 or 2035, Yeast Lab L31, BrewTek CL-620 or CL-660).

Ferment at:
45-55° (4-13°C). Transfer to secondary after 7-10 days, condition at 35-50°F (2-10°C) for 4-8 weeks.

Prime with:
3/4 cup (170 ML) of CORN SUGAR and bottle condition for 2 months at below 60°F (16°C).

VIENNA

WIENERMALZ LAGER

Vienna and Oktoberfest lagers are "cousins" in much the same fashion that German and Czech pilseners are related; Viennas are drier and more hop-accented than Oktoberfests.. The Vienna style is credited to Anton Dreher, one of the innovators of lager brewing. The style was hugely popular in the Victorian era.

The recipe calls for Vienna malt, but Munich malt can be substituted for it without radically changing the finished beer.

OG 1051 TG 1013 ABV 5% SRM 12 IBU 28

Heat 6-1/2 gallons (25 L) of water to 137°F (58°C)

WATER SUPPLY:	TREAT WATER
Soft	1-1/2 TEASPOON OF GYPSUM, ACIDIFY TO pH 7.2
Moderately sulfate	1/2 TEASPOON OF GYPSUM, ACIDIFY TO pH 7.2
Moderately carbonate	1/2 TEASPOON OF GYPSUM, ACIDIFY TO pH 7.2
Highly sulfate	ACIDIFY TO BELOW pH 7.2
Highly carbonate	ACIDIFY TO BELOW pH 7.2

4-3/4 LBS (2.2 KG) VIENNA MALT
1 OZ (28 GRAMS) 80°L CRYSTAL
1/4 LB (.11 KG) 55°L CRYSTAL

Crush the malt. Mash-in to 153-4°F (67°C) with 1-1/2 gallons (5.7 L) of liquor at 168 °F (76°C). After 1 hour begin to runoff sweet wort to the kettle. Heat sparge liquor to 172°F (78°C). Sparge the mash with 1-3/4 gallons (6.6 L) liquor. Add the remaining liquor to the kettle to bring the total volume to 5-3/4 gallons (22 L)

Add:
3.3 LBS (1.5 KG) LIGHT MALT EXTRACT

KETTLE SCHEDULE:
1.25 HBU HALLERTAU as soon as the wort comes to a boil,
2.5 HBU HALLERTAU after 45 minutes,
2.5 HBU HALLERTAU after 60 minutes,
5 HBU HALLERTAU and
1/2 TSP (2.5 ML) IRISH MOSS after 1 hour and fifteen minutes,
KETTLE KNOCKOUT at 1-1/2 hours.

Transfer through wort chiller into carboy, aerating the wort.
5-1/4 gallons (20 L) of wort should be collected at sg 1051.

Pitch with:
2 PKGS of lager yeast (10-14 grams dry yeast) or liquid yeast (Wyeast 2308 or 2206, Yeast Lab L32 or L33, or BrewTek CL-680).

Ferment at:
40-55°F (4-13°C). Transfer to secondary after 7-12 days, condition at 35-50°F (2-10°C) for 4-8 weeks.

Prime with:
2/3-3/4 cup (150-170 ML) of CORN SUGAR and bottle condition for 2 months at below 60°F (16°C).

MÄRZEN/OKTOBERFEST

OCTANE OBERFEST

Visions of beer tents, sausages and fat men playing tubas pop into mind at the mention of Oktoberfest, but it's the Oktoberfest beer that is at the heart of all the oom-pah. Don't wait until October to make a Märzen. This is a great beer to brew and drink year 'round if you have the ability to ferment at cool temperatures, even during the warmer weather of the summer months.

The big maltiness of this robust, sweet style of lager is its claim to fame, and why it is a popular beer at pub breweries year 'round.

OG 1061 TG 1015 ABV 6% SRM 14 IBU 28

Heat 6-3/4 gallons (25.5 L) of water to 137°F (58°C)

WATER SUPPLY:	TREAT WATER
Soft	1 TEASPOON OF GYPSUM, ACIDIFY TO pH 7.2
Moderately sulfate	ACIDIFY TO BELOW pH 7.2
Moderately carbonate	ACIDIFY TO BELOW pH 7.2
Highly sulfate	DILUTE 1:1, ACIDIFY TO BELOW pH 7.2
Highly carbonate	BOIL, ACIDIFY TO BELOW pH 7.2

2-1/4 LBS (1 KG) PILSNER MALT
1/2 LB (.23 KG) CARAPILS
2 LBS (.9 KG) MUNICH MALT
1/2 LB (.23 KG) 55°L CRYSTAL

Crush the malt. Mash-in to 122°F (50°C) with 1-3/4 gallons (6.6 L) of liquor at 137°F (58°C). Cover and hold. After 15 minutes raise the temperature to 154°F (67°C). After 1 hour begin to runoff sweet wort to the kettle. Heat sparge liquor to 172°C (78°C). Sparge the mash with 2 gallons (7.6 L) liquor. Add the remaining liquor to the kettle to bring the total volume to 5-3/4 gallons (22 L)

Add:
3.3 LBS (1.5 KG) AMBER MALT EXTRACT
1 LB (.45 KG) LIGHT DME

KETTLE SCHEDULE:
1.5 HBU TETTNANG as soon as the wort comes to a boil,
3 HBU SPALT after 45 minutes,
2.5 HBU TETTNANG after 60 minutes,
2.5 HBU SPALT and
1/2 TSP (2.5 ML) IRISH MOSS after 1 hour and fifteen minutes,
KETTLE KNOCKOUT at 1-1/2 hours.

Transfer through wort chiller into carboy, aerating the wort.
5-1/4 gallons (20 L) of wort should be collected at sg 1061.

Pitch with:
2 PKGS of lager yeast (10-14 grams dry yeast) or liquid yeast (Wyeast 2308 or 2206, Yeast Lab L32 or L33 BrewTek CL-680).

Ferment at:
40-55°F (4-13°C). Transfer to secondary after 7-12 days, condition at 35-50°F (2-10°C) for 4-8 weeks.

Prime with:
2/3-3/4 cup (150-170 ML) of CORN SUGAR and bottle condition for 2 months at below 60°F (16°C).

TRADITIONAL BOCK

REBOCK

One of the best things to happen to winter is the availability of Bock beers. One of the best things about homebrewing is that you don't have to wait until winter to enjoy a bock. You can brew it anytime. Winterbock, Springbock, even Summerbock. Any time of year is appropriate for Rebock.

OG 1073 TG 1018 ABV 7.2% SRM 21 IBU 25

Heat 6-1/2 gallons (25 L) of water to 137°F (58°C)

WATER SUPPLY:	TREAT WATER
Soft	1-1/2 TEASPOONS OF GYPSUM
Moderately sulfate	1/2 TEASPOON OF GYPSUM
Moderately carbonate	1/2 TEASPOON OF GYPSUM
Highly sulfate	OK AS IS
Highly carbonate	ACIDIFY TO BELOW 7.0

3 LBS (1.4 KG) MUNICH MALT
1-1/2 LBS (.68 KG) 55°L CRYSTAL
1/2 LB (.23 KG) CARAPILS
1/8 LB (57 GRAMS) CHOCOLATE MALT

Crush the malt. Mash-in to 122°F (50°C) with 1-3/4 gallons (6.6 L) of liquor at 137°F (58°C). Cover and hold. After 15 minutes raise the temperature to 151°F (66°C). After 1 hour begin to runoff sweet wort to the kettle. Heat sparge liquor to 172°F (78°C). Sparge the mash with 1-3/4 gallons (6.6 L) liquor. Add the remaining liquor to the kettle to bring the total volume to 5-3/4 gallons (22 L)

Add:
6.6 LBS (3 KG) LIGHT MALT EXTRACT.

KETTLE SCHEDULE:
1.25 HBU HALLERTAU as soon as the wort comes to a boil,
2.5 HBU HALLERTAU after 45 minutes,
3.75 HBU HALLERTAU after 60 minutes, and
1/2 TSP (2.5 ML) IRISH MOSS after 1 hour and fifteen minutes
KETTLE KNOCKOUT at 1-1/2 hours.

Transfer through wort chiller into carboy, aerating the wort.
5-1/4 gallons (20 L) of wort should be collected at sg 1073.

Pitch with:
2 PKGS of lager yeast (10-14 grams dry yeast) or liquid yeast (Wyeast 2308 or 2206, Yeast Lab L32 or L33, BrewTek CL-680).

Ferment at:
40-55°F (4-13°C). Transfer to secondary after 7-12 days, condition at 35-50°F (2-10°C) for 4-8 weeks.

Prime with:
2/3-3/4 cup (150-170 ML) of CORN SUGAR and bottle condition for 2 months at below 60°F (16°C).

HELLESBOCK

BEELZEBUB BOCK

A strong, light-colored lager, a Hellesbock has a deep malt richness that is spiced by the high alcohol content and restrained hopping. Its flavor is a reflection of the season it is brewed for: springtime. Full, rich, and bursting with flavor, Maibock is a celebration of renewal and life.

The devil of the thing for the brewer is to keep everything in balance when the flavors are this big. Don't be deterred by this, just remember, brewing is an art, and the artist needs to be in touch with their medium. If you follow tradition and brew this beer in late winter, you ought to be at your peak form this late in the brewing season. This brew can be the masterwork of your year's output.

OG 1071 TG 1018 ABV 7% SRM 5 IBU 25

Heat 6-1/2 gallons (25 L) of water to 137°F (58°C)

WATER SUPPLY:	TREAT WATER
Soft	1/2 TEASPOON GYPSUM AND ACIDIFY TO pH 7.0
Moderately sulfate	ACIDIFY TO BELOW pH 7.0
Moderately carbonate	ACIDIFY TO BELOW pH 7.0
Highly sulfate	DILUTE 1:1 AND ACIDIFY TO BELOW 7.0
Highly carbonate	BOIL OR DILUTE 1:1 AND ACIDIFY TO BELOW 7.0

4 LBS (1.8 KG) PILSNER MALT
1/2 LBS (.23 KG) CARAPILS

Crush the malt. Mash-in to 122°F (50°C) with 1-1/2 gallons (5.7 L) of liquor at 137°F (58°C). Cover and hold. After 15 minutes raise the temperature to 154°F (68°C). After 1 hour begin to runoff sweet wort to the kettle. Heat sparge liquor to 172°F (78°C). Sparge the mash with 1-1/2 gallons (5.7 L) liquor. Add the remaining liquor to the kettle to bring the total volume to 5-3/4 gallons (22 L)

Add:
6.6 LBS (3 KG) EXTRA LIGHT MALT EXTRACT

KETTLE SCHEDULE:
2 HBU PERLE as soon as the wort comes to a boil,
3 HBU PERLE after 45 minutes,
1.5 HBU SPALT after 60 minutes, and
1/2 TSP (2.5 ML) IRISH MOSS after 1 hour and fifteen minutes,
KETTLE KNOCKOUT at 1-1/2 hours.

Transfer through wort chiller into carboy, aerating the wort.
5-1/4 gallons (20 L) of wort should be collected at sg 1071.

Pitch with:
2 PKGS of lager yeast (10-14 grams dry yeast) or liquid yeast (Wyeast 2308 or 2206, Yeast Lab L32 or L33, or BrewTek CL-680).

Ferment at:
40-55°F (4-13°C). Transfer to secondary after 7-12 days, condition at 35-50°F (2-10°C) for 4-8 weeks.

Prime with:
2/3-3/4 cup (150-170 ML) of CORN SUGAR and bottle condition for 2 months at below 60°F (16°C).

DOPPELBOCK

SEEULATOR

A Doppelbock should have a strong malt character with a noticeable alcoholic warmth and spiciness. Seeulator Doppelbock is no exception. The soothing, warming effect of this beer will gradually lull you into a pleasant state of nirvana. Enjoy it, but don't overdo it, or it will be "see you later".

OG 1082 TG 1021 ABV 8% SRM 20 IBU 20

Heat 6-3/4 gallons (25.5 L) of water to 137°F (58°C)

WATER SUPPLY:	TREAT WATER
Soft	1/2 TEASPOON GYPSUM AND ACIDIFY TO pH 7.2
Moderately sulfate	ACIDIFY TO BELOW pH 7.2
Moderately carbonate	ACIDIFY TO BELOW pH 7.2
Highly sulfate	ACIDIFY TO BELOW pH 7.2
Highly carbonate	ACIDIFY TO BELOW pH 7.2

3-3/4 LBS (1.7 KG) MUNICH MALT
1-1/2 LBS (.68 KG) 80°L CRYSTAL
1/8 LB (57 GRAMS) CHOCOLATE MALT

Crush the malt. Mash-in to 122°F (50°C) with 1-3/4 gallons (6.6 L) of liquor at 137°F (58°C). Cover and hold. After 15 minutes raise the temperature to 152°F (67°C). After 1 hour begin to runoff sweet wort to the kettle. Heat sparge liquor to 172°C (78°C). Sparge the mash with 2 gallons (7.6 L) liquor. Add the remaining liquor to the kettle to bring the total volume to 5-3/4 gallons (22 L)

Add:
6.6 LBS (3 KG) LIGHT MALT EXTRACT
1 LB (.45 KG) AMBER DME

KETTLE SCHEDULE:
1.5 HBU MT HOOD as soon as the wort comes to a boil,
2.5 HBU MT HOOD after 45 minutes
1.5 HBU HALLERTAU after 60 minutes, and
1/2 TSP (2.5 ML) IRISH MOSS after 1 hour and fifteen minutes,
KETTLE KNOCKOUT at 1-1/2 hours.

Transfer through wort chiller into carboy, aerating the wort.
5-1/4 gallons (20 L) of wort should be collected at sg 1082.

Pitch with:
2 PKGS of lager yeast (10-14 grams dry yeast) or liquid yeast (Wyeast 2308 or 2206, Yeast Lab L32 or L33, or BrewTek CL-680).

Ferment at:
40-55°F (4-13°C). Transfer to secondary after 7-12 days, condition at 35-50°F (2-10°C) for 4-8 weeks.

Prime with:
2/3-3/4 cup (150-170 ML) of CORN SUGAR and bottle condition for 2 months at below 60°F (16°C).

CHAPTER 13

MASH/ALL-GRAIN RECIPES

AMERICAN WHEAT ALE

LAWN BOY

From the land that gave the world lawnmower beer, microbrewers have established a respectable alternative — lawnmower wheat ale. Just the thing to quench your thirst while you're manicuring the half acre astride the John Deere 12-horse.

OG 1042   TG 1008   ABV 4.5%   SRM 3   IBU 15

Heat 7-1/4 gallons (27.5 L) of water to 145°F (63°C).

WATER SUPPLY:	TREAT WATER:
Soft	ACIDIFY TO BELOW pH 7.0
Moderately sulfate	ACIDIFY TO BELOW pH 7.0
Moderately carbonate	ACIDIFY TO BELOW pH 7.0
Highly sulfate	DILUTE 1:1 AND ACIDIFY TO BELOW pH 7.0
Highly carbonate	BOIL OR DILUTE 1:1; ACIDIFY TO BELOW pH 7.0

4-3/4 LBS (2.2 KG) LAGER MALT
2-1/2 LBS (1.1 KG) WHEAT MALT

Crush the malt. Mash-in the malt to 135°F (57°C) with 2-3/4 gallons (10.4 L) of liquor at 145°F (63°C). Cover and hold for 15 minutes, then apply heat to raise the temperature of the goods to 148-9°F (65°C). Cover and hold, maintaining the temperature as necessary. After 1-1/2 hours begin to run-off sweet wort to kettle. Heat sparge liquor to 172°F (78°C). Sparge mash with 3-3/4 gallons of 172°F (78°C) liquor. Pour the remaining 3/4 gallon (2.8 L) of liquor into the kettle, to collect 6 gallons (23 L) of sweet wort at sg 1037.

KETTLE SCHEDULE:
1.75 HBU CASCADE as soon as the wort comes to a boil,
1.75 HBU CASCADE after 45 minutes, and
1/2 TSP (2.5 ML) IRISH MOSS after 1 hour and fifteen minutes,
KETTLE KNOCK-OUT at 1-1/2 hours.

Transfer through wort chiller into carboy, aerating the wort.
5-1/4 gallons (20 L) of wort should be collected at sg 1042.

Pitch with:
2 PKGS of neutral ale yeast (10-14 grams dry yeast) or liquid yeast (Yeast Lab A07, BrewTek CL-10 or CL-400,Wyeast 1007). Lager yeast may be be used instead.

Ferment at:
60-68°F (16-20°C). Transfer to secondary after 5-7 days, condition at 40-60°F (5-16°C) for 2 weeks.

Prime with:
3/4 - 1 cup (170-230 ML) of CORN SUGAR and bottle condition for 1 month at down to 33°F (1°C), but in any case at below 65°F (18°C).

ENGLISH BROWN ALE

NEW DUBLIN BROWN ALE

Ah, brown ale! Is there **anyone** who doesn't like brown ale? We've never met them, if there is such a person.

Flavorful, malty and well-rounded, with hints of richness, roastiness, and even nuttiness, this style is never overwhelming. Malty beer styles demand a lot of the brewer; with no big hop character to camouflage defects, don't oversparge this brew, or let the fermentation temperature get out of hand.

OG 1045   TG 1012   ABV 4.3%   SRM 18   IBU 20

Heat 7-1/4 gallons (27.5 L) of water to 160°F (71°C).

WATER SUPPLY:	TREAT WATER:
Soft	1/2 TSP (2.5 ML) OF GYPSUM
Moderately sulfate	OK AS IS
Moderately carbonate	ACIDIFY TO BELOW pH 7.2
Highly sulfate	DILUTE 1:1 OR BOIL
Highly carbonate	DILUTE 1:1, OR BOIL, AND ACIDIFY

6-3/4 LBS (3.1 KG) PALE MALT
1/4 LB (.11 KG) CARAPILS MALT
1/2 LB (.23 KG) CRYSTAL MALT
1/3 LB (.15 KG) CHOCOLATE MALT

Crush the malt. Mash-in the malt to 150°F (65°F) with 2-1/2 gallons (9.5 L) of liquor at 160°F (71°C). Cover and hold. After 1-1/4 hours begin to run-off the sweet wort to kettle. Heat sparge liquor to 172°F (78°C). Sparge mash with up to 4 gallons (15 L) of 172°F (78°C) liquor, but don't let the runoff pH rise over pH 5.8. If you sparge with 4 gallons (15 L), you will have about 3/4 gallon (2.8 L) of liquor left over; add all the remaining liquor to the kettle to collect 6 gallons (23 L) of sweet wort at sg 1038.

KETTLE SCHEDULE:
1.25 HBU GOLDINGS as soon as the wort comes to a boil,
1.25 HBU FUGGLES after 45 minutes,
1.25 HBU GOLDINGS after 60 minutes,
2.5 HBU FUGGLES and
1/4 TSP (1.2 ML) IRISH MOSS after 1 hour and fifteen minutes
KETTLE KNOCK-OUT at 1-1/2 hours.

At your option, adding:
1 OZ (28 G) FUGGLES at knock-out will nicely accent this brew with a worty aromatic hoppiness, although the brew will no longer be true to style.

Transfer through wort chiller into carboy, aerating the wort.
5-1/4 gallons (20 L) of wort should be collected at sg 1045.

Pitch with:
2 PKGS of malty/neutral ale yeast (10-14 grams dry yeast) or liquid yeast (Yeast Lab A05, BrewTek CL-20 or CL-130, Wyeast 1087).

Ferment at:
65-68°F (18-20°C). Transfer to secondary after 4-6 days, condition at 50-60°F (10-16°C) for 2-3 weeks.

Prime with:
2/3 cup (150 ML) of CORN SUGAR and bottle condition for 1 month at below 65°F (18°C).

ENGLISH MILD ALE

MR. ROGER'S LOCAL

The venerable pub ale, sort of a "mild" porter. This beer is rich and yet mellow, sweet but roasty, a true beverage of moderation and brownbird of happiness. The Buddha surely contemplated mild ale!

Don't be fooled, however; this can be just about the hardest style of beer to brew, because it is a "soft" beer style, yet it has enough characterful ingredients that if anything is overdone or off, it will overwhelm the flavor. Mash temperature and thickness are also important, to acheive the lower fermentablility required to leave some fullness in this low-gravity brew. So get in touch with your inner self before brewing this mellow ale!

OG 1036   TG 1011   ABV 3.3%   SRM 20   IBU 18

Heat 7 gallons (26.5 L) of water to 165°F (74°C).

WATER SUPPLY:	TREAT WATER:
Soft	1/2 TSP (2.5 ML) OF GYPSUM
Moderately sulfate	OK AS IS
Moderately carbonate	ACIDIFY TO BELOW pH 7.2
Highly sulfate	DILUTE 1:1 OR BOIL
Highly carbonate	DILUTE 1:1, OR BOIL, AND ACIDIFY TO 7.2

5-1/4 LBS (2.4 KG) MILD ALE OR PALE ALE MALT
3/4 LB (.34 KG) CRYSTAL MALT
1/4 LB (.11 KG) CARAMEL-120 MALT
1/4 LB (.11 KG) CHOCOLATE MALT

Crush the malt. Mash-in the malt to 155-156°F (68°C) with 1-3/4 gallons (6.6 L) of liquor at 168°F (76°C). Cover and hold. After 3/4 of an hour begin to run-off sweet wort to kettle. Heat sparge liquor to 172°F (78°C). Sparge mash with 3-1/4 gallons (12.3 L) of 172°F (78°C) liquor; add the remaining 2 gallons (7.6 L) of liquor to your kettle for 6 gallons (23 L) of sweet wort at sg 1032.

KETTLE SCHEDULE:
1.25 HBU GOLDINGS as soon as the wort comes to a boil,
1.25 HBU FUGGLES after 45 minutes,
2.5 HBU GOLDINGS after 60 minutes,
1.25 HBU FUGGLES and
1/4 TSP (1.2 ML) IRISH MOSS after 1 hour and fifteen minutes,
KETTLE KNOCK-OUT at 1-1/2 hours.

Transfer through wort chiller into carboy, aerating the wort.
5-1/4 gallons (20 L) of wort should be collected at sg 1033.

Pitch with:
2 PKGS of malty ale yeast (10-14 grams dry yeast) or liquid yeast
(Yeast Lab A05, BrewTek CL-20 or CL-130,Wyeast 1087).

Ferment at:
68-72°F (20-22°C). Transfer to secondary after 4-5 days, condition at 50-60°F (10-16°C) for 2-3 weeks.

Prime with:
1/2 - 2/3 cup (115-150 ML) of CORN SUGAR and bottle condition for 1 month at below 65°F (18°C).

AMERICAN BROWN ALE

EUGENE BROWN

Hops, hops, hops! Whodathunk twenty years ago that Americans would take a liking to **bitter** beer? So the AHA had to come up with a new beer style for those hophead brewers from places like Oregon, Washington and Texas. Texas? Hops? Its' a wonderful time in the timeline to be a homebrewer!

OG 1050   TG 1012   ABV 5%   SRM 18   IBU 36

Heat 7-3/4 gallons (29.5 L) of water to 165°F (74°C).

WATER SUPPLY:	TREAT WATER:
Soft	2 TSP (10 ML) GYPSUM, 1/2 TSP (2.5 ML) TABLE SALT
Moderately sulfate	1/2 TSP (2.5 ML) OF GYPSUM
Moderately carbonate	1 TSP (5 ML) GYPSUM, 1/2 TSP (2.5 ML) TABLE SALT
Highly sulfate	OK AS IS
Highly carbonate	ACIDIFY TO BELOW 7.2

7-1/2 LBS (3.4 KG) LAGER MALT
1 LB (.45 KG) LIGHT CRYSTAL MALT
1/4 LB (112 G) CHOCOLATE MALT

Crush the malt. Mash-in the malt to 150-152°F (67°C) with 3 gallons (11.4 L) of liquor at 165°F (74°C). Cover and hold. After 1-1/4 hours begin to run-off sweet wort to kettle. Heat sparge liquor to 172°F (78°C). Sparge mash with 4-3/4 gallons (18 L) of 172°F (78°C) liquor to collect 6-1/4 gallons (24 L) of sweet wort at sg 1042.

KETTLE SCHEDULE:
1.5 HBU WILLAMETTE as soon as the wort comes to a boil,
1.5 HBU WILLAMETTE and
3 HBU GALENA after 45 minutes,
1.5 HBU WILLAMETTE after 60 minutes,
3 HBU WILLAMETTE and
1/4 TSP (1.2 ML) IRISH MOSS after 1 hour and fifteen minutes,
1/2 OZ (14 GRAMS) CHINOOK (6.5 HBU) at KETTLE KNOCK-OUT after 1-1/2 hours.

Transfer through wort chiller into carboy, aerating the wort.
5-1/4 gallons (20 L) of wort should be collected at sg 1050.

Pitch with:
2 PKGS of dry ale yeast (10-14 grams dry yeast) or liquid yeast (Yeast Lab A06, BrewTek CL-260, Wyeast 1056)

Ferment at:
68-72°F (20-22°C). Transfer to secondary after 4-5 days, condition at 50-60°F (10-16°C)for 2 weeks.

Prime with:
3/4 cup (170 ML) of CORN SUGAR and bottle condition for 1 month at below 65°F (18°C).

SCOTTISH LIGHT

HORNE'S 60 SHILLING ALE

Even today, Scottish brewers retain the 19th century price-per-barrel in shillings (that's 12 pence, 20 shillings to a Pound Sterling) to define the OG of their brews. This is roughly the Scots' equivalent of an English Mild Ale.

The hallmark of Scottish brewing is the use of a small amount of roasted barley as the primary coloring and flavoring of their ales, and a light touch on the hops, probably because the growing season in Scotland is too short for cultivating hops; consequently their price was prohibitive, especially given the legendary frugality of the Scots.

So don your kilt (what **does** one wear under a kilt?), inflate the bagpipes, and get ready to brew a real Celtic ale!

OG 1033   TG 1010   ABV 3%   SRM 14   IBU 16

Heat 7 gallons (26.5 L) of water to 168°F (76°C).

WATER SUPPLY:	TREAT WATER:
Soft	2 TSPS (10 ML) GYPSUM,
	1/2 TSP (2.5 ML) TABLE SALT
Moderately sulfate	1/2 TSP (2.5 ML) OF GYPSUM
Moderately carbonate	1/2 TSP (2.5 ML) GYPSUM,
	1/2 TSP (2.5 ML) TABLE SALT
Highly sulfate	OK AS IS
Highly carbonate	ACIDIFY TO BELOW 7.2

4-3/4 LBS (2.2 KG) PALE MALT
1/2 LB (.23 KG) CARAPILS MALT
1 OZ (28 G) CHOCOLATE MALT
1 OZ (28 G) ROASTED BARLEY
1/2 LB (.23 KG) FLAKED BARLEY

Crush the malt. Mash-in to 155-156°F (68°C) with 2 gallons (7.6 L) of liquor at 168°F (76°C). Cover and hold. After 3/4 of an hour begin to run-off the sweet wort to the kettle. Heat sparge liquor to 172°F (78°C). Sparge mash with 3-1/4 gallons (12.3 L) of 172°F (78°C) liquor. Pour the remaining 1-3/4 gallons (6.6 L) of liquor into the kettle, to collect 6 gallons (23 L) of sweet wort at sg 1029.

KETTLE SCHEDULE:
1.25 HBU GOLDINGS as soon as the wort comes to a boil,
1.25 HBU GOLDINGS after 45 minutes,
1.25 HBU FUGGLES after 60 minutes, and
1/4 TSP (1.2 ML) IRISH MOSS after 1 hour and fifteen minutes, KETTLE KNOCK-OUT at 1-1/2 hours.

Transfer through wort chiller into carboy, aerating the wort.
5-1/4 gallons (20 L) of wort should be collected at sg 1033.

Pitch with:
2 PKGS of neutral ale yeast (10-14 grams dry yeast) or liquid yeast (Yeast Lab A05, BrewTek CL-160, Wyeast 1087).

Ferment at:
60-68°F(16-20°C). Transfer to secondary after 4-6 days, condition at 50-60°F (10-16°C) for 2-3 weeks.

Prime with:
1/2 cup (115 ML) of CORN SUGAR and bottle condition for 1 month at below 65°F (18°C).

SCOTTISH HEAVY

DUNCAN'S 70 SHILLING HEAVY

Duncan Kellock has the best job in the world — head brewer at Maclay's Thistle Brewery in Alloa. The brewery is like a museum of 19th century brewing, complete with domed kettles and enormous wood-framed, copper-lined open fermenters. In the cellars, rows of ale cask-condition just yards from the brewery taps.

This beer is named for him, and commemorates the preservation of old beer styles and brewing techniques. Step back in time, and brew Duncan's Heavy!

OG 1036   TG 1012   ABV 3.2%   SRM 14   IBU 16

Heat 7 gallons (26.5 L) of water to 168°F (76°C).

WATER SUPPLY:	TREAT WATER:
Soft	2 TSPS (10 ML) GYPSUM, 1/2 TSP (2.5 ML) TABLE SALT
Moderately sulfate	1/2 TSP (2.5 ML) OF GYPSUM
Moderately carbonate	1/2 TSP (2.5 ML) GYPSUM, 1/2 TSP (2.5 ML) TABLE SALT
Highly sulfate	OK AS IS
Highly carbonate	ACIDIFY TO BELOW 7.2

5-1/4 LBS (2.4 KG) PALE MALT
3/4 LB (.34 KG) CARAPILS MALT
2 OZ (57 G) ROASTED BARLEY
1/2 LB (.23 KG) FLAKED BARLEY

Crush the malt. Mash-in to 155-156°F (68°C) with 2-1/4 gallons (8.5 L) of liquor at 168°F (76°C). Cover and hold. After 3/4 of an hour begin to run-off the sweet wort to the kettle. Heat sparge liquor to 172°F (78°C). Sparge mash with 3-1/2 gallons (13.2 L) of 172°F (78°C) liquor. Pour the remaining 1-1/4 gallons (4.7 L) of liquor into the kettle, to collect 6 gallons (23 L) of sweet wort at sg 1032.

KETTLE SCHEDULE:
1.25 HBU FUGGLES as soon as the wort comes to a boil,
1.25 HBU FUGGLES after 45 minutes,
2.5 HBU FUGGLES after 60 minutes, and
1/2 TSP (2.5 ML) IRISH MOSS after 1 hour and fifteen minutes,
KETTLE KNOCK-OUT at 1-1/2 hours.

Transfer through wort chiller into carboy, aerating the wort.
5-1/4 gallons (20 L) of wort should be collected at sg 1036.

Pitch with:
2 PKGS of neutral ale yeast (10-14 grams dry yeast) or liquid yeast (Yeast Lab A05, BrewTek CL-160, Wyeast 1728).

Ferment at:
60-68°F(16-20°C). Transfer to secondary after 4-6 days, condition at 50-60°F (10-16°C)for 2-3 weeks.

Prime with:
1/2 cup (115 ML) of CORN SUGAR and bottle condition for 1 month at below 65°F (18°C).

SCOTTISH EXPORT

JOHN BARLEYCORN 80 SHILLING EXPORT

T'will make a man forget his woe
T'will heighten all his joy
T'will make the widow's heart to sing,
Though the tear were in her eye.

Then let us toast John Barleycorn,
Each man a glass in hand;
And may his great prosperity
Ne'er fail in old Scotland!

— Rabbie Burns

OG 1045   TG 1012   ABV 4.3%   SRM 15   IBU 18

Heat 7-1/4 gallons (27.5 L) of water to 165°F (74°C).

WATER SUPPLY:	TREAT WATER:
Soft	2 TSPS (10 ML) GYPSUM,
	1/2 TSP (2.5 ML) TABLE SALT
Moderately sulfate	1/2 TSP (2.5 ML) OF GYPSUM
Moderately carbonate	1/2 TSP (2.5 ML) GYPSUM,
	1/2 TSP (2.5 ML) TABLE SALT
Highly sulfate	OK AS IS
Highly carbonate	ACIDIFY TO BELOW 7.2

7-3/4 LBS (3.5 KG) PALE MALT
2-1/2 OZ (71 G) ROASTED BARLEY

Crush the malt. Mash-in to 153°F (67°C) with 2-3/4 gallons (10.4 L) of liquor at 165°F (74°C).
Cover and hold. After 1 hour begin to run-off the sweet wort to the kettle. Heat sparge
liquor to 172°F (78°C). Sparge mash with 4 gallons (15 L) of 172°F (78°C) liquor. Pour the
remaining 1/2 gallon (1.9 L) of liquor into the kettle, to collect 6 gallons (23 L) of sweet wort
at sg 1039.

KETTLE SCHEDULE:
1.25 HBU GOLDINGS as soon as the wort comes to a boil,
2.50 HBU FUGGLES after 45 minutes,
1.25 HBU FUGGLES after 60 minutes, and
1/4 TSP (1.2 ML) IRISH MOSS after 1 hour and fifteen minutes,
KETTLE KNOCK-OUT at 1-1/2 hours.

Transfer through wort chiller into carboy, aerating the wort.
5-1/4 gallons (20 L) of wort should be collected at sg 1045.

Pitch with:
2 PKGS of neutral ale yeast (10-14 grams dry yeast) or liquid yeast (Yeast Lab A05, BrewTek
CL-160, Wyeast 1728).

Ferment at:
60-68°F(16-20°C). Transfer to secondary after 4-6 days, condition at 50-60°F (10-16°C) for
2-3 weeks.

Prime with:
2/3 cup (150 ML) of CORN SUGAR and bottle condition for 1 month at below 65°F (18°C).

ORDINARY BITTER

BULL & BLADDER BITTER

The Bull & Bladder Ale is an English Ordinary - the style that British pubs pump out by the hogshead. Its conservative starting gravity and alcohol content make it the ideal session beer. It is neither overly filling or strongly inebriating, so it won't spoil either your appetite or your judgement when you have your mother-in-law over for dinner, and she might even like it!

OG 1036   TG 1012   ABV 3.2%   SRM 10   IBU 25

Heat 7 gallons (26.5 L) of water to 168°F (76°C).

WATER SUPPLY:	TREAT WATER:
Soft	3 TSPS (15 ML) GYPSUM,
	1/2 TSP (2.5 ML) TABLE SALT
Moderately sulfate	1 TSP (5 ML) OF GYPSUM
Moderately carbonate	1 TSP (5 ML) GYPSUM,
	1/2 TSP (2.5 ML) TABLE SALT
Highly sulfate	ACIDIFY TO BELOW 7.0
Highly carbonate	ACIDIFY TO BELOW 7.0

5-1/4 LBS (2.4 KG) PALE MALT
1/2 LB (.23 KG) WHEAT MALT
1/3 LB (.15 KG) CRYSTAL MALT
1/4 LB (.11 KG) DARK CRYSTAL (C-80) MALT

Crush the malt. Mash-in the malt to 156°F (69°C) with 2 gallons of liquor at 168°F (76°C). Cover and hold. After 3/4 of an hour begin to run-off the sweet wort to kettle. Heat sparge liquor to 172°F (78°C). Sparge mash with 3-1/2 gallons (13.2 L) of 172°F (78°C) liquor. Pour the remaining 1-1/2 gallons (5.7 L) of liquor into the kettle, to collect 6 gallons (23 L) of sweet wort at sg 1032.

KETTLE SCHEDULE:
1.25 HBU GOLDINGS as soon as the wort comes to a boil,
2.5 HBU FUGGLES after 45 minutes,
1.25 HBU GOLDINGS after 60 minutes,
1.25 HBU FUGGLES and
1/4 TSP (1.2 ML) IRISH MOSS after 1 hour and fifteen minutes, and 1/2 OZ (14 GRAMS) FUGGLES at KETTLE KNOCK-OUT after 1-1/2 hours boil.

Transfer through wort chiller into carboy, aerating the wort.
5-1/4 gallons (20 L) of wort should be collected at sg 1036.

Pitch with:
2 PKGS of fruity/diacetyl ale yeast (10-14 grams dry yeast) or liquid yeast (Yeast Lab A04, A08, BrewTek CL-160, CL-120, CL-130, CL-170, Wyeast 1028).

Ferment at:
68-72°F (20-22°C). Transfer to secondary after 3-4 days, condition at 50-60°F (10-16°C) for 1-2 weeks, adding 3/4 - 1 OZ (21-28 G) FUGGLES 7 days before bottling.

Prime with:
1/2 cup (115 ML) of CORN SUGAR and bottle condition for 1 month at below 65°F (18°C).

EXTRA SPECIAL BITTER

DOG & DEVIL ESB

The strongest of Bitters, ESBs are still of relatively usual alcohol content by American standards. The Dog & Devil recipe is a good choice for those who appreciate a full-flavored British ale.

As with other British ale recipes, the flaked barley (or wheat, as the case may be) in the recipe is for improved head retention, but the brew will not be dramatically altered if pale malt is substituted in its stead. The water treatment is for a London version; for a "Burton" ale use the treatment given for Champion Reserve IPA, or for a Yorkshire example, use the liquor treatment shown for Old No. 7 Pale Ale.

OG 1048   TG 1012   ABV 4.7%   SRM 13.5   IBU 30

Heat 7-3/4 gallons (29.5 L) of water to 160°F (71°C).

WATER SUPPLY:	TREAT WATER:
Soft	1/2 TSP (2.5 ML) OF GYPSUM
Moderately sulfate	OK AS IS
Moderately carbonate	ACIDIFY TO BELOW 7.2
Highly sulfate	DILUTE 1:1
Highly carbonate	BOIL OR DILUTE 1:1; ACIDIFY TO BELOW 7.2

7-1/4 LBS (3.3 KG) PALE MALT
2/3 LB (.3 KG) LIGHT CRYSTAL (C-35) MALT
3/4 LB (.34 KG) FLAKED BARLEY
1 OZ (28 G) CHOCOLATE MALT

Crush the malt. Mash-in the malt to 150-152°F (66°C) with 3 gallons (11.4 L) of liquor at 160°F (71°C). Cover and hold. After 1-1/4 hours begin to run-off sweet wort to kettle. Heat sparge liquor to 172°F (78°C). Sparge mash with 4-3/4 gallons (18 L) of 172°F (78°C) liquor to collect 6-1/4 gallons (24 L) of sweet wort at sg 1040.

KETTLE SCHEDULE:
1.25 HBU GOLDINGS as soon as the wort comes to a boil,
3.75 HBU GOLDINGS after 45 minutes,
2.5 HBU FUGGLES after 60 minutes,
1.25 HBU GOLDINGS and 1/4 TSP (1.2 ML) IRISH MOSS after 1 hour and fifteen minutes,
and 1/2 OZ (14 G) FUGGLES at KETTLE KNOCK-OUT after 1-1/2 hours boil.

Transfer through wort chiller into carboy, aerating the wort.
5-1/4 gallons (20 L) of wort should be collected at sg 1048.

Pitch with:
2 PKGS of fruity/diacetyl ale yeast (10-14 grams dry yeast) or liquid yeast (Yeast Lab A04, A08, BrewTek CL-160, CL-120, CL-130, CL-170, or Wyeast 1028, 1087).

Ferment at:
68-72°F (20-22°C). Transfer to secondary after 3-4 days, condition at 50-60°F (10-16°C) for 2 weeks, adding
1 OZ (28 G) FUGGLES 7 days before bottling.

Prime with:
2/3 cup (150 ML) of CORN SUGAR and bottle condition for 1 month at below 65°F (18°C).

CLASSIC PALE ALE

OLD NO. 7 PALE ALE

The number 7 is a mystical number, and Old No. 7 is an enigmatic brew. It is an easy ale for the uninitiated to learn to like, but complex and individualistic enough for even the most jaded to enjoy.

It is an ideal ale for brewers limited by very hard water to brew; addition of a little chocolate malt will make it a chewier ale, and able to overcome a great deal of carbonate hardness without any other acidification. If your water supply is highly sulfate, this should probably be your "house" ale. Other good ale recipes for brewers with these waters are IPAs and ESBs.

Dry hop this with 1 or 2 ounces (28-57 grams) of Fuggles for an aromatic enigma.

OG 1050   TG 1012   ABV 5%   SRM 10.5   IBU 35

Heat 7-3/4 gallons (29.5 L) of water to 165°F (74°C).

WATER SUPPLY:	TREAT WATER:
Soft	2 TSP (10 ML) GYPSUM,
	1/2 TSP (2.5 ML) TABLE SALT
Moderately sulfate	1/2 TSP (2.5 ML) OF GYPSUM
Moderately carbonate	1 TSP (5 ML) GYPSUM,
	1/2 TSP (2.5 ML) TABLE SALT
Highly sulfate	OK AS IS
Highly carbonate	ACIDIFY TO BELOW 7.0

7-3/4 LBS (3.5 KG) PALE MALT
3/4 LB (.34 KG) CRYSTAL MALT
1/2 LB (.23 KG) FLAKED WHEAT

Crush the malt. Mash-in to 150-152°F (67°C) with 3 gallons (11.4 L) of liquor at 165°F (74°C). Cover and hold. After 1-1/4 hours begin to run-off sweet wort to kettle. Heat sparge liquor to 172°F (78°C). Sparge mash with 4-3/4 gallons (18 L) of 172°F (78°C) liquor to collect 6-1/4 gallons (24 L) of sweet wort at sg 1042.

KETTLE SCHEDULE:
1.25 HBU GOLDINGS as soon as the wort comes to a boil,
3.75 HBU GOLDINGS after 45 minutes,
3.75 HBU FUGGLES after 60 minutes,
2.5 HBU GOLDINGS and
1/4 TSP (1.2 ML) IRISH MOSS after 1 hour and fifteen minutes, and 3/4 OZ (21 G) FUGGLES at KETTLE KNOCK-OUT after 1-1/2 hours.

Transfer through wort chiller into carboy, aerating the wort.
5-1/4 gallons (20 L) of wort should be collected at sg 1050.

Pitch with:
2 PKGS of fruity/diacetyl ale yeast (10-14 grams dry yeast) or liquid yeast (Yeast Lab A03, A04, BrewTek CL-120, CL- 130, CL-160, CL-170, or Wyeast 1028, 1098).

Ferment at:
68-72°F (20-22°C). Transfer to secondary after 3-5 days, condition at 55-60°F (13-16°C) for 1-3 weeks.

Prime with:
3/4 cup (170ML) of CORN SUGAR and bottle condition for 1 month at below 65°F (18°C).

INDIA PALE ALE

CHAMPION RESERVE IPA

More hops! Hops that fill your mouth with hop bitterness and hop flavor, and hops that perfume the air with their aroma. IPAs are the showcase of hops. Many brewers have developed signature hop synergetics in their India Pale Ales, creating intriguing aromatic blends, oftentimes employing non-traditional varieties.

If you choose to use traditional British varieties, late-hop and dry-hop with East Kent Goldings for a citric sharpness, or Fuggles for rounder, more floral aromatics. Alternate or blend the two for greater complexity.

Be sure to "Burtonize" your water for this brew, to get the cleanest and most pleasant bitterness from the hops.

OG 1058   TG 1014   ABV 6%   SRM 13   IBU 48

Heat 8 gallons (30 L) of water to 165°F (74°C). Only 2-3 teaspoons (10-15 ML) of gypsum will dissolve into your water, unless it is saturated with CO_2...the solution is to add the rest directly to wort in the kettle. Check your liquor pH, and acidify it if it is over pH 7.0.

WATER SUPPLY:	TREAT WATER:
Soft	6 TSPS (30 ML) GYPSUM, 1/4 TSP (1.2 ML) TABLE SALT
Moderately sulfate	4 TSPS (20 ML) GYPSUM, 1/4 TSP (1.2 ML) TABLE SALT
Moderately carbonate	5 TSPS (25 ML) GYPSUM, 1/4 TSP (1.2 ML) TABLE SALT
Highly sulfate	UP TO 3 TSPS (15 ML) OF GYPSUM
Highly carbonate	UP TO 3 TSPS (15 ML) OF GYPSYM, ACIDIFY TO 7.0

9 LBS (4.1 KG) PALE MALT
1/2 LB (.23 KG) CARAPILS MALT
3/4 LB (.34 KG) CRYSTAL MALT
1/4 LB (.11 KG) FLAKED BARLEY

Crush the malt. Mash-in to 150-152°F (67°C) with 3-1/4 gallons (12.3 L) of liquor at 165°F (74°C). Cover and hold. After 1-1/4 hours begin to run-off sweet wort to kettle. Heat sparge liquor to 172°F (78°C). Sparge mash with 4-3/4 gallons (18 L) of 172°F (78°C) liquor to collect 6-1/4 gallons (24 L) of sweet wort at sg 1050.

KETTLE SCHEDULE:
1.75 HBU CASCADE as soon as the wort comes to a boil,
4 HBU PERLE and
3.5 HBU CASCADE after 45 minutes,
5.25 HBU CASCADE after 60 minutes,
1/2 TSP (2.5 ML) IRISH MOSS after 1 hour and fifteen minutes, and 1-1/2 OZ (35 G) PERLE at KETTLE KNOCK-OUT after 1-1/2 hours boil.

Transfer through wort chiller into carboy, aerating the wort.
5-1/4 gallons (20 L) of wort should be collected at sg 1050.

Pitch with:
2 PKGS of fruity/diacetyl ale yeast (10-14 grams dry yeast) or liquid yeast (Yeast Lab A03, A07, BrewTek CL-120, CL-130, CL-170, or Wyeast 1028, 1098).

Ferment at:
68-72°F (20-22°C). Transfer to secondary after 3-5 days, condition at 50-60°F (10-16°C) for 2 weeks, adding
3/4 TO 1 OZ (21-28 grams) CASCADE dry hops one week before bottling.

Prime with:
3/4 cup (170 ML) of CORN SUGAR and bottle condition for 1 month at below 65°F (18°C).

ROBUST PORTER

SHOREDITCH PORTER

There is not much dispute about the claim that Ralph Harwood created the Porter style at his brewery in Shoreditch, London, in 1722. There is a great deal of controversy over whether it was to replicate a mix of three different-colored ales, or a blend of fresh and soured ale, or was just a new, darker ale made possible by new, hotter-roasting iron kilns.

There is not much dispute about Shoreditch Porter; it is a Porter in the 18th-century style that London became famous for.

Homebrewers are responsible for the renewed interest in many archaic and indigenous beers. There is even an antiquarian beer club in Durden Park, outside London, that researches and recreates historical styles.

OG 1052   TG 1012   ABV 5.3%   SRM 35   IBU 30

Heat 7-3/4 gallons (29.5 L) of water to 160°F (71°C).

WATER SUPPLY:	TREAT WATER:
Soft	1/2 TSP (2.5 ML) OF GYPSUM
Moderately sulfate	OK AS IS
Moderately carbonate	ACIDIFY TO BELOW 7.2
Highly sulfate	DILUTE 1:1
Highly carbonate	BOIL OR DILUTE 1:1; ACIDIFY TO BELOW 7.2

7-1/4 LBS (3.3 KG) PALE MALT
1-1/2 LBS (.68 KG) (.68 KG) CRYSTAL MALT
1/4 LB (.11 KG) CARAMEL-120 MALT
1/2 LB (.23 KG) CHOCOLATE MALT
1 OZ (28 G) BLACK MALT

Crush the malt. Mash-in the malt to 149-150°F(66°C) with 3 gallons (11.4 L) of liquor at 160°F (71°C). Cover and hold. After 1-1/2 hours begin to run-off the sweet wort to the kettle. Heat sparge liquor to 172°F (78°C). Sparge mash with 4-3/4 gallons (18 L) of 172°F (78°C) liquor to collect 6-1/4 gallons (24 L) of sweet wort at sg 1044.

KETTLE SCHEDULE:
3 HBU GALENA as soon as the wort comes to a boil,
3 HBU GALENA after 45 minutes,
1/4 TSP (1.2 ML) IRISH MOSS after 1 hour and fifteen minutes, and 1/2 OZ (14 G) WILLAMETTE at KETTLE KNOCK-OUT after 1-1/2 hours' boil.

Transfer through wort chiller into carboy, aerating the wort.
5-1/4 gallons (20 L) of wort should be collected at sg 1052.

Pitch with:
2 PKGS of fruity/diacetyl ale yeast (10-14 grams dry yeast) or liquid yeast (Yeast Lab A03, A05, BrewTek CL-130, CL-240, or Wyeast 1968, 1028).

Ferment at:
65-72°F (18-22°C). Transfer to secondary after 3-6 days, condition at 50-60°F (10-16°C) for 2-3 weeks.

Prime with:
1/2 - 2/3 cup (115-150 ML) of CORN SUGAR and bottle condition for 1 month at below 65°F (18°C).

BROWN PORTER

POOR RICHARD'S PORTER

Ben Franklin began his illustrious career as writer, inventor, statesman and humanitarian writing under the nom d'plume "Poor Richard". Some of his more memorable credos include "Beer is Proof that there is a God", and the motto of the Vermont Pub and Brewery, "All Things in Moderation".

Whether the venerable Mr. Franklin lived by this last maxim is questionable; he did, after all, sire 17 illegitimate children. Perhaps he considered that to be a moderate number...or perhaps he thought of children as we do Porter: there can never be enough!

OG 1045   TG 1010   ABV 4.6%   SRM 35   IBU 20

Heat 7-1/2 gallons (28.5 L) of water to 160°F (71°C).

WATER SUPPLY:	TREAT WATER:
Soft	1/2 TSP (2.5 ML) OF GYPSUM
Moderately sulfate	OK AS IS
Moderately carbonate	ACIDIFY TO BELOW 7.2
Highly sulfate	DILUTE 1:1
Highly carbonate	BOIL OR DILUTE 1:1; ACIDIFY TO BELOW 7.2

6-1/4 LBS (2.8 KG) PALE MALT
2/3 LB (.34 KG) CRYSTAL MALT
1/2 LB (.23 KG) CHOCOLATE MALT
2-1/2 OZ (71 G) ROAST BARLEY
1/2 LB (.23 KG) FLAKED BARLEY

Crush the malt. Mash-in to 149-150°F(66°C) with 2-3/4 gallons (10.4 L) of liquor at 160°F (71°C). Cover and hold. After 1-1/2 hours begin to run-off the sweet wort to the kettle. Heat sparge liquor to 172°F (78°C). Sparge mash with 4-1/4 gallons (16 L) of 172°F (78°C) liquor. Pour the remaining 1/2 gallon (1.9 L) of liquor into the kettle to collect 6-1/4 gallons (24 L) of sweet wort at sg 1038.

KETTLE SCHEDULE:
1.5 HBU WILLAMETTE as soon as the wort comes to a boil,
3.3 HBU WILLAMETTE after 45 minutes,
1/4 TSP (1.2 ML) IRISH MOSS after 1 hour and fifteen minutes, and 1/4 OZ (7 G) WILLAMETTE after 1 hour and twenty-five minutes.
KETTLE KNOCK-OUT at 1-1/2 hours.

Transfer through wort chiller into carboy, aerating the wort.
5-1/4 gallons (20 L) of wort should be collected at sg 1040.

Pitch with:
2 PKGS of ale yeast (10-14 grams dry yeast) or liquid yeast (Yeast Lab A03, BrewTek CL-130, or Wyeast 1028).

Ferment at:
65-72°F(18-22°C). Transfer to secondary after 3-6 days, condition at 50-60°F (10-16°C) for 2-3 weeks.

Prime with:
2/3 cup (150 ML) of CORN SUGAR and bottle condition for 1 month at below 65°F (18°C).

CLASSIC DRY STOUT

OLD DUBLIN STOUT

"Stout Porter", indeed. Other countries have a National Bird, or a National Flowering Shrub, or a Poet Laureate, but the Gaels have a National Drink, "Irish Stout", and consequently they have poets by the hundreds!

A County Cork poet who winters in Burlington, Vermont, Greg Delanty, is known to have a pint of stout now and then. Given the winters in Vermont, one would do well to have Guinness flowing through the veins! It's not for naught that stout is the beverage of choice for many marathoners, combining electrolyte replacement and carbohydrate-packing in a more inviting package than pasta and Croc-Aid. So the next time it threatens to rain all weekend, get out your brewkit and steam up the windows brewing Old Dublin Stout!

OG 1044   TG 1010   ABV 4.5%   SRM 60   IBU 33

Heat 7-1/2 gallons (28.5 L) of water to 160°F (71°C).

WATER SUPPLY:	TREAT WATER:
Soft	1/2 TSP (2.5 ML) OF GYPSUM
Moderately sulfate	OK AS IS
Moderately carbonate	OK AS IS
Highly sulfate	OK AS IS
Highly carbonate	ACIDIFY TO BELOW 7.2

4-3/4 LBS (2.2 KG) PALE MALT
1 LB (.45 KG) CRYSTAL MALT
1/4 LB (.11 KG) CARAMEL-120 MALT
1 LB (.45 KG) CHOCOLATE MALT
1/2 LB (.23 KG) ROAST BARLEY
1/2 LB (.23 KG) FLAKED WHEAT

Crush the malt. Mash-in to 149-150°F (66°C) with 2-3/4 gallons (10.4 L) of liquor at 160°F (71°C). Cover and hold. After 1-1/2 hours begin to run-off the sweet wort to the kettle. Heat sparge liquor to 172°F (78°C). Sparge mash with 4-3/4 gallons (18 L) of 172°F (78°C) liquor to collect 6-1/4 gallons (24 L) of sweet wort at sg 1037.

KETTLE SCHEDULE:
1.5 HBU WILLAMETTE as soon as the wort comes to a boil,
6.5 HBU CHINOOK after 45 minutes,
KETTLE KNOCK-OUT at 1-1/2 hours.

Transfer through wort chiller into carboy, aerating the wort.
5-1/4 gallons (20 L) of wort should be collected at sg 1037.

Pitch with:
2 PKGS of mildly fruity ale yeast (10-14 grams dry yeast) or liquid yeast (Yeast Lab A05, BrewTek CL-240, or Wyeast 1084).

Ferment at:
65-72°F (18-22°C). Transfer to secondary after 3-6 days, condition at 50-60°F (10-16°C) for 2-3 weeks.

Prime with:
2/3 (150 ML) cup of CORN SUGAR and bottle condition for 1 month at below 65°F (18°C).

SWEET STOUT

MILK-CHOCOLATE STOUT

A Dry Stout may inspire Irish poets, but it is English milk stout that the Bard of Beer, Michael Jackson, is inspired to compare to Oloroso sherry.

The Sweet Stout style is rich, rounded and smooth, with a roasty-chocolate aroma and flavor. Milk-Chocolate Stout is a balm for the weary, a caress for the depressed, and a cure for what ales you!
OG 1050   TG 1016   ABV 4.5%   SRM 40   IBU 24

Heat 7-1/2 gallons (28.5 L) of water to 165°F (74°C).

WATER SUPPLY:	TREAT WATER:
Soft	1/2 TSP (2.5 ML) OF GYPSUM
Moderately sulfate	OK AS IS
Moderately carbonate	OK AS IS
Highly sulfate	DILUTE UP TO 1:1
Highly carbonate	ACIDIFY TO BELOW 7.2

6 LBS (2.7 KG) PALE MALT
1/2 LB (.23 KG) CARAPILS MALT
1 LB (.45 KG) CRYSTAL MALT
3/4 LB (.34 KG) CHOCOLATE MALT
3 OZ (85 G) ROAST BARLEY

Crush the malt. Mash-in to 149-150°F (66°C) with 3 gallons of liquor at 165°F (74°C). Cover and hold. After 1 hour begin to run-off the sweet wort to the kettle. Heat sparge liquor to 172°F (78°C). Sparge mash with 4-1/2 gallons of 172°F (78°C) liquor to collect 6-1/4 gallons (24 L) of sweet wort at sg 1042.

KETTLE SCHEDULE:
1.5 HBU WILLAMETTE as soon as the wort comes to a boil,
3.5 HBU NUGGET after 45 minutes,
1/2 LB (.23 KG) LACTOSE and
KETTLE KNOCK-OUT at 1-1/2 hours.

Transfer through wort chiller into carboy, aerating the wort.
5-1/4 gallons (20 L) of wort should be collected at sg 1050.

Pitch with:
2 PKGS of mildly fruity ale yeast (10-14 grams dry yeast) or liquid yeast (Yeast Lab A05, A06, BrewTek CL-240, or Wyeast 1084).

Ferment at:
65-72°F (18-22°C). Transfer to secondary after 4-6 days, condition at 50-60°F (10-16°C) for 2-3 weeks.

Prime with:
1/2 cup (115 ML) of CORN SUGAR and bottle condition for 1 month at below 65°F (18°C).

IMPERIAL STOUT

CATHERINE THE GREAT TIPPLE

Catherine must have been great, given all the practice she is reported to have had. Undoubtedly, when she was sated with other worldly pleasures, she sent to the kitchens for a magnum of Imperial Stout, a beverage worthy of both her title and her appetites.

Catherine the Great Tipple is **not** the beer to introduce your mother-in-law to your homebrew with, or at least we don't think it is. You and your spouse, however, may just enjoy a Tipple when your mother-in-law **isn't** around. If you happen to have any essence of oyster, infuse some of that into this recipe, for an Imperial aphrodisiac!

OG 1085   TG 1024   ABV 8%   SRM 75   IBU 58

Heat 8-3/4 gallons (33 L) of water to 165°F (74°C).

WATER SUPPLY:	TREAT WATER:
Soft	6 TSPS (30 ML) GYPSUM, 1/4 TSP (1.2 ML) TABLE SALT
Moderately sulfate	4 TSPS (20 ML) GYPSUM, 1/4 TSP (1.2 ML) TABLE SALT
Moderately carbonate	5 TSPS (25 ML) GYPSUM, 1/4 TSP (1.2 ML) TABLE SALT
Highly sulfate	UP TO 3 TSPS (15 ML) (15 ML) OF GYPSUM
Highly carbonate	UP TO 3 TSPS (15 ML) OF GYPSYM, ACIDIFY TO 7.0

11-1/4 LBS (5.1 KG) PALE MALT
1 LB (.45 KG) DARK CRYSTAL (C-80) MALT
1 LB (.45 KG) CHOCOLATE MALT
1 LB (.45 KG) ROAST BARLEY

Crush the malt. Mash-in to 150-152°F (67°C) with 4-1/4 gallons (16 L) of liquor at 165°F (74°C). Cover and hold. After 1 hour begin to run-off the sweet wort to the kettle. Heat sparge liquor to 172°F (78°C). Sparge mash with 4-1/2 gallons (17 L) of 172°F (78°C) liquor.

Add:
3.3 LBS (1.5 KG) LIGHT MALT EXTRACT. There should be 6-1/3 gallons (24.5 L) of sweet wort at sg 1070 in the kettle at the start of the boil.

KETTLE SCHEDULE:
1.25 HBU WILLAMETTE as soon as the wort comes to a boil,
6.5 HBU CHINOOK after 45 minutes,
12 HBU PERLE after 1 hour,
2.5 HBU WILLAMETTE and
1/4 TSP (1.2 ML) IRISH MOSS after 1 hour and fifteen minutes,
KETTLE KNOCK-OUT at 1-1/2 hours.

Transfer through wort chiller into carboy, aerating the wort.
5-1/4 gallons (20 L) of wort should be collected at sg 1085.

Pitch with:
2-3 PKGS of mildly fruity ale yeast (10-14 grams dry yeast) or liquid yeast (Yeast Lab A05, BrewTek CL-240, or Wyeast 1098).

Ferment at:
65-68°F (18-20°C). Transfer to secondary after 5-7 days, condition at 55-65°F (13-18°C) for 3-5 weeks.

Add:
1 OZ (28 G) CHINOOK dry hops 1 week before bottling.

Prime with:
2/3 cup (150 ML) of CORN SUGAR and bottle condition for 2-6 months at below 65°F (18°C).

OLD ALE

OLD GODESGOOD STRONG ALE

Before the scientific revolution of the 19th century, brewers and brewsters had no real idea of what yeast was, but they knew enough to collect the frothy barm from a ferment and imbue their new wort with it. Medieval brewers in Spain called it "los almos", or little souls. In merry old England, brewsters thanked the heavens for the "Godesgood", or God-is-good, that gave life to their worts.

Over the centuries barley, kilning, hops, mashing and fermentation techniques have changed, but Old Ale has remained part of the lexicon of brewing.

OG 1065 TG 1016 ABV 6.4% SRM 13 IBU 35

Heat 8 gallons (30 L) of water to 165°F (74°C).

WATER SUPPLY:	TREAT WATER:
Soft	2 TSPS (10 ML) GYPSUM,
	1/2 TSP (2.5 ML) TABLE SALT
Moderately sulfate	1/2 TSP (2.5 ML) OF GYPSUM
Moderately carbonate	1/2 TSP (2.5 ML) GYPSUM,
	1/2 TSP (2.5 ML) TABLE SALT
Highly sulfate	OK AS IS
Highly carbonate	ACIDIFY TO BELOW 7.2

10-1/2 LBS (4.8 KG) PALE MALT
1/2 LB (.23 KG) CRYSTAL MALT
1/2 LB (.23 KG) AMBER MALT

Crush the malt. Mash-in the malt to 149-150°F(66°C) with 3-3/4 gallons (14 L) of liquor at 165°F (74°C). Cover and hold. After 1 hour begin to run-off the sweet wort to the kettle. Heat sparge liquor to 172°F (78°C).

Sparge mash with 4-1/4 gallons (16 L) of 172°F (78°C) liquor to collect 6-1/4 gallons (24 L) of sweet wort at sg 1050.

KETTLE SCHEDULE:
1.25 HBU GOLDINGS as soon as the wort comes to a boil,
6 HBU NUGGET after 45 minutes,
2.5 HBU GOLDINGS after 60 minutes, and
1/4 TSP (1.2 ML) IRISH MOSS after 1 hour and fifteen minutes,
KETTLE KNOCK-OUT at 1-1/2 hours.

Transfer through wort chiller into carboy, aerating the wort.
5-1/4 gallons (20 L) of wort should be collected at sg 1065.

Pitch with:
2 PKGS of neutral ale yeast (10-14 grams dry yeast) or liquid yeast (Yeast Lab A05, BrewTek CL-160, or Wyeast 1728).

Ferment at:
60-68°F (16-20°C). Transfer to secondary after 4-6 days, condition at 50-60°F (10-16°C) for 2-3 weeks.

Prime with:
2/3 cup (150 ML) of CORN SUGAR and bottle condition for 1 month at below 65°F (18°C).

SCOTCH ALE

LAIRD OF THE BORDERS WEE HEAVY

This recipe is for a 90 shilling ale. It is named in honor of Laird Peter Maxwell Stewart, 20th Laird of Traquair House, at Innerleithen in the Scottish Borders. The laird resurrected the 16th century brewery under the manor house to brew four-barrel batches of "the rarest ale in the world", the 90/- Traquair House Ale.

The "new" copper, built in 1736, the open coolships and unlined, open oak fermenters, nearly two centuries old, yield a nectar of malt from the cobblestone and dirt-floored brewery. The brewery ought to be an inspiration to every homebrewer who questions whether their equipment can produce world-class brews!

OG 1080   TG 1022   ABV 7.5%   SRM 14.5   IBU 30

Heat 8-1/2 gallons (32 L) of water to 165°F (74°C).

WATER SUPPLY:	TREAT WATER:
Soft	2 TSPS (10 ML) GYPSUM,
	1/2 TSP (2.5 ML) TABLE SALT
Moderately sulfate	1/2 TSP (2.5 ML) OF GYPSUM
Moderately carbonate	1/2 TSP (2.5 ML) GYPSUM,
	1/2 TSP (2.5 ML) TABLE SALT
Highly sulfate	OK AS IS
Highly carbonate	ACIDIFY TO BELOW 7.2

13-1/2 LBS (6.2 KG) PALE MALT
1/2 LB (.23 KG) AMBER MALT
1-1/2 OZ (35 G) ROAST BARLEY

Crush the malt. Mash-in the malt to 154-155°F (68°C) with 4-1/4 gallons (16 L) of liquor at 165°F (74°C). Cover and hold. After 1 hour begin to run-off the sweet wort to the kettle. Heat sparge liquor to 172°F (78°C). Sparge mash with 4-1/4 gallons (16 L) of 172°F (78°C) liquor to collect 6-1/4 gallons (24 L) of sweet wort at sg 1067.

KETTLE SCHEDULE:
1.25 HBU GOLDINGS as soon as the wort comes to a boil,
6 HBU CHINOOK after 45 minutes,
1/2 TSP (2.5 ML) IRISH MOSS after 1 hour and fifteen minutes,
KETTLE KNOCK-OUT at 1-1/2 hours.

Transfer through wort chiller into carboy, aerating the wort.
5-1/4 gallons (20 L) of wort should be collected at sg 1080.

Pitch with:
2 PKGS of neutral ale yeast (10-14 grams dry yeast) or liquid yeast (Yeast Lab A05, BrewTek CL-160, or Wyeast 1087).

Ferment at:
60-68°F (16-20°C). Transfer to secondary after 5-8 days, condition at 50-60°F (10-16°C) for 3-5 weeks.

Prime with:
1/2 - 2/3 (115-150 ML) cup of CORN SUGAR and bottle condition for 3-6 months at below 65°F (18°C).

BARLEYWINE

SLEEPWALKER BARLEYWINE

This barleywine is a great choice for a brew with a meal. It is the perfect accompaniment for red meat or cheeses, is wonderful as a digestif, or for that surreal twist, have one as a nightcap and dream in technicolor.

Dry-hop a batch with 1 oz (28 grams) each of Cascades and Fuggles, one or two weeks before bottling, for an overwhelming experience each time you open a bottle!

OG 1096   TG 1024   ABV 9.5%   SRM 18   IBU 65

Heat 8-1/2 gallons (32 L) of water to 165°F (74°C).

WATER SUPPLY:	TREAT WATER:
Soft	1 TSP (5 ML) OF GYPSUM
Moderately sulfate	OK AS IS
Moderately carbonate	ACIDIFY TO BELOW pH 7.2
Highly sulfate	DILUTE 1:1 OR BOIL
Highly carbonate	DILUTE 1:1, OR BOIL, AND ACIDIFY

8-1/4 LBS (3.7 KG) PALE MALT
1-1/2 LBS (.68 KG) WHEAT MALT
2-1/4 LBS (1 KG) CRYSTAL MALT

Crush the malt. Mash-in the malt to 150°F (66°C) with 4-1/4 gallons (16 L) of liquor at 165°F (74°C). Cover and hold. After 1-1/2 hours begin to run-off sweet wort to kettle. Heat sparge liquor to 172°F (78°C). Sparge mash with 4-1/4 gallons (16 L) of 172°F (78°C) liquor to collect 6-1/4 gallons (24 L) of sweet wort at sg 1077.

Stir into your kettle:
3.3 LBS (1.5 KG) LIGHT MALT SYRUP
1 LB (.45 KG) BREWER'S CORN SUGAR

KETTLE SCHEDULE:
4.5 HBU BULLION as soon as the wort comes to a boil,
4.5 HBU BULLION after 45 minutes,
5 HBU FUGGLES after 60 minutes,
7.5 HBU FUGGLES and
1/2 TSP (2.5 ML) IRISH MOSS after 1 hour and fifteen minutes,
1 OZ (28 G) FUGGLES after 1 hour and twenty-five minutes,
KETTLE KNOCK-OUT at 1-1/2 hours.

Transfer through wort chiller into carboy, aerating the wort.
5-1/4 gallons (20 L) of wort should be collected at sg 1096.

Pitch with:
3 PKGS of fruity ale yeast (15-25 grams dry yeast) or liquid ale yeast; ask at your homebrew shop for a strain that will match a particular character that you may desire; otherwise Yeast Lab A02 will give good results.

Ferment at:
66-72°F (18-22°C). Transfer to secondary after 2-3 days, condition at 60-65°F (16-18°C) for 2-4 weeks.

Prime with:
1/2 cup (115 ML) of CORN SUGAR for two volumes of CO_2, and bottle condition for 2-3 months at below 65°F (18°C). Lay some bottles down at cool cellar temperatures (40-60°F/ 22-42°C) for two or three years to fully mature!

FLANDERS' BROWN ALE

OUDENAARDE BROWN ALE

Brown ales from Flanders have an ideosyncratic sweet-and-sour flavor that is character-istic of the yeast strains used, and historically included a limited bacterial fermentation. To really duplicate the style, you need to use one of the yeast strains specified below, but a reasonable approximation can be obtained just by the lactic acid addition.

The recipe employs a mix of sucrose and glucose, with an added touch of dark molasses, to replicate the flavor of dark Belgian "candi" sugar. If you have access to real Belgian candi, though, replace these with 1lb. amber or dark candi. The complexity of this beer makes it an ideal accompaniment to a wide range of foods.

OG 1053   TG 1010   ABV 5.3%   SRM 14   IBU 24

Heat 7-1/4 gallons (27.5 L) of water to 160°F (71°C).

WATER SUPPLY:	TREAT WATER:
Soft or Moderately sulfate	OK AS IS
Moderately carbonate	OK AS IS
Highly sulfate	DILUTE 1:1 AND ACIDIFY TO BELOW 7.2
Highly carbonate	DILUTE 1:1, OR BOIL, AND ACIDIFY

5-1/4 LBS (2.4 KG) PALE MALT
3/4 LB (.34 KG) WHEAT MALT
1/2 LB (.23 KG) CRYSTAL MALT
1/4 LB (.11 KG) CARAMEL-120 (VERY DARK CRYSTAL) MALT
1/4 LB (.11 KG) FLAKED WHEAT
1/4 LB (.11 KG) OATMEAL

Crush the malt. Mash-in the malt to 148-149°F (65°C) with 2-3/4 gallons (10.4 L) of liquor at 160°F (71°C). Cover and hold. After 1-1/2 hours begin to run- off the sweet wort to kettle. Heat sparge liquor to 172°F (78°C).

Sparge mash with 3-1/2 gallons (13.2 L) of 172°F (78°C) liquor. Add the remaining 1 gallon (3.8 L) of liquor to the ketttle to collect 6 gallons (23 L) of sweet wort at sg 1040. Stir into your kettle:

1/2 LB (.23KG) BREWER'S CORN SUGAR
1/2 LB (.23 KG) TABLE SUGAR
1/2 CUP (115 ML) DARK MOLASSES

KETTLE SCHEDULE:
1.5 HBU MT HOOD as soon as the wort comes to a boil,
2 HBU PERLE after 45 minutes, 2 HBU PERLE after 60 minutes,
1.25 HBU GOLDINGS and
1/2 TSP (2.5 ML) IRISH MOSS after 1 hour and fifteen minutes,
ADJUST pH WITH LACTIC ACID AT KETTLE KNOCK-OUT, after 1-1/2 hour boil.

Transfer through wort chiller into carboy, aerating the wort.
5-1/4 gallons (20 L) of wort should be collected at sg 1050.

Pitch with:
2 PKGS of fruity ale yeast (10-14 grams dry yeast) or liquid yeast (Yeast Lab A08, BrewTek CL-320, or Wyeast 1565).

Ferment at:
65-72°F (18-22°C). Transfer to secondary after 5-7 days, condition at 50-60°F (10-16°C) for 4-8 weeks.

Prime with:
3/4 cup (170 ML) of CORN SUGAR and bottle condition for 1-2 months at below 65°F (18°C).

DUBBEL

FAT ABBOT ALE

Belgian monks, and the commercial breweries that copy this style, invariably brew with dark candi sugar rather than dark malts to color and flavor their brews, but the combination of malts and sugar in this recipe gives a reasonable approximation.

If you have access to dark **candi** sugar, replace the amber and light-crystal malts with pale malt, and the corn and table sugar with the candi sugar. The yeast strain should give a hint of butteriness (diacetyl) to your brew. This beer always seems to come out better if you shave your head in the fashion of a monk's tonsure and speak French while brewing it.

OG 1060   TG 1010   ABV 6.5%   SRM 12   IBU 20

Heat 8 gallons (30 L) of water to 160°F (71°C).

WATER SUPPLY:	TREAT WATER:
Soft or Moderately sulfate	OK AS IS
Moderately carbonate	ACIDIFY TO BELOW 7.2
Highly sulfate	DILUTE 1:1 AND ACIDIFY TO BELOW 7.2
Highly carbonate	DILUTE 1:1, OR BOIL, AND ACIDIFY

7-1/2 LBS (3.4 KG) PALE MALT
1 LB (.45 KG) WHEAT MALT
1/2 LB (.23 KG) C-35 MALT
3/4 LB (.34 KG) BROWN MALT

Crush the malt. Mash-in the malt to 148-149°F (65°C) with 3-1/2 gallons (13.2 L) of liquor at 160°F (71°C). Cover and hold. After 1-1/2 hours begin to run-off sweet wort to kettle. Heat sparge liquor to 172°F (78°C).

Sparge mash with 4-1/2 gallons (17 L) of 172°F (78°C) liquor to collect 6-1/4 gallons (24 L) of sweet wort at sg 1051. Stir into your kettle:

1/2 LB (.23 KG) BREWER'S CORN SUGAR
1/2 LB (.23 KG) TABLE SUGAR

KETTLE SCHEDULE:
1-1/4 HBU GOLDINGS as soon as the wort comes to a boil,
1-1/4 HBU GOLDINGS after 45 minutes,
2-1/2 HBU GOLDINGS after 60 minutes,
1-1/4 HBU GOLDINGS and
1/4 TSP (1.2 ML) IRISH MOSS after 1 hour and fifteen minutes,
KETTLE KNOCK-OUT at 1-1/2 hours.

Transfer through wort chiller into carboy, aerating the wort.
5-1/4 gallons (20 L) of wort should be collected at sg 1060.

Pitch with:
2 PKGS of fruity/diacetyl ale yeast (10-14 grams dry yeast) or Belgian liquid yeast (Wyeast 1214, Yeast Lab A08, BrewTek CL-300 or CL-340).

Ferment at:
65-68°F (18-20°C). Transfer to secondary after 5-8 days, condition at 55-60°F (13-16°C) for 3-6 weeks.

Prime with:
3/4 cup (170 ML) of CORN SUGAR and bottle condition for 1 month at below 65°F (18°C).

BELGIAN TRIPEL

STANDUP TRIPLE

The origins of Tripels and Dubbels likely rests in antiquity, when brewers didn't sparge in the modern sense, but mashed the same grains three consecutive times. The first mash produced xxx ale, the second xx, and the third a weak common beer.

This style is the domain of the Trappist monasteries of Belgium. Not your everyday lawnmower beer, a Tripel demands contemplation, and makes an excellent nightcap.

OG 1080   TG 1012   ABV 9.0%   SRM 4   IBU 22

Heat 8-1/4 gallons (31 L) of water to 145°F (63°C).

WATER SUPPLY:	TREAT WATER:
Soft or Moderately sulfate	OK AS IS
Moderately carbonate	ACIDIFY TO BELOW 7.0
Highly sulfate	DILUTE 1:1 AND ACIDIFY TO BELOW 7.0
Highly carbonate	DILUTE 1:1, OR BOIL, AND ACIDIFY

10-1/2 LBS (4.8 KG) LAGER MALT
1 LB (.45 KG) WHEAT MALT

Crush the malt. Mash-in the malt to 131°F (55°C) with 4 gallons (15 L) of liquor at 145°F (63°C). After 15-20 minutes, apply heat to raise the temperature of the mash to 148-149°F (65°C). Cover and hold. After 1 hour raise the temperature to 160°F (71°F) over ten minutes, and hold for another 20 minutes. Run-off the sweet wort to the kettle. Heat sparge liquor to 172°F (78°C). Sparge mash with 4-3/4 gallons (18 L) of 172°F (78°C) liquor to collect 6-1/4 gallons (24 L) of sweet wort at sg 1056.

Stir into your kettle:
1-1/4 LB (.57 KG)S BREWER'S CORN SUGAR
1/2 LB (.23 KG) TABLE SUGAR

KETTLE SCHEDULE:
2 HBU PERLE as soon as the wort comes to a boil,
1.5 HBU STYRIAN GOLDINGS after 45 minutes,
2 HBU PERLE after 60 minutes,
1.25 HBU SAAZ and
1/2 TSP (2.5 ML) IRISH MOSS after 1 hour and fifteen minutes,
KETTLE KNOCK-OUT at 1-1/2 hours.

Transfer through wort chiller into carboy, aerating the wort.
5-1/4 gallons (20 L) of wort should be collected at sg 1080.

Pitch with:
2 PKGS of fruity ale yeast (10-14 grams dry yeast) or Belgian liquid yeast (Yeast Lab A08, BrewTek CL-300 or CL-340 or Wyeast 1214).

Ferment at:
65-68°F (18-20°C). Transfer to secondary after 5-8 days, condition at 55-60°F (13-16°C) for 4-8 weeks.

Prime with:
3/4 cup (170 ML) of CORN SUGAR and bottle condition for 2-4 months at below 65°F (18°C).

WIT

CHEVAL BLANC

Pierre Celis revived this refreshing "white" Belgian ale style at the Hoegaarden Brewery near Louvain. It has since become a popular style not only with Belgian brewers, but in America as well.

Originally brewed with unmalted wheat, our recipe combines flaked wheat and malted wheat. Why? Because unmalted wheat in a mash reacts about the same as wallpaper paste would; it glues it together, making sparging difficult, if not impossible. Malting and the flaking process both reduce the complexity and the adhesive qualities of wheat. Even so, at almost 40% wheat, you can expect the sparging from this recipe to run slowly.

OG 1048   TG 1010   ABV 5%   SRM 4   IBU 19

Heat 6-1/2 gallons (25 L) of water to 160°F (71°C).

WATER SUPPLY:	TREAT WATER:
Soft or Moderately sulfate	OK AS IS
Moderately carbonate	ACIDIFY TO BELOW 7.0
Highly sulfate	DILUTE 1:1 AND ACIDIFY TO BELOW 7.0
Highly carbonate	DILUTE 1:1, OR BOIL, AND ACIDIFY

4-1/2 LBS (2 KG) PILSENER MALT
2-1/2 LBS (1.1 KG) WHEAT MALT
1/2 LB (.23 KG) FLAKED WHEAT

Crush the malt. Mash-in the malt to 148-149°F (65°C) with 2-1/2 gallons (9.5 L)of liquor at 160°F (71°C). Cover and hold. After 1-1/2 hours begin to run- off sweet wort to kettle. Heat sparge liquor to 172°F (78°C).

Sparge mash with 3 gallons (11.4 L) of 172°F (78°C) liquor to collect about 4-1/2 gallons (17 L) of sweet wort; dilute with the remaining 1-1/2 gallons (5.7 L) of liquor to collect 6 gallons (23 L) at sg 1041.

Stir into your kettle:
1/4 LB (.11 KG) TABLE SUGAR, and
1/4 LB (.11 KG) BREWER'S CORN SUGAR, or 1/2 LB (.23 KG) OF LIGHT CANDI SUGAR

KETTLE SCHEDULE:
1.5 HBU STYRIAN GOLDINGS as soon as the wort comes to a boil,
2 HBU PERLE after 45 minutes,
1.25 HBU FUGGLES after 60 minutes, and
1/2 OZ (14 G) CORIANDER SEEDS,
1/4 OZ (7 G) DRIED ORANGE PEEL, and
1/2 TSP (2.5 ML) OF CITRIC ACID AT KETTLE KNOCK-OUT, after 1-1/2 hour boil.

Transfer through wort chiller into carboy, aerating the wort.
5-1/4 gallons (20 L) of wort should be collected at sg 1048. The citric acid is to help reduce the wort acidity to 4.5 or so, to achieve the characteristic tartness of Wit beer.

Pitch with:
1 PKG of neutral ale yeast (7-14 grams dry yeast) or Belgian liquid yeast (Yeast Lab A08 or W52, Wyeast 3944, or BrewTek CL-390).

Ferment at:
60-68°F (16-20°C). Transfer to secondary after 5-7 days, condition at 50-65°F (10-18°C) for 2-3 weeks.

Prime with:
1 cup (.23 L)of CORN SUGAR and bottle condition for 1-2 months at below 65°F (18°C).

CALIFORNIA COMMON BEER

FRITZ LAGER

If Maytag appliances weren't as reliable as their ads claim, Anchor Brewing's Fritz Maytag might have had to become a repairman to keep the family business going, and he might not have rescued the last San Francisco Steam® Beer brewery, and the style just might have been forgotten. The world would be a less wonderful place.

Fortunately, the dean of the craft-brewing revival did rescue Anchor from oblivion, and California Common Beer has been among homebrewers' favorite beers ever since. So steam up the kitchen brewing this **hoppy** beer. Be sure to use a lager yeast strain that doesn't give a lot of "solventy" flavors at the high temperatures the beer ferments at.

OG 1052   TG 1012   ABV 5.3%   SRM 13   IBU 30

Heat 7-3/4 gallons (29.5 L) of water to 165°F (74°C).

WATER SUPPLY:	TREAT WATER:
Soft	OK AS IS
Moderately sulfate	OK AS IS
Moderately carbonate	ACIDIFY TO BELOW pH 7.2
Highly sulfate	DILUTE 1:1
Highly carbonate	BOIL, AND ACIDIFY TO BELOW pH 7.2

8-1/4 LBS (3.7 KG) LAGER MALT
1 LB (.45 KG) CRYSTAL MALT

Crush the malt. Mash-in the malt to 149-150°F (66°C) with 3 gallons (11.4 L) of liquor at 165°F (74°C). Cover and hold. After 1-1/4 hours begin to run-off sweet wort to kettle. Heat sparge liquor to 172°F (78°C).

Sparge mash with 4-3/4 gallons (18 L) of 172°F (78°C) liquor to collect 6-1/4 gallons (24 L) of sweet wort at sg 1044.

KETTLE SCHEDULE:
 1.25 HBU GOLDINGS as soon as the wort comes to a boil,
 1.75 HBU NORTHERN BREWER after 30 minutes,
 1.75 HBU NORTHERN BREWER after 45 minutes,
 3.5 HBU NORTHERN BREWER after 60 minutes,
 1.75 HBU NORTHERN BREWER and
 1/4 TSP (1.2 ML) IRISH MOSS after 1 hour and fifteen minutes,
KETTLE KNOCK-OUT at 1-1/2 hours.

Transfer through wort chiller into carboy, aerating the wort.
5-1/4 gallons (20 L) of wort should be collected at sg 1052.

Pitch with:
2 PKGS of dry lager yeast (10-14 grams dry yeast) or liquid yeast (Yeast Lab L35, BrewTek CL-690, or Wyeast 2112).

Ferment at:
63-65°F (17-18°C). Transfer to secondary after 4-7 days, condition at 35-50°F (2-12°C) for 2-3 weeks.

Prime with:
3/4 cup (170 ML) of CORN SUGAR and bottle condition for 1 month at below 65°F (18°C).

WEIZEN

BEETLEJUICE/BETELGEUSE

Even if you've never seen the movie, this is still a great beer to brew. Weizens have loads of eccentric character, unlike their rather straight-forward American counterparts. Speaking of eccentric, did you know that astronomers named a huge star in the constellation Orion "Beetlejuice"?

OK, so let's brew Beetlejuice! You don't need to go out and collect several hundred beetles and distill their vital juices to brew this beer, but you can if you really want to.

OG 1052   TG 1012   ABV 5.3%   SRM 4   IBU 12

Heat 8 gallons (30 L) of water to 165°F (74°C).

ADJUST ALL WATER SUPPLIES TO BELOW pH 7.0 BEFORE BREWING

WATER SUPPLY:	TREAT WATER:
Soft	1 TSP (5 ML) GYPSUM,
	1 TSP (5 ML) TABLE SALT
Moderately sulfate	1/2 TSP (2.5 ML) GYPSUM,
	1 TSP (5 ML) TABLE SALT
Moderately carbonate	1 TSP (5 ML) GYPSUM,
	1/2 TSP (2.5 ML) TABLE SALT
Highly sulfate	DILUTE 1:1, 1/2 TSP (2.5 ML) TABLE SALT
Highly carbonate	BOIL; 1/2 TSP (2.5 ML) TABLE SALT

4-1/2 LBS (2 KG) 6-ROW LAGER MALT
4-1/2 LBS (2 KG) WHEAT MALT

Crush the malt. Mash-in the malt to 131-133°F (56°C) with 2-1/2 gallons (9.5 L) of liquor at 165°F (74°C). After 15 minutes, add another 1 gallon (3.8 L) of liquor to raise the temperature of the goods to 146-148°F (64°C). After 20 minutes gently apply heat to raise the temperature of the goods to 155-158°F (68-70°C). Cover and hold. After 1/2 hour begin to run-off sweet wort to kettle. Heat sparge liquor to 172°F (78°C). Sparge mash with 4-1/2 gallons (17 L) of 172°F (78°C) liquor to collect 6-1/2 gallons (25 L) of sweet wort at sg 1042.

KETTLE SCHEDULE:
2 HBU PERLE as soon as the wort comes to a boil,
1.25 HBU SAAZ after 90 minutes,
1/2 TSP (2.5 ML) IRISH MOSS after 1 hour and forty-five minutes.
KETTLE KNOCK-OUT at 2 hours.

Transfer through wort chiller into carboy, aerating the wort.
5-1/4 gallons (20 L) of wort should be collected at sg 1052.

Pitch with:
2 PKGS of dry ale yeast (10-14 grams dry yeast) or liquid yeast (Yeast Lab W51, BrewTek CL-920, Wyeast 3068).

Ferment at:
65-72°F (18-22°C). Transfer to secondary after 4-6 days, condition at 35-55°F (2-13°C) for 2-3 weeks.

Prime with:
3/4 - 1 cup (170-230 ML) of CORN SUGAR and bottle condition for 1 month at below 65°F (18°C).

DUNKELWEIZEN

SCHWARZ UND WEISS

Nothing is black-and-white about brewing, except the fact that beer is wonderful. Brewing is wonderful, too, but there is absolutely nothing black-and-white about it. Brewing has a scientific basis, but it requires an artful touch, and a "feel" for the beer. Even so, things don't always proceed as planned.

Always let "the artist within you" have a say when you have to make brewing decisions. Don't let the crazy bugger go wild, though, because brewing **is** a science as well. You need to balance Yin and Yang. Art and Science. Black and White. Schwarz und Weiss.

OG 1052 TG 1012 ABV 5.3% SRM 19 IBU 14

Heat 8 gallons (30 L) of water to 165°F (74°C).

WATER SUPPLY:	TREAT WATER:
Soft	1 TSP (5 ML) GYPSUM,
	1/2 TSP (2.5 ML) TABLE SALT
Moderately sulfate	1/2 TSP (2.5 ML) OF TABLE SALT
Moderately carbonate	1/2 TSP (2.5 ML) GYPSUM,
	1/2 TSP (2.5 ML) TABLE SALT
Highly sulfate	DILUTE 1:1, ADJUST ACIDITY TO pH 7.2
Highly carbonate	BOIL, ADJUST ACIDITY TO pH 7.2 OR BELOW

4-1/4 LBS (1.9 KG) 6-ROW LAGER MALT
4-1/2 LBS (2 KG) WHEAT MALT
1/4 LB (113 G) CHOCOLATE MALT
2 OZ (57 G) BLACK MALT

Crush the malt. Mash-in the malt to 131-133°F (56°C) with 2-1/2 gallons (9.5 L) of liquor at 165°F (74°C). After 15 minutes, add another 1 gallon (3.8L) of liquor to raise the temperature of the goods to 146-148°F (64°C). After 10 minutes apply heat to raise the temperature of the goods to 152-153°F (67°C). Cover and hold. After 1 hour begin to run-off sweet wort to kettle. Heat sparge liquor to 172°F (78°C). Sparge mash with 4-1/2 gallons (17 L) of 172°F (78°C) liquor to collect 6-1/2 gallons (25 L) of sweet wort at sg 1042.

KETTLE SCHEDULE:
2 HBU PERLE as soon as the wort comes to a boil,
1.25 HBU SAAZ after 90 minutes,
1/2 TSP (2.5 ML) IRISH MOSS
after 1 hour and forty-five minutes,
KETTLE KNOCK-OUT at 2 hours.

Transfer through wort chiller into carboy, aerating the wort.
5-1/4 gallons (20 L) of wort should be collected at sg 1052.

Pitch with:
2 PKGS of dry ale yeast (10-14 grams dry yeast) or liquid yeast (Yeast Lab W51, BrewTek CL-920, Wyeast 3068).

Ferment at:
65-72°F (18-22°C). Transfer to secondary after 4-6 days, condition at 35-55°F (2-13°C) for 2-3 weeks.

Prime with:
3/4 - 1 cup (170-230 ML) of CORN SUGAR and bottle condition for 1 month at below 65°F (18°C).

DÜSSELDORF ALT

ZUM RUMDUM ALTBIER

Altbiers are essentially like pale ales and steam beer in color and flavor, but use "continental" ingredients and alt (ale) yeast in a warm fermentation, followed by cold conditioning. "Alt" means old in German, and refers to the beers and brewing style that preceded the lager brewing revolution in Germany.

OG 1048   TG 1012   ABV 4.7%   SRM 15   IBU 30

Heat 7-1/2 gallons (28.5 L) of water to 165°F (74°C).

WATER SUPPLY:	TREAT WATER:
Soft	1-1/2 TSP (7.4 ML) GYPSUM, 1/2 TSP (2.5 ML) SALT
Moderately sulfate	1/2 TSP (2.5 ML) GYPSUM, 1/2 TSP (2.5 ML) TABLE SALT
Moderately carbonate	1/2 TSP (2.5 ML) GYPSUM, 1/2 TSP (2.5 ML) TABLE SALT
Highly sulfate	ACIDIFY TO BELOW pH 7.2
Highly carbonate	BOIL, ACIDIFY TO BELOW pH 7.2

7-1/4 LBS (3.3 KG) LAGER MALT
3/4 LB (340 G) CRYSTAL MALT
1/2 LB (227 G) CARAMEL-120 MALT

Crush the malt. Mash-in to 149-150°F (66°C) with 3 gallons (11.4 L) of liquor at 165°F (74°C). Cover and hold. After 1 hour begin to run-off sweet wort to kettle. Heat sparge liquor to 172°F (78°C). Sparge mash with 4 gallons (15 L) of 172°F (78°C) liquor. Pour the remaining 1/2 gallon (1.9 L) of liquor into your kettle, for 6-1/4 gallons (24 L) of sweet wort at sg 1040.

KETTLE SCHEDULE:
1.5 HBU TETTNANG as soon as the wort comes to a boil,
3.5 HBU NORTHERN BREWER after 45 minutes,
3 HBU TETTNANG after 60 minutes,
1.5 HBU TETTNANG and
1/4 TSP (1.2 ML) IRISH MOSS after 1 hour and fifteen minutes,
KETTLE KNOCK-OUT at 1-1/2 hours.

Transfer through wort chiller into carboy, aerating the wort.
5-1/4 gallons (20 L) of wort should be collected at sg 1048.

Pitch with:
2 PKGS of ale yeast (10-14 grams dry yeast) or liquid yeast (Yeast Lab A06, BrewTek CL-400, Wyeast 1338).

Ferment at:
60-68°F (16-20°C). Transfer to secondary after 4-8 days, condition at 35-55°F (2-13°C) for 3-6 weeks.

Prime with:
3/4 - 7/8 cup (170-190 ML) of CORN SUGAR and bottle condition for 2 months at below 60°F (16°C).

KÖLSCH

HAUSBRAUEREI LITEN

What's pale in color, has a winey aroma with just a hint of hops, a lightly fruity flavor and a dry finish? Kölsch! Homebrew Lite! Summer-weather homebrew!

The weather of the British Isles being what it is, there isn't an English counterpart to the pale beers of America and Continental Europe. It never gets hot enough in England for anyone with tastebuds to **want** to drink a light-flavored beer. In Germany, on the other hand, there are Kölsch and Weizen, in Belgium Wit beer, and in America...well, in America that's why homebrewers brew British, Belgian and German style beers.

OG 1044 TG 1010 ABV 4.5% SRM 3.5 IBU 25

Heat 8 gallons (30 L) of water to 165°F (74°C).

WATER SUPPLY:	TREAT WATER:
Soft	ACIDIFY TO BELOW pH 7.0
Moderately sulfate	ACIDIFY TO BELOW pH 7.0
Moderately carbonate	BOIL, ACIDIFY TO BELOW pH 7.0
Highly sulfate	DILUTE AT LEAST 1:1, ACIDIFY TO BELOW 7.0
Highly carbonate	BOIL, DILUTE 1:1, ACIDIFY TO BELOW pH 7.0

6-1/4 LBS (2.8 KG) LAGER MALT
1-1/2 LBS (.68 KG) WHEAT MALT

Crush the malt. Mash-in to 149-150°F (66°C) with 2-3/4 gallons (10.4 L) of liquor at 165°F (74°C). Cover and hold. After 1-1/4 hours begin to run-off sweet wort to kettle. Heat sparge liquor to 172°F (78°C). Sparge mash with 4 gallons (15 L) at 172°F (78°C). Pour the remaining 1-1/4 gallons of liquor into the kettle, to collect just less than 6-1/4 gallons (24 L) of sweet wort at sg 1037.

KETTLE SCHEDULE:
1.25 HBU TETTNANG as soon as the wort comes to a boil,
2.5 HBU TETTNANG after 30 minutes,
3.75 HBU TETTNANG after 60 minutes,
1/2 TSP (2.5 ML) IRISH MOSS after 1 hour and fifteen minutes, and 1/4 OZ (7 g) TETTNANG after 1 hour and twenty-five minutes, KETTLE KNOCK-OUT at 1-1/2 hours.

Transfer through wort chiller into carboy, aerating the wort.
5-1/4 gallons (20 L) of wort should be collected at sg 1044.

Pitch with:
2 PKGS of ale yeast (10-14 grams dry yeast) or liquid yeast (Yeast Lab L32, L33, BrewTek CL-450, Wyeast 1007).

Ferment at:
55-68°F (13-20°C). Transfer to secondary after 4-7 days, condition at 35-50°F (2-12°C) for 3 weeks.

Prime with:
3/4 cup (170 ML) of CORN SUGAR and bottle condition for 1 month at below 60°F (16°C).

FRUIT BEER

BLUEBERRY CREAM ALE

We hope that you've brewed one of the fruit-beer recipes by the time you've gotten this far into the book, because it is such an intriguing style of beer. The first time that a lot of American homebrewers were exposed to a fruit beer was at the 1984 AHA conference. Michael Jackson featured a Kriek at a beer tasting. Many attitudes changed from purists' disdain to greed - they had to have more of this strange brew!

A decade later, fruit beers are not at all so strange to Americans. Brew up a batch at anytime of year, because it is a style that knows no season...only fruit does. If blueberries are not in season, try sour cherries or raspberries or any of the other berries, including cranberries, or use peaches, or currants, or watermelon, or...

For ease, the fruit is added at kettle knock-out. If you wish to pursue old-world fruit beers, buy a book on lambic brewing.

OG 1060   TG 1012   ABV 6.2%   SRM 4   IBU 16

Heat 7 gallons (26.5 L) of water to 160°F (71°C).

WATER SUPPLY:	TREAT WATER:
Soft	1-1/2 TSP (7.4 ML) OF GYPSUM, ACIDIFY TO pH 7.0
Moderately sulfate	ACIDIFY TO BELOW pH 7.0
Moderately carbonate	1/2 TSP (2.5 ML) OF GYPSUM, ACIDIFY TO pH 7.0
Highly sulfate	ACIDIFY TO BELOW pH 7.0
Highly carbonate	BOIL, ACIDIFY TO BELOW pH 7.0

6-1/4 LBS (2.8 KG) LAGER MALT
1 LB (454 G) CARAPILS MALT
1 LB (454 G) FLAKED WHEAT

Crush the malt. Mash-in to 149-150°F (66°C) with 2-3/4 gallons (10.4 L) of liquor at 165°F (74°C). Cover and hold. After 1 hour begin to run-off sweet wort to kettle. Heat sparge liquor to 172°F (78°C). Sparge mash with 4 gallons (15 L) of 172°F (78°C) liquor to collect 5-3/4 gallons (21 L) at sg 1037.

KETTLE SCHEDULE:
1.5 HBU MT HOOD as soon as the wort comes to a boil,
1.5 HBU MT HOOD after 45 minutes,
1.5 HBU MT HOOD and
1/2 TSP (2.5 ML) IRISH MOSS after 1 hour and fifteen minutes,
10 LBS (4.5 KG) CRUSHED BLUEBERRIES and KETTLE KNOCK-OUT at 1-1/2 hours.
Allow blueberries to steep for 1/2 hour, then

transfer through wort chiller into carboy, aerating the wort. 5-1/4 gallons (20 L) of wort should be collected at sg 1060.

Pitch with:
2 PKGS of ale yeast (10-14 grams dry yeast) or liquid yeast (Yeast Lab A08, A07, BrewTek CL-300, Wyeast 1087).

Ferment at:
60-68°F (16-19°C). Transfer to secondary after 5-8 days, condition at 50-60°F (10-16°C) for 3-5 weeks.

Prime with:
3/4 - 7/8 cup (170-190 ML) of CORN SUGAR and bottle condition for 1 month at below 60°F (16°C).

RAUCHBIER

RAUCHEN ROLL BRAU

Very few beers have the depth or intensity of flavor to let them stand up and be counted as accompaniments to flavorful foods; this one does. Smoked beers go especially well with fried foods, cheeses, and red meats. Of course, you don't have to have a meal to enjoy this beer.

This style of smoked beer should be very smoky, mouthfilling, and finish very dry. Smoked malts are not just limited to rauch brewing, however; peat, beechwood, alder or fruitwood-smoked malts can add a new dimension to many full-flavored beer styles if you are interested in experimenting further. Generally, the more the smoked malt, the less the hops that you will need to balance the sweetness of the malt.

This beer can be brewed as a lager, but is all the more interesting with a little ale fruitiness. It should always be conditioned cold.

OG 1050   TG 1015   ABV 4.6%   SRM 16   IBU 22

Heat 7-3/4 gallons (29.5 L) of water to 168°F (75°C).

WATER SUPPLY:	TREAT WATER:
Soft	1-1/2 TSP (7.4 ML) OF GYPSUM
Moderately sulfate	1/2 TSP (2.5 ML) OF GYPSUM
Moderately carbonate	1 TSP (5 ML) OF GYPSUM
Highly sulfate	OK AS IS
Highly carbonate	ACIDIFY TO 7.2

5-1/2 LBS (2.5 KG) LAGER MALT
2 LBS (.9 KG) GERMAN "MEDIUM" SMOKED MALT
3/4 LB (340 G) WHEAT MALT
1/2 LB (227 G) AMBER MALT
1 OZ (28 G) CHOCOLATE MALT

Crush the malt. Mash-in to 155-156°F (68°C) with 3 gallons (11.4 L) of liquor at 168°F (75°C). Cover and hold. After 1 hour begin to run-off sweet wort to kettle. Heat sparge liquor to 172°F (78°C). Sparge mash with 4-3/4 gallons (18 L) of 172°F (78°C) liquor to collect 6-1/4 gallons (24 L) of sweet wort at sg 1042.

KETTLE SCHEDULE:
2 HBU PERLE as soon as the wort comes to a boil,
2 HBU PERLE after 45 minutes,
2 HBU PERLE after 60 minutes,
1/4 TSP (1.2 ML) IRISH MOSS after 1 hour and fifteen minutes,
KETTLE KNOCK-OUT at 1-1/2 hours.

Transfer through wort chiller into carboy, aerating the wort.
5-1/4 gallons (20 L) of wort should be collected at sg 1050.

Pitch with:
2 PKGS of ale yeast (10-14 grams dry yeast) or liquid yeast (Yeast Lab A01, A05, BrewTek CL-240, Wyeast 1007).

Ferment at:
55-65°F (13-18°C). Transfer to secondary after 5-10 days, condition at 35-50°F (2-12°C) for 4-6 weeks.

Prime with:
2/3 - 3/4 cup (170-190 ML) of CORN SUGAR and bottle condition for 2 months at below 60°F (16°C).

LAGER

AMERICAN PREMIUM LAGER

CORN QUEEN LAGER

OK so this is America, and virgins don't hand-pick our hops (see Zatec Wirgin Pilsner page 251), but hey, any homecoming queen can harvest a hundred acres of corn a day from atop a twin-diesel John Deere! Corn is king, and America is home to the King of Beers, so beer should have corn in it, right? Right. At least when it comes to Corn Queen Lager!

We don't have a label for this beer, but we trust that trusty homebrewers will remedy that. Send us Corn Queen labels!

OG 1048   TG 1010   ABV 5%   SRM 2.5   IBU 16

Heat 7-1/2 gallons (28.5 L) of water to 145°F (63°C).

WATER SUPPLY:	TREAT WATER:
Soft	1-1/2 TSP (2.5 ML) GYPSUM, ACIDIFY TO BELOW 7.0
Moderately sulfate	ACIDIFY TO BELOW pH 7.0
Moderately carbonate	ACIDIFY TO BELOW pH 7.0
Highly sulfate	ACIDIFY TO BELOW pH 7.0
Highly carbonate	BOIL, ACIDIFY TO BELOW pH 7.0

6-1/4 LBS (2.8 KG) 6-ROW LAGER MALT
2 LBS (.9 KG) CORN FLAKES

Crush the malt. Mash-in with the corn flakes and 2-1/2 gallons (9.5 L) of liquor to 131-135°F (56-57°C) for a combined protein/beta-amylase rest. In the meantime heat the remaining liquor to 172°F (78°C). After 20 minutes, add 1/2 gallon (3.8 L) of liquor, and apply heat, to raise the temperature of the goods to 149-150°F (66°C). Cover and hold. After 3/4 of an hour, raise the temperature over 10 minutes to 158-160°F (70-71°C) and hold the temperature for 15 minutes. Run off the sweet wort to the kettle. Sparge mash with 4-1/2 gallons (17 L) of 172°F (78°C) liquor to collect 6-1/4 gallons (24 L) of sweet wort at sg 1040.

KETTLE SCHEDULE:
1.5 HBU CLUSTER as soon as the wort comes to a boil,
1.5 HBU CLUSTER after 45 minutes,
1.5 HBU CLUSTER after 60 minutes,
1/2 TSP (2.5 ML) IRISH MOSS after 1 hour and fifteen minutes,
KETTLE KNOCK-OUT at 1-1/2 hours.

Transfer through wort chiller into carboy, aerating the wort.
5-1/4 gallons (20 L) of wort should be collected at sg 1048.

Pitch with:
2 PKGS of lager yeast (10-14 grams dry yeast) or liquid yeast (Yeast Lab L34, L31, BrewTek CL-620, CL-690, Wyeast 2035).

Ferment at:
50-60°F (10-16°C). Transfer to secondary after 6-10 days, condition at 35-50°F (2-12°C) for 2-4 weeks.

Prime with:
3/4 - 7/8 cup (170-190 ML) of CORN SUGAR and bottle condition for 1 month at below 60°F (16°C).

CREAM ALE/LAGER

OTTAQUEECHIE CREAM ALE

Cream Ale is such a great style of beer because: 1) you can use any kind of yeast you like to brew it, 2) you can use any kind of hops you like to brew it, and 3) you can brew it too.

So what is a Cream Ale? It is like an American pilsener in color, hop rate and carbonation, and it is cold-conditioned (lagered). What is different about Cream Ale is that it is always fermented "warm". Ottaqueechie Cream Ale is named for the "Queechie" river nearby in Vermont, which is a great place to enjoy a Cream Ale while fishing, swimming or canoeing.

OG 1048   TG 1012   ABV 4.7%   SRM 4   IBU 20

Heat 7-3/4 gallons (29.5 L) of water to 160°F (71°C).

WATER SUPPLY:	TREAT WATER:
Soft	1-1/2 TSP (7.4 ML) OF GYPSUM, ACIDIFY TO pH 7.0
Moderately sulfate	ACIDIFY TO BELOW pH 7.0
Moderately carbonate	1/2 TSP (2.5 ML) OF GYPSUM, ACIDIFY TO pH 7.0
Highly sulfate	ACIDIFY TO BELOW pH 7.0
Highly carbonate	BOIL, ACIDIFY TO BELOW pH 7.0

6-1/4 LBS (2.8 KG) LAGER MALT
1 LB (454 G) CARAPILS MALT
1 LB (454 G) CORN FLAKES

Crush the malt. Mash-in to 149-150°F (66°C) with 2-3/4 gallons (10.4 L) of liquor at 165°F (74°C). Cover and hold. After 1 hour begin to run-off sweet wort to kettle. Heat sparge liquor to 172°F (78°C). Sparge mash with 4-1/4 gallons (16 L) of 172°F (78°C) liquor. Pour remaining 1/2 gallon (1.9 L) of liquor into kettle to collect 6-1/4 gallons (24 L) of sweet wort at sg 1040.

KETTLE SCHEDULE:
1.5 HBU MT HOOD as soon as the wort comes to a boil,
2 HBU PERLE after 45 minutes,
2 HBU PERLE and
1/2 TSP (2.5 ML) IRISH MOSS after 1 hour and fifteen minutes,
KETTLE KNOCK-OUT at 1-1/2 hours.

Transfer through wort chiller into carboy, aerating the wort.
5-1/4 gallons (20 L) of wort should be collected at sg 1048.

Pitch with:
2 PKGS of ale yeast (10-14 grams dry yeast) or liquid yeast (Yeast Lab A07, A08, A02, L35, BrewTek CL-260, CL-450, Wyeast 1007).

Ferment at:
60-68°F (16-20°C). Transfer to secondary after 4-7 days, condition at 35-50°F (2-12°C) for 3-6 weeks.

Prime with:
3/4 - 7/8 (170-190 ML) cup of CORN SUGAR and bottle condition for 1 month at below 60°F (16°C).

DORTMUND EXPORT

MEIN KELLER SUDZWERKS XX EXPORT

Here's a great recipe to brew in **your** cellar suds-works. Call it a Dort, call it an Export, it's a rose of a beer by any name.

The Dortmund style is kissing-cousins with the Pilsner family, but fuller, and with a faint mineral character. For homebrewers with moderately-carbonate to highly-sulfate water, it is the logical choice to brew instead of a Pilsener.

OG 1052 TG 1012 ABV 5.3% SRM 5 IBU 32

Heat 7-3/4 gallons (29.5 L) of water to 165°F (74°C).

WATER SUPPLY:	TREAT WATER:
Soft	1-1/2 TSP (7.4 ML) GYPSUM,
	1/2 TSP (2.5 ML) SALT
Moderately sulfate	1/2 TSP (2.5 ML) TABLE SALT
Moderately carbonate	1/2 TSP (2.5 ML) OF TABLE SALT
Highly sulfate	OK AS IS
Highly carbonate	1/2 TSP (2.5 ML) SALT, ACIDIFY TO BELOW 7.0

8-3/4 LBS (4 KG) LAGER MALT
1/2 LB (227 G) CARAPILS MALT

Crush the malt. Mash-in to 149-150°F (66°C) with 3-1/4 gallons (12.3 L) of liquor at 165°F (74°C). Cover and hold. After 1-1/4 hours begin to run-off sweet wort to kettle. Heat sparge liquor to 172°F (78°C). Sparge mash with 4-1/2 gallons of 172°F (78°C) liquor to collect 6-1/4 gallons (24 L) of sweet wort at sg 1044.

KETTLE SCHEDULE:
1.25 HBU HALLERTAU as soon as the wort comes to a boil,
4 HBU PERLE after 45 minutes,
3.75 HBU HALLERTAU after 60 minutes,
2.5 HBU HALLERTAU and
1/4 TSP (1.2 ML) IRISH MOSS after 1 hour and fifteen minutes,
KETTLE KNOCK-OUT at 1-1/2 hours.

Transfer through wort chiller into carboy, aerating the wort.
5-1/4 gallons (20 L) of wort should be collected at sg 1052.

Pitch with:
2 PKGS of lager yeast (10-14 grams dry yeast) or liquid yeast (Yeast Lab L31, L34, BrewTek CL-660, Wyeast 2042).

Ferment at:
45-55°F (7-13°C). Transfer to secondary after 7-12 days, condition at 35-50°F (2-12°C) for 4-8 weeks.

Prime with:
3/4 cup (170 ML) of CORN SUGAR and bottle condition for 2 months at below 60°F (16°C).

MUNICH HELLES

SMALLBRAUHAUS HELL

Side-by-side a Pilsener and a Helles do not appear very different. They are, however, about as different as light lagers could be.

If you like the flavor of malt, and overall softness, this is the brew for you. If you can, use genuine Bohemian lager (or pilsner) malt to brew Smallbrauhaus Hell, because no other malt will give it the full maltiness that characterizes the Munich beers. If you do use one of these malts, you must at least step-mash it. Decoction mashing will bring the soft maltiness out even further.

OG 1048   TG 1014   ABV 4.5%   SRM 5   IBU 22

Heat 7-1/2 gallons (28.5 L) of water to 168°F (76°C).

WATER SUPPLY:
Soft
Moderately sulfate
Moderately carbonate
Highly sulfate
Highly carbonate

TREAT WATER:
1/2 TSP (2.5 ML) GYPSUM ACIDIFY TO pH 7.0
ACIDIFY TO BELOW pH 7.0
ACIDIFY TO BELOW pH 7.0
DILUTE 1:1, ACIDIFY TO BELOW pH 7.0
DILUTE 1:1, ACIDIFY TO BELOW pH 7.0

6 LBS (2.7 KG) LAGER MALT
2-1/2 LBS (1.1 KG) MUNICH MALT

Crush the malt. Mash-in to 154-155°F (68°C) with 3 gallons (11.4 L) of liquor at 168°F (76°C). Cover and hold. After 1 hour begin to run-off sweet wort to kettle. Heat sparge liquor to 172°F (78°C). Sparge mash with 4-1/2 gallons of 172°F (78°C) liquor to collect 6-1/4 gallons (24 L) of sweet wort at sg 1042.

If you are step-mashing, heat liquor to 145°F (63°C) instead of 168°F (76°C) and mash in with 2-1/2 gallons of liquor to 131-135°F (56-57°C) for a combined protein/beta-amylase rest. In the meantime heat the remaining liquor to 172°F (78°C). After 15 minutes, add 1/2 gallon (1.9 L) of liquor, and apply heat, to raise the temperature of the goods to 156-158°F (69°C). Cover and hold for 3/4 hour, and sparge as above.

KETTLE SCHEDULE:
1.25 HBU HALLERTAU as soon as the wort comes to a boil,
2.5 HBU HALLERTAU after 45 minutes,
2.5 HBU HALLERTAU after 60 minutes,
1.25 HBU HALLERTAU and
1/4 TSP (1.2 ML) IRISH MOSS after 1 hour and fifteen minutes,
KETTLE KNOCK-OUT at 1-1/2 hours.

Transfer through wort chiller into carboy, aerating the wort.
5-1/4 gallons (20 L) of wort should be collected at sg 1048.

Pitch with:
2 PKGS of lager yeast (10-14 grams dry yeast) or liquid yeast (Yeast Lab L32, L33, BrewTek CL-620, Wyeast 2178).

Ferment at:
45-55°F (7-13°C). Transfer to secondary after 7-10 days, condition at 35-50°F (2-12°C) for 4-8 weeks.

Prime with:
3/4 cup (170 ML) of CORN SUGAR and bottle condition for 2 months at below 60°F (16°C).

GERMAN PILSENER

HOPFEN UND MALZ PILS

Hops and malt says it all. Before lager brewing, yeastiness in one of its myriad forms was a character of all beer. In the 19th century, Pilsener lager became the rage around the world, not just because it was a clear, haze-free, golden beer, but because the style of brewing let the flavor of malt and hops stand alone for the first time.

This recipe employs a protein/maltose rest in a step-mash. Use fresh, fragrant German hops and "continental" malt for brewing Hopfen und Malz Pils, and use a very neutral lager yeast strain to capture the real character of a Deutscher Pils.

OG 1048   TG 1012   ABV 4.7%   SRM 3   IBU 35

Heat 7-1/2 gallons (28.5 L) of water to 145°F (63°C).

WATER SUPPLY:	TREAT WATER:
Soft	1 TSP (5 ML) OF GYPSUM, ACIDIFY TO BELOW 7.0
Moderately sulfate	ACIDIFY TO BELOW pH 7.0
Moderately carbonate	ACIDIFY TO BELOW pH 7.0
Highly sulfate	DILUTE 1:1, AND ACIDIFY TO BELOW pH 7.0
Highly carbonate	DILUTE 1:1, AND ACIDIFY TO BELOW pH 7.0

7-1/2 LBS (3.4 KG) EUROPEAN LAGER OR PILSNER MALT
1/2 LB (227 G) CARAPILS MALT
1/2 LB (227 G) VIENNA MALT

Crush the malt. Mash-in with 2-3/4 gallons (10.4 L) of liquor to 131-135°F (56-57°C) for a combined protein/beta-amylase rest. In the meantime heat the remaining liquor to 172°F (78°C). After 15 minutes, add 1 quart (.95 L) of liquor, and apply heat, to raise the temperature of the goods to 156-158°F (69-70°C). Cover and hold. After 3/4 of an hour begin to run-off sweet wort to kettle. Sparge mash with 4-1/2 gallons (17 L) of 172°F (78°C) liquor to collect 6-1/4 gallons (24 L) of sweet wort at sg 1040.

KETTLE SCHEDULE:
1.5 HBU MT HOOD as soon as the wort comes to a boil,
4.5 HBU NORTHERN BREWER after 45 minutes,
3 HBU MT HOOD after 60 minutes,
2.5 HBU TETTNANG and
1/4 TSP (1.2 ML) IRISH MOSS after 1 hour and fifteen minutes,
KETTLE KNOCK-OUT at 1-1/2 hours.

Transfer through wort chiller into carboy, aerating the wort.
5-1/4 gallons (20 L) of wort should be collected at sg 1048.

Pitch with:
2 PKGS of lager yeast (10-14 grams dry yeast) or liquid yeast (Yeast Lab L31, L35, BrewTek CL-660, CL-620, Wyeast 2007).

Ferment at:
45-55°F (7-13°C). Transfer to secondary after 7-10 days, condition at 35-50°F (2-12°C) for 4-6 weeks.

Prime with:
3/4 cup (170 ML) of CORN SUGAR and bottle condition for 2 months at below 60°F (16°C).

BOHEMIAN PILSENER

ZATEC WIRGIN PILSENER

Saaz hops are undisputedly the finest lager hops in the world. Some would have it that it is not just the hop itself, or the soil, or the weather conditions around Zatec (Zaht-k) that make Saaz (Zotz) hops the finest, but that it is because they are hand-picked by wirgins (virgins).

Zatec Wirgin emulates the original Pilsner as closely as possible; you only need to add reasonable fermentation-temperature control to produce your own Wirgin Urquell.

OG 1048   TG 1012   ABV 4.7%   SRM 4   IBU 36

Heat 7-1/2 gallons (28.5 L) of water to 145°F (63°C).

WATER SUPPLY:	TREAT WATER:
Soft	ACIDIFY TO BELOW pH 7.0
Moderately sulfate	ACIDIFY TO BELOW pH 7.0
Moderately carbonate	BOIL, AND ACIDIFY TO BELOW pH 7.0
Highly sulfate	BREW DORTMUND
Highly carbonate	BREW DORTMUND

6-3/4 LBS (3.1 KG) PILSENER MALT
1/2 LB (227 G) CARAPILS MALT
1 LB (454 G) VIENNA MALT

Crush the malt. Mash-in with 2-1/2 gallons (9.5 L) of liquor to 131-135°F (56-57°C) for a combined protein/beta-amylase rest. In the meantime heat the remaining liquor to 172°F (78°C). After 15 minutes, add 1/2 gallon of liquor, and apply heat, to raise the temperature of the goods to 158-160°F (70-71°C). Cover and hold. After 3/4 of an hour begin to run-off sweet wort to kettle.
Sparge mash with 4-1/2 gallons of 172°F (78°C) liquor to collect 6-1/4 gallons (24 L) of sweet wort at sg 1040.

KETTLE SCHEDULE:
1.5 HBU MT HOOD as soon as the wort comes to a boil,
3.75 HBU SAAZ after 45 minutes,
2.5 HBU SAAZ after 60 minutes,
3.75 HBU SAAZ and
1/4 TSP (1.2 ML) IRISH MOSS after 1 hour and fifteen minutes,
1 OZ (28 G) SAAZ and KETTLE KNOCK-OUT at 1-1/2 hours.

Transfer through wort chiller into carboy, aerating the wort.
5-1/4 gallons (20 L) of wort should be collected at sg 1048.

Pitch with:
2 PKGS of lager yeast (10-14 grams dry yeast) or liquid yeast (Yeast Lab L31, L33, BrewTek CL-600, Wyeast 2124).

Ferment at:
45-55°F (7-13°C). Transfer to secondary after 7-10 days, condition at 35-50°F (2-12°C) for 4-8 weeks.

Prime with:
3/4 cup (170 ML) of CORN SUGAR and bottle condition for 2 months at below 60°F (16°C).

MUNICH DUNKEL

BIERBAUCH LAGER

Our Beerbelly Lager is a Munich Dunkel, a virtual celebration of malt and maltiness. Traditionally decoction mashed, the repeated boiling of the Bavarian malt brings out "malty" flavors in a manner that infusion and step-mashing cannot really replicate.

However you may choose to mash this brew, it still gives a good malty flavor, with a mild roastiness. It's a perfect choice for homebrewers that are cursed with highly carbonate water. And if your idea of a fashion statement is developing a beerbelly, this is the beer to do it with.

OG 1052   TG 1015   ABV 4.9%   SRM 18   IBU 23

Heat 7-3/4 gallons (29.5 L) of water to 168°F (76°C).

WATER SUPPLY:	TREAT WATER:
Soft	1/2 TSP (2.5 ML) OF GYPSUM
Moderately sulfate	OK AS IS
Moderately carbonate	OK AS IS
Highly sulfate	OK AS IS
Highly carbonate	ACIDIFY SPARGE WATER TO BELOW 7.2

4-3/4 LBS (2.2 KG) LAGER MALT
3 LBS (1.4 KG) MUNICH MALT
3/4 LB (340 G) CRYSTAL MALT
2/3 LB (284 G) BROWN MALT
1 OZ (28 G) CHOCOLATE MALT
1 OZ (28 G) BLACK MALT

Crush the malt. Mash-in to 153-154°F (67°C) with 3-1/4 gallons (12.3 L) of liquor at 168°F (76°C). Cover and hold. After 1 hour begin to run-off sweet wort to kettle. Heat sparge liquor to 172°F (78°C). Sparge mash with 4-1/2 gallons (17 L) of 172°F (78°C) liquor to collect 6-1/4 gallons (24 L) of sweet wort at sg 1044.

KETTLE SCHEDULE:
1.5 HBU MT HOOD as soon as the wort comes to a boil,
2 HBU PERLE after 45 minutes,
3 HBU MT HOOD after 60 minutes,
1.5 HBU HALLERTAU and
1/4 TSP (1.2 ML) IRISH MOSS after 1 hour and fifteen minutes,
KETTLE KNOCK-OUT at 1-1/2 hours.

Transfer through wort chiller into carboy, aerating the wort.
5-1/4 gallons (20 L) of wort should be collected at sg 1052.

Pitch with:
2 PKGS of lager yeast (10-14 grams dry yeast) or liquid yeast (Yeast Lab L32, L33, BrewTek CL-620, Wyeast 2178).

Ferment at:
45-55°F (7-13°C). Transfer to secondary after 7-10 days, condition at 35-50°F (2-12°C) for 4-8 weeks.

Prime with:
2/3 - 3/4 cup (150-170 ML) of CORN SUGAR and bottle condition for 2 months at below 60°F (16°C).

SCHWARZBIER

BLACKGOLD SCHWARZPILS

Pilseners are by definition light-gold to straw colored, but many a German brauerei, large and small, produces dark lagers, or Schwarzbier. The dark lagers from Beck, Heineken, St. Pauli Girl and Michelob are all of this style. Although they are dark to the point of approaching black, none of them is as full or as satiating as a Munich Dunkel. They are more appropriately called Schwarzpils.

This recipe is for a dark Pilsner, and yields a delicious brew that is unusually crisp for a beer of this color. It is a favorite of patrons of the Vermont Pub & Brewery under the Black Bear Lager name.

OG 1048   TG 1012   ABV 4.7%   SRM 20   IBU 30

Heat 7-3/4 gallons (29.5 L) of water to 165°F (74°C).

WATER SUPPLY:	TREAT WATER:
Soft	UP TO 1-1/2 TSP (7.4 ML) OF GYPSUM
Moderately sulfate	OK AS IS
Moderately carbonate	OK AS IS
Highly sulfate	OK AS IS
Highly carbonate	ACIDIFY TO BELOW 7.2

7-1/2 LBS (3.4 KG) LAGER MALT
3/4 LB (340 G) DARK CRYSTAL MALT
2 OZ (57 G) CHOCOLATE MALT
2 OZ (57 G) BLACK MALT

Crush the malt. Mash-in to 150-152°F (66-67°C) with 3 gallons (11.4 L) of liquor at 165°F (74°C). Cover and hold. After 1 hour begin to run-off sweet wort to kettle. Heat sparge liquor to 172°F (78°C). Sparge mash with 4-3/4 gallons (18 L) of 172°F (78°C) liquor to collect 6-1/4 gallons (24 L) of sweet wort at sg 1040.

KETTLE SCHEDULE:
1.5 HBU MT HOOD as soon as the wort comes to a boil,
2 HBU PERLE after 45 minutes,
4 HBU PERLE after 60 minutes,
5 HBU SAAZ and
1/4 TSP (1.2 ML) IRISH MOSS after 1 hour and fifteen minutes,
KETTLE KNOCK-OUT at 1-1/2 hours.

Transfer through wort chiller into carboy, aerating the wort.
5-1/4 gallons (20 L) of wort should be collected at sg 1048.

Pitch with:
2 PKGS of lager yeast (10-14 grams dry yeast) or liquid yeast (Yeast Lab L31, L35, BrewTek CL-660, CL-620, Wyeast 2007).

Ferment at:
45-55°F (7-13°C). Transfer to secondary after 7-10 days, condition at 35-50°F (2-12°C) for 4-8 weeks.

Prime with:
3/4 cup (170 ML) of CORN SUGAR and bottle condition for 2 months at below 60°F (16°C).

VIENNA

INNSBRUCK ALPEN SPEZIAL

This is such a great style of beer that it is nice to have two subcategories to brew to, the only differences being that Vienna interpretations tend to be somewhat more bitter and slightly lower in gravity than Oktoberfests.

For authenticity this recipe uses Styrian Goldings hops and Vienna malt, and so should you. For a richer version, replace the lager malt in the recipe with Vienna malt. Keep the mash thickness tight to conserve the limited enzyme strength of the Vienna malt. This interpretation is incredibly full and rounded in flavor.

OG 1052   TG 1013   ABV 5.1%   SRM 12   IBU 25

Heat 7-3/4 gallons (29.5 L) of water to 145°F (63°C).

WATER SUPPLY:	TREAT WATER:
Soft	1-1/2 TSP (7.4 ML) OF GYPSUM, ACIDIFY TO pH 7.2
Moderately sulfate	1/2 TSP (2.5 ML) OF GYPSUM, ACIDIFY TO pH 7.2
Moderately carbonate	1/2 TSP (2.5 ML) OF GYPSUM, ACIDIFY TO pH 7.2
Highly sulfate	ACIDIFY TO BELOW pH 7.2
Highly carbonate	ACIDIFY TO BELOW pH 7.2

4-3/4 (2.2 KG) LBS LAGER MALT
4 LBS (1.8 KG) VIENNA MALT
1/4 LB (113 G) LIGHT CRYSTAL MALT
1/4 LB (113 G) CARAMEL-120 MALT

Crush the malt. Mash-in with 3 gallons (11.4 L) of liquor to 131-135°F (55-57°C) for a combined protein/maltose rest. In the meantime heat the remaining liquor to 172°F (78°C). After 15 minutes, add 1/2 gallon (2.4 L) of liquor, and apply heat, to raise the temperature of the goods to 158-160°F (70-71°C). Cover and hold. After 3/4 of an hour begin to run-off sweet wort to kettle. Sparge mash with 4-1/4 gallons (16 L) of 172°F (78°C) liquor to collect 6-1/4 gallons (24 L) of sweet wort at sg 1044.

KETTLE SCHEDULE:
1.5 HBU STYRIAN GOLDINGS as soon as the wort comes to a boil,
2 HBU PERLE after 45 minutes,
3 HBU STYRIAN GOLDINGS after 60 minutes,
1.5 HBU STYRIAN GOLDINGS and
1/4 TSP (1.2 ML) IRISH MOSS after 1 hour and fifteen minutes,
1/4 OZ (7 G) STYRIAN GOLDINGS after 1 hour and 25 minutes,
KETTLE KNOCK-OUT at 1-1/2 hours.

Transfer through wort chiller into carboy, aerating the wort.
5-1/4 gallons (20 L) of wort should be collected at sg 1052.

Pitch with:
2 PKGS of lager yeast (10-14 grams dry yeast) or liquid yeast (Yeast Lab L32, L33, BrewTek CL-640, Wyeast 2042).

Ferment at:
45-55°F (7-13°C). Transfer to secondary after 7-10 days, condition at 35-50°F (2-12°C) for 4-8 weeks.

Prime with:
3/4 cup (170 ML) of CORN SUGAR and bottle condition for 2 months at below 60°F (16°C).

ROCKTOBERFEST

Does anybody really like oompah music? We don't think so. Oompah-pah, oompah-pah, oompah-pah, ooh, let's have another litre. We think that the Munich beer halls just play it to make you drink more.

What we need here in America is a **Rock**toberfest. Sort of like a Woodstock with homebrew. We could get maybe 500,000 homebrewers or so to show up. Everybody could bring a batch of Rocktoberfest Märzen. All we need is a place. Hey! Ask your spouse! Can we have it at your house?

OG 1058   TG 1014   ABV 5.8%   SRM 14   IBU 24

Heat 8 gallons (30 L) of water to 145°F (63°C).

WATER SUPPLY:	TREAT WATER:
Soft	1 TSP (5 ML) OF GYPSUM, ACIDIFY TO pH 7.2
Moderately sulfate	ACIDIFY TO BELOW pH 7.2
Moderately carbonate	ACIDIFY TO BELOW pH 7.2
Highly sulfate	DILUTE 1:1, ACIDIFY TO BELOW pH 7.2
Highly carbonate	BOIL, ACIDIFY TO BELOW pH 7.2

8-3/4 LBS (4 KG) LAGER MALT
1 LB (454 G) LIGHT CRYSTAL MALT
1/4 LB (113 G) CRYSTAL MALT
1/4 LB (113 G) CARAMEL-120 MALT

Crush the malt. Mash-in with 3 gallons (11.4 L) of liquor to 131-135°F (56-57°C) for a combined protein/maltose rest. In the meantime heat the remaining liquor to 172°F (78°C). After 15 minutes, add 1/2 gallon (1.9 L) of liquor, and apply heat, to raise the temperature of the goods to 158-160°F (71°C). Cover and hold. After 3/4 of an hour begin to run-off sweet wort to kettle. Sparge mash with 4-1/2 gallons (17 L) of 172°F (78°C) liquor to collect 6-1/4 gallons (24 L) of sweet wort at sg 1049.

KETTLE SCHEDULE:
1 HBU HALLERTAU as soon as the wort comes to a boil,
2 HBU HALLERTAU after 45 minutes,
4 HBU PERLE after 60 minutes,
1 HBU HALLERTAU and
1/4 TSP (1.2 ML) IRISH MOSS after 1 hour and fifteen minutes,
1/4 OZ (7 G) HALLERTAU and KETTLE KNOCK-OUT at 1-1/2 hours.

Transfer through wort chiller into carboy, aerating the wort.
5-1/4 gallons (20 L) of wort should be collected at sg 1058.

Pitch with:
2 PKGS of lager yeast (10-14 grams dry yeast) or liquid yeast (Wyeast 2042, Yeast Lab L32, L33, BrewTek CL-640, CL-680).

Ferment at:
45-55°F (7-13°C). Transfer to secondary after 7-10 days, condition at 35-50°F (2-12°C) for 4-8 weeks.

Prime with:
3/4 cup (170 ML) of CORN SUGAR and bottle condition for 2 months at below 60°F (16°C).

TRADITIONAL BOCK

EMPEROR OF LEBANON BOCK

One of the advantages of home brewing is that one is not subject to stupid laws governing the sale of alcohol. Here in New Hampshire, beer containing more than 6% alcohol by volume cannot be sold. But, hey, we can **homebrew** it! Another good reason to homebrew, as if you needed one.

When you brew this recipe, plan on being patient - lagers need to be lagered and bottle-conditioned to mature. Big lagers like this require you to have big-time patience. Traditionally brewed as a seasonal beer, a bock like Emperor of Lebanon was brewed in late autumn and consumed during the coldest months of winter, but don't be afraid to brew this any time of year that you can maintain cold fermentation and lagering temperatures.

OG 1070   TG 1018   ABV 6.8%   SRM 20   IBU 24

Heat 8-1/2 gallons (32 L) of water to 165°F (74°C).

WATER SUPPLY:	TREAT WATER:
Soft	1-1/2 TSP (7.4 ML) OF GYPSUM
Moderately sulfate	1/2 TSP (2.5 ML) OF GYPSUM
Moderately carbonate	1/2 TSP (2.5 ML) OF GYPSUM
Highly sulfate	OK AS IS
Highly carbonate	ACIDIFY TO BELOW 7.0

8-1/4 LBS (3.7 KG) LAGER MALT
3 LBS (1.4 KG) MUNICH MALT
1 LB (454 G) LIGHT CRYSTAL MALT
3 OZ (84 G) CHOCOLATE MALT
2 OZ (57 G) BLACK MALT

Crush the malt. Mash-in to 152°F (67°C) with 4 gallons (15 L) of liquor at 165°F (74°C). Cover and hold. After 1 hour begin to run-off sweet wort to kettle. Heat sparge liquor to 172°F (78°C). Sparge mash with 4-1/2 gallons of 172°F (78°C) liquor to collect 6-1/3 gallons (24.5 L) of sweet wort at sg 1058.

KETTLE SCHEDULE:

1.5 HBU MT HOOD as soon as the wort comes to a boil,
2 HBU PERLE after 45 minutes,
3 HBU MT HOOD after 60 minutes,
3 HBU MT HOOD and
1/4 TSP (1.2 ML) IRISH MOSS after 1 hour and fifteen minutes,
KETTLE KNOCK-OUT at 1-1/2 hours.

Transfer through wort chiller into carboy, aerating the wort.
5-1/4 gallons (20 L) of wort should be collected at sg 1070.

Pitch with:

2 PKGS of lager yeast (10-14 grams dry yeast) or liquid yeast (Yeast Lab L32, L33, BrewTek CL-640, Wyeast 2178).

Ferment at:

45-55°F (7-13°C). Transfer to secondary after 10-14 days, condition at 35-50°F (2-12°C) for 4-8 weeks.

Prime with:

2/3 - 3/4 cup (150-170 ML) of CORN SUGAR and bottle condition for 2 months at below 60°F (16°C).

BILLYBUCK MAIBOCK

Springtime blonde bocks enjoy the widest popularity of all the big beers because they are soft, rounded and malty. This recipe will even appeal to industrial-beer drinkers.

A Maibock like this should be a masterwork of balancing the malt against the hops and strong alcohol flavors. Temperature control is very important to this end, because if a perceptible amount of "higher" alcohols are produced by a too-warm fermentation, this style does not have enough hops or roastiness to camouflage them, and their harsh flavors would spoil the malty softness that characterizes this style. If you cannot ferment below 55°F (13°C), use Wyeast 2042, Yeast Lab L35, or BrewTek CL-680.

OG 1066   TG 1014   ABV 6.8%   SRM 5   IBU 25

Heat 8-1/4 gallons (31 L) of water to 165°F (74°C).

WATER SUPPLY:	TREAT WATER:
Soft	1/2 TSP (2.5 ML) GYPSUM AND ACIDIFY TO pH 7.0
Moderately sulfate	ACIDIFY TO BELOW pH 7.0
Moderately carbonate	ACIDIFY TO BELOW pH 7.0
Highly sulfate	DILUTE 1:1 AND ACIDIFY TO BELOW 7.0
Highly carbonate	BOIL OR DILUTE 1:1, AND ACIDIFY TO BELOW 7.0

11-3/4 LBS (5.3 L) LAGER MALT

Crush the malt. Mash-in to 150°F (66°C) with 4 gallons (15 L) of liquor at 165°F (74°C). Cover and hold. After 1-1/2 hours begin to run-off sweet wort to kettle. Heat sparge liquor to 172°F (78°C). Sparge mash with 4-1/4 gallons (16 L) of 172°F (78°C) liquor to collect 6-1/4 gallons (24 L) of sweet wort at sg 1055.

This recipe is improved by using Continental Pilsner malt in place of U.S. lager malt. Pilsner malt should be step-mashed, or decoction mashed. To step-mash, heat liquor to 140°F (60°C) instead of 165°F (74°C) and mash in to 131-132°F (56°C) for a protein rest. After 15 minutes apply heat to raise the temperature of the goods to 155°F (68°C), and proceed to heat the sparge liquor to 172°F (78°C).

KETTLE SCHEDULE:
1.25 HBU HALLERTAU as soon as the wort comes to a boil,
2 HBU PERLE after 30 minutes,
3.75 HBU HALLERTAU after 45 minutes,
2.5 HBU HALLERTAU and
1/4 TSP (1.2 ML) IRISH MOSS after 1 hour and fifteen minutes,
KETTLE KNOCK-OUT at 1-1/2 hours.

Transfer through wort chiller into carboy, aerating the wort.
5-1/4 gallons (20 L) of wort should be collected at sg 1066.

Pitch with:
2 PKGS of lager yeast (10-14 grams dry yeast) or liquid yeast (Yeast Lab L32, L33, BrewTek CL-640, Wyeast 2178).

Ferment at:
45-55°F (7-13°C). Transfer to secondary after 7-12 days, condition at 35-50°F (2-12°C) for 4-6 weeks.

Prime with:
3/4 cup (170 ML) of CORN SUGAR and bottle condition for 2 months at below 60°F (16°C).

DOPPELBOCK

SAINT LUBRICATOR

The difference between bocks and American high-test "malt liquors" is that bocks have fullness and flavor. Saint Lubricator has plenty of flavor; this is a **big** beer, sort of the barleywine of lagers.

Brewing history has it that doppelbock was brewed by monks and consumed during Lenten fasting. Undoubtedly this regimen inspired many religous visions. German doppelbocks adhere to the convention of appending the suffix "...ator" to the brand name, in deference to the Salvator ("Savior"). Homebrewers aren't bound by tradition to such a schedule, but it is a pretty safe wager that most doppelbocks are still brewed and consumed during the winter months.

OG 1075   TG 1018   ABV 7.5%   SRM 18   IBU 24

Heat 8-1/2 gallons (32 L) of water to 165°F (74°C).

WATER SUPPLY:	TREAT WATER:
Soft	1/2 TSP (2.5 ML) GYPSUM AND ACIDIFY TO pH 7.2
Moderately sulfate	ACIDIFY TO BELOW pH 7.2
Moderately carbonate	ACIDIFY TO BELOW pH 7.2
Highly sulfate	ACIDIFY TO BELOW 7.2
Highly carbonate	ACIDIFY TO BELOW 7.2

9 LBS (4.1 KG) LAGER MALT
3-1/2 LBS (1.6 KG) MUNICH MALT
3/4 LB (340 G) DARK CRYSTAL MALT
2-1/2 OZ (71 G) CHOCOLATE MALT

Crush the malt. Mash-in to 150°F (66°C) with 4-1/4 gallons (16 L) of liquor at 165°F (74°C). Cover and hold. After 1-1/4 hours begin to run-off sweet wort to kettle. Heat sparge liquor to 172°F (78°C). Sparge mash with 4-1/4gallons (16 L) of 172°F (78°C) liquor to collect 6-1/4 gallons (24 L) of sweet wort at sg 1063.

KETTLE SCHEDULE:
1 HBU HALLERTAU as soon as the wort comes to a boil,
2 HBU PERLE after 30 minutes,
1 HBU HALLERTAU after 45 minutes,
2 HBU PERLE after 60 minutes,
2.5 HBU HALLERTAU and
1/4 TSP (1.2 ML) IRISH MOSS after 1 hour and fifteen minutes,
KETTLE KNOCK-OUT at 1-1/2 hours.

Transfer through wort chiller into carboy, aerating the wort.
5-1/4 gallons (20 L) of wort should be collected at sg 1075.

Pitch with:
2 PKGS of lager yeast (10-14 grams dry yeast) or liquid yeast (Yeast Lab L32, L33, BrewTek CL-640, Wyeast 2178).

Ferment at:
45-55°F (7-13°C). Transfer to secondary after 7-12 days, condition at 35-50°F (2-12°C) for 4-8 weeks.

Prime with:
2/3 - 3/4 (150-170 ML) cup of CORN SUGAR and bottle condition for 2 months at below 60°F (16°C).

CHAPTER 14

KEGGING

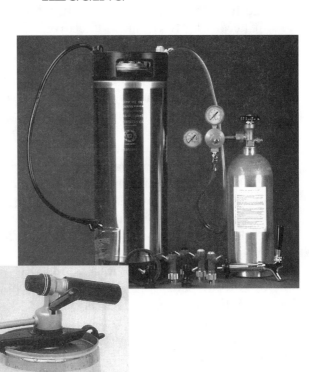

Pressure barrels come in many sizes, from Quoin's 2-1/4 gallon "Party Pig" to 5 gallon soda kegs. Regardless of which one you use, they are all filled the same way: Mix your priming sugar, although less than for bottling (1/2 to 2/3 as much) and add it to the keg. Rack your finished beer into the keg and close it according to the manufacturer's directions. Let the beer naturally carbonate as you would for bottled beer, allowing 2 to 3 weeks for conditioning.

Most kegs have some provision for maintaining carbonation during dispensing, either by connection to a CO_2 tank, or means of CO_2 bulbs or pressure pouches. The "Party Pig" has the advantage of being just right for half of a 5-gallon batch, and its CO_2 pouch system does not allow the gas to come in contact with the beer, preserving the "natural" carbonation due to priming. It is a convenient size for a refrigerator or for a picnic cooler, and its tap is built right in. The 5-liter *mini-keg* system, on the other hand, is even smaller, and thus fits even more easily almost anywhere. It takes less time to empty one, too, so you can vary your choice of draft beer more frequently. It requires an exterior tap, either a hand-operated air pump or a CO_2 pressure tap. The CO_2 tap not only aids in dispensing the beer but also helps to keep the beer fresh by filling the head space as the keg is emptied. The 5-gallon soda-keg system accepts a whole batch of home brew. It's bigger and it's more expensive too. The stainless-steel keg uses a 5-to-20 lb. CO_2 tank and regulator to provide blanket pressure for dispensing. Since three or four soda kegs fit into a standard refrigerator, some homebrewers set up systems able to serve several of their brews at controlled temperatures, with faucets mounted right on the refrigerator. These homebrewers rarely leave their homes, and are very popular in the brewing community.

Both the 5-liter and 5-gallon kegs can be artificially carbonated by simply forcing the blanket pressure into the solution, obviating the need for priming the batch and waiting for it to come into condition.

Kegging choices come down to what you feel best suits your needs and your budget. Either way, just think of all the bottles you won't be washing!

REAL ALE

Another option in kegging is "beer from the wood", or real ale. Real ale is "cask" conditioned and served under its own pressure from a keg or a barrel ("cask"). This is the way British ales are traditionally served. You can serve your beer this way too. There is very little difference in preparation, but a big difference in taste.

This difference arises from the method of dispensing the beer. With no outside CO_2 pressure being applied, after the first few pours air needs to be allowed into the keg for the beer to be dispensed. Air reacts with the beer, changing its flavor. The carbonation level will also be much softer, with less "prickliness" to distract from the beer's true flavor.

The first step, and possibly the most important one, is the priming of your real ale. Lower carbonation levels in the finished beer mean lower priming rates, so use only 1/3 to 1/2 of what you would normally use to prime a batch. Add finings at the same time you prime the beer. After fining and priming, the beer should be kept at fermentation temperatures for 5 to 14 days, depending on how "young" you prefer your real ale.

Cask-conditioned ales are often dry-hopped in the keg. In fact, most, if not all pale ales and bitters are dry-hopped. This is done to add a fresher hop aroma and flavor to the beer.

Dry hop with only the freshest whole leaf hops or "type 100" hop plugs. The hops should be bagged because loose leaf hops and pellets will clog the tap, and can't usually be cleared without disassembling. Put 1/2-2 oz. (14 - 57 grams) of aroma hops in a sterilized muslin bag. A few sterilized marbles in the bag will help submerge them. Add this bag to the cask when you fine and prime the beer.

After 1 to 2 weeks your "real ale" will be ready to serve. Don't serve your beer at too cool a temperature. Real ales are best appreciated when served between 52° and 61°F (11°-16°C), because you are able to better taste the beer when it is not as cold. After conditioning draw off beer until you have dispensed all the trub that has settled to the bottom of the keg. If you are using a **soda keg**, lay it on its side with the "out" side or liquid outlet on top and the "in" side or gas inlet on the bottom. Reverse the fittings so that the beer is tapped through the "in" plug and the keg is vented through the "out" plug. Controlling the air intake will control the beer flow.

Be forewarned that real ale will only last a few days, so plan

IN   OUT

SODA KEG

to drink it while it's in its prime. If it will be consumed all at one time, the cask can be vented for the whole time it is being served. If you want to enjoy it at a slower pace, over 3-5 days, pull off only a couple of pints each day. You can continue tapping a couple of pints a day until either the carbonation level drops or the pour slows down, at which point you will have to start venting the keg.

KEGGING PROCEDURES

Now that we've had a look at options, let's go over a few kegging basics. Remember the basic sanitation procedures? Well, the same apply to kegs as do to bottles, except that stainless steel is not as inert as glass. Stainless can pit and corrode over time if it is left exposed to strong chlorine solutions.

Use plenty of elbow grease and clean your keg out well, then sanitize as usual, using either an iodophor-type sterilant or the basic homebrewer's chlorine solution. Don't use a strong chlorine solution. When using heat to sanitize kegs, make sure the keg is vented to relieve the pressure so that it will not build up as the keg is heated.

Purging Air From Kegs

A good general rule to follow with any kegging system that uses an external CO_2 source is to purge the "keg" of air, by displacing the air in the keg with CO_2. This drastically reduces the effects of oxidation. When you rack finished beer into the keg, the inevitable splashing will be in a CO_2 atmosphere, instead of harmful air. Purging works because CO_2 is heavier than air, and to some extent drops to the bottom of the keg pushing the air upwards. There is inevitably some mixing of the gases, but purging does effectively reduce oxidation. Just apply CO_2 pressure to your keg, wait until it is pressurized to about 10-15 psi, and then relieve the pressure from the top of the keg through the "in" plug.

If you fill your keg with homebrewer's sanitizing solution the day before you fill it with beer, you can very effectively purge the keg by simply pushing the sanitizer out with CO_2 pressure.

Fining

The finings that we have talked about before will work for kegging as well. Finings are added directly to the cask or keg for real ale, but in all other circumstances should be added to the secondary fermenter so that clear beer can be drawn into the keg. An additional way to help clear your beer is to cool it. If you are able to put the whole batch in a cooler or refrigerator, the chilling will drop yeast and proteins out of suspension.

Priming

Smaller amounts of priming sugar are needed when kegging to achieve the same carbonation levels as in bottles. A good guideline to follow is :

Low Carbonation (as in most British styles), use 1/3 to 1/2 cup (75-115 ml) corn sugar.

Medium Carbonation (as in most European lagers and ales), use 1/2 cup (115 ml) corn sugar.

High Carbonation (American lagers, wheat and fruit beers), use 3/4 cup (170 ml) of corn sugar.

Filtering

Some of you may want to serve absolutely clear and brilliant beer, with no yeast sediment. Filtering your beer will make it clearer and more attractive, but on the other hand, it can strip your beer of some body and flavor. If this doesn't bother you, read on.

To filter, you will need to have a few additional items beyond the basic CO_2 tank, keg and lines. You will need an additional keg, two "out" fittings lines to connect the two kegs, and of course a filter. There are several types of filters available , but the most common are trap-type cartridge filters , and plate-and-frame type sheet filters.

The cheapest and easiest filter arrangement to use is a cartridge filter. These are basically the same as the one you may have under your sink. The big difference is in the filter cartridge. Home water filters usually have activated-charcoal cartridges, which are great for filtering out large particles and organics, but not for filtering beer. What you want for filtering homebrew is a cartridge that eliminates particles down to .5 microns. If you filter any finer than that, you risk stripping the proteins in beer that give it body and a rich head.

OK, how do you go about filtering? First, chill your (uncarbonated) beer overnight. Chilling your beer will help the excess proteins to congeal, forming a filterable chill haze. While your beer is chilling, sterilize your kegs, filter and attendant tubing and fittings. You can sterilize everything at once by filling one keg with 4 gallons (15 L) of water and 1 ounce of chlorine bleach. Pressurize the keg to 5-10 psi with CO_2 and push all of the chlorine mixture through the filter, into the second keg, and then down the drain. The CO_2 will purge the air from the entire system.

Rack your chilled, uncarbonated beer into one sterilized keg. Pressurize the full keg to 5 psi to seal it. Connect the second keg up through the filter. Apply CO_2 pressure slowly to the full keg while bleeding off pressure from the empty keg. You want the beer to flow through the filter slowly and at an even pace. When you have finished filtering, take everything apart and clean it immediately. It is a good idea to store your filter with a weak chlorine solution in it to prevent bacterial contamination. Filtered beer is artificially carbonated, as explained below.

ARTIFICIAL CARBONATION

An advantage to soda canister kegging is that you can forego priming by artificially carbonating your beer. You can rack your finished beer into the keg and use CO_2 pressure to reach the desired level of carbonation. Chilling the beer and the keg before filling, and shaking it after, dissolves the CO_2 into the beer within minutes. Otherwise, it will take two to five days to carbonate the beer in the keg, depending upon its temperature.

Use the chart below to determine the proper level of carbonation. All you need to know is the temperature that the beer is at, and you can carbonate your beer to whatever level you desire. As you know, particular styles of beer are best suited by specific levels of carbonation. A general guideline is:

British Ales: 1.8 to 2.2 volumes.
Lagers and German ales: 2.5 volumes.
American-style lagers and ales: 2.6 to 2.8 volumes.
Wheat beers and fruit ales: 3.0 volumes.

Guideline for degrees of carbonation at various beer temperatures.

| | Pounds per Square Inch | | | | | | | | | | | | | | |
	1	2	3	4	5	6	7	8	9	10	11	12	13	14	15
30	1.82	1.92	2.03	2.14	2.23	2.36	2.48	2.60	2.70	2.82	2.93	3.02			
31	1.78	1.88	2.00	2.10	2.20	2.31	2.42	2.54	2.65	2.76	2.86	2.96			
32	1.75	1.85	1.95	2.05	2.15	2.27	2.38	2.48	2.59	2.70	2.80	2.90	3.00	3.11	3.21
33		1.81	1.91	2.01	2.10	2.23	2.33	2.43	2.53	2.63	2.74	2.84	2.96	3.06	3.15
34		1.78	1.86	1.97	2.06	2.18	2.28	2.38	2.48	2.58	2.69	2.79	2.90	3.00	3.09
35			1.83	1.93	2.02	2.14	2.24	2.34	2.43	2.52	2.63	2.73	2.83	2.93	3.02
36			1.79	1.88	1.98	2.09	2.19	2.29	2.38	2.47	2.57	2.67	2.77	2.86	2.96
37				1.84	1.94	2.04	2.14	2.24	2.33	2.42	2.52	2.62	2.71	2.80	2.90
38				1.80	1.90	2.00	2.10	2.20	2.29	2.38	2.48	2.57	2.66	2.75	2.85
39					1.86	1.96	2.06	2.15	2.25	2.34	2.43	2.52	2.61	2.70	2.80
40					1.83	1.92	2.01	2.10	2.20	2.30	2.39	2.47	2.56	2.65	2.75
41					1.79	1.88	1.97	2.06	2.16	2.25	2.34	2.43'	2.52	2.60	2.70
42					1.75	1.85	1.94	2.02	2.12	2.21	2.30	2.39	2.48	2.56	2.65
43					1.72	1.81	1.90	1.99	2.08	2.17	2.26	2.34	2.43	2.52	2.61
44					1.69	1.78	1.87	1.95	2.04	2.13	2.22	2.30	2.39	2.47	2.56
45					1.66	1.75	1.84	1.91	2.00	2.08	2.17	2.26	2.34	2.42	2.51
46					1.62	1.71	1.80	1.88	1.96	2.04	2.13	2.22	2.30	2.38	2.47
47					1.59	1.68	1.76	1.84	1.92	2.00	2.09	2.18	2.26	2.34	2.42
48					1.56	1.65	1.73	1.81	1.89	1.96	2.05	2.14	2.22	2.30	2.38
49					1.53	1.62	1.70	1.79	1.86	1.93	2.01	2.10	2.18	2.25	2.34
50					1.50	1.59	1.66	1.74	1.82	1.90	1.98	2.06	2.14	2.21	2.30
51						1.57	1.64	1.71	1.79	1.87	1.95	2.02	2.10	2.18	2.26
52						1.54	1.61	1.68	1.76	1.84	1.92	1.99	2.06	2.14	2.22
53						1.51	1.59	1.66	1.74	1.81	1.89	1.96	2.03	2.10	2.18
54							1.56	1.63	1.71	1.78	1.86	1.93	2.00	2.07	2.15
55							1.53	1.60	1.68	1.75	1.82	1.89	1.97	2.04	2.12
56							1.50	1.57	1.65	1.72	1.79	1.86	1.93	2.00	2.08
57								1.54	1.62	1.70	1.77	1.83	1.90	1.97	2.04
58								1.51	1.59	1.67	1.74	1.80	1.87	1.94	2.01
59									1.56	1.64	1.71	1.77	1.84	1.91	1.98
60									1.54	1.62	1.69	1.75	1.82	1.88	1.95

To use this chart: First find the temperature of your beer along the outside vertical edge. Look across until you reach the carbonation level desired (the numbers in the grid express the volumes of carbon dioxide; 1 L of beer containing 3 L of carbon dioxide at standard temperature and pressure is said to contain 3 volumes of carbon dioxide). Then look up to the top of that column to find the required pressure, and set your regulator accordingly.

						Pounds per Square Inch									
16	17	18	19	20	21	22	23	24	25	26	27	28	29	30	
															30
															31
															32
3.25															33
3.19															34
3.12	3.22														35
3.05	3.15	3.24													36
3.00	3.09	3.18	3.27												37
2.94	3.03	3.12	3.21												38
2.89	2.98	3.07	3.16	3.25											39
2.84	2.93	3.01	3.10	3.19	3.28										40
2.79	2.88	2.96	3.05	3.14	3.23										41
2.74	2.83	2.91	3.00	3.09	3.18	3.26									42
2.69	2.78	2.86	2.95	3.04	3.13	3.21									43
2.64	2.73	2.81	2.90	2.99	3.07	3.16	3.24								44
2.60	2.69	2.77	2.86	2.94	3.02	3.11	3.19								45
2.55	2.64	2.72	2.81	2.89	2.98	3.06	3.15	3.23							46
2.50	2.59	2.67	2.76	2.84	2.93	3.02	3.09	3.18							47
2.46	2.54	2.62	2.71	2.79	2.88	2.96	3.04	3.13							48
2.42	2.50	2.58	2.67	2.75	2.83	2.91	3.00	3.07	3.15						49
2.38	2.46	2.54	2.62	2.70	2.78	2.86	2.94	3.02	3.10	3.17					50
2.34	2.42	2.49	2.57	2.65	2.74	2.82	2.90	2.97	3.05	3.13	3.19				51
2.30	2.38	2.45	2.53	2.61	2.68	2.76	2.84	2.92	3.00	3.06	3.13	3.22			52
2.26	2.34	2.41	2.49	2.57	2.64	2.71	2.79	2.86	2.94	3.01	3.09	3.16			53
2.22	2.30	2.37	2.45	2.52	2.59	2.66	2.74	2.81	2.89	2.96	3.04	3.10	3.17		54
2.19	2.26	2.33	2.40	2.47	2.54	2.62	2.69	276	2.83	2.89	2.97	3.04	3.11	3.18	55
2.15	2.22	2.29	2.36	2.43	2.50	2.57	2.64	2.71	2.78	2.85	2.92	2.99	3.06	3.13	56
2.11	2.18	2.25	2.32	2.39	2.46	2.53	2.60	2.66	2.73	2.80	2.87	2.94	3.00	3.08	57
2.08	2.15	2.21	2.28	2.35	2.42	2.48	2.55	2.62	2.69	2.75	2.82	2.88	2.95	3.02	58
2.04	2.11	2.17	2.24	2.31	2.38	2.43	2.50	2.57	2.64	2.70	2.77	2.84	2.91	2.97	59
2.01	2.08	2.14	2.21	2.27	2.34	2.40	2.47	2.53	2.60	2.66	2.73	2.79	2.86	2.92	60

This chart was adapted from reference 2 and "Solubility of Carbon Dioxide in Beer: Pressure–Temperature Relationships," courtesy of Zahm and Nagel Co. Inc. (Rochester, New York).

CHAPTER 15

"YUCCH! WHAT WENT WRONG??!!"
TROUBLE-SHOOTING

The keys to brewing good beer are knowledge, attention to detail and sanitation. (It also helps to be organized and prepared.) If a brew has not turned out as you expected it to, or you've got a bad batch on your hands, don't be too quick to blame it on the ingredients. You just might have cut corners once too often.

Everyone makes mistakes, but if you want to brew good beer, don't make it a habit. You're doing the right thing now, looking for that piece of information that will define for you what the problem is, and how you got it, so that you can correct it before you brew again.

In the meantime, you've got this problem batch of beer. Can you save it? Probably not. Can you prevent the same thing happening again? Most definitely.

This chapter should help you sort out what your problem is, and it probably will if you have followed our oft-repeated advice and kept good brew records. If you haven't, start now. In the meantime, if you're feeling bad about losing a five-gallon batch, we have a story that ought to at least make you feel less bad. Misery loves company, right?

The Seven Barrel Brewery is named for our batch size. We brew seven barrels, 217 gallons, 8.2 hectoliters per batch. That's about what an industrial brewery spills every day before lunch, but for us, that's a lot of beer.

We brew it in this great tower brewhouse. It has rakes in the mash tun, a decoction kettle, a pipe matrix that lets us pump anything anywhere, and it has temperature controllers on everything. We designed, installed, bricked, wired, plumbed and polished it. We knew this brewery inside-out before we ever even brewed in it. When we did brew in it, it was great. We congratulated ourselves on the great brewery we had; it was everything a brewer could ask for.

The first nine batches went great. OK, so the old, used wort chiller we had slapped in because we had it leaked, but we were going to get around to replacing it soon. It was no big deal. Then, out of the blue, three batches in a row contaminated. Without sampling or testing, we zeroed right in on our leaky wort chiller. We knew this brewery cold, and we knew that had to be our problem. So, geniuses that we are, we shut down the brewery and ordered a new wort chiller. We were going to fall way behind our brewing schedule, but there was nothing we could do but wait. When the new chiller arrived, we installed it, tore down and sanitized the whole brewery, and brewed three batches right in a row. The problem was solved, right?

Wrong. They all contaminated. Three more batches down the tubes. We shut down again and pulled the brewery apart from top to bottom again. We cleaned and sterilized everything. We re-engineered a couple of things that maybe, just possibly, could cause a problem. We boosted up the wort chilling system so that the temperature dropped faster and we could pitch sooner. Confident that we had eliminated all possible sources of infection, we reassembled the brewery. The following brew went through with no problem. So did the next. Good thing, because we were running out of beer. No problem, though, we had it beat!

Or so we thought. Come brew #18, the bacteria were back. They outnumbered the yeast in the fermenter! Frustrated, we took samples. There was no contamination in the wort chiller or in the stainless tubing. We knew that the fermenter had been sterile. The brew was picking up the infection between the transfer line and the fermenter, but the only thing there was a ten-foot brewers' hose. It couldn't be that, because we always kept it full of sterilant between brews. Well, we hadn't sterilized it after brew #17, because we were brewing again the next day, but it had still been attached at both ends, so it couldn't have picked up the contamination overnight. And we had taken it apart, inspected, cleaned and sterilized it twice, most recently only two brews ago. Hadn't we? Who did clean it, anyway? You didn't do it? I didn't do it. You were supposed to do it. You didn't do it? Do you mean...

We unclamped the hose barbs and stripped them out. And there was our contamination. The hose-barb at one end had been clamped incorrectly; the clamp had been tightened on halfway up the barb, allowing a pocket to form between the inserted end of the barb, the inside of the hose and the clamp. The bacteria had a safe port against our sanitizing storm. It was rudimentary, elementary, fundamental stupidity.

The wort chiller probably was the source of the original contamination, but by sloppily clamping the hose incorrectly in the first place, and then skipping it in the brewery teardown, we had violated two of the inviolable rules of brewing. Our oversights cost us 1,519 gallons of beer down the tubes.

PROBLEMS AND SOLUTIONS

If something detracts from the aroma, flavor or appearance of your beer, it's a problem. To correct the problem, you need to focus on what is wrong. Exactly what is "different" about it? Define the problem as accurately as you are able. Don't drink the whole batch or dump it and then go problem-solving two weeks later. Have that beer, and its brew record, in hand as you read this chapter. Swirl the brew, sniff it, taste it and think about it while you read. You can't solve the problem if you don't know what it is. You won't know what it is if you can't separate the particular defect out from similar symptoms.

SMELLS "DIFFERENT"

Smells skunky:
The beer is "lightstruck". The more heavily-hopped a beer is, the more susceptible a beer is to being lightstruck. Don't cut back on hops to get rid of the problem, though. Keep your beer out of direct sunlight and away from strong fluorescent light. Bottle into brown bottles; clear and green bottles do not filter out harmful light rays as well.

Smells like cheap wine:
Reduce the temperature that you ferment at by at least 5°F(3°C). If the aroma and flavor persists, change the type of yeast that you are using.

Smells like green apples:

Let the beer age. If it is from the yeast strain, the aroma and flavor will subside. If it is from a bacterial infection, it may get worse. If it does, in the future, close all windows and avoid racking and bottling in any drafts.

Smells like cream corn:

DMS (dimethyl sulfide, which is what you smell) is part of the round flavor of most beers, even though its level may be so low that you cannot distinguish it. Lager malt has more potential for giving DMS aroma than Pale malt does. In any case, most yeast strains generally reduce DMS levels during fermentation to reasonable levels, but some yeast strains reduce it less than others. If you don't like the aroma, or it is inappropriate for the beer style, try switching yeast strains.

The DMS may arise from undermodified malt, probably combined with a combination of some of the following circumstances: an inadequate boil, either in terms of time or intensity, taking too long a time to cool the hot wort down, letting the hot wort get aerated, or too slow a fermentation. Review your brew log to determine which remedies to apply. Some wort bacteria produce an aroma very much like DMS, so see the next two entries, below.

Smells like celery or parsnips:

See cream corn above and cabbage below. Decide which one is more like your problem, since celery/parsnip aromas can be related to one or the other. If the aroma is intense, you can bet your wort got contaminated.

Smells like cabbage cooking:

Your wort or yeast culture got contaminated. Assuming that you remembered to boil the wort, the bacteria responsible got into your wort after it cooled below 170°F. The bacteria multiplies incredibly quickly, and although normal yeast fermentation robs them of nutrients and they die off, their flavor trail remains. Pay more attention to sanitizing your equipment, and don't rack your beer in a drafty area. If you only clean your kitchen once every spring, look for a new hobby.

Smells like overcooked vegetables:

Did you boil your extract brew for at least 45 minutes? If you mashed, did you boil the wort for an hour-and-a-half? Under-boiled wort can cause this aroma.

Most likely the problem is due to bacterial contamination. Is there a discolored ring around the neck of the bottles? Did you notice the smell before the beer started fermenting vigorously? This aroma is usually associated with contaminated wort, rather than a contaminant that got started in the beer, indicating that you need to improve your brewing hygiene in the period after the wort boil.

If you are culturing and/or repitching your yeast from brew-to-brew, the bacteria may be harbored in your yeast culture; try pitching a different yeast culture.

Smells musty:

This is a relatively uncommon occurrence, but when it is encountered it is most often due to moldy ingredients. When this is the case, the mustiness is generally accompanied by some amount of solventy aromas. Taste and smell your ingredients before you brew with them.

If you brew in a musty cellar you should suspect air-or-waterborne- fungi, which oftentimes contribute a woody flavor as well. Move your brewery! Sanitize all your fermenting equipment overnight with a solution of 1/2 oz (15 ml) of bleach per gallon of water.

Smells fruity:

Depending on the beer style, these "esters" may very well be appropriate. If they aren't, or you don't like the aromatics, you may want to change yeast strains, since some strains produce more fruity esters than others. Fruity aromatics develop when the yeast are using oxygen in the early stage of fermentation to reproduce. Reducing the initial fermentation temperature 5°F(3°C) or so, reducing the aeration of the wort and/or reducing the amount of yeast pitched are all remedies for reducing fruitiness.

Smells like butterscotch:

"Diacetyl", the buttery aroma, is characteristic of many yeast strains. It is appropriate in many ales, and is usually considered out-of-place in a lager. If you don't like it, you can switch yeast strains, leave the beer in the primary fermenter for two or three days longer before racking it to secondary, or use less adjuncts in the recipe. Diacetyl aroma can be greatly reduced by forcing a 5°F(3°C) lower temperature at the start of fermentation and a 5°F warmer temperature near the end, or by letting the beer sit at, or slightly above, the fermentation temperature two or three days after fermentation has ended.

Smells solventy:

Specific yeast strains produce acetone-like aromas at higher temperatures, sometimes with band-aid aromas as well. Most often these flavors can be avoided by lowering the fermentation temperature 5°F(3°C) or so.

These aromas may be the calling card of wild yeast that have contaminated a brew. If you suspect this, improve upon your sanitation.

Solventy aromas may get picked-up from plastic equipment, and is a likely cause if the equipment is not food-grade plastic.

A synergetic effect is often created when the brew has a lot of dark roasted grains in the recipe, accentuating solventy aromas.

SMELLS BAD

Smells like bandaids:

Most often due to overzealous sanitizing with bleach. Unless you use bleach at a dilution of 1 fluid ounce to 4 gallons of water (2 ml/liter), or less, you must rinse equipment with sterile water after it has soaked in bleach.

If your water supply is drawn from a low-lying area or from surface water and it is heavily chlorinated, your water may be the source of the flavor. It can usually be eliminated by boiling all your brewing water for 10-30 minutes.

Smells like rotten eggs:

Fermenting beer will often smell like rotten eggs, but the aroma is driven off by carbon dioxide generation. Check your brew record; if the fermentation proceeded at relatively cool temperatures and/or it was too slow and weak to drive off the hydrogen sulfide, that is the problem.

The problem is accentuated if the boil was insufficient. If neither solution improves things to your satisfaction, switch to a yeast strain that is less sulfury.

If the problem is bacterial in origin, it will be accompanied by other indicators, such as off-flavors and residues in the bottle. Try to identify accompanying problems, and refer to those entries.

Smells like burnt matches:

Too slow a fermentation, usually due to too low a fermentation temperature.

Smells like burnt rubber:

Usually due to "autolyzed" yeast, aka dead yeast, decomposing in your beer. The solution in most cases is simple; transfer your beer to a secondary fermenter to condition it, and don't let it lager extensively on top of sediment.

Some yeast strains are more prone to autolyzing than others. You may want to switch to a hardier strain.

Smells like rancid butter:

You've got trouble. The bacteria responsible is very difficult to get rid of. Inspect your equipment, looking for any tiny deposits called "beerstone". Soak them with a detergent solution, and then scrub them away. Soak all your fermenting equipment, including the wort chiller, in strong sanitizer for at least a week, or thoroughly dampen and heat-sterilize equipment in an oven at 200°F (95°C) for two hours. If you have been repitching yeast, go to a new culture.

TASTES "DIFFERENT"

Tastes cidery:

If you are using sugar in your brew, don't, or reduce it drastically.

Close windows and doors when racking and bottling, and avoid drafty areas. Avoid stirring or other agitation of your fermenting or conditioning beer.

Tastes bitter:

In rare instances, due to nitrates in water. If your water has a mineral, rotten aroma, don't use it to brew with.

Most often due to overhopping, or boiling a large percentage of the hops for over an hour, extracting harshly-bitter hop acids.

Tastes like sherry:

This is part of the profile of strong, well-aged ales. It is due to oxidation, and usually takes several months in the bottle to develop. The usual solution is to fill your bottles more, leaving as little headspace as possible, and avoid splashing wort and beer around, except during aeration at pitching.

TASTES BAD

Tastes harsh/astringent:

Reduce the time that you are boiling your hops if the beer is very bitter as well.

Rack beer to secondary for aging if you aren't, be more careful about carrying along "trub" sediment if you are.

Crush grain less intensely and acidify your sparge water, or stop sparging earlier if you are mashing. Do not collect runoff after the pH rises to 5.8.

If there is a vinegar, green-apple, or rancid-butter aroma as well, you may not be sanitizing your brewing equipment well enough, or you may be picking up a contamination at racking or bottling; avoid drafty areas when transferring beer.

Tastes husky/grainy:

If you are using grain adjuncts in the kettle, remove them before the wort boils, and don't leave them in the wort for as long a time. If you are mashing, don't crush the grains so intensely that the husks become shreds. Acidify your sparge water and don't collect runoff after the pH rises to 5.8. Don't oversparge the spent grains. Stop sparging once the density drops to SG 1012. It is also possible that the flavor is from husks burning against the sides of your mash pot.

Tastes like wet cardboard:

Always due to oxidation. It is especially noticeable in beers that are light in color and flavor and have become oxidized. You may be picking up the problem by oxidizing the wort (or the mash), but it is more likely to occur after fermentation has subsided. Do not splash fermented beer around! The other common cause is underfilling bottles. Always use necked bottles, and fill them to within at least 3/4" (20 mm) of the top of the bottle.

Tastes sour:

The first possibility to eliminate is that you have gotten carried away acidifying your brew water. If the wort pH after the boil is below 5.0, reduce your water acidification.

Acidic bacterial contamination is usually accompanied by a vinegar or grainy/sweaty aroma, and cloudiness in the beer. Sanitize your fermentation equipment and avoid drafts when racking wort.

Tastes vinegary:

Close windows and doors when racking and bottling, and avoid drafty areas. Avoid exposing your beer to air. Sanitize your brewing equipment.

Tastes metallic:

Most often due to the presence of iron in the brewing water, or from contact with rusty/oxidized steel equipment.

Otherwise, possibly due to extraction of malt fats by oversparging.

TOO THIN:

If the brew has no body, it may be that you need to create a less fermentable extract. If you are adding adjunct sugars, add less, or even better, add none or next to none. If you are mashing, shorten the mash time or raise the temperature.

Step and decoction mash brewers encountering thinness should reduce the duration of the protein rest, and/or raise its temperature up into the mid-130°'s F (57-58°C).

TOO SWEET:

Is the TG higher than the recipe/style called for? Change yeast to a more attenuative strain. If it is a mash brew, it may be that the mash temperature was too high or the duration too short. Review the brewing log against the recipe.

Another possibility is that the yeast was shocked by a sudden temperature change during fermentation. Again, your brew record should indicate this.

NO HEAD:
Beer is carbonated, but it has no head:
Did you substitute a lot of sugar in the recipe? Beer needs malt, barley, wheat or oatmeal to contribute proteins that make up the head.

If you mashed, did you let the mash rest at 118-140°F (48-60°C) for a long time? Or was your sparging runoff over pH 5.8, and the gravity under 1012?

Is your glass clean? Did any oily or fatty substance get into your brew? Could the bottles or your glass have had an oily residue in them?

Beer is flat and has no head:
Did you prime the beer at bottling? Did you inadvertently "pasteurize" it and kill off the yeast? See below, and reprime the bottles.

Beer is flat and sweet:
There may not have been enough yeast in the beer at bottling to ferment the sugar and carbonate the beer. If the beer was chilled soon after bottling, it may have been too cold for the yeast to carbonate it. Let the batch warm up to room temperature for two weeks or so, and see if it has carbonated. If it hasn't, mix 1/4 cup of corn sugar with a package of yeast in a quart of sterilized body- temperature water, uncap your bottles, add a tablespoon of the primer to each bottle, recap, and let it sit at room temperature for at least another two weeks.

WON'T HOLD A HEAD:
Is the beer carbonated? The "flatter' the beer, the less well it will hold a head.

The less hops that are in a recipe, the less head the beer will hold.

If the beer fermented-out in a just a couple of days, it will hold a head less well than if fermentation took longer.

Also see the entry for "Beer is carbonated, but has no head".

CLOUDY:
Chill a bottle of the brew, and then let it warm up to room temperature. If it gets more cloudy as it gets cold and clears up as it warms, it is "chill haze". Chill haze is caused by proteins. Change either your malt or your mashing program.

Check for a ring of residue in the neck of the bottle, and any "off" aroma, especially a vinegar smell. These things indicate contamination, and the solution, again, is better sanitation.

GUSHES WHEN BOTTLE IS OPENED:

The beer is overcarbonated, for one reason or another.

Let future brews ferment out fully before bottling; there should be no bubbling in the airlock for at least a few days before bottling.

Check your brew record. Did you add too much priming sugar?

Check the necks of your bottles. Is there a "ring around the collar?" If there is, the beer is contaminated. You may not be sanitizing your brewing equipment well enough, or you may be picking up a contamination at racking or bottling; avoid drafty areas when transferring beer. If your water has a lot of iron in it, the beer will usually taste metallic as well, and you will see "rust" where your faucet drips. If so, you need to find a new source of brewing water.

CHAPTER 16

JUDGING YOUR BEER AND ANYONE ELSE'S

"I brew better beer than <u>that</u>!"

S o, you've brewed a whole bunch of different beers, tried a lot of the styles you like, experimented with some different combinations, and you're doing pretty well. At least, you like your beer, your spouse does too, and all your friends and neighbors as well, BUT... how can you know if you really are brewing good stuff? That's easy.

Enter it into a homebrewing competition. We've mentioned several times that our kit recommendations and our recipes are based on AHA style guidelines. Lest you think that's just namedropping to make our book seem more impressive, let us reassure you — there are literally hundreds of local, regional, nationwide and even international beer tastings and judging events every year, sponsored by clubs and associations that are sanctioned by the American Homebrewers Association, the Home Wine and Beer Trade Association or the Beer Judge Certification Program. In order for all that to work together, they really did define a set of standards as to color, gravity and strength, flavor characteristics, clarity, etc. Brews entered into sanctioned contests are judged by panels of trained beer enthusiasts. Most judges come from the ranks of highly-qualified homebrewers. They have undergone training programs and passed a very tough test to become judges. Still others are just enthusiasts, people like you who just like beer, and like it well enough to have become certified competition judges.

Go back and look at World Beer Styles in chapter 5. Those numbers are the standard parameters. We warned you — you are free to change the recipes, experiment with any ingredient you want, BUT... to be in the category, it's got to be at least close to the right color, the right alcoholic strength, the right balance of bitter/sweet, the right carbonation...

In a competition, beer is judged on the following bases:

Aroma: right balance of malt and other fermentables and hop bouquet, and other aromas characteristic of the style.

Appearance: Appropriate color, appropriate clarity, head, etc.

Flavor: Balance of malt and hops, and other appropriate flavors, appropriate mouth-feel or texture, length and intensity of after-taste.

Body: Is it full or is it thin? Is it appropriate for the beer style?

ENTRY/RECIPE FORM

American Homebrewers Association
SANCTIONED COMPETITION PROGRAM

BREWER(S) INFORMATION ••

Name(s) _____

Street Address _____

City _____ State _____ Zip _____

Phone (h) (_____) _____ Phone (w) (_____) _____

Are you a member of an AHA Registered Homebrew Club? ☐ Yes ☐ No

If so, what is its name? _____ (Please spell out the full club name. Do not abbreviate)

ENTRY INFORMATION ••

Name of Brew_____ Special Ingredients/Classic Style: _____

Category/Subcategory (print full names)_____ _____

Category _____ Subcategory _____ _____

Recipe is: ☐ Malt Extract Only ☐ Malt Extract & Grain ☐ All-grain ☐ Mead ☐ Cider ☐ Saké

For Mead, Cider, Saké: ☐ Dry ☐ Medium ☐ Sweet

INGREDIENTS AND PROCEDURES ••

Number of U.S. gallons brewed for this recipe_____

WATER TREATMENT Type(s) _____

Amount(s) _____

YEAST CULTURE ☐ Liquid ☐ Dried

Did you use a starter? ☐ Yes ☐ No

Brand and Type _____

YEAST NUTRIENTS Type_____

Brand _____

Amount _____

CARBONATION Type_____

Amount _____

Use of Kegs? _____

BOILING TIME_____

SPECIFIC GRAVITIES Original _____

Terminal _____

FERMENTATION Duration (days) Temperature

Primary _____ _____

Secondary _____ _____

Other _____ _____

DATE THIS BREW WAS BOTTLED_____

HOPS:

TYPE	PELLETS OR WHOLE?	AMOUNT (OZ.)	% A ACID	USE (BOIL, DRY, ETC.)	TIME

MALT (GRAIN, EXTRACTS AND/OR OTHER FERMENTABLES):

TYPE/BRAND	AMOUNT (LBS.)	USE (STEEP/MASH)	TIME	TEMP.

Type of Fermenter (glass, plastic, etc.) _____

_____

_____

_____

© AHA/SCP 5/95

AMERICAN HOMEBREWERS ASSOCIATION • PO Box 1679 • Boulder, Colorado 80306-1679 • U.S.A. • (303) 447-0816 • FAX (303) 447-2825

Judging is based on comparison to the guidelines of the beer style categories, not on an arbitrary head-to-head basis with other beers entered into the contest. In other words, a judge is considering not just how good the beer is but how well it fits into the category. Is it a reasonable representation of the style? Judges look for off-flavors, inappropriate esters, inadequate or overdone carbonation, excessive or insufficient bitterness, etc. A good judge will also point out good qualities and make constructive suggestions as to how to improve the beer. On the whole, judges are more interested in promoting good brewing and appreciation for diversity of styles. Judges also get to taste a lot of good beer, obviously.

On a less upbeat note, judges must be able to recognize faults in the beers that they are judging. Remember the list of problems that we listed in the last chapter? The value of having your beer judged is not just in having your already inflated ego swollen by reinforcement. If there are defects in your beer, it helps to have an impartial judge point them out. The intention here is not to burst your bubble, but to improve your brewing skills and your understanding of styles. Most judges will suggest remedies for problems that they perceive in your entry.

If you are perfectly happy drinking your own brew and don't really see how it could be improved on, then our best advice may be to leave well enough alone. There really is something to be said for "I like my beer just fine the way it is." Don't enter any competitions, because ignorance really can be bliss. Once you have learned to recognize defects, you may never quaff your own or anyone else's beer with as much pure enjoyment as you are now.

On the other hand, there is a point in brewer's education where you will learn more, faster, by getting expert feedback. One way to get this is to join your nearest homebrewing club. Clubs usually meet monthly and sponsor their own competitions as well. Sanctioned competitions provide homebrewers with the best analysis of their beer that they are ever likely to get. The persons analyzing your beer are trained, experienced and unbiased. The more competitions you enter, the more feedback you will get.

Another step in the continuing education of the homebrewer is to become a judge yourself. You don't just become a recognized judge by volunteering your services. There is a test to pass first, and you have to study for it to pass it. What you need to learn to become a judge is also invaluable brewer-training: the parameters of beer styles, how to taste beer, and the aromas and flavors that occur in beer and how they can be controlled. The Beer Judge Certification Program (BJCP) is the best vehicle for the beer enthusiast to learn about beer and beer styles, and to learn the criteria of what makes a good beer. Judges accumulate experience points leading to different levels of certification. If you are interested in learning more about the BJCP or about entering your brew into a contest, contact your local homebrew supply shop, homebrewing club, or the program administrators. Keep an eye on the calendars in trade publications such as <u>Zymurgy</u> and <u>Brew Your Own</u> for scheduled BJCP tests, or contact the program and inquire how you can become involved.

CHAPTER 17

THE SEVEN BARREL BREWERY

Here at the original Seven Barrel Brewery, we have a remarkable relationship with homebrewers. It's partly because we are a brewpub, where consumers can interact with the brewery itself. When you are sitting at our bar, you see yourself reflected in the copper of the eight serving tanks that tower above the backbar. You are face-to-face with the tanks that the fresh beer is being drawn from. On any given day, the brewer may be filling one of the serving tanks from the fermenters located just on the other side of the lab.

If the brewer is not there, he's probably in the brew tower, which is visible from both inside and outside the building. From crushing the malt in the mill, to mashing, sparging, boiling the wort and finally chilling it, the whole brewhouse operation is visible and easy to understand.

And finally, it's partly because we brew at a size that is not far removed from homebrewing. Our brewery is very traditional, but pretty sophisticated as well. It's large by homebrewing standards, but small enough that we encounter many of the same challenges that every kitchen brewer does. We aren't so large that we get malt in by the carload. We lug sacks of grain up the brewhouse stairs. There is an advantage to this, because it encourages diversity. We use English ale malts for our British-style ales. We use German lager malts for our lager brews, and US or Canadian malts in our domestic beers.

We crush our grains in a two-roll mill. After we set the crush, it takes us about fifteen minutes to mash-in a seven barrel batch. As the crushed grain falls from the mill's hopper into the combination mash/lauter tun it is sprayed with the hot liquor. Sensors in thermowells on one side of the tun give us an accurate temperature reading, so it is a simple matter to adjust the liquor flow to hit the strike temperature of the mash.

When the mill is running, we always run the mash mixer to get a good distribution of temperature and mash thickness. The mixer, which is a combination of rakes and cutting blades that rotate around a central shaft, has a stirring paddle that drops down to just above the false bottom. The mixer is hydraulically driven. This gives us a wide speed band that can be adjusted to suit the task at hand. We never have a problem with balled starch or varying mash thickness. When the last of the grist has been crushed and run in, the temperature from top-to-bottom of the tun is always absolutely uniform.

As a rule, grain homebrewers probably have better temperature dispersion in their mashes than most other small breweries do. The scale of mixing seven or ten pounds of grain gives a homebrewer a great deal of control. In the usual seven-barrel-or-larger infusion mash tun, it is impossible to mix the mash well enough with a paddle to get even temperatures.

Most small commercial breweries don't have any mixing paddles in their mash tuns, because they are expensive, and they aren't an "off- the-shelf" item. We had to design ours ourselves, and were fortunate to know Yvon and Norman of Stainless Steel Specialists in Montreal. These two guys not only build breweries for a living, but they homebrew themselves. They had the ability to fabricate a very practical mash-mixer.

Our mash tun has no heat source. It is, however, well insulated and closed on the top. If we close the manhole, it maintains the strike temperature for as long as we've ever needed it to.

If we are doing a step-mash, we dough-in thick for the protein rest, and then raise the temperature for the saccharification rest with boiling water from the copper. For decoction mashes, we open the side outlet of the mash tun, just above the false bottom, and drop mash into the old decoction kettle. It has a gas burner under it, a temperature controller and its own mixing paddle. We can set the strike temperature on the controller and the burner will turn-down when it is reached, so we can hit each of the rest temperatures accurately. It sounds pretty sophisticated, but we know homebrewers that have even more high-tech controllers on their mash tuns, that can be programmed for a series of rests, and then just run it.

Decoctions are returned by drawing them through the bottom outlet of the kettle into the brewhouse pump, and back up through the valve on the side of the tun, so that the boiled mash mixes in low in the tun, and is dispersed from there. This reduces hot-side aeration and oxidation of the mash, a real consideration for all brewers when mixing a mash. It is also important so that the strike temperature of the next rest can be reached quickly. With this configuration, the temperature stabilizes by the time the last of the decoction is pumped in.

When we finish mashing, we reach down with a hooked rod and pull the paddle up through the mash and hook it up out of the way. It's not exactly NASA technology, but this is a case where simplicity is elegance. It works just fine, and a mechanical system would be more Rube-Goldberg-than-common-sense for such a simple operation.

With the paddle out of the way, the mixer is configured to rake the mash bed during sparging. If we are running an infusion mash, we are careful not to knock the air out of the mash mixing it, and we rarely operate the rakes during the runoff. If it is a step or decoction mash, the spent grains would set if they weren't raked, so we set the hydraulics to turn the rakes very slowly, exposing every part of the filter bed to within six inches of the false bottom to the flow of sparge water.

Kitchen mash-brewers should follow the same rules; hit the strike temperature and then let an infusion float. Where the mash program calls for more than one rest, rake the filterbed, but don't rake it so deeply that draff is washed through and into the kettle.

Our false bottom isn't very sophisticated; it's just a 2-piece perforated plate, but Yvon selected the perf correctly, and the false bottom gives more resistance to the runoff flow than the mash does, so that the mash is less inclined to pull down tight. Even so, we need to be careful when there is an appreciable amount of wheat or oats in the grain bill to avoid a stuck mash.

We start heating the wort in the copper during the sparge. Because the copper is gas-fired, we have the option of carmelizing the first wort in the bottom of the copper if the recipe calls for it. The burner has enough BTU output to boil it over, so we have to pay attention and adjust the burner's output as the wort approaches boiling. We always add a half-pound or so of whole hops to the wort as it comes to a boil, because the hops help break the surface tension of the wort, which reduces the protein froth. This lets us keep a violent boil under control, which coagulates proteins better than a less-intense boil would, without boiling-over.

We use a two-stage wort chiller, something that is not available to homebrewers, but is not really needed on the smaller scale. We cool the wort first with municipal water that we then recover and use for cleaning and brewing. We then chill the wort with glycol in the second stage, to get the wort down to the proper pitching temperature. Counter-flow wort chillers accomplish the same thing just fine for homebrewers, and creating fifteen gallons or so of clear wastewater in the process is no great environmental crime.

The wort is run to one of our eight conical fermenters. Homebrewers can pretty well replicate conical fermenters with the Yeast Collection Cap and an inverted carboy. Both configurations are nice because they eliminate the need for transferring to a secondary fermenter. Instead of racking off the trub, you just drain it away. What homebrewers don't have readily available is variable temperature control. Our fermenters are fitted with sensors and cooling jackets, so we can set a temperature and it will be maintained. This is probably the biggest advantage that commercial brewers have over homebrewers. Depending on the beer style and the yeast strain, we will set different temperatures to encourage or discourage flavors that are temperature-sensitive.

Another great advantage we enjoy is a rudimentary lab, and probably its biggest advantage is that we know how much yeast we are pitching, and how many cells the culture grows to. Both of these things also have a huge effect on "yeast" flavors. In all the homebrewing recipes in this book we recommend pitching rates, because we know how important they are by our own experience.

We also know from experience how important time is to the different beer styles. Some styles should be consumed "young", others benefit from extensive conditioning. Here is where homebrewers have a huge advantage over commercial brewers. Fermenting and storage tanks are incredibly expensive for commercial brewers. The decision to buy enough tanks so that there is the capacity to let beers condition properly is not cheap. Our eight fermenters give us the freedom to really lager, in practice as well as in name, but many commercial breweries do not have this luxury.

Homebrewers are not faced with this constraint, because carboys are relatively inexpensive.

And that brings us back to our serving tanks. Besides being able to brew seasonal beers at our whim, without having to pay set-up costs for special labels, carriers and cases as packaging breweries are faced with, we have absolute control over the beer right up to the point that you drink it. We don't have to worry about out-of-date beer still on the shelves, or how it may have been mishandled before it got there. Pub brewing has its own share of challenges, but it also gives us incredible control at the same time as it gives us unparalleled freedom to brew diverse styles of beer.

Only homebrewers enjoy less constraints than we do. How do we feel about that? Go for it!

We hope that you enjoyed this book. More importantly, we hope that it has enabled you to learn to brew, and to enjoy brewing as much as you enjoy your homebrewed beer.

Finally, we would like to thank homebrewers everywhere, because it was homebrewers who founded the beer renaissance that is happening today, and it is homebrewers that will keep it happening.

WEIGHTS AND MEASURES

To use Weights and Measures: If you want to convert 3 quarts to liters, look down the left column until you find 1 quart; look across the row until you find the equivalent in liters, .946. 3 quarts x .946 liter = 2.838 liters.

VOLUME

1 milliliter = .001 liter = .034 fluid ounce

1 teaspoon = .17 fluid ounce = 1/3 tablespoon = 5 milliliters

1 tablespoon = 1/2 fluid ounce = 15 milliliters

1 fluid ounce = 2 tablespoons = 30 milliliters

1 cup = 8 fluid ounces = 229 milliliters = .2286 liters

1 pint = 16 fluid ounces = 2 cups = 473 milliliters = .473 liters

1 dry pint = 33.6 cubic inches = 550 milliliters

1 Imperial pint = 19.22 fluid ounces = 20 Imp fl oz = 568 milliliters

1 quart = 32 fluid ounces = 4 cups = 946 milliliters = .946 liter

1 liter = 33.8 fluid ounces = 1.06 quarts = .2642 gallons = 1000 ml

1 dry quart = 1.16 liquid quarts = 67.2 cubic inches = 1.1 liters

1 gallon = 128 fluid ounces = 4 quarts = 231 cubic inches = 3.785 liters

1 Imperial gallon = 160 Imperial ounces = 1.2 US gallons = 4.55 liters

1 bushel = 32 dry quarts = 35.2 liters

1 Keg = 1/2 barrel = 15.5 gallons = 58.7 liters

1 hectoliter = 26.42 gallons = 100 liters

1 barrel = 31 gallons = 1.17 hectoliters

1 Imperial barrel = 43.2 US gallons = 1.4 US barrels = 1.64 hectoliters

WEIGHT

1 milligram = .001 gram

1 centigram = .01 gram

1 gram = 1000 milligrams = .035 ounces avoir.

1 ounce = 28.35 grams

1 pound = 16 ounces avoir. = 453.59 grams

1 kilogram = 1000 grams = 35.27 ounces avoir. = 2.205 lbs

LINEAR MEASURE

1 millimeter = .039 inches = .001 meter

1 centimeter = .3937 inches = .01 meter

1 inch = 25.44 millimeters

1 foot = 12 inches = .305 meters

1 yard = 36 inches = 3 feet = .914 meters

1 meter = 1000 millimeters = 39.37 inches =3.28 feet = 1.09 yards

SQUARE MEASURE

1 square inch = 6.4516 square centimeters
1 square foot = 144 square inches = .093 square meters

PRESSURE

1 VOLUME OF CO_2 = .195 grams of CO_2/100 grams of beer at 50°F

1 ATMOSPHERE = 14.7 psi = .968 kilograms/square centimeter
   at 50°F

CONVERSIONS

°Centigrade	°Fahrenheit	°Centigrade	°Fahrenheit
0	32	30	86
1	34	35	95
2	36	40	104
3	37	45	113
4	39	50	122
5	41	55	131
6	43	60	140
7	45	65	149
8	46	66	151
9	48	67	153
10	50	68	154
11	52	69	156
12	54	70	158
13	55	71	160
14	57	74	165
15	59	75	167
16	61	76	169
17	63	77	171
18	64	78	172
19	66	80	176
20	68	85	185
21	70	90	194
22	72	95	203
25	77	100	212

°C to °F: °C x 9 / 5 + 32
°F to °C: °F - 32 X 5 / 9

APPROXIMATE CONVERSIONS:

ALCOHOL ESTIMATION:

OG - TG X .1275 = %ABV   %ABW X 1.25 = %ABV
OG - TG X .102 = %ABW   %ABV X .8 = %ABW

3/4 CUP CORN SUGAR = 2/3 CUP TABLE SUGAR = 1 CUP DME = 2.5 VOLUMES/CO_2

REPLACE EACH CUP OF TABLE SUGAR IN A RECIPE WITH 1-1/3 CUPS OF DME TO ACHIEVE ROUGHLY THE SAME ALCOHOL CONTENT, AND INCREASE THE TG 1001.5.

REPLACE EACH CUP OF CORN SUGAR IN A RECIPE WITH 1-1/4 CUPS OF DME TO ACHIEVE ROUGHLY THE SAME ALCOHOL CONTENT AND INCREASE THE TG 1001.3.

IRISH MOSS: 1 GRAM = 1/4 TEASPOON

WATER SALTS: 1 TEASPOON:
                 GYPSUM = 3-3/4 grams
                 CALCIUM CHLORIDE = 3-1/2 grams
                 TABLE SALT = 6-1/2 grams
                 EPSOM SALT = 4-1/2 grams
                 CHALK = 1-3/4 grams

CARBONATION

The Carbon Dioxide pressure that carbonates beer increases with temperature. Although the amount of CO_2 doesn't change, the pressure does. If bottled beer is let warm up, it may gush upon opening, or even explode if it is over carbonated:

VOLUMES OF CO_2 =

	@40°F	@50°F	@60°F	@70°F	@80°F
2	= 7 psi	= 11 psi	= 16 psi	= 20 psi	= 25 psi
2.5	= 12 psi	= 18 psi	= 23 psi	= 28 psi	= 34 psi
3	= 18 psi	= 24 psi	= 30 psi	= 36 psi	= 42 psi

HYDROMETER CORRECTIONS

Homebrewers measure Specific Gravity at 60°F (15.56°C). To correct readings taken at temperatures other than 60°F:

50°F/10°C	-1000.7	120°F/49°C	+1010	160°F/71°C	+1022
70°F/21°C	+1001	130°F/54°C	+1013	170°F/77°C	+1025
80°F/27°C	+1002	140°F/60°C	+1016	190°F/88°C	+1033
90°F/32°C	+1004	150°F/65°C	+1018	212°F/100°C	+1040

Specific Gravity, the metric system for measuring density, is based upon water at 60°F being sg 1.000. Brewers drop the decimal point, so that wort at sg 1.050 becomes 1050, or "ten-fifty", and beer at 1.012 becomes 1012, or "ten-twelve". To make sg calculations, brewers drop the 1. and make the calculations using the decimal fractions (50, 12, etc) as if they were whole numbers (Attenuation of beer at TG 1012, OG 1050: 50 - 12 = 38. Attenuation was 1038. ABV: 38 X .1275 = 4.8%).

USEFUL INFORMATION

The boiling point of water at sea level is 212°F. The boiling point drops almost 2°F for each 1,000' increase in altitude. If you live at 4,000' above sea level, water will boil at 205°F.

Beer weighs roughly 8.4 pounds per gallon, water weighs 8.33 lbs/gal. To find the weight of wort or beer, multiply its specific gravity by 8.33.

One cup of whole malt weighs approximately 5 ounces.

To find the volume of a cylinder in fluid quarts, multiply:

(radius x radius) 3.1416) height) /58.

1 milligram per liter = 1 part per million

INGREDIENTS: COLOR AND UTILIZATION

	SRM COLOR 1 LB/1GAL	EXTRACT 1 LB/1GAL	S.G. INCREASE 1 LB IN 1 GAL
2-row Pale Malt	2.5	.68*	1030.7
2-row Mild Ale Malt	2.7	.67*	1030
2-row Lager Malt (US)	1.5	.68*	1030.7
6-row Lager Malt	1.5	.67*	1030
2-row Pilsener Malt	1.3	.69*	1031.5
6-row Diastatic Malt	1.5	.66*	1030.3
Wheat Malt	2	.70*	1032
Carapils Malt	10	.67*	1030.7
Caramel-35 Malt	35	.65*	1030.3
Caramel-55 Malt	55	.65*	1029.5
Caramel-80 Malt	80	.65*	1028.2
Caramel-120 Malt	120	.65*	1027.8
Vienna Malt	4	.67*	1030.3
Munich Malt	8	.67*	1030.3
Amber Malt	35	.65*	1030.3
Brown Malt	60	.65*	1029.5
Chocolate Malt	475	.65*	1029.5
Black Malt	600	.63*	1029

ADJUNCTS

Roast Barley	600	.64*	1029
Flaked Barley	1.5	.55*	1022.5
Flaked Wheat	2	.72*	1033.5
Corn Flakes	1	.76*	1034.8
Rice	.5	.76*	1034.8
Oatmeal	1	.54*	1022

KETTLE ADDITIONS

Rice Syrup	1	.84	1039.5
Light DME	2.5	.97	1045.6
Amber DME	25	.97	1045.6
Dark DME	40	.97	1045.6
Light Malt Syrup	3.5	.78	1036.6
Amber Malt Syrup	35	.78	1036.6
Dark Malt Syrup	50	.78	1036.6
Corn Sugar/Glucose	1	.90	1042.3
Table Sugar/Sucrose	.5	1.00	1047
Lactose	.5	.90	1042.3
Honey	3.5	.76	1035.7

*Extract potentials listed for grains are based upon the values that maltsters quote: Extract, Coarse Grind, As Is Basis. This means that the stated value reflects the moisture content of the grain at the time of testing. Maltsters also quote Extract, Coarse Grind, Dry Basis, but this value is misleading, since grains are never at 0% m.c. Usual m.c. is about 5%. Dry-basis quotes, then, are about 5%, or 1002 higher than As-Is quotes.

The extract values for the grains assume that they are being mashed, and that mash efficiency is 87%; if grains are added directly to the kettle, add s.g 1004.5 to the values given in column 3.

The Kettle Additions, such as sugar and malt extract, are not adjusted for moisture content, or for mash utilization, since they are always added directly to the kettle.

The color contributions listed will give fairly accurate SRM beer color up to a wort color of about 10°SRM. Multiply the pounds used by the color value, and add the totals up. Above 10°SRM, the SRM color will be progressively lighter than predicted. Lovibond color (°L) and SRM color are virtually identical.

1HBU = 1 OZ. (28 GRAMS) OF A 1% ALPHA-ACID HOP

HOP UTILIZATION diminishes the later in the boil that a hop addition is made, and the higher that wort specific gravity is. These factors must be adjusted for when planning hop additions to a beer. At 30% utilization (.30 in the chart), 1 HBU can be expected to give 22.5 Bitterness Units to the finished beer. If a hop addition to a wort at 1050 or below will only be boiled for 15 minutes, then utilization will only be 8% (.08), and the Bitterness Units would be: (22.5/.30).08 = 6 Bitterness Units per HBU.

There are mitigating factors that this chart cannot account for, such as the intensity of the boil, and the time that elapses between the end of the boil and wort chilling. Your actual utilization may be greater or less than the chart indicates. If you are using whole hops rather than pellets, you can expect your utilization to be as little as 80% of the values given here, so utilization of hops added 45 minutes before kettle knock-out to a wort at 1048 might be 22% instead of 28%.

MINUTES AT UP TO SG:

BOILING:	1050	1065	1075	1085	1095	1105	1115	1125
Hop utilization can be expected to be:								
90	.32	.30	.29	.27	.26	.25	.24	.23
60	.30	.29	.27	.26	.25	.24	.23	.23
45	.28	.26	.25	.24	.23	.22	.21	.20
30	.17	.16	.15	.15	.14	.13	.13	.12
20	.11	.10	.10	.10	.09	.09	.08	.08
15	.09	.08	.08	.08	.07	.07	.07	.07
10	.07	.07	.06	.06	.06	.05	.05	.05
5	.05	.05	.05	.05	.05	.04	.04	.04
0	.05	.05	.04	.04	.04	.04	.04	.04

This chart is based upon the authors' experience and various sources, especially "Recipe Formulation Calculations for Brewers", Martin P. Manning, Brewing Techniques, 2 (1), 44-55 and "Calculating Hop Bitterness in Beer", Jackie Rager, Zymurgy, 13 (4), 53-54.

For most homebrewers' purposes, the utilization chart can be extrapolated to this simple table:

1 HBU in boiling wort for: Will increase IBUs:

	2 gallons	**5 gallons**
0 minutes	.5 IBU	.7 IBU
5 minutes	.5 IBU	.7 IBU
15 minutes	1.0 IBU	1.25 IBUs
20 minutes	1.1 IBUs	1.5 IBUs
30 minutes	1.75 IBUs	2.4 IBUs
45 minutes	2.8 IBUs	4.0 IBUs
60 minutes	3.25 IBUs	4.25 IBUs
90 minutes	3.25 IBUs	4.5 IBUs

2 GALLONS = 7.6 LITERS, 5 GALLONS = 18.93 LITERS

So, if you want to get 18 IBUs from a hop addition at 45 minutes in a five-gallon boil, using a 5% alpha-acid hop, then:

Look up the utilization, intersecting the 5 gallon column and the 5 minute row; it gives you utilization of 4.0 IBUs per HBU of hops added.

IBUs divided by utilization equals HBUs, divided by Alpha-Acid equals ounces of hops that you should add.

18 divided by 4.0 equals 4.5; divided by 5 equals .9 ounces of 5% alpha-acid hops.

ASSOCIATIONS

American Homebrewers Association, Box 1679, Boulder, CO 80306-1679. (303) 447 0816

Beer Judge Certification Program, AHA, Boulder, CO 80306-1679.

Beer Drinkers of America, 150 Paularino Ave, Suite 190, Costa Mesa, CA 92626.

PERIODICALS: HOMEBREWING

Brewing Techniques, Box 3222, Eugene, OR 97403. (503) 683-1916.

Brew Your Own, 216 F Street, Suite 160, Davis, CA, 95616. (916) 758-4596

Zymurgy, AHA, Box 1679, Boulder, CO 80306-1679. (303) 447-0816.

PERIODICALS: BEER

All About Beer, 1627 Marion Ave #41, Durham, NC 27705 (919) 490-0589.

Beer, The Magazine, 1080 B Street, Hayward, CA 94541.

What's Brewing, Campaign for Real Ale (CAMRA), 34 Alma Road, St Albans, Herts AL1 3BW, England

FURTHER READING

Eckhardt, Fred. Essentials of Beer Style. Portland, OR: Fred Eckhardt Associates, 1989. ISBN 0-9606302-7-9

Jackson, Michael. The Beer Companion. Philadelphia, PA: Running Press. ISBN 1-56138-288-4

Jackson, Michael. The World Guide to Beer. Philadelphia, PA: Running Press. ISBN 0-84971-292-6

Jackson, Michael. The Simon and Schuster Pocket Guide to Beer. New York, NY: Simon and Schuster. ISBN 0-671-61460

Line, Dave. Brewing Beers Like Those You Buy. Ann Arbor, MI: G.W. Kent, Inc. ISBN 0-9619072-3-1

Miller, Dave. Brewing the World's Great Beers. Pownal, VT: Storey Communications, Inc. ISBN 0-88266-775-0

Noonan, Gregory J. Brewing Lager Beer. Boulder, CO: Brewers Publications. ISBN 0-937381-01-2

Papazian, Charlie. The Home Brewer's Companion. New York, NY: Avon Books. ISBN 0-380-77287-6

BREWLOG: BEERKITS

BREW #_____ DATE:_____/_____/_____

KIT_____

ADD EXTRACT _____ of_____ ____ of_____

KETTLE BOIL, TIME_____ VOLUME_____

AROMA HOPS, TIME _____ TYPE _____ AMOUNT _____

IRISH MOSS _____OZ

KETTLE KNOCK-OUT, TIME_____

PITCHING, TIME_____ TEMP_____ YEAST_____ AMOUNT_____

              DATE   TEMP   S.G.   NOTES

           _____/_____ _____ _____   _____

BOTTLING _____/_____ PRIMING_____ T.G._____

              TEMP

EVALUATION_____/_____ _____

AROMA:_____

_____

FLAVOR:_____

_____

1-10 SCALE, 5 IS NEUTRAL OR AVERAGE. HEAD_____ LACE_____ DMS_____

DIACETYL_____ SWEET_____ MALTY_____ ROASTY_____ SULPHUR_____

BITTER_____ HOPPY_____ ESTERS_____ PHENOL_____ FUSELS_____

SMOOTHNESS_____ FULLNESS_____ CLARITY_____ OVERALL_____

BREWLOG: EXTRACTS

BREW #_____ NAME:_____ DATE:_____/_____/_____

TARGETS: OG_____ TG_____ ABV_____ SRM_____ IBU_____

LIQUOR: TEMP_____ VOLUME_____ TREATMENT_____

MALT EXTRACT _____ of_____   ____ of_____

ADJUNCTS _____ of_____   ____ of_____

KETTLE BOIL _____ VOLUME_____ S.G._____ pH_____

	TIME	AMOUNT		TYPE	%AA	HBU	BU
HOPS	_____	_____	of _____	at _____	=_____	=_____
HOPS	_____	_____	of _____	at _____	=_____	=_____
HOPS	_____	_____	of _____	at _____	=_____	=_____
HOPS	_____	_____	of _____	at _____	=_____	=_____

IRISH MOSS _____OZ   IBU TOTAL:_____

TIME

KNOCK-OUT _____ VOLUME_____ S.G._____ pH_____

PITCHING _____ TEMP_____YEAST_____ AMOUNT_____

	DATE	TEMP	S.G.	NOTES
RACKING	____/_____	_____	_____	_____
FININGS	____/_____	_____		_____
BOTTLING	____/_____	PRIMING		_____ T.G._____

TEMP   ACTUAL OG/TARGET

EVALUATION_____/_____ _____ EXTRACT EFFICIENCY_____

AROMA:_____

FLAVOR:_____

1-10 SCALE, 5 IS NEUTRAL OR AVERAGE. HEAD_____ LACE_____ DMS_____

DIACETYL_____ SWEET_____ MALTY_____ ROASTY_____ SULPHUR_____

BITTER_____ HOPPY_____ ESTERS_____ PHENOL_____ FUSELS_____

SMOOTHNESS_____ FULLNESS_____ CLARITY_____ OVERALL_____

BREWLOG: PARTIAL MASH

BREW #_____ NAME:_____ DATE:_____/_____/_____

TARGETS: OG_____ TG_____ ABV_____ SRM_____ IBU_____

MASH, MALT + ADJUNCTS: _____ of_____ _____ of_____

_____ of_____ _____ of_____ _____ of_____

MASH LIQUOR: TEMP_____ VOLUME_____ TREATMENT_____

SPARGE LIQUOR: TEMP_____ VOLUME_____ TREATMENT_____

	TIME	MASH TEMP	pH	IODINE	DEPTH
MASH IN	_____	_____	_____		_____
30 MINUTES	_____	_____	_____	_____	
45 MINUTES	_____	_____	_____	_____	
END	_____	_____	_____	_____	

MALT EXTRACT + ADJUNCTS:_____ of_____ _____ of_____

_____ of_____ _____ of_____ _____ of_____

KETTLE BOIL _____ VOLUME_____ S.G._____ pH_____

	TIME	AMOUNT	TYPE	%AA	HBU	BU
HOPS	_____	_____	of _____	at _____	=_____	=_____
HOPS	_____	_____	of _____	at _____	=_____	=_____
HOPS	_____	_____	of _____	at _____	=_____	=_____
HOPS	_____	_____	of _____	at _____	=_____	=_____

IRISH MOSS _____OZ   IBU TOTAL:_____

                TIME

KNOCK-OUT _____VOLUME_____ S.G._____ pH_____

PITCHING _____ TEMP_____YEAST_____ AMOUNT_____

	DATE	TEMP	S.G.	NOTES
RACKING	____/____	_____	_____	_____
FININGS	____/____	_____		_____
BOTTLING	____/_____	PRIMING_____	T.G._____	

                TEMP

ACTUAL OG/TARGET

EVALUATION____/____ _____ EXTRACT EFFICIENCY_____

AROMA:_____

FLAVOR:_____

1-10 SCALE, 5 IS NEUTRAL OR AVERAGE. HEAD_____ LACE_____ DMS_____

DIACETYL_____ SWEET_____ MALTY_____ ROASTY_____ SULPHUR_____

BITTER_____ HOPPY_____ ESTERS_____ PHENOL_____ FUSELS_____

SMOOTHNESS_____ FULLNESS_____ CLARITY_____ OVERALL_____

BREWLOG: FULL MASH

BREW #_____ NAME:_____ DATE:_____/_____/_____

TARGETS: OG_____ TG_____ ABV_____ SRM_____ IBU_____

MALT + ADJUNCTS: _____ of_____   _____ of_____

_____ of_____   _____ of_____   _____ of_____

MASH LIQUOR: TEMP_____ VOLUME_____   TREATMENT_____

SPARGE LIQUOR: TEMP_____ VOLUME_____   TREATMENT_____

	TIME	MASH TEMP	pH	IODINE	DEPTH
MASH IN	_____	_____	_____		_____
30 MINUTES	_____	_____	_____	_____	
45 MINUTES	_____	_____	_____	_____	
END	_____	_____	_____	_____	
SPARGE	_____	_____	_____	_____	_____
RUNOFF END	_____	_____	_____	_____	

KETTLE BOIL _____ VOLUME_____ S.G._____ pH_____

	TIME	AMOUNT		TYPE	%AA	HBU	BU
HOPS	_____	_____	of _____	at _____	=	_____ =	_____
HOPS	_____	_____	of _____	at _____	=	_____ =	_____
HOPS	_____	_____	of _____	at _____	=	_____ =	_____
HOPS	_____	_____	of _____	at _____	=	_____ =	_____

IRISH MOSS _____OZ   IBU TOTAL:_____

                    TIME

KNOCK-OUT _____ VOLUME_____ T.G._____ pH_____

PITCHING _____ TEMP_____YEAST_____ AMOUNT_____

	DATE	TEMP	S.G.	NOTES
RACKING	_____/_____	_____	_____	_____
FININGS	_____/_____	_____		_____
BOTTLING	_____/_____	PRIMING_____		T.G._____

                    TEMP   ACTUAL OG/TARGET

EVALUATION_____/_____ _____ EXTRACT EFFICIENCY_____

AROMA:_____

FLAVOR:_____

1-10 SCALE, 5 IS NEUTRAL OR AVERAGE. HEAD_____ LACE_____ DMS_____

DIACETYL_____ SWEET_____ MALTY_____ ROASTY_____ SULPHUR_____

BITTER_____ HOPPY_____ ESTERS_____ PHENOL_____ FUSELS_____

SMOOTHNESS_____ FULLNESS_____ CLARITY_____ OVERALL_____

INDEX

AAU, 6, 48
Adjuncts, 38, 41-42, 44, 72, 80, 134, 136, 138, 143, 272, 275, 296
Alcohol, 6, 54, 62, 81, 293
Alkalinity, 51-54, 147
Alpha acids, 47
Altitude, 295
American Homebrewers, 19, 60, 62, 244, 280, 300
Anaerobic, 7
Anchor, 104
Aroma, 7, 20, 28, 70, 126, 138, 270, 271-272, 280
Astringent, 275

Bacterial, 130, 264, 271-273, 276
Bacterial infections, 9
Beer kits, 18
Beta acid, 7
Beta-amylase, 7, 138, 155
Big Book of Brewing, 48
Bitterness, 9, 47, 48, 282, 298
Black patent malt, 44, 83, 181
Boiling, 27, 56, 295, 298
Bottle brush, 72
Bottle capper, 16
Bottle washer, 75
Bottle-aging, 188
Bottles, 16, 270
Bottling, 33
BrewCap, 72
Brewhouse efficiency, 139, 286

Calcium, 142, 147
Calcium carbonate, 147-150
Calcium chloride, 294
Calcium Sulfate, 8, 53
Capper, 75
Caps, 16
Caramel, 39, 42
Caramel malts, 42, 138
Carbon dioxide, 19, 31, 273, 294
Carbonates, 20, 294
Carbonation, 7, 32, 81, 125, 194, 260, 263-264, 282, 294
Carboy brush, 72
Carboys, 71
Cherries, 130, 244
Chill haze, 264, 277
Chiller, 79
Chloride, 51-53

Chlorine, 23, 262
Chocolate malt, 44, 296
Citric acid, 54, 147
Clarifying agent, 57
Clarity, 53-54, 280
Cleaning, 26
Cloudy, 277
Cold break, 7
Color, 39, 125, 138, 280, 296, 297
Contamination, 23, 28, 55, 72, 142, 264, 269, 272, 275-278
Corn, 45, 246
Corn sugar, 20-21, 46, 296
Crystal malt, 40-43

Decanting, 7
Decoction, 7, 137, 156-159, 164, 276, 287-288
Detergent, 25, 33, 274
Dextrine, 46
Dextrinization, 154
Dextrins, 8, 20, 137, 141
Dextrose, 46
Diacetyl, 8, 54, 175, 272
Diastatic enzymes, 137, 141, 150
Draft beer, 260

Enzymes, 20, 135, 137, 142, 162
Epsom salt, 294
Esters, 47, 54, 56, 194, 272, 282

Fermentation, 8, 21, 26, 31, 32, 55-56, 72-73, 80, 126, 130, 147, 154
Finings, 8, 54, 57, 261, 263
Finishing hops, 21, 28
Flaked grains, 45
Fruits, 124, 129, 135

Gelatin, 56-57, 130, 141

Hardness, water, 52, 203, 209, 225
Head retention, 42, 45, 57, 224
Herbs, 65, 128, 129
Homebrew Bitterness Units (HBUs), 48
Hop utilization, 49, 298
Hot break, 7
Hydrogen sulfide, 273
Hydrometer, 9, 16, 35, 80, 81, 294

Infections, *See* Bacterial infections
Infusion mash, 137, 138, 151, 153, 155, 156, 159, 287-288

INDEX

International Bitterness Units (IBU), 48
Iodine, 142-143, 147, 149, 152-153
Iodophor, 262
Irish Moss, 9, 54
Iron, 276, 278
Isinglass, 56-57

Judging beer, 79, 127, 280

Kegging, 259-264
Kilning, 9, 20, 40, 138-139

Lactic acid, 54, 147, 235
Lactose, 46
Lagering, 7, 9, 76
Lauter tun, 10, 149, 159, 163-166, 286
Lautering, 10, 163-165
Line, Dave, 48
Liquid yeast, 55-56
Lovibond, 10, 297
Lupulin, 47-48

Malting, 10, 20, 40, 136
Malto-dextrin, 46
Maltose, 7, 20, 141
Maltotriose, 20
Mash tun, 10 149, 152, 157, 287
Milled grain, 8
Munich malt, 42-43, 157

Oats, 45, 288
Overcarbonated beer, 278
Oxidation, 10, 15, 47, 163, 262, 275, 287
Oxygen, 29, 272

Pale malt, 42, 137-139, 224
pH, 51, 53, 57, 70, 166, 275-277
Papers, 167
Phosphoric acid, 54
Pilsener malt, 39, 41, 138-139, 156,
    205, 206, 249-250, 253
Polysaccharides, 20, 141
Primary fermentation, 10, 71, 272
Priming, 10, 32-35, 130, 261, 263-264
Priming bucket, 15
Protein rest, 153-157
Proteins, 40-42, 137, 154, 277
Proteolytic, 137, 155

Racking, 10, 35, 71-72, 271, 274, 278
Racking cane, 15, 34-35, 72

Raspberries, 244
Recipe formulation, 124, 299
Records, 127
Rehydration, 10
Roasted barley, 44
Rotten eggs aroma, 273
Runoff, 144, 147, 160, 163, 275, 277, 288
Rye, 45

Saccharification, 141-142, 154, 156, 287
Sanitation, 25-26, 29, 262, 277
Scale, 72
Secondary fermenter, 11, 71, 80, 130, 263,
    274, 289
Sediment, 11, 33, 35
Siphon, 15, 34-35, 70, 72, 80-81
Smoke, 65, 110, 200, 245
Smoked flavored beers, 110, 131, 200
Sodium Chloride, 53
Sour flavors, 276
Sourmash, 157
Sparging, 11, 140, 143, 148, 151, 159-160
Spices, 192
Starches, 39, 45, 136-137, 140, 156, 162
Steeping, 40
Step mash, 153-154, 163

Tannins, 144
Trub, 11, 29, 261, 275, 289

Vegetables, 131
Vienna malts, 42, 139, 157, 209, 254

Water filters, 24, 264
Wheat, 192
Wheat beer, 65, 194
Wheat malt, 39, 159
Wort, 19-25, 28-30, 134, 140
    Boiling, 3, 286-288
Wort chillers, 74, 288

Yeast, 1, 19-21
Yeast, culturing, 272
Yeast, lager, 54, 56, 73
Yeast, respiration, 6
Yeast, wild, 9, 22, 140